Strategies for Vertical Integration

Strategies for Vertical Integration

Kathryn Rudie Harrigan
Columbia University

LexingtonBooks
D.C. Heath and Company
Lexington, Massachusetts
Toronto

Library of Congress Cataloging in Publication Data

Harrigan, Kathryn Rudie.
  Strategies for vertical integration.

  Bibliography: p. 347
  Includes index.
  1. Trusts, Industrial—United States. 2. Consolidation and merger of
corporations—United States. 3. Corporation planning—United States.
I. Title. II Title: Vertical integration.
HD2785.H36 1983   658.1'6   83–47513
ISBN 0–669–06694–x

Published simultaneously in Canada

Printed in the United States of America

International Standard Book Number: 0–669–06694–x

Library of Congress Catalog Card Number: 83–47513

Contents

Figures

Tables

Foreword

Strategies for Vertical Integration is a landmark book. It is the most-comprehensive study of the important topic of vertical integration done in recent years. Moreover, it gives added importance to the analysis of vertical integration in the design of business strategy. It provides the strategist with an analytical tool to help sharpen and expedite decisions about this basic issue. Three features make the book especially valuable. First, a *new conceptual model* illuminates the questions that must be answered, and suggests the factors that should be weighed when vertical integration is undertaken. The model makes it clear that vertical integration is not a single characteristic but is composed of four dimensions—breadth, stages, degree, and form—each requiring careful attention. In addition to flagging these dimensions, the model lists the array of potential determinants of a wise choice.

Most previous studies of vertical integration focused on a particular issue, such as antitrust, or stressed a few variables, such as the capacity load factor. The new model shows that the decision is more complex, and yet can be structured to incorporate the diverse elements.

The second important feature of the book is that *fresh data* are presented throughout. Harrigan draws data from sixteen industries that were selected to represent differences in such things as type of products and industry maturity. Then within each industry she examines integration actions taken by 192 specific companies and the reasons for such actions. Managers who knew the specific circumstances were interviewed, and the data were cross-checked. This is not a hypothetical deductive study, nor is it based on remote reports. Rather, the database is a remarkable collection of information about recent company actions and the conditions prompting them.

Few studies of business practice are based on such a rich array of clinical material. Moreover, the field information has a structure representation that adds credibility to conclusions drawn from it.

The third important feature of Harrigan's study is that it is very *timely*. Four current social-economic developments are pushing vertical integration toward center stage. First, deregulation is opening up possibilities for realignments. More movement is tolerated. Of course, upon close examination, additional integration may turn out to be unwise. But with the drift toward deregulation the options for more, or less, integration are at least being considered.

In addition, diversification strategy is being reassessed. Mere conglomerates of businesses are out of fashion. Instead, the various units of a diversified corporation are expected to reinforce each other in some manner. And vertical integration is a prime source of such synergy. Consequently Harrigan's model and observations contribute directly to the current reexamination of corporate portfolios.

Further, productivity has become vital to company survival, especially in international competition. The ample capacity existing in many industries makes low cost and better service critically important. Vertical integration can be a major source of such advantages—or, as Harrigan notes, in declining and volatile industries *less* integration may improve a company's competitive position. Vertical integration, then, is a two-edged sword that must be employed with dexterity if it is to improve productivity.

Finally, industry restructuring is moving at a rapid pace in financial services, office equipment, and other sectors. The delegation of responsibility in these areas is constantly changing. Many firms in such industries are redefining the scope of their activities. In this setting, vertical-integration choices are likely to spell success or disaster.

The publication of Harrigan's study now is particularly opportune. Deregulation, more-cautious diversification, the press for productivity, and industry restructuring accentuate the value of gaining a better grasp on vertical integration. The book will become a basic guide for both scholars and practitioners.

William H. Newman
Director, Strategy Research Center
Graduate School of Business
Columbia University

Preface

This book and its companion study of strategies for declining businesses represent an effort to test ideas about competitive strategy that have been a part of the recent intellectual flourishing of the field of strategic management in academia. As such, it draws on the research tradition of industrial economists such as Markham, MacKie, and Tennant—who used case studies to examine patterns of rivalry in diverse industries—and on theories of industry and competitor analysis advanced by scholars of both economics and corporate strategy, such as Porter and others. Its approach to the strategic issues surrounding vertical integration is a robust hybrid of economics and case-study idiosyncracies. It examines the strategy decisions of individual business units and it generalizes about patterns of strategy formulation observed by comparing the behaviors of firms within and across several industries.

The intention of such a hybrid study is to acknowledge the context in which firms formulate strategies while embracing the richness of understanding available by examining competitors' diverse solutions to common problems. The behaviors examined here are motivated in part by firms' needs to be sure that their products never lacked the necessary inputs (materials, components, research, or labor) or the most advantageous presentations to their markets (physical distribution, market research, or incorporation in more complex products). Their solutions to these problems are grouped together in this book to create some generic strategies for vertical integration. Any make-or-buy decision that firms evaluate is a part of these strategies, including decisions to subcontract research, wholesaling (or retailing) services, or other activities that firms could someday perform themselves. The *when* and *why* of these make-or-buy decisions is of particular interest in this study, as is the *what happened?*

The chapters are laid out in a uniform and straightforward format that enables readers to skim those industries of lesser interest and savor the details of particularly intriguing industry evolutions. Following some introductory remarks in chapter 1, the generic strategies and strategy model are introduced in chapter 2. The major forces affecting strategy choices for vertical integration are presented there and are echoed in the third section of each industry chapter and also in the generalizations of chapter 12.

Business practitioners may wish to jump immediately to the generalizations and policy implications of chapters 12 and 13, and to digest the strategy model in chapter 2 for greater understanding later. They may skim the analyses of each industry initially and then return for the details surrounding those industries that interest them most.

Academicians will note that separating the industry data from the analysis facilitates a more-objective evaluation of the strategy model. A snapshot of industry conditions in 1981 and a brief history of how industry participants forced these conditions to evolve reinforce a key finding of this study: different types of vertical-integration strategies are more appropriate at different times and in light of various factors that can be changed. Moreover, vertical integration can be used skillfully as a competitive weapon because exploitation of the many dimensions comprising vertical strategies can offer some innovative solutions to supply and distribution issues, tantamount to the currently popular concept of niche strategies.

Finally, public policymakers will note that although government is never explicitly named as an industry participant in the industry studies, it has been an important force for firms to reckon with in formulating strategies of vertical integration. A clearer understanding of this force and of the benefits that some forms of vertical integration can provide should suggest a need for more enlightened policies of economic regulation.

Acknowledgments

Funding for travel, telephone interviews, and administrative assistance was made possible by a grant from the Strategy Research Center, Columbia Business School. I am deeply grateful to the corporations whose support of the Strategy Research Center enabled me and other researchers to undertake scholarly investigations in the field of strategic management.

This project would not have been completed when it was without the assistance of my industrious research associates: Paul A. Gelburd (currently employed by Booz Allen & Hamilton), Stanley W. Herman, Mary Ellen Waller (U.S. Foreign Service), Kris Ishibashi (Metro-North Division, New York Metropolitan Transit Authority), and Kurt Feuerman (Bank of New York), all M.B.A.s from Columbia Business School. They buffered me from exhausting hours of photocopying and assembling background materials, and on many occasions they conducted field interviews with me in order to compile the data for each industry study. Their contributions are noted at the beginning of each chapter for which they assisted. I also thank Harold Hamman Martin (Shearman and Sterling, New York) for legal-research assistance.

My students at Columbia have helped me substantially to clarify my understanding of vertical integration. In particular, I thank Dean Hoke Simpson and Dr. James Coakley of Executive Programs for their valuable assistance and research support. I thank the members of the 68th Executive Program in Business Administration and their faculty directors, William H. Newman and David Lewin, for allowing me to present my ideas in that program. My M.B.A. classes have also provided helpful criticisms of these ideas, and I thank them for reading early drafts of this material. I am grateful also to the instructors who taught my materials in other sections of the core business-policy course and provided suggestions concerning their improvement.

I received enthusiastic assistance from Dr. Marianne Devanna, the most-helpful administrator of the Strategy Research Center's funds, and from Carol Landes and her intrepid staff in the Office of Support Services where hours of taped interview notes were transcribed to create source files for the industry studies. Special accolades go to Joy Glazener, the superstar who singlehandedly prepared this manuscript and its voluminous predecessors.

My colleagues, Donald C. Hambrick, Ian C. MacMillan, and John O'Shaughnessy, among others, all provided useful comments on the manuscript at various stages and in many forms. Many corporate executives (who must remain anonymous) commented on the background papers, interview notes, chapters, and supporting materials in several rounds of extremely useful feedback. My greatest intellectual debt, however, is owed to William H. Newman, the Samuel H. Bronfman Professor Emeritus of Democratic Business Enterprise and Director of the Strategy Research Center. In addition to supporting my research, Bill has commented extensively on the many drafts of each chapter and offered thoughtful suggestions concerning the strategy model and interpretation of the results I obtained. He has remained most enthusiastic in his support of this research effort by virtue of his interest in its progress, my findings, and their presentation. The shortcomings in the manuscript are mine alone, but the merits must be shared with my supportive and brilliant colleagues at Columbia.

1 Issues of Vertical-Integration Strategy

Managers need a ready supply of raw materials and a ready market for their firms' outputs. Although firms could own their supplying and distributing units, that solution is a deceptively simple one which overlooks other ways of controlling adjacent industries. Many arrangements might be used to control these risks and manage vertical relationships, and all are forms of *vertical integration*.

Strategic Questions concerning Vertical Integration

Which integration strategies work best under different competitive conditions? Although vertical integration is one of the first diversification strategies firms consider, it is not clear that vertical strategies that may have worked well in the past can work as well when certain competitive factors change. What are the factors that influence the best degree, stages, breadth, or form of vertical integration and how do they affect profitability?

Vertical integration has been a key force in the development of high productivity and managerial sophistication. Ownership of ore mines, ships, foundries, rolling mills, and fabricating plants was necessary for steel companies to lower costs and improve productivity in the 1890s, and Ford Motor Company's vertical-integration strategy in 1910 provided affordable automobiles to large numbers of consumers. Vertical integration has lost some of its attraction recently, however, because many managers resent having to buy from sister units. Yet our research has indicated that broad or high degrees of integration can be rewarding in situations where quality or cost objectives are stressed.

A New Concept of Strategies for Vertical Integration

The old image of vertical integration as operations that are 100 percent owned and physically interconnected and that supply 100 percent of the firm's needs is outmoded.[1] Vertical integration can vary in breadth, stages, degree, and form.

1

The *breadth* of vertical integration is determined by which activities a firm might perform in-house, including design, production, and distribution.[2] For example, television-receiver manufacturers are more broadly integrated if they make their own electronic components, picture tubes, and power supplies; sell television receivers through their own retail outlets; and service their television receivers with their own fleet of repair persons than are firms that only make their own electronic components. Both types of television makers would be considered vertically integrated.

Each technologically distinct activity—in our example, electronic components, picture tubes, and power supplies—may involve several steps (or conversions) which the firm itself may or may not undertake. These are *stages* of vertical integration. For example, the stages of integration for television-receiver firms that produce not only picture tubes but also the glass envelopes which encase them, connectors, capacitors, and other ordinarily purchased components are greater than those for firms that assemble picture tubes from sourced components. Both types of firms would be considered vertically integrated, but those involved in more stages of activity would behave differently under adverse competitive conditions than less-integrated firms. Moreover, business units are typically concerned primarily with stages of activity adjacent to their central missions, but their parents may push the stages of corporate involvement much farther. Thus, the proper stage of integration is more an issue of corporate than business-unit strategy.

The *degree* of integration is a separate issue for each activity, and companies that are highly integrated perform nearly 100 percent of a given activity in-house. Firms having lower degrees of internal integration purchase (or sell) some part of the service or material needed from outsiders. Firms owning business units with potential buyer-seller relationships can encourage high internal sales (or not) depending upon their corporate strategies.

The *form* a vertical relationship takes affects the amount of asset exposure and flexibility a venture possesses. Although firms may prefer outright ownership of trading partners, there are situations where joint ventures (or no ownership) may be preferable.

The key to successful use of vertical integration is determining how broadly integrated the firm should be at a particular time, how many stages of production to engage in, how much of each task should be done internally, and what form the venture should take. Although no particular degree, breadth, stages, or form of vertical integration is best for all firms under all circumstances, this study identifies conditions where certain combinations of strategies work better than others.

The Benefits of Vertical Integration

Vertical integration should be considered from two viewpoints: internal benefits and costs, and effects on competitive posture. Internal benefits affect the profitability of the strategy, and strengths in competitive posture enable firms to be more responsive to changes in market needs and less vulnerable to the maneuvers of competitors.

Internal Benefits of Vertical Integration

The principal benefits of vertical integration are economies of integration and cost reductions made possible by improved coordination of activities. Firms sometimes knowingly undertake a more costly degree of integration than may be required to cut costs, however, for the following reasons.

First, although integration economies can include cost savings by eliminating duplicate sources of overhead, it may also be possible to bypass certain steps in production or distribution, thereby saving the costs of services no longer needed. (For example, selling one's own wares could save some advertising costs and avoiding wholesalers may yield higher profit margins.) These savings are not universal, however. Some technologies offer little opportunity for cost reduction, and integration would actually *increase* total costs for a few.

In addition, costly and time-consuming tasks such as price shopping, communicating design details, or negotiating contracts could be circumvented through vertical integration if the goods and services in question must be purchased routinely. But too much integration injures strategic flexibility when industry structures change, and firms can lose their competitive edge by not keeping aware of market costs.

Competitive Posture Advantages of Vertical Integration

Vertical integration can be used to gain, first, improved marketing and technological intelligence; second, superior control of one's environment; and third, product-differentiation advantages which competitors cannot replicate easily. Vertical integration gives firms an improved ability to forecast cost or demand changes, thereby reducing anxieties concerning events they cannot foresee. The power to guarantee supplies of raw materials or markets for products through integration strengthens firms against other opportunistic firms lurking in adjacent industries.

Vertical integration can provide intelligence concerning demand (especially about consumers' changing tastes) which enables firms to change product mixes quickly. Common ownership of production stages enables firms to make technological adaptations efficiently in all stages so that investment expectations can be brought to convergence rapidly. Although shared technological information enhances innovation, particularly where the transformation process is complex and its stages are technologically interdependent, these competitive advantages can be lost as the basis for competition evolves. Then the special access to suppliers or distributors created by vertical integration is nullified.

Many firms use vertical integration defensively, to attain greater control of their environments. For example, when nonintegrated buyers find they are dependent upon suppliers who are also their competitors, they often neutralize their suppliers' market power by also integrating. Other firms use vertical integration to penetrate markets where their products are substantially different from those they are intended to replace. In order to prove to potential customers that the substitute produce is viable (or to overcome resistance to new processes), firms integrate downstream to ultimate consumers, as Celanese did from wood pulp to the fabrication of rayon garments when it introduced man-made fibers in the 1920s, or as ALCOA did when existing metals fabricators were reluctant to use aluminum in their products.

Firms can use vertical integration to add value to an otherwise indistinguishable product by creating special qualities that command premium prices, such as higher service levels, customized development of special components, or coordination of raw-material qualities. Irreplicable differentiation advantages explain much of the costly integration observed in some industries.

A Caveat Regarding Strategies of Vertical Integration

Being broadly or highly integrated is not riskless, however, and it may be more costly than the benefits it yields not only because the technologies of some plants require large volumes of throughput to be efficient, but also because firms sometimes integrate to attain illusory benefits.[3] Thus, a manager's integration strategy will be rationalized in retrospect, rather than beforehand as this study suggests. For example, managers might integrate because the opportunity to do so arose, the new business is close to one they know, and they believe diversifying in this manner will stabilize net income. Firms may have excess assets or managers to deploy, or see integration as a means to move into a better business segment or as a means to attract business to their primary segment. Because integration could be as likely to amplify the variability of returns as to diversify this risk, firms should reassess their integration strategies frequently in terms of excess-capacity costs versus market-share or profitability goals, and compare the loss of technological, marketing, or other competitive intelligence, with the synergies gained from high degrees of integration. Access to suppliers or customers could become constrained; technological changes could make existing processes obsolete; and business units that were nurtured could become uneconomical burdens if structural changes are not monitored and fitting adjustments in integration are not made over time. An integration strategy must account for limitations in an organization's capability to change as well as limitations in the environment where it competes.

Some firms hold vertically related business units apart, thereby forgoing the synergies that integration could provide. Others combine vertically related tasks imprudently, thinking synergies will occur automatically. Neither approach is foolproof because such firms often have not considered the competitive reasons why integration should occur, nor conditions which reduce their needs for broad or high degrees of integration.

In summary, vertical strategies must be variegated, permitting firms to make or buy components or services as needed, depending upon whether there is any benefit in doing so. Rather than own and operate vertically related businesses to capture synergies (or integration economies), however, firms that use high degrees of integration often do so to compensate for weak competitive positions. It is fitting therefore that strategists ask important questions concerning their firm's future such as: When should the firm vertically integrate? Which industry traits most substantially influence the profitability potential of vertical integration? In which competitive environment would many forms of vertical integration be clearly inappropriate? How can the firm maximize the benefits of vertical integration while minimizing its risks?

The framework developed and tested below considers how firms should assess the make versus buy question as their situations change. It addresses strategies that differ in magnitude from the incremental decisions pondered in cost-reduction campaigns, however, because the former requires large investments ratified by finance committees or chief strategists. Changes in such strategies can be so massive as to change an industry's structure as well as a firm's role within it because they alter crucial buyer-supplier relationships. These strategic changes (and the integration framework) are developed in chapter 2. The contributions of this study are illuminated in the following section, which explains how previous studies have overlooked key dimensions of the vertical-strategy problem and how this study differs from them.

Motives for Vertical Integration:
Where Previous Studies Fail

Previous studies do not provide useful guidance for managers about vertical integration because their findings are conflicting and unclear. (Some of the incompleteness that characterizes these studies is relevant for government regulators also, but that is not the focus of this particular study of vertical integration.) This section summarizes the attempts of economic and antitrust studies to cope with integration. Shortfalls in strategic management literature are also discussed.

Market-Power Theories

The principal shortcoming of market-power theories is that they see only one form that integration might assume. Usually, in these studies, the integrated firm is a monopolist, at one stage in the vertical chain, seeking to extend its market power to other markets (thereby erecting entry barriers and decreasing consumer welfare). Such integration is anticompetitive because it makes entry difficult for new competitors, forecloses markets to nonintegrated firms, and facilitates price discrimination.

    Much antitrust law echoes this viewpoint,[4] but recent studies contest the extent to which vertical integration raises a firm's market power.[5] (If firms possess market power by virtue of their integrated posture, it is usually for a temporary period only. Earlier studies have de-emphasized or ignored the changing balance of bargaining power between buyers and suppliers which occurs as an industry's structure evolves.[6] With few exceptions,[7] the economic theory of integration underlying regulatory policies assumed that the form of integration was homogeneous and its reward the same under all conditions.[8] It did not recognize that the degree, stages, breadth, and form, as well as the timing, of each firm's vertical integration could vary for diverse reasons.[9]

Theories of Market Failure

A second body of economic theory explains vertical integration as an action managers undertake because the market cannot allocate resources in a manner that adequately alleviates uncertainty.[10] Vertical integration is viewed by this group as being management's attempt to overcome contractual difficulties and other uncertainties. Briefly, the *market-failure* theorists argue that because there are costs associated with the market system, such as search costs to obtain relevant prices, negotiation costs to contract for purchases, and governmental (or regulatory) costs imposed on market transactions which vertical integration might alleviate, many firms prefer to be integrated.[11]

The market-failure theories do not go far enough in developing investment ramifications to be useful to managers because they ignore the realities of industry structure and corporate strategies. In brief, economic treatments of market failure de-emphasize the activities of firms that used means other than vertical integration to overcome the information gap this theory describes. Thus, they ignore different firms' interesting and useful strategic responses to market imperfections.

In summary, market-failure theories do not recognize the strategic attributes that temper the extent to which firms will (or will not) integrate the operations of adjacent business units. Because they have not allowed for firms to choose integration strategies of dissimilar degree, stages, breadth, or form, they have not been very helpful when placed against a backdrop of volatile competition.

Overgeneralized Theories of Integration

The third group of economic studies is flawed because it used few observations to reach its conclusions. These scholars have largely ignored the diverse market traits which affect a firm's varying needs for integration. For example, Stigler's conclusion that firms integrate early to achieve the greatest competitive advantage was overstated.[12] Although some firms obtained critical raw materials, distribution channels, and marketing intelligence through early integration, there are too many cases in which integration did not occur in the embryonic phase of an industry's development for this strategy to be touted as an option appropriate for all. Late integration and no integration have also given firms strategic advantages in some industries. (Indeed, the environment most closely resembling the one Stigler hypothesized is the lesser-developed country (LDC) where little infrastructure exists and early integration might be needed.[13])

Shortfalls in Strategic Management Literature

Finally, the strategic-management literature has suffered from a lack of rigor and a shortsighted portrayal of the ways in which firms might manage important vertical relationships. The *product-life-cycle* (PLC) literature takes a broad-brush approach to the topic of vertical integration that does not distinguish between different types of products and their individual needs for vertical control.[14] The literature on the contingency theory of strategy formulation limits vertical integration to established industries and does not distinguish between firms of varying market share.[15] Rumelt and others have concluded that vertical integration is not highly profitable,[16] a recent Profit Impact of Market Share (PIMS) based study concluded that there is little advantage to being more vertically integrated than one's competitors,[17] and the very firms that Chandler described in glowing terms have been called "dinosaurs" in the seventies.[18]

In summary, none of these studies recognized that the strategic needs of competitors could vary, as could their abilities to manage some forms of integration (by virtue of their sales volumes or other critical attributes). Like the economic studies, these early studies assumed firms integrate at the same time and in the same ways, thereby overgeneralizing the implications of their findings. Among strategy researchers, Porter comes closest to suggesting that profitability differences exist among firms with diverse vertical-integration strategies.[19] Unfortunately, he does not match strategy alternatives with environments where they might be most appropriate, distinguish among differing needs for vertical integration at different phases in an industry's development, nor acknowledge how corporate strategies temper integration.

Summary of the inadequacies of previous studies. The shortcomings sketched above are substantial because it is difficult to generalize about integration without considering firms' objectives and market positions as well as their industries. The combination of corporate needs and competitive conditions which make one vertical strategy better than another at a particular time may change; as a result, strategies which were once effective become disadvantageous. The simplified views I have described are scarcely adequate because differences in industry structures, in vertical needs, and in other previously overlooked characteristics are too important to the development of an appropriate integration strategy to be ignored. All firms do not use vertical integration identically, nor should they. Their needs for vertical integration will differ initially and shift in different ways as each industry evolves. Most importantly, there are several ways firms might use vertical integration. A firm need not be fully integrated and may not want to be physically integrated at all. Given the firm's bargaining power and other competitive strengths, its broader strategic needs, and the requirements of its industry at a particular time, some approaches to vertical integration may be more suitable than others. This study suggests matching integration strategies with these factors and testing that framework by using industry data.

The Research Problem

Given these shortcomings and unanswered questions concerning vertical strategies, a study is needed that identifies the differences among competitive environments and advances what is known about their hospitality for various integration strategies, and such a study should go beyond the single-goal single-environment, hence single-strategy, treatment of vertical integration. Previous research has failed to recognize the roles of competitors' strategic postures, the firm's corporate strategy, and industry conditions. What is needed is a study of vertical integration that identifies these variations and how they affect integration (and *dis*-integration) within dynamic environments. This section explains the study's scope. It sketches the principal factors comprising the strategy framework, explains how it was tested, and outlines the chapters which follow.

The study analyzes transactions between strategic business units, an approach which differs in scope from economists' studies which measured *value-added* (a popular economic index of vertical integration comprised of the difference between selling price and cost of materials which is commonly examined at the two- or four-digit Standard Industrial Classification (SIC) code industry level). This methodology is appropriate because it examines relationships between firms' strategies and the environments in which they implement those strategies. Briefly, the framework argues that if firms follow particular generic strategies, certain outcomes will be more likely to occur. Specifically, the vertical-integration experiences of firms studied are assessed for their success or failure in meeting several goals, and firms which followed the framework's strategies were expected to attain greater success. The predictive power of the framework was evaluated by comparing these expected consequences with actual outcomes.

Figure 1-1 diagrams the principal factors affecting integration-strategy choices. These are:

Uncertainty concerning sales growth and industry development,

Industry traits affecting how firms compete,

Company attributes creating bargaining power vis-à-vis buyers and suppliers,

Corporate missions for the business unit or chain of businesses.

The research design was longitudinal as well as cross-sectional, and it used a medium-grained approach that captured the important nuances of several industries examined. (The methodology facilitates the generalizabil-

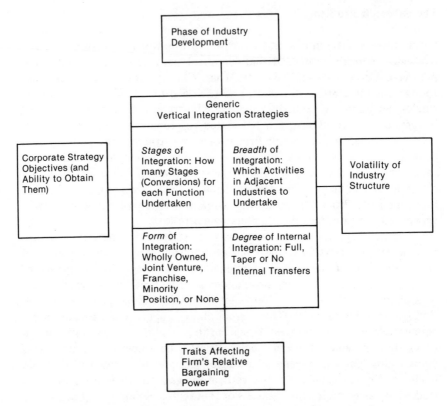

Figure 1-1. Variables Predicting Changes in Strategies for Vertical Integration

ity of findings, as do *coarse-grained* PIMS-based studies, yet it captures the complexities of firms' strategic decisions, as do *fine-grained* case studies.) The details of this design are explained in chapter 3. Briefly, different vertical-integration strategies were observed by studying firms which were vertically integrated (including firms which have disintegrated and the units they spun off), customers and suppliers which were not integrated, and representatives of industry trade associations. A combination of library research and quantitative analysis corroborated the findings from field studies.

The theory, data, and subsequent analyses are presented in industry studies which detail the variables identified in the vertical integration strategy framework. Firms' vertical-integration strategies are tracked and compared within each sample industry. The history of vertical integration and firms' performance within each industry are then analyzed (using the framework posited in chapter 2). A subsequent section abstracts the common patterns of vertical-integration behavior across the several industries studied, investigates their variances, and extrapolates meaningful changes likely to occur with respect to vertical integration in the future. The implications of the study's findings are presented in a separate, concluding chapter.

Notes

1. I am indebted to William H. Newman for assistance in developing this section.

2. I am indebted to Dr. David J. Springate, Societé Générale pour l'Energie et les Resources, Geneva, for comments concerning vertical integration and diversification which are developed in this section.

3. The *old* phenomenon of vertical integration has been described in Dennison, F., "Technical Influences on Vertical Integration," *Economica,* vol. 7 (March 1925), pp. 27–36; Frank, L.K., "The Significance of Industrial Integration," *Journal of Political Economy,* vol. 33 (April 1925), pp. 179–195; Jewkes, J., "Factors in Industrial Integration," *Quarterly Journal of Economics,* vol. 44 (August 1930), pp. 621–638; Dennison, S.R., "Vertical Integration and the Iron and Steel Industry," *Economic Journal,* vol. 49 (June 1939), pp. 244–258; Livesay, H.C. and Porter, P.G., "Vertical Integration in American Manufacturing, 1899–1948," *Journal of Economic History,* vol. 29 (September 1969), pp. 494–500.

4. For a history of current antitrust policy, see Adelman, Morris A., "Integration and Antitrust Policy," *Harvard Law Review,* vol. 63 (November 1949), pp. 27–77; Bork, Robert, "Vertical Integration and the Sherman Act: The Legal History of an Economic Misconception," *University of Chicago Law Review,* vol. 22 (Autumn 1954), pp. 157–201; Comanor, William, "Vertical Mergers, Market Power, and Antitrust Laws," *American Economic Review,* vol. 57 (May 1967), pp. 259–262; McGee, John S. and Bassett, Lowell R., "Vertical Integration Revisited," *Journal of Law and Economics,* vol. 19 (April 1976), pp. 17–38; Louis, Martin B., "Vertical Distributional Restraints Under 'Schwinn' and 'Sylvania'—An Argument for the Continuing Use of a Partial per se Approach," *Michigan Law Review,* vol. 75, no. 2 (December 1976), pp. 257–310; Louis, Martin B., "Vertical Distribution Restraints After 'Sylvania': A Postscript and Comment," *Michigan Law Review,* vol. 76, no. 2 (December 1977), pp. 265–280; Metzger, Michael B., "Schwinn's Swan Song," *Business Horizons,* vol. 21, no. 2 (April 1978), pp. 52–56; Weisberg, David E., "Continental TV v. GTE Sylvania: Implications for Horizontal as well as Vertical Restraints on Distributors," *Business Lawyer,* vol. 33, no. 3 (April

1978), pp. 1757–1769; Blair, Roger and Kaserman, David, "Vertical Integration, Tying and Antitrust Policy," *American Economic Review,* vol. 68 (June 1978), pp. 397–402; Anon., "Antitrust Treatment of Intraband Territorial Restraints within a Dual Distribution System," *Texas Law Review,* vol. 56, no. 8 (November 1978), pp. 1486–1511; Kaserman, David, "Theories of Vertical Integration: Implications for Antitrust Policy," *Antitrust Bulletin,* vol. 23 (Fall 1978), pp. 483–510; Marx, Thomas G., "An Analysis of the Economic Issues Raised in Continental TV versus GTE Sylvania," *Akron Business and Economic Review,* vol. 10, no. 1 (Spring 1979), pp. 7–11; Zelek, Eugene R., Jr.; Stern, Louis W.; Dunfee, Thomas W., "A Rule of Reason Decision Model after Sylvania," *California Law Review,* vol. 58, no. 1 (January 1980), pp. 13–47; Altschuler, Stuart, "Sylvania, Vertical Restraints, and Dual Distribution," *Antitrust Bulletin,* vol. 25, no. 1 (Spring 1980), pp. 1–102; Zelenitz, A., "The Attempted Promotion of Competition in Related Goods Markets: The Ford-Autolite Divestiture Case," *Antitrust Bulletin,* vol. 25, no. 1 (Spring 1980), pp. 103–124; and Posner, Richard A., "The Next Step in the Antitrust Treatment of Restricted Distribution: Per Se Legality," *University of Chicago Law Review,* vol. 48, no. 1 (Winter 1981), pp. 6–26.

5. Spengler, Joseph J., "Integration and Antitrust Policy," *Journal of Political Economy,* vol. 68 (August 1950), pp. 347–352; and Carlton, Dennis, "Vertical Integration in Competitive Markets Under Uncertainty," *Journal of Industrial Economics,* vol 27 (March 1979), pp. 189–209.

6. See Palamountain, Joseph C., Jr., *The Politics of Distribution* (Cambridge, Massachusetts: Harvard University Press, 1955); Kaysen, Carl and Turner, D.F., *Antitrust Policy* (Cambridge, Massachusetts: Harvard University Press, 1959).

7. For a discussion of quasi-integration policies, see Blois, K.J., "Vertical Quasi-Integration," *Journal of Industrial Economics,* vol. 20 (July 1972), pp. 253–272; Blois, K.J., "Quasi-Integration as a Mechanism for Controlling External Dependencies," *Management Decision* (UK), vol. 18, no. 1 (1980), pp. 55–63.

8. See, for example, Adelman, M.A., "Concept and Statistical Measurement of Vertical Integration," in National Bureau of Economic Research (conference report), *Business Concentration and Price Policy* (Princeton: Princeton University Press, 1955), pp. 281–330; Laffer, Arthur B., "Vertical Integration by Corporations 1929–1965," *Review of Economics and Statistics,* vol. 51 (February 1969), pp. 91–93; Warren-Boulton, Frederick R., "Vertical Control with Variable Proportions," *Journal of Political Economy,* vol. 82 (July/August 1974), pp. 783–802; Bernhardt, I., "Vertical Integration and Demand Variability," *Journal of Industrial Economics,* vol. 25, no. 3 (March 1977), pp. 213–229; Perry, Martin K., "Vertical Integration: The Monopsony Case," *American*

Economic Review, vol. 68 (September 1978), pp. 561–570; Shepherd, William G., *The Economics of Industrial Organization* (Englewood Cliffs, N.J.: Prentice-Hall, Inc., 1979); and Blair, R.D.; Kaserman, D.L., "Vertical Control with Variable Proportions: Ownership Integration and Contractual Equivalent," *Southern Economic Journal,* vol. 46, no. 4 (April 1980), pp. 1118–1128.

9. *Market power* was an important explanatory variable in Parker, Russell C., "Vertical Integration by Grocery Retailers: A Market Structure Analysis," unpublished doctoral dissertation, University of Wisconsin, 1962; Crandall, Robert W., "Vertical Integration in the United States Automobile Industry," unpublished doctoral dissertation, Northwestern University, 1968; Clarke, William Alan, "Vertical Integration in the Aluminum Industry," unpublished doctoral dissertation, Rutgers University, 1974; Litman, Barry R., "Vertical Integration and Performance of the Television Networks," unpublished doctoral dissertation, Michigan State University, 1976; Perry, Martin K., "The Theory of Vertical Integration by Imperfectly Competitive Firms," unpublished doctoral dissertation, Stanford University, 1976; Flaim, Theresa A., "The Structure of the U.S. Petroleum Industry: Concentration, Vertical Integration, and Joint Activities," unpublished doctoral dissertation, Cornell University, 1977; Mommsen, Jack T., "Vertical Integration in the Nuclear Fuel Cycle," unpublished doctoral dissertation, University of Santa Clara, 1977; and Maddigan, Ruth J., "The Impact of Vertical Integration on Business Performance," unpublished doctoral dissertation, Indiana University, 1979. Only this last study recognized that integration can be dynamic.

10. For a sampling of the information-economies literature, see Williamson, Oliver, "The Vertical Integration of Production: Market Failure Considerations," *American Economic Review,* vol. 61 (May 1971), pp. 112–123; Williamson, Oliver E., *Markets and Hierarchies,* N.Y.: Free Press, 1975; Arrow, K.J., "Vertical Integration and Communications," *The Bell Journal of Economics,* vol. 6, no. 1 (Spring 1975), pp. 173–183; Blair, Roger and Kaserman, David L., "Uncertainty and the Incentive for Vertical Integration," *Southern Economic Journal,* vol. 26 (July 1978), pp. 266–272; and Globerman, Steven, "Markets, Hierarchies, and Innovation," *Journal of Economic Issues,* vol. 14, no. 4 (December 1980), pp. 977–998.

11. Coase, Ronald H., "The Nature of the Firm," *Economics,* November 1937, pp. 386–405. This is the popular view of firms' motives for integration which is also found in Weik, James L., "An Analysis of the Relation of Vertical Integration and Selected Attitudes and Behavioral Relationships in Competing Channel Systems," unpublished doctoral dissertation, Michigan State University, 1969.

12. Stigler, George J., "The Division of Labor Is Limited by the

Extent of the Market," *Journal of Political Economy,* vol. LIX, no. 3 (June 1951), pp. 185–193; Etgar, M., "A Test of the Stigler Theorem," *Industrial Organization Review,* vol. 5, nos. 2-3 (1977), pp. 135–137; Tucker, Irvin B. and Wilder, Ronald P., "Trends in Vertical Integration in the U.S. Manufacturing Sector," *Journal of Industrial Economics,* vol. 26 (September 1977), pp. 81–94; Maddigan, "The Impact of Vertical Integration on Business Performance," 1979.

13. I am indebted to William H. Newman for making this distinction clear to me. See also Leff, Nathaniel H., "Industrial Organization and Entrepreneurship in the Developing Countries: The Economic Groups," *The Journal of Business,* vol. 51 (July 1978), pp. 661–675.

14. The treatment by Wasson is typical of this literature. Wasson, Chester R., *Dynamic Competitive Strategy and Product Life Cycles* (St. Charles, Ill.: Challenge Books, 1974).

15. Hofer, Charles W., "Toward a Contingency Theory of Business Strategy," *Academy of Management Journal,* vol. 18 (December 1975), pp. 784–810.

16. Levitt, T., "Dinosaurs Among the Bears and Bulls," *Harvard Business Review,* vol. 53, no. 1 (January-February 1975), pp. 41–53; see also Scott, Bruce, "Stages of Corporate Development Part I," Boston Intercollegiate Case Clearinghouse, 1965; and Peterson, R.D., "Galbraith's Obviated Market: Some Empirical Evidence," *Journal of Economic Issues,* vol. 14, no. 2 (June 1980), pp. 291–308; compare with Rumelt, Richard P., *Strategy, Structure, and Economic Performance* (Boston: Division of Research, Graduate School of Business Administration, Harvard University, 1974).

17. MacMillan, Ian C., Hambrick, Donald C., and Day, Diane, "The Association Between Profit Performance and Strategic Attributes for the Four Cells of the BCG Matrix," *Academy of Management Journal,* December 1982. See also MacMillan, Ian C., Hambrick, Donald C., and Pennings, Johannes M., "Backward Vertical Integration and Interorganizational Dependence—A PIMS Based Analysis of Strategic Business Units," working paper, Columbia University, 1982; Pennings, Johannes M., Hambrick, Donald C., and MacMillan, Ian C., "Interorganizational Dependence and Forward Integration," working paper, Columbia University, 1982; and Buzzell, Robert D., "Is Vertical Integration Profitable?" *Harvard Business Review* (January-February 1983), pp. 92–102.

18. Chandler, Alfred D., Jr., *The Visible Hand: The Managerial Revolution in American Business* (Cambridge, Mass.: Harvard University Press, 1977).

19. Porter, Michael E., *Competitive Strategy: Techniques for Analyzing Industries and Competitors* (New York: Free Press, 1980).

2

The Model of Vertical-Integration Strategy: The Conceptual Framework

What are the strategy alternatives for vertical integration? What should firms weigh most heavily in choosing a vertical strategy? This chapter presents a framework explaining how the factors presented in figure 1–1 affect integration-strategy choices individually, and in combination with the other dimensions comprising the strategy framework. A section is devoted to each factor and the final section of chapter 2 combines the effects of the entire strategy framework.

What Are the Alternatives?

How can firms best manage their needs for secure supplies and access to distribution channels? There are several strategies for vertical integration, but some are particularly tricky to manage because they require firms to assume much of the responsibility for upstream and downstream services (or supplies) that would otherwise have been purchased. Unless strategic requirements make full integration a necessity, firms should transfer some of the risk of vertical integration to outside parties.

Firms may need a broad and fully integrated strategy to attain corporate objectives regarding market share or technological leadership. A major risk of embracing high degrees of internal integration is the loss of asset inflexibility through imprudent vertical arrangements. Some firms give up more than they must. Strategies requiring high degrees of integration (and many stages) are particularly risky in volatile environments where demand is slowing or declining, but if other conditions within an industry are conducive to full integration—if firms' corporate-strategy needs mandate it and their business units can manage it—this could be an advantageous vertical-integration strategy.

For each resource needed (breadth), firms choose whether to produce or consume all or part of their requirements internally (degree), which components or services to perform upstream or downstream (stages), and how much of each business to own (form). Firms evaluate incremental make-or-buy decisions continually as competitive conditions evolve,[1] but they change their vertical strategies by deciding whether to increase or decrease their breadth, stages, or degree of integration through acquisition or de novo activity (or divestiture); build capacity to maintain internal transfers as sales volumes increase; or change ownership form or control of a vertical unit. In the presence of favorable industry and internal traits, adequate control over sequential industries can be exerted without ownership expense, and this analysis is appropriate for each activity considered for integration.

The breadth of vertical integration—that is, which activities the firm will control internally—is determined by the nature of the product (especially its differentiability) and other industry traits, by the phase of industry development, and to a lesser extent by the missions of the business units involved. The *stages* of integration for each activity are suggested by corporate-wide strategy, demand, and industry traits. The *form* integration takes is determined by strategy objectives, bargaining-power relationships, and uncertainty of demand. The *degree* of vertical integration—how much of each activity is performed internally—will be determined not only by current competitive conditions and relative bargaining power, but also by expectations about future conditions, based upon industry development and forecasts. An embryonic industry, for example, is more risky for high degrees of integration because many structural relationships are not yet established and there is high uncertainty about future demand. Therefore, a joint-venture form of integration (or a research contract) might be a more appropriate strategy than 100 percent ownership.

Typically, under various conditions four generic vertical-integration strategies seem appropriate, each representing differing degrees of internal investment and transfers, and each implying differing degrees of bargaining power with adjacent industries. Each generic strategy represents differing degrees of risk aversion; desires for control; and objectives for market share, long-term profitability, or other forms of leadership that help maximize long-term wealth. Use of these generic strategies at different stages in the vertical chain makes the analysis more complex. These strategies are: full integration, tapered integration, quasi-integration, and nonintegration.

The strategies are explained below. A subsequent section develops hypotheses concerning when these generic strategies are appropriate.

Fully Integrated Strategies

Fully integrated firms buy or sell all of their requirements for a particular material or service internally. They have the highest degree of internal integration, and the sequent units are frequently fully owned subsidiaries.[2]

Fully integrated firms are frequently market-share leaders, particularly if minimum-efficient-scale plants are large. Because the diseconomies associated with running underutilized plants may be high, fully integrated firms often pursue high market-share goals to avoid operating inefficiently. The balance problems associated with full integration would seem to make the strategy a rarity,[3] except in continuous-technology businesses where feedstocks are interconnected with processing plants. Even in such industries, the decision of whether to purchase feedstocks from a supplier or to obtain them internally can have significant strategic implications. Nevertheless, some firms prefer not to use outsiders.

Because fully integrated firms capture more value-added, they should capture more of the profit that would be built into each transfer price were the stages of production separate. In fact, full integration is riskier than taper integration because the firm is less diversified and more sensitive to economic fluctuations. That means when industries that are vertically linked are depressed, fully integrated firms suffer most. Full integration also risks operating diseconomies because of imbalances between upstream and downstream technologies. Thus full integration is a two-edged sword. Firms are assured of a sufficient supply of materials, but costs that would be variable under a purchasing contract are converted to fixed costs; more assets are at stake; and the diseconomies incurred could be larger using this strategy.

Full integration is used when there are *contract difficulties,* that is, when factor prices are so wildly unpredictable that no independent economic entity would write a long-term contract to supply the desired materials. Full integration is also used when firms believe they must protect nonpatented proprietary processes from competitive espionage by integrating, when components must be engineered carefully and manufactured to fit an assembly precisely, when firms desire to supervise all stages of quality control tightly, and when interconnection (or coordination) gives integration cost advantages.

Full integration works best when price competition is not fierce enough for diseconomies to matter; no significant diseconomies are incurred with imbalance; capacity expansions are not *lumpy* (causing sizable disequilibrium); the firm enjoys cost advantages due to access to scarce resources that offset any imbalance costs; and it matters little if the firm is cut off from the market intelligence or technological improvements of outsiders. If the environment is a stable one, more internal integration can be undertaken successfully. Note that a firm need not *own* 100 percent of an entity to be fully integrated for that particular need. In most cases where operating diseconomies are substantial and lack of external intelligence will harm strategic flexibility, full integration is not advisable. Firms should seek tapered integration instead.

Taper-Integrated Strategies

As figure 2–1 indicates, taper-integrated firms rely on outsiders for a portion of their requirements. Taper integration means they produce or distribute a portion of their requirements internally but purchase or sell the remainder through specialized suppliers, distributors, or competitors that are not so integrated. Although taper integration gives firms the advantage of full-capacity utilization, outsiders (who have absorbed the uncertainties of irregular demand) may charge them premium prices for supplies and services, or give their needs low priority, depending upon firms' bargaining power.

Although vertical integration is generally expected to offer lower coordination costs, lower raw materials prices, and higher margins in distribution, there are several reasons *not* to produce or distribute all things internally, particularly in a volatile environment. Tapered integration allows firms to monitor, and put to use, the research-and-development advances of outside suppliers; it also buffers them from strikes or shortages which they might face alone if fully integrated. As a long-term customer of outsiders, firms often receive favored treatment in the event of rationing and can sometimes purchase products they usually make in-house for resale in order to maintain customer goodwill during disasters or the shutdown of their own plants.

Tapered integration creates bargaining power because firms can use their knowledge of suppliers' or distributors' cost structures to extract lower prices from them (provided they keep some of their own plant capacity free to make credible threats of not buying from outsiders). Taper integration works well when firms' activity levels are large enough to justify one plant of efficient scale but not two plants, and can be easier to manage than full integration.

Taper integration can be used whenever physical interconnection need not occur, and it works best where firms can add substantial value to the materials they produce or distribute, raw materials are abundant or subcontractors are readily available, and underutilized capacity does not incur meaningful diseconomies because the benefits outweigh the costs. Leasing arrangements or obtaining components from licensed overseas agents are other ways to extend the firm's capacity when demand increases sharply.

Taper integration may be necessary if technologies incur substantially increasing costs beyond some level of production or if additional capacity is available only in great lumps that cannot be used efficiently without stealing sales from competitors and risking price wars. It assumes that an outside supply of (or market for) excess resources will be readily available. If instead the firm will face substantial discrimination in its external transactions, more internal integration or higher diseconomies may occur.

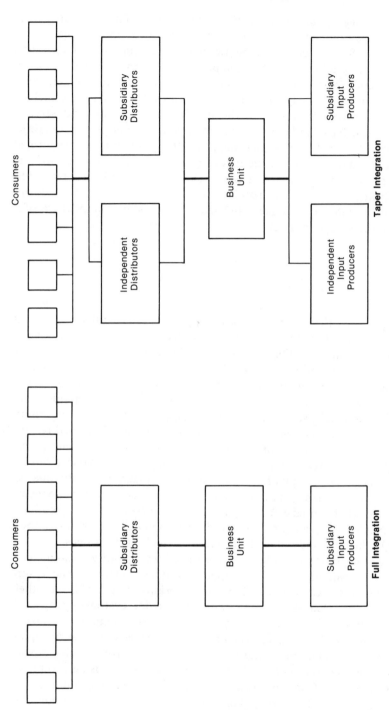

Figure 2–1. An Illustration of Generic Strategies

Note: In both full integration and taper integration, the stages of integration are greater than if only two stages of operations were joined. No assumptions concerning the form of integration are shown here.

Degree of integration: In summary, many firms prefer to transfer some degree of materials or services internally. The other option—that is, *no internal transfers*—is developed below, but first the importance of a high degree of integration must be reemphasized. Because balance between upstream and downstream operations may be difficult to achieve, taper integration is more likely to be used than full integration. Nevertheless, some competitive circumstances dictate that all materials and services should be transferred in-house, even if doing so forces one plant in the vertical chain to operate below efficient capacity. *Which* activities are performed in-house depends in part on the nature of existing infrastructure and the type of product in question. For each task performed in-house, two additional strategic decisions are required: first, how far upstream or downstream to be integrated (stages) and second, how much internal transfer occurs at each stage (degree).

Quasi-Integrated Strategies

Quasi-integrated firms need not own 100 percent of the adjacent business units in question, but they may consume or distribute all, some, or none of the outputs or inputs of the adjacent, quasi-integrated unit. The manner in which firms control adjacent units without fully owning them can be highly variegated, and there are many cases in which they may treat others' assets as if they were their own. Quasi-integration is a bonding of autonomous units which may take several forms, including cooperative ventures, minority equity investments, loans or loan guarantees, prepurchase credits, specialized logistical facilities, or merely an understanding of customary relationships. Downstream quasi-integration arrangements enable firms to retain a network of qualified distributors to manage quality images. Upstream arrangements, such as take-or-pay contracts or *kanban,* an inventory control system used effectively in many Japanese assembly operations, enable production planners to balance inventorying costs against known shipping schedules and reduce their needs for high buffer stocks.

Quasi-integration provides many of the advantages of vertical integration without assuming the risks and rigidity of full ownership. Using it, suppliers and customers can develop close working relationships to their mutual benefit. Quasi-integration can even provide customers with such bargaining power that suppliers may court them using nonprice incentives.

Quasi-integration is useful when risks from new technologies or capital requirements are quite high, and it offers the competitive-scanning advantages of taper integration for a lower ownership stake. It is an acceptable strategy where the firm's product offering or corporate mission does not require tight control of component quality. (Under certain conditions, quasi-integration can also yield integration economies, although these should not be overrated due to the higher administrative costs of managing quasi-integrated relationships.) Quasi-integration can lock firms into relatively inflexible identifications with particular suppliers and customers, a factor that may prove significant if these partner firms should prove to be strategically sick themselves, and can impede their abilities to shift tactics quickly in a volatile market. Although many quasi-integration arrangements involve contracts extending the depreciable life of the assets in question, expensive problems can arise where these contracts have failed to spell out obligations arising from unforeseen contingencies.

Nonintegrated Strategies

Strategies for obtaining materials and markets that require *no* internal transfers and *no* ownership stakes are like contracts. Most frequently, firms simply purchase the raw materials or assemblies as needed, but custom-design services as well as marketing representation may also be purchased in this manner. Because virtually every activity firms perform internally could also be provided by outside suppliers, fabricators, wholesalers, and marketing representatives, a knowledge of this network of services is crucial when firms must disintegrate or must go to external markets.

Nonintegrated strategies are attractive when firms are reluctant to buy specialized assets. This is especially true when the minimum efficient scale of facilities is large but a firm's needs are not. When environmental conditions are turbulent, nonintegrated strategies lower a firm's overhead and breakeven point. They are also attractive when delivery schedules can be agreed upon well in advance, but at little risk to either party. Nonintegration is particularly attractive when a firm's strong bargaining position can persuade outsiders to perform research-and-development or marketing tasks at costs well below what the firm itself might incur.

Ownership and internal transfers should rarely be used in highly volatile industries or when firms can use their bargaining power to shift the risk to suppliers or distributors. Successful nonintegration assumes the availability of numerous subcontractors whose products and services equal or exceed the quality of the firm's own, but if subcontractors are scarce, outsiders may gain bargaining power over the firm in a way that is disadvantageous to the firm's strategic flexibility.

The Use of Generic Strategy Alternatives

The strategies for vertical integration explained above offer a significant contrast to the homogeneous prescriptions of the contingency model and the simplified propositions developed by antitrust courts and economists. Moreover, as this section explains, the use of these strategies over time contrasts significantly with the model posited by Stigler and ratified by subsequent economic studies. A richer use of vertical integration is made feasible by incorporating the differences among competitors' attributes, market positions, and industry structures, as opposed to what a simplified analysis might suggest. Several strategies for vertical integration do exist and should be considered because the nature of firms' operating environments and other strategic variables differ.

The generic strategies are *not* intended to be static. When competitive conditions or other factors change, adjustments in the degree, breadth, stages, or form of vertical integration should follow. A change in strategy may also alter integration, as firms move in and out of integrated positions. For example, General Telephone and Electronics (which stopped semiconductor production in 1969 or earlier) purchased EMI Semi Inc. in 1979 because it again recognized its need for the design of custom-integrated circuits in telecommunications.

Finally, firms should reduce their ownership and deal with outsiders when they face too much uncertainty in demand, when there are few economies in their currently integrated stance, or when outsiders can offer better values than the firm can. When the *strategic window* that favored integration has closed,[4] and the cost of emulating competitors' vertically integrated structures is no longer justified, firms should also consider reducing the degree, breadth, stages, or form of their integration if declining demand creates problems beyond the firm's control or if the integrated units could operate more cheaply apart.[5] Dis-integrating early could give firms an advantage over those competitors locked into less-economic forms of integration. And decreasing breadth could lower costs by substituting outside suppliers' or distributors' services for functions previously done inside, thus lowering overhead from administrative salaries, avoiding diseconomies due to underutilized facilities, or giving firms bargaining advantages when creating specialized outsiders to supply their needs. A key review point for reducing integration is when corporate cash outlays are required to upgrade existing vertically integrated technologies, and business units that are not self-sufficient become a cash trap.

Predictive Variables for Vertical-Integration Strategies

Firms adopt different strategies for vertical integration because they are in industries that differ in volatility;[6] they have attained differing degrees of bargaining power with respect to upstream and downstream industries; and they possess otherwise dissimilar but germane competitive needs. This section suggests how the factors introduced in chapter 1 affect vertical strategies. Each group of factors is developed in turn, and hypotheses concerning them are presented. Finally, these dimensions are combined to illustrate the hypothesized effects of their interactions within the strategy framework tested in later chapters. Four groups of forces influence a firm's vertical strategies at a particular time. The first two affect the riskiness of the environment a firm faces—that is, phase of industry development and industry structure. The other two indicate a firm's ability to undertake certain types of vertical strategies—that is, bargaining power and corporate strategy.

Phase of Industry Development

The perceived riskiness of demand conditions changes as an industry develops an infrastructure and as certain patterns of competition become recognized as being more successful than others.[7] When conditions are stable, more internal integration (degree) can be easily undertaken than when the means of satisfying markets is changing rapidly. When the risks of launching an embryonic industry are quite high, firms may form joint ventures or undertake to provide an infrastructure themselves. Ordinarily, integration would be low both early and late in an industry's evolution, as figure 2–2 indicates. Also instability in demand can discourage high internal integration, and this instability may be variability associated with macroeconomic fluctuations or industry growth and evolution. Some industries such as the construction industry are inherently cyclical or extremely vulnerable to economic fluctuations, and others such as the aerospace industry are stultified by governmental policies. The effect of industry development on firms' needs for integration is discussed below.

Embryonic Industries. Ordinarily, firms would not enjoy sales volumes adequate for high integration in embryonic industries because underutilized capacity would be too costly until demand was established. Although firms may perform their research and development internally at this early stage, other integrations would be risky unless excess outputs could be used in nonembryonic businesses.[8] Forward integrations may occur within embryonic industries out of necessity, in order to prove the worth of new products to ultimate consumers. By contrast, in industries like automobile manufacturing, assemblers (GM, Ford, and Chrysler) first let outside suppliers invest in research and development to produce new components, like the electronic fuel-injection (EFI) system, and when the technological design was proven and uncertainties reduced, the assemblers produce the new components in-house. Thus the automotive assemblers persuade outsiders to bear the risks of failure in EFI production.

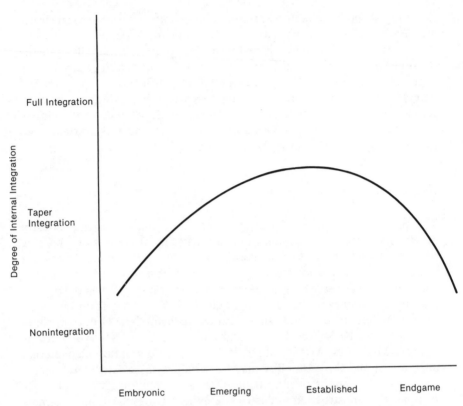

Figure 2–2. Degree of Internal Integration Hypothesized to Be Most Appropriate as Industries Develop (Holding Other Factors Constant)

In summary, few stages, little internal transfer, and joint ventures are more likely to be used in embryonic settings as a means of sharing risks or obtaining capital. Firms in embryonic industries should build small pilot plants, pressure outside suppliers to perform research and development for components not produced internally, and pursue relatively low degrees of internal integration for the remainder, given the high uncertainty associated with this phase.

Emerging Industries. As more competitors enter an emerging industry, the advantages of undertaking more activities, more-integrated stages, and higher degrees of integration become clearer, particularly as it forces an industry's structure from one of trading relationships to one of greater customer specialization and lower production costs. More activities, stages, or tries because when throughput volumes approach that of efficient plants, of minimum efficient scale, the experience curve lowers average costs dramatically, and sales grow more rapidly. Although imbalances between upstream and downstream facilities are still likely to be a problem during this phase, integration can offer innovative processes that replace labor with lower-cost capital, secrecy in protecting nonpatentable production processes and designs, and components or services created especially for the firm's needs. Firms can maintain a window on competitive developments by taper integrating their engineering and component production at this time. Internal research and development will enable them to respond to design improvements faster than firms relying on outside research results.

In summary, when an industry is young and demand is expected to exceed the depreciable life of assets used to integrate various activities, firms can undertake highly integrated strategies without fear that dis-integration will be difficult to achieve later. If sales volumes permit firms to attain scale economies in each stage of production, broader integration involving more stages can occur as an industry's structure grows more clearly defined.

Established Industries. It may become even more advantageous to be broadly integrated as an industry matures and sales volumes become stable. At this time also, integration may create scale economies by eliminating intermediate steps and using continuous-manufacturing processes. When sales volumes stabilize, firms can better forecast their activity levels and ascertain how more value-added could be retained using vertical integration. But as industry-trading relationships become more established, firms entering late may be required to be more integrated than they may wish to overcome foreclosure to raw-materials or distribution outlets created by the existing firms' vertical arrangements.

There is a transition point in established industries where attitudes regarding integration need reevaluation, however. Changes in market share become rare and small (unless competitive errors are made). New firms pursuing *leadership* objectives skim the benefits of earlier firms' integrations and supplant them upon entry. Corporate pressures to *harvest* businesses in established industries increase as industry growth slows. As managers' attentions become focused upon near-term profitability targets and as requests for new-capital allocations become more difficult to justify, vertical strategies become difficult to change. This is a time when managers should become critical of their integrated positions and assess whether some reductions should occur to prevent vertically integrated assets from acting as exit barriers.

Endgame Industries. Reductions in the degree, breadth, stages, or form of vertical integration should begin as industries progress toward the endgame. Firms contemplating increases at a time when competitors are disintegrating should be forewarned that changes in certain industry factors make this strategy risky in endgame. Although cast-off assets could be purchased cheaply, caution should be exercised when electing to go against the pack in vertical strategies at this time.[9] In brief, little broad or full integration should occur in the late stages of endgame because the risks of imbalance and corresponding operating diseconomies are too great. Although some loyal users who are facing high switching costs continue to demand the products of declining businesses, their sensitivity to price increases eventually overcomes their switching-cost barriers and they cease to consume these products. Intermediate customers abrogate long-term contracts to use firms' products if they cannot pass on their higher costs to ultimate consumers. The distribution channels forged with careful vertical agreements deteriorate and crumble. This is a time when intelligence becomes crucial, timing delicate, and vertical integration becomes a millstone rather than an advantage.

Summary: Hypotheses concerning Vertical-Integration
Strategies and Phase of Industry Development

In summary, the most likely pattern of vertical strategies over time should be the inverse of the *U-shape* Stigler posited. Less integration will occur in the early-embryonic and late-endgame phases; high degrees of integration become commonplace as industries grow and become more established. Early integration is a means to reduce customer uncertainties regarding new products, to undertake tasks no other supplier or distributor would perform, or to create a new way of reaching the ultimate consumer. In most cases, specialized suppliers or distributors are better suited to do these things on a contractual basis for the firm until uncertainties concerning demand and viability are resolved. Full integration in late maturity is a means of creating component sources and marketing outlets for late entrants who find existing suppliers or distributors already under contract to competitors. Thus competitive motivations other than lowering cost may create broad patterns of integration in established industries.

Uncertainty increases the riskiness of making a premature commitment to high degrees of integration. Because integrated production processes require balanced activity levels both upstream and downstream, firms in industries characterized by cyclical demand (such as textiles), or in industries that are sensitive to variances in the levels of disposable income (such as vacation homes), should forgo integrations that the framework suggests are otherwise appropriate for their industry's phase of development. This

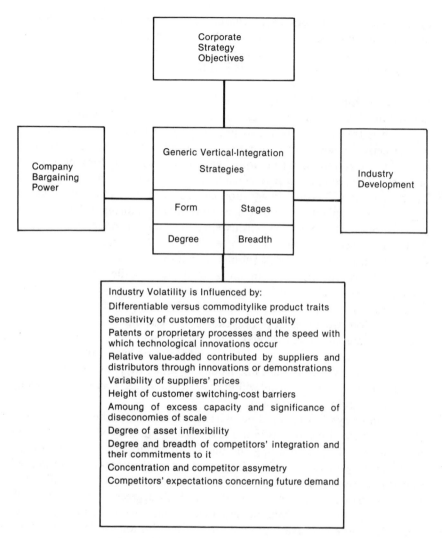

Figure 2–3. Factors Determining Volatility of Industry Structure

analysis differs, however, when firms develop businesses in newly developing nations where no infrastructure exists.

Volatility of Industry Structure

An industry's volatility may be inferred from the presence of certain structural traits (sketched in figure 2–3) and competitive practices that increase the likelihood that industry discipline will degenerate to price-cutting and other competitive tactics that devastate long-term profitability. Volatile industries are created by key industry factors such as the attributes of products, customers, suppliers, manufacturing conditions, and competitors. The effects of these attributes are explained below.

Product Attributes. Other factors held constant, the most important product attribute to consider with respect to industry volatility and vertical integration is the variety of models produced. Integration is generally more cost effective if few models using standardized components are produced than if the business unit functions like a job shop in making customized products. The second factor to consider is the importance of product quality to customers. Vertical integration can buttress this competitive advantage by freeing plant space to concentrate manufacturing either on components that customers deem sensitive in determining product quality or on those components offering the best economics. This knowledge can also suggest whether in-house units should market the products in question, and may even prevent firms from entrapment in volatile rounds of style changes, superficial feature changes or other costly ways of competing. Where trade secrets protect some aspect of a firm's products, higher degrees of integration are necessary. For example, Polaroid stopped buying its negative materials from Kodak when Polaroid's instant-photography patent expired. Too much proprietary information was embodied in the negative to allow competitors like Kodak to make it. Thus, where innovation is important, fewer firms will license technologies, thereby foreclosing competitors from copying them.

In summary, firms should purchase components (or the product itself) where life cycles are short, as in the case of toys, but if a competitive advantage is achieved by controlling the quality of inputs and precision of the manufacturing process, higher degrees of internal integration are needed even where short life cycles predominate. In consumer products, distribution is the critical function to control, and high degrees of integration will be necessary to protect brand images unless firms possess sufficient control over sales representatives' presentations, distribution outlets, incentives paid to sales forces' or other activities associated with differentiating their products.[10] Contracts or quasi-integration practices involving substantial outside activities are appropriate forms of vertical integration if product quality does not matter.

Supplier Attributes. Other factors held constant, the most significant supplier attributes with respect to industry volatility and vertical integration are their relative value-added contributions and the volatility of their prices.[11] If suppliers frequently improve their raw materials' or components' attributes, the industry will be more volatile because more frequent product updates will occur. Accordingly, if firms contemplate a high degree of internal backward integration, some imperfection in existing suppliers must justify this investment. Perhaps they do so because firms need tight control over the quality and design of their components and cannot contract for these services, or they face uncertain availability of their raw materials and resources. They may face competitors who are also suppliers and who will not deal with them, or frequent product improvements that require close coordination of manufacturing processes and raw material attributes. Although firms frequently integrate to acquire an assured flow of future deliveries, rather than to lower the average cost of production, many suppliers are particularly innovative or efficient and firms can purchase a portion of their needs from them to gain the fruits of their research-and-development expenditures. Taper integration would also enable firms to grasp suppliers' true manufacturing costs and use this information to create bargaining power to offset price increases.[12]

In summary, taper integration is preferable to full backward integration when firms need control of their raw materials but suppliers innovate frequently. If quasi-integration arrangements for backward integration are used, more internal research and development should be used to keep firms' operations coordinated and aware of technological improvements which may require rapid internal responses.

Customer Attributes. Other factors held constant, the customer attributes that are most important with respect to industry volatility and vertical integration are their value-added distribution activities[13] and the height of their switching-cost barriers. Because wholesalers and marketing representatives are specialists in distribution services, firms should have viable rationales for committing their assets to high degrees of forward integration where the same results could be achieved using contracts. The ways in which firms' products have been marketed suggest their differentiability and the role downstream firms play in enhancing that image for ultimate customers. If the product needs advertising, product and packaging improvements, installation, demonstration aids, or other promotional services that increase the costliness of using in-house marketing, then the use of outsiders to share these tasks could reduce tied-up capital and operating costs.[14] But exclusive marketing arrangements are ultimately more expensive because they mean excluding other firms from a function where widespread participation is frequently desirable. They are undesirable except for specialized products, and then are acceptable only if the firm is not cut off from marketing intelligence, merchandising innovations, or other value-adding activities that downstream firms could offer.

If customer-switching costs are low, a firm's ability to control demand for its products and to hold customers will be lower unless it creates other forms of value-added to hold them. Sometimes, firms can tailor their technology to suit users' needs or use quasi-integration agreements to raise switching-cost barriers to intermediate customers. Or, in competitive-bidding contests, firms might team up with consulting engineers that specify their unique products to increase switching costs. In summary, greater degrees of vertical control should be used where carefully controlled marketing could create a quality image. If customers' purchases are based upon price considerations rather than differentiating traits, lower degrees of internal integration could be acceptable unless integration economies were gained by integrating forward.

Manufacturing Technology Attributes. Other factors held constant, the technological attributes of greatest interest to a firm contemplating internal vertical relationships are the sizes of adjacent industry plants, the magnitude of diseconomies incurred if its throughput is not balanced, the degree of asset inflexibility, and the nature of experience curves associated with these plants. Firms use subcontractors to handle dangerous materials or perform tasks needing very specialized pieces of machinery because they can frequently perform these manufacturing steps as well as the firms, but without tying up underutilized in-house resources. Other circumstances favoring use of outside producers include unionized-labor-force inflexibility, high supervisions costs, or other conditions where lower productivity results from performing the task in-house, as well as Environmental Protection Agency or Occupational Safety and Health Administration regulations that would make plant modifications prohibitively expensive. Finally, if technology is changing rapidly, using outsiders to produce components or perform an intermediate step reduces the risk of being stuck with obsolete machines.

If there are sizable penalties associated with operating a plant at less than the most optimal scale (MOS), a firm's balance requirements increase and it will want to keep its assets utilized efficiently by assuring supplies of materials or markets for its outputs. But if a plant's output cannot be consumed entirely by downstream units, a firm is forced to enter merchant activities, a type of business it may prefer to avoid.

By buying simple components outside, a firm may keep its critical, skilled laborers employed and attain full utilization of an efficient-sized plant. But when taper integration exposes it to the uncertainties of relying on outside suppliers for a portion of its needs, a firm risks foreclosure if competitors obtain control of its suppliers or distributors.

Asset inflexibility frequently plagues highly integrated firms because their assets are specialized and function as *exit barriers,* preventing firms from easily changing to alternative technologies.[15] Thus, in manufacturing technology, being highly specialized may give a firm a lower cost per unit[16] but it increases industry volatility because capital-intensive, interconnected technologies make a firm reluctant to dis-integrate or exit when growth slows. The resulting excess capacity destroys the industry's pricing discipline. One way to hurdle exit barriers is to force review points in the make-or-buy decision whenever assets are fully depreciated or made obsolete. Firms in the late maturity phase of an industry's life should consider if expected demand exceeds the economic life of the new assets proposed, and if excess capacity plagues the industry. If both these cases are true, the firm might consider buying from competitors as a prelude to exit.

When products are subject to experience-curve economies, firms integrating late must spend heavily to overtake existing manufacturing volumes and push further down the industry-experience curve. By waiting, such firms gain intelligence concerning false starts and problems that pioneering firms have encountered, but to do so they frequently must offer a low-priced product intended to capture market share quickly, unless they innovate.

In summary, industry volatility will be increased by rapid rates of technological change, excess capacity, and by the high exit barriers some vertically integrated firms face. When conditions are volatile, fewer stages, integrated activities, and lower degrees of integration should be used.

Competitor Attributes. Other factors held constant, the competitor attributes that are most important to industry volatility and integration are the degree of a competitor's vertical integration, the amount of industry concentration, and a competitor's expectations concerning future demand. Vertically integrated competitors use foreclosure in lieu of price competition to squeeze out nonintegrated firms by denying them access to materials, markets, innovations, intelligence, or other competitive advantages.

Industries will be more volatile if dissimilar strategic groups compete for the same customers' sales, and price competition is more likely to erupt if competitive signalling is blurred by a fragmented industry structure. When more than one type of strategic group tries to serve the same group of customers, the potential for a volatile competitive environment is amplified. Because a firm's high-market-share goals lead to large plants and high degrees of internal integration, such competitors have vested interests in keeping their large plants filled. If troubled, they tend to expand their capacity to protect their downstream units, and narrowly diversified firms pose a special exit-barrier problem because such so-called dominant verticals compete fiercely. They face extremely high exit barriers, because any reductions in the breadth, stages, or degree of their integrations are dissolutions of their corporate entity. Thus dominant verticals generally behave more like mavericks than widely diversified firms, and are more likely to bloody the entire industry unless these firms can recognize how mutually dependent they are upon each other to maintain order.

If minimum-efficient-plant sizes are large, the number of firms in an industry will be few, and thus they will be more likely to use high degrees of internal integration as their industry matures. Similarly, if the product cannot be differentiated effectively, low operating costs become an important basis for competition and the industry will be more concentrated. High integration is especially likely in concentrated industries where integration economies are significant and firms can achieve focal points in pricing easily.

A competitor's expectations about the nature and duration of demand will greatly influence its vertical-integration behavior as it expands plant capacity, lets a contract for bidding, strengthens outside distributors' incentives, or undertakes other competitive activities. If there is great uncertainty among firms about demand, they will be more likely to create a chaotic industry environment by undertaking activities which foreclose each other from access to suppliers or distributors.

In summary, a firm's vertical-integration strategy will be driven, in part, by those of its competitors. If competitors use high degrees of internal integration and create relationships which foreclose some firms, they may integrate (in defense) even where other considerations do not warrant such high degrees of internal integration. The result is chaotic price cutting.

Summary of Factors Influencing Industry Volatility

Industries are volatile when first, several firms from different strategic groups that serve the same customer group expand capacity to protect their integrated structures, second, competitive signalling has been poor in the past, third, fringe competitors frequently use price-cutting to fill their plants, or fourth, maverick competitors are pricing below their costs because they cannot dis-integrate or take other actions to reduce their overhead. A volatile environment would also be characterized by high product differentiation, frequent process innovations, or low switching costs and loyalties among ultimate consumers. Such an industry would be characterized by erratic or cyclical demand and low industry-wide profits until excess capacity is retired. Thin profitability and rounds of price-cutting are outward signs that competition is volatile within the industry, and patterns of erratic demand signal imbalances exist in upstream or downstream units as well as units operating within the troubled industry. If few outlets exist for dumping excess output, industries in which firms are highly integrated are more likely to exacerbate price wars to dispose of such excess capacity (and inventory buildup), assuming such firms do not resort to dis-integration until demand has become clearly stagnant. Such industries also have high exit barriers but low entry barriers.

By contrast, stable environments have: low product differentiation, infrequent product improvements, high customer-switching costs, and few strategic groups—where all major firms are similarly integrated and recognize their interdependence with respect to the activities of other competitors. Accordingly, in such environments competitive signals are clear and easily understood, firms expand their vertical capacities sparingly, and there is no history of price competition. In these environments, major firms tend to be broadly diversified and not particularly stymied by the need to reduce high levels of internal transfers. Price wars erupt less frequently and last for shorter periods.

High degrees of integration and more-integrated stages and activities are more likely to succeed when firms enjoy monopoly or monopsony conditions in downstream or upstream industries. They will be more successful if firms have the opportunity to serve specialized markets by differentiating products, to limit competitive incursions by raising entry or mobility barriers, to obtain cost advantages using technologies subject to significant integration economies, and to take advantage of conditions of increasing concentration, as well as other structural traits that reduce the likelihood that competition will become volatile. Less integration and fewer stages (or activities) are appropriate under conditions of high uncertainty, where the industry is volatile, and where products must be modified frequently, because when competitors must change tactics rapidly, a highly vertically integrated posture could reduce firms' abilities to maneuver.

Summary: Hypotheses About Factors Influencing Industry Volatility and Vertical-Integration Strategies

The five attributes developed in this section illustrate the relative attractiveness of an industry. Figure 2–4 depicts the degree of internal integration appropriate for various phases of industry development and under various conditions of industry volatility. Less internal integration is appropriate under conditions of high uncertainty, volatility, and frequent product modification. More internal integration is appropriate when industry conditions are less volatile and uncertain.

Bargaining Power

This section explains how bargaining power affects the type of internal integration a firm must undertake in order to secure access to suppliers and distribution without damaging its strategic flexibility. One way to reduce asset exposure and inflexibility is to reduce ownership stakes in supplying or distributing business units. Another way is to use the firm's bargaining power to persuade sequent businesses to assume those duties the firm wishes to avoid.[17]

Any firm that hopes to reap the advantages of vertical integration must possess internal strengths that are appropriate for the integration strategy it chooses. Bargaining power is foremost among these. Firms that possess bargaining power have influenced the prices, terms, and shipping schedules of suppliers and distributors; influenced the styling and promotional policies of downstream firms; obtained superior information concerning desired product traits, preferred product mix, and trends in ultimate buyers' tastes

Volatility of Industry Structure

		Low Volatility Low Uncertainty	High Volatility High Uncertainty
	Embryonic	Nonintegration or Quasi-Integration (few internal transfers)	Nonintegration
	Emerging	Quasi-Integration (with some internal transfers) or Taper Integration (and full ownership)	Quasi-Integration (with some internal transfers)
	Established	Full Integration or Taper Integration (and full ownership)	Taper Integration (and full ownership) or Quasi-Integration (some internal transfers)
	Endgame	Taper Integration (and full ownership) or Nonintegration	Nonintegration

Phase of Industry Development

Figure 2–4. Degree of Internal Integration and Ownership Hypothesized to Be Most Appropriate per Phase of Industry Development and Volatility of Industry Structure (Holding Other Factors Constant)

from distributors' sales representatives; or urged distributors to perform expensive missionary-selling tasks to help introduce these new products. But aside from the many services firms can induce their suppliers or distributors to perform, bargaining power is crucial because it reduces the firm's asset inflexibility.

Which factors determine who has bargaining power?[18] Other factors held constant, the most important determinants of bargaining power are: product specificity to the industry in question, the existence of alternative outlets or sources of supply, the ability to self-manufacture, and the dependence of the supplier (or distributor) upon the business unit. If firms possess great bargaining power with respect to suppliers or distributors they require less integration, but if a firm's suppliers or distributors possess bargaining power, it must have greater degrees of integration to attain the control desired. (These and other determinants of bargaining power are diagrammed in figure 2–5.)

Business units possess bargaining power if no other industry consumes

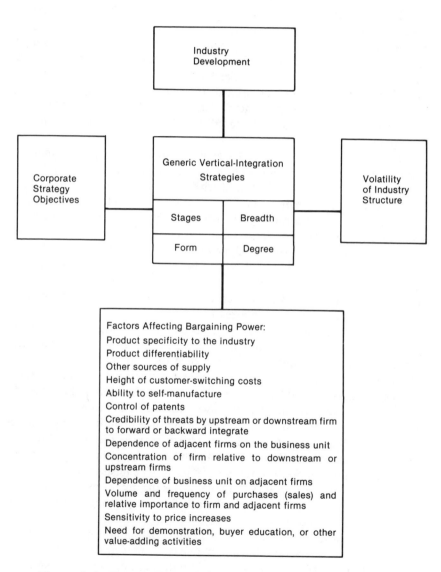

Figure 2–5. Factors Determining Company's Bargaining Power

the product being supplied. For example, automobile manufacturers have never backward integrated into tire production because tires are clearly dependent upon automobiles as consumers. Although suppliers which produce a unique or customized component should possess some bargaining power over customers, their market power may be negated if several alternative sources of supply exist.

The better the alternative capacity, quality, and reliability offered by *other* potential suppliers of a component, the greater bargaining power the business unit has over a particular supplier. Business units can play suppliers against each other to obtain lower prices, and if subcontractors can be easily controlled—as in the case of garment manufacturers who use assemblers—less integration may be needed. (Garment makers' high bargaining power over assemblers enables them to specify penalties to be paid by piecerate firms for excessive use of materials supplied by the garment firms, for example.)

The business unit possesses bargaining power over adjacent industry participants if it can communicate a credible threat that it will integrate backward, or forward, if displeased with them. (For example, Ford once decided to manufacture its own glass to protect against interruptions in supply, and as a result of this entry, the price per square foot of glass dropped from a maximum of two dollars to as low as twenty-five cents.) Whether the threat of self-manufacture is credible or not depends upon the minimum-efficient scale of the plant that would be needed to supply the business units' needs. If no significant entry barriers exist to prevent the business unit from executing its threat of self-manufacture, it possesses bargaining power. It need not integrate to exert that power.

Whenever the business unit can act as a bottleneck to entities upstream or downstream, it possesses bargaining power. For example, in the automobile industry, the assemblers pay for special tools, dies, jigs, and fixtures which they supply to their component manufacturers. Ownership of these assets gives assemblers the power to stipulate how the tools will be used, to control how many units are produced with the tools, and to move the tools between plants, as needed, in order to even out their manufacturing requirements. Also, since the automobile assemblers own the dies needed to produce these components, they control the abilities of supplier firms to participate in the after-market for automotive parts. The business unit also possesses bargaining power over the supplier if it is the only consumer of a nonstandardized design, or the supplier's facilities and personnel are unsuited to produce other kinds of output.

Suppliers or distributors can exert countervailing power over the business unit if they have acceptable alternative customers or can communicate a credible threat that they will integrate into the business unit's market. The business unit will be dependent upon them if it buys or sells a large percentage of key materials to one firm, if there are few alternative suppliers of the needed products or services, or if the business unit faces high switching costs in changing suppliers or distributors. Whenever firms must share trade secrets with suppliers the potential to exert bargaining power exists. Suppliers who recognize their dependence upon a business unit may seek to temper its bargaining power by gaining control of key resources (such as a patent, trade secret, or materials). Distributors frequently band together in buying groups to represent a larger volume of the business unit's sales in order to counter its bargaining power.

In summary, if firms do not possess adequate bargaining power to maintain control over resources, they must frequently integrate to obtain this power. If firms do not possess adequate bargaining power to negotiate these services with independent downstream firms they may use quasi-integration to control them legally, without ownership, but firms in relatively weaker bargaining positions often must use higher degrees of ownership to obtain supplies or access to customers.

Summary: Hypotheses Concerning Relative Bargaining Power (With Respect to Suppliers and Customers) and Strategies for Vertical Integration

Higher degrees of internal integration and increased ownership are needed when firms cannot control access to suppliers or customers through bargaining power. Ownership of supplying or distributing operations is highest in established industries where the firm's bargaining power is low and industry conditions are stable. In each case, the balance in bilateral bargaining power is determined by who needs whom. If there are tasks firms cannot perform internally with skill and economy equal to that of outsiders, firms possessing bargaining power can obtain these skills inexpensively without investing in specialized assets by using contracts to control adjacent industries. But firms that do not possess bargaining power must instead use some form of ownership to control them or pay relatively higher prices. Highly integrated strategies are risky in volatile industries because they amplify a firm's exposure to the fluctuations of demand and competition, but firms with little bargaining power may be forced to use them for defensive reasons.

Corporate-Strategy Objectives for the Business Unit

As figure 2-6 indicates, corporate-level review of integration policies is needed to attain acceptable risk-return performance for the business unit in

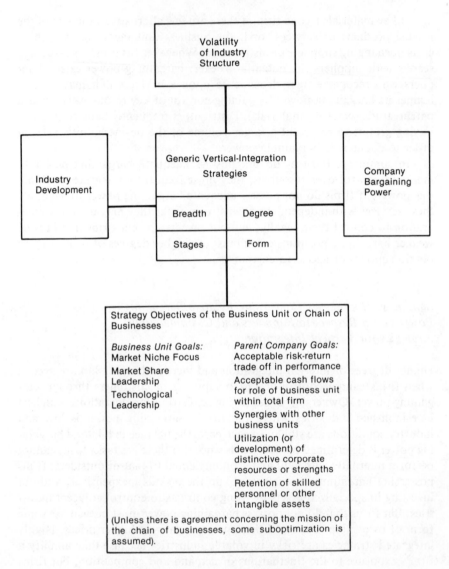

Figure 2-6. Strategy Objectives

question, to maintain acceptable cash flows from the business units, to maximize synergies from sharing resources with other business units, to utilize (or develop) distinctive corporate strengths or resources, and to retain skilled personnel and other intangible assets through carefully designed

opportunities for integration. Business units are likely to define their objectives in terms of near-term profit-maximization, market-share targets, or
technology-leadership objectives (as well as other specialized niche positions). In reconciling business-unit goals with corporate objectives, competitive thrusts involving leadership positions (either cost or technological
leadership)[19] are better suited to higher degrees of integration than are business units pursuing a focus strategy for reasons explained below.

Corporate review of vertical strategies is needed lest firms suffer product obsolescence (due to a lack of contact with customers), technological
lags (from a lack of access to research and development and innovations),
cash drains (created by the cost of maintaining out-of-date integration),
excessive fixed costs and high breakeven points (from incurring unjustified
costs to build an integrated position), and organizational ennui. Thus cor-
porate-integration strategies use market forces to create intracompany competition, frequently by maintaining loosely coupled bonds between adjacent
units rather than stronger bonds.

Business Unit Goals. In selecting its strategy, the strategic business unit
(SBU) identifies the domain it seeks and which differential advantages it has
to serve that domain. When the business unit selects the strategic thrusts
necessary to achieve its product and market objectives (and the timing of
moves to capture its domain), it may envision advantages of vertical integration that require intraorganizational negotiations. Because many managers prefer to eschew buying from their sister business units, they try to
exert control over outsiders instead, but there are circumstances in which
high internal integration would be preferable to going outside.

Firms pursuing *leadership* objectives seek either market-share leadership (which is usually achieved through cost leadership), or technological
leadership (which is usually achieved through either strong product differentiation or continuing innovation). Firms pursuing *focus* objectives seek a
selective market niche they can serve well through differentiated product
attributes, service, location, or other qualities that are not universally
demanded by the entire market.

Business units pursuing a focus strategy seek high-margin niches to
serve by virtue of distinctive competence. Because their goal is frequently to
maximize near-term profits, such business units seek integration that may
be narrower or of a lesser degree than a corporate perspective considering
capabilities not bounded by markets might advocate. For example,
although the marketing of established, branded products may often be
achieved more profitably by using distribution agents rather than a costly
sales force (or owned stores), channel effectiveness may be weak when the
parent firm tries to introduce new products for a sister unit by using the
business unit's marketing channels. By cutting back marketing expenses on

its mature and stable products, the business unit has made the parent firm ill-prepared to launch the new ones which incur heavy roll-out costs.

Business units pursuing leadership goals may seek high market shares attained through cost leadership. Large sales volumes could enable them to exploit the manufacturing *and* integration economies which frequently accrue to vertically integrated postures. Thus business units negotiate with upstream (or downstream) units to arrange the least costly means of satisfying demand, an arrangement that can include broad and high integration in some industries.

The dangers in asset inflexibility that such leadership strategies promote make corporate review imperative. In addition to the higher breakeven points and penalties for excess capacity created by these arrangements, such activities may require more cash or administrative resources than the parent firm is willing to allocate to business units in particular industry settings. Figure 2-7 illustrates the integration trade-offs that a volatile industry setting could impose upon cost-leadership objectives, for example.

Other business units pursuing a leadership strategy seek positions of

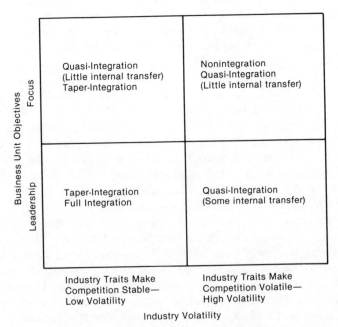

Figure 2-7. Appropriate Degree of Internal Integration per Degree of Industry Volatility and Business-Unit Objectives (Holding Other Factors Constant)

technological leadership that offer long-term profitability from the halo effect of commercializing technological breakthroughs. The markets these business units seek are specialized and price insensitive in some cases. (In other cases, technological leaders innovative and license their discoveries for large market-share applications.) In either case technological leadership strategies prosper from high degrees of integration in the activities that are integrated. Their technological strengths (or quality images) emanate from the excellent intelligence about innovation and demand provided by integration.

Corporate-profitability pressures create a dilemma for technological-leadership strategies, because as the most effective users of breakthroughs in processes, components, or designs, these business units seek integration; parent firms facing profitability problems encourage them to use contracts or other low-cost arrangements instead. Although contracts may be lower in cost, high internal integration is more desirable if trade secrets must be protected. If research and development is important to business units' strategic objectives (and if they lack the power to control outsiders), only small-volume, well-understood component requirements should be farmed out to job shops, and sensitive, high-technology inputs should be produced internally.

Parent Corporation Goals. Whatever objectives a business unit hopes to pursue must be consistent with the mission selected by corporate management for that unit. Because vertical integration can be costly if used imprudently, corporate strategists must scrutinize the advantages they hope to capture by condoning (or denying) the creation of certain vertical relationships. Because vertical integration may be part of a larger strategy involving shared resources and experience-curve economies for some components, corporate strategists must sustain some vertical relationships and maximize their effectiveness.

Some vertical integrations risk joining industries that possess similar sensitivities to economic conditions. Other integrations are risky because they create mobility or exit barriers by substituting new technologies and products for obsolete ones. Both conditions could damage corporate profitability or strategic flexibility.

Although certain operating improvements are available to firms progressing down the experience curve through vertical integration, these improvements often require capital expenditures which the parent firm may be loath to undertake. Thus, increasing the degree, breadth, stages, or form of integration in a business unit that the parent firm is harvesting is inconsistent with corporate objectives and less likely to occur.

Some vertical integrations improve long-term synergies for the entire firm although they appear to penalize a particular business unit. Supply-side economies, for example, can often be gained by sharing manufacturing facilities for components that could be used in several dissimilar products. Yet the organization that coordinates both the supply-side and market-segmentation strategies a particular strategic business unit faces must be complex (as must be the control system). Although the synergies obtained from this complexity may be substantial, the costs of expensive organizations may not be justified by the economies and market intelligence attained. The firm may be thrust into businesses it did not intend to enter, or diseconomies may occur by linking organizational cultures that are not compatible.[20]

To the extent that vertical integration can increase or enhance innovation by sharing of technological information common to separate stages of an industry, corporate management will be more likely to sanction vertical integration, especially if it promises to create or make use of strengths the firm values. Briefly, firms that view themselves as research-and-development oriented will be more likely to condone high degrees of in-house research, and firms that view themselves as marketing firms will be more likely to approve the creation of substantial in-house marketing-research and advertising staffs.

The most scarce resource firms possess is their entrepreneurial ability. Rather than seeing their mix of businesses as streams of cash flows, parent firms can consider them reservoirs of capabilities. Thus vertical integration should be encouraged where personnel with crucial skills (or other scarce capabilities) might otherwise not be retained.

Summary: Hypotheses Concerning Business-Unit and
Corporate Goals and Vertical-Integration Strategies

Vertical integration is risky in unstable environments, yet corporate objectives urge business units to undertake such integrations if advantages due to synergies or exploitation of key corporate strengths are anticipated. Accordingly, these corporate objectives will increase the degree, breadth, stages, or form of vertical integration beyond the recommendations of the strategy framework. Doing so will also increase the corporation's riskiness; however, this decision is appropriate when considered in the portfolio of other ventures the corporation is funding. Cash-flow requirements will reduce the expected degree, breadth, stages, or form of vertical integration when operating economies from integration are not substantial, because corporate objectives reduce vertical integration for business units that the strategy framework suggests could be more highly—or more completely—integrated.

A Simplified Strategy Framework

The strategy framework that has been developed in this chapter is summarized in figures 2-8 through 2-11. These simplified frameworks summarize those relationships hypothesized to be significant to the need for stable access to supplies, resource personnel and distribution while minimizing the riskiness some strategies for vertical integration entail and striving toward generic business-unit objectives as the industry's structure evolves. Figure 2-8 suggests appropriate strategies for embryonic businesses, given the presence or absence of the traits developed in previous sections. Figure 2-9 illustrates how the strategy options change as the industry's structure becomes better articulated, and figure 2-10 shows the range of strategies for vertical

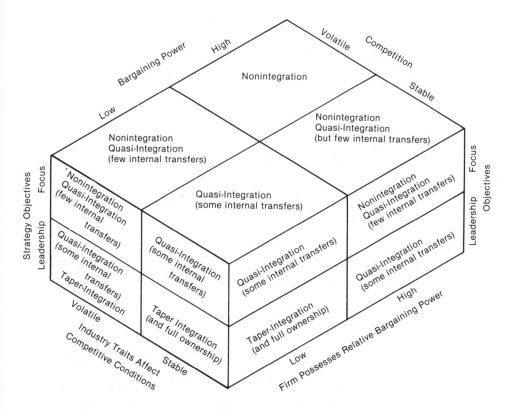

Figure 2-8. An Illustration of the Strategy Framework for Vertical Integration with Embryonic Industries

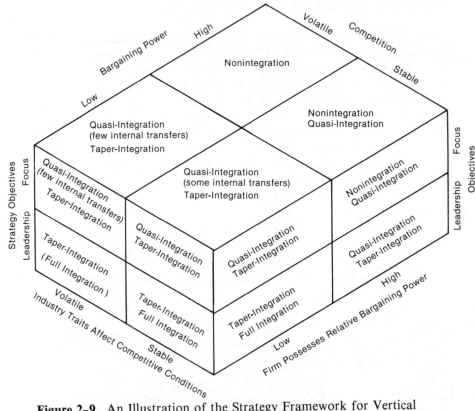

Figure 2-9. An Illustration of the Strategy Framework for Vertical Integration within Emerging Industries

integration within established settings. Figure 2-11 suggests strategies for vertical integration within endgame, or declining, industries.

The Model's Predictions

The strategic framework suggests that certain generic strategies are more likely to be successful depending upon first, the relative probability that a particular industry will undergo radical technological changes or severe price warfare, second, the ability of the firm to cajole or pressure suppliers or distributors into performing value-adding tasks for the firm, thus providing it with competitive advantages, and third, the degree of uncertainty surrounding sales growth, industry infrastructure, and other market traits. Interpretive examples of the strategy framework are given below.

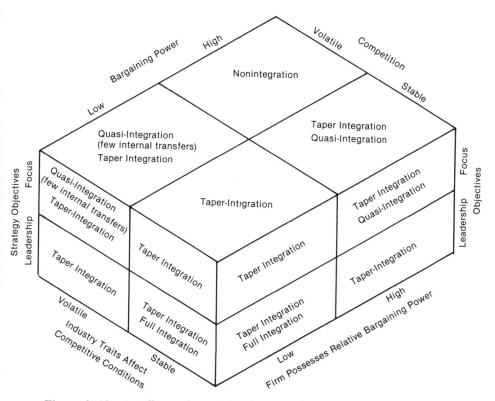

Figure 2-10. An Illustration of the Strategy Framework for Vertical Integration within Established Industries

Briefly, a stable competitive environment has low variability in the growth rate of sales and an established industry infrastructure. There are few process innovations to upset relative price advantages, high customer-switching costs, high entry barriers, and little excess capacity. Where there is excess capacity, the diseconomies are not substantial and competitors see the industry similarly, hence they act like a stable oligopoly. Within these industries, bargaining power enables firms to transfer to adjacent firms a greater portion of overhead and expense associated with ensuring that they have access to components and distribution channels. Thus it is not necessary to invest in strategies calling for high degrees of integration, and more tasks could be entrusted to highly specialized suppliers or merchandisers. If integration is necessary, it is less risky than in volatile environments. An unfavorable environment, by contrast, creates a situation where firms cannot command the power necessary to persuade firms in adjacent industries

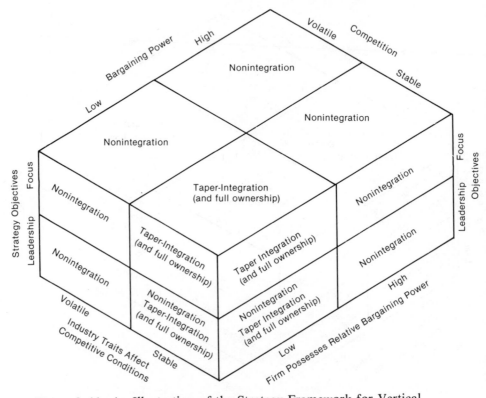

Figure 2–11. An Illustration of the Strategy Framework for Vertical Integration within Endgame Industries

to carry a portion of their overhead. Whether an industry is volatile or not, and whether a firm possesses bargaining power or not depends upon the industry and corporate traits developed in the strategy framework using the analysis presented above.

From this framework, it should be evident that different competitors within the same industry could each execute strategies for vertical integration that are appropriate for them, but different from one another. The following considerations temper the framework's recommendation: first, if a business were pursuing large market-share targets, it may use more internal integration than the strategic matrix might suggest would be advisable; second, if it were pursuing profitability goals using product quality, it may use more internal upstream and less downstream integration than the strategic matrix might recommend, holding other factors constant; and third, if the firm were seeking technological leadership, it might seek more integration even in the embryonic phase of industry development. The choice of strategies is discussed below.

If the firm either cannot find suppliers or distributors to perform the tasks it requires, it requires complete secrecy due to the uniqueness of its technological products, or requires complete and total control of its products from raw materials to consumers for quality-assurance purposes in a stable environment that has a modest and regular growth rate, established product traits, and few maverick competitors, or possesses other favorable industry characteristics, the firm should seek high degrees of internal integration both upstream and downstream, or full integration, provided it is willing to make the investments in assets and personnel to support this strategy choice. This is a risky strategy, but a bold one, which could be rewarding if executed correctly because it offers the potential of lowest unit costs where integration economies are substantial.

Tapered integration offers a safety valve in that both stages of the vertical chain need not be perfectly in balance. Tapered integration is a prudent strategy when the environment is volatile and demand is erratic because the fluctuations in demand can be carried by outsiders. It is a less risky response to a bargaining position of relative weakness than is full integration.

Firms that are in a strong bargaining position could use *quasi-integration* to control external firms' activities as if they were owned by the firm. Executed correctly, this strategy can represent a relatively inexpensive method of leveraging the breadth of a firm's operations and reducing its uncertainty.

Ownership or internal transfers may not be appropriate when the firm's competitive environment is volatile and its bargaining power is high. A strategy of *nonintegration* requires little financial stake in adjacent industries and affords maximum strategic flexibility should the firm wish to alter its mix of products or size of operations. Exit is easiest from this strategic arrangement.

The Timing of Vertical-Integration Strategies

The frameworks in figures 2–8 through 2–11 indicates that the appropriate degree of internal integration will change over time due to changes in risk or uncertainty and demand or sales growth. High degrees of internal integration offer temporary state-of-the-art advantages that must be weighed against the advantages of being flexible to exploit the next technological innovation. Sales volumes and structural conditions are generally too uncertain to justify high degrees of internal integration in embryonic industries, but vertical integration may be a rationalizing device. Industry leaders may integrate vertically in an embryonic industry to forge order in a chaotic environment and to obtain lower operating costs first. Vertical integration becomes an entry barrier as an industry's structure emerges. Firms that can afford to enter integration frequently prefer to allow thinly capitalized pioneers to test the competitive waters for them. These competitors skim the benefits of the early entrants' investment but bear little of the risk associated with the embryonic phase by integrating during the emerging phase, instead.

As growth rates slow and industry structures become established, backward integration has been used to force out thinly capitalized firms. Consequently some firms integrate for defensive reasons. Balance is easiest to achieve in mature industries and thus more firms use integration there than in other settings. Integration can be risky in volatile mature industries, however, because too much (or too little) output risks over- or under-production, adverse market reactions, or imbalances that leave excess capacity or costly inventories to be absorbed. In declining markets, integrated assets become exit barriers as the take-or-pay contract willingly signed to guarantee supplies becomes increasingly costly to honor, and the highly specific and durable assets erected to streamline manufacturing processes become outmoded overnight by technological breakthroughs. In these times, firms using lower degrees and forms of integration will find the endgame easier to manage.

Summary of the timing of changes in vertical integration. Each firm that integrates tries to control its need for certainty, but if competitive conditions and demand variability become *too* unfavorable for it to endure, the firm will face increasing pressures to dis-integrate, or to retreat to lesser forms of integration. Restructuring a firm's strategies to include quasi-control relationships will minimize its exit barriers, reduce breakeven targets, and create more-streamlined strategic postures. Although it may seem desirable for firms to wait to see what happens as their industry evolves before selecting an integration strategy, waiting could be suboptimal. If the firm needs integration to control some aspect of its product policy, it should build a pilot plant and learn about its suppliers *early*, before competitors can match this advantage with their own experience.

In summary, less internal investment in vertical integration may be better than more. The firm should keep one foot in the competitive arena of each of its businesses, even the integrated ones, by using a less than fully integrated strategy. The integration strategy selected should consider the industry structure and the demand characteristics of the vertical chain as well as the characteristics of the firms under study. By recognizing the basic patterns that match strategy alternatives with the determinant variables (sketched above), firms could better select and execute an optimal strategy for vertical integration.

Notes

1. This chapter has benefited from exposure to Porter, *Competitive Strategy: Techniques for Analyzing Industries and Competitors* (New York: Free Press, 1980). The make-or-buy decision becomes a corporate one when: the size of the investment exceeds the discretion levels of a business unit's authority, corporate-control needs treat the adjacent units as separate reporting (and planning) entities, or corporate synergies can be maximized by thinking of formerly separate business units together.

2. Firms that are fully integrated with respect to a particular raw material or service need not own 100 percent of the sequent business unit. Joint ventures exist where one partner to the venture obtains its requirements from it while the other partner obtains other benefits, such as access to technology, experience, or cash. Many business arrangements are possible.

3. Firms always purchase small amounts of needed supplies on an infrequent basis to meet emergency needs. (Distress sales of unsold merchandise clear inventories on an irregular basis in fully integrated firms.) Firms which usually transferred 95 percent of their materials internally and which did not seem to consider outside markets as routine trading partners were considered fully integrated with respect to a material or service for the purposes of this study.

4. Abell, Derek, *Defining the Business: The Starting Point of Strategic Planning* (Englewood Cliffs, N.J.: Prentice-Hall, 1980).

5. Harrigan, Kathryn Rudie, *Strategies for Declining Businesses,* D.C. Heath, Lexington, 1980; see also Harrigan, Kathryn Rudie, "Strategy Formulation in Declining Industries," *Academy of Management Review,* vol. 5, no. 4 (October 1980), pp. 599–604; and Harrigan, Kathryn Rudie, "Strategies for Declining Businesses," *Journal of Business Strategy,* vol. 1, no. 2 (Fall 1980), pp. 20–34.

6. Although a volatile competitive environment could be characterized by rapid technological changes in product configurations, aggressive advertising campaigns, and other efforts to capture sales from other firms, environments characterized by fierce price-cutting (due to slowing sales growth, excess manufacturing capacity, or other factors causing a breakdown of competitive discipline) are the most damaging type of *volatile* industry settings.

7. The vertical-integration study does not address the issue of whether the *objective environment* or the *perceived environment* is more useful (or relevant) in strategy research. This issue has been developed elsewhere. See Child, J., "Organizational Structure, Environment and Performance— The Role of Strategic Choice," *Sociology,* vol. 6 (1972): pp. 1–22; Duncan, R., "Characteristics of Organizational Environments and Perceived Environmental Uncertainty," *Administrative Science Quarterly,* vol. 17 (1972):

pp 313–322; Aldrich, H., and Pfeffer, J., "Environments of Organization," *Annual Review of Sociology,* vol. 2 (1976): 79–105; and Hambrick, D.C., "Environmental Scanning, Organizational Strategy and Executive Roles: A Study in Three Industries," unpublished doctoral dissertation, Pennsylvania State University, May 1979.

8. Stigler, George, J., "The Division of Labor is Limited by the Extent of the Market," *Journal of Political Economy,* vol. LIX, no. 3 (June 1951), pp. 185–193; Tucker, Irvin B., and Wilder, Ronald P., "Trends in Vertical Integration in the U.S. Manufacturing Sector," *Journal of Industrial Economics,* vol. 26 (September 1977), pp. 81–94.

9. Harrigan, K.R., "Strategies for Declining Businesses," unpublished doctoral dissertation, Graduate School of Business Administration, Harvard University, 1979, see chapter 10.

10. Sometimes forward acquisitions are made to improve the firm's image in its distribution channels or to foreclose competitors from access to ultimate consumers through distribution outlets. For example, Culbro Corporation was seeking better access to shelf space when the firm acquired Havatampa Cigar, a major distributing company and hoped to obtain superior access to shelf space by owning this distribution company. Other brands were subsequently relegated to less-desirable positions on the cigar racks after this acquisition.

11. The author has benefited from exposure to the ideas presented in Porter, Michael E., "Consumer Behavior, Retailer Power, and Market Performance in Consumer Goods Industries," *Review of Economics and Statistics,* vol. 56 (November 1974), pp. 419–435; Porter, Michael E., *Interbrand Choice, Strategy, and Bilateral Market Power* (Cambridge, Mass.: Harvard University Press, 1976); and Porter, *Competitive Strategy,* 1980, in preparing this section.

12. Within industries where the prices of raw materials are regulated, backward integration to control prices would be ineffective. Nevertheless, one study of petroleum-refinery integration into crude-oil production has found this activity reduces shareholders' perceived risks of the company. (Mead, D.E., "The Effect of Vertical Integration on Risk in the Petroleum Industry," *Quarterly Review of Economics and Business,* vol. 18, no. 1 (Spring 1978), pp. 83–90). Another form of risk reduction in the oil industry, the joint venture, shares the costs of seismic shootings to locate oil in offshore tracts for bidding in lease sales. Oil firms also frequently share the costs of offshore exploratory drilling to participate in developing several sites.

13. The value added by downstream firms can vary from mere order taking (low value added) to consumption of the product in-house for use in other product (high value added).

14. Using distributors (or dealers) will require that some demonstration

aids, exhibits, cutaways, etc., are supplied by the manufacturer. Thus the savings in marketing expense to roll out a product are minimal.

15. Other factors held constant, the presence of high economic exit barriers would deter firms from dis-integrating in a timely fashion and result in opportunity costs being incurred. Economic exit barriers are factors which will keep a firm invested in a suboptimal posture even when it earns subnormal on the investment. Although they may assume many forms (such as the costs associated with shutting down a plant, breaking a supply contract, or facing a loss on disposal where there is a thin resale market for the plant and assets), the effect of exit barriers is to keep excess capacity operating. Exit barriers also continue vertical relationships which may have become uneconomic to sustain.

The factors that influence the *height* of economic exit barriers are predominantly characteristics relating to the products' manufacturing technology: capital intensity, asset specificity, age of the assets (extent to which their value has been depreciated), and technological or operating reinvestment requirements. If the expenditures for other types of investments—advertising, research and development, or plant improvements—were not expensed previously, they too could constitute economic exit barriers. See Caves, Richard E., and Porter, Michael E., "Barriers to Exit," in David P. Qualls and Robert T. Masson, eds., *Essays in Industrial Organization in Honor of Joe S. Bain* (Cambridge, Mass.: Ballinger, 1976): chapter 3; Porter, Michael E., "Please Note Location of Nearest Exit: Exit Barriers and Strategic and Organizational Planning," *California Management Review,* vol. 19, no. 2 (Winter 1976), pp. 21–33; Harrigan, Kathryn Rudie, "The Effect of Exit Barriers Upon Strategic Flexibility," *Strategic Management Journal,* vol. 1, no. 2 (April–June 1980 1980(a)), pp. 165–176; Harrigan, Kathryn Rudie, "Deterrents to Divestiture," *Academy of Management Journal,* vol. 24, no. 2 (June 1981), pp. 306–323; Harrigan, Kathryn Rudie, "Exit Decisions in Mature Industries, *Academy of Management Journal,* vol. 25, no. 4 (December 1982), pp. 707–732.

16. As Chandler has noted, the major determinant of the growth of the firm is its manufacturing technology. Certain capital-intensive technologies possess substantial scale economies which, if pursued, propel the firm to even more rapid growth. The major opportunities for vertical integration occurred only with changes in technology (or major shifts in markets), when firms could nurture new scale economies. Because the fully integrated enterprise flourished when it used capital-intensive, energy-consuming, continuous, or large-batch production, changes in production techniques leading to larger minimum-efficient-scale technologies in the steel and cement industries, for example, were critical in promoting the vertical relationships which developed there. The need to sustain competitive advan-

tages made imperative the vertical control of economic activities which fed (or received) the throughput of efficient plants. Moreover, these technological innovations did not just replace labor, they changed the nature of operations by introducing fully integrated competitors which were better equipped to exploit these opportunities. Thus, the continuous-process industries such as steel, petroleum, and petrochemicals; food processing (especially meatpacking and flour milling), cigarette, cement and concrete manufacturing; aluminum, rubber, copper, wood, and paper products; and inorganic chemicals would be expected to be more frequently vertically integrated by virtue of technological innovation. See Chandler, Alfred D., Jr., *The Visible Hand: The Managerial Revolution in American Business* (Cambridge, Mass.: Harvard University Press, 1979).

17. Porter, Michael E., *Interbrand Choice, Strategy and Bilateral Market Power* (Cambridge, Mass.: Harvard University Press, 1976).

18. I am indebted to William H. Newman and Ian C. MacMillan for assistance in developing this section.

19. These generic strategies—that is, cost leadership, focus, and differentiation—are developed in Porter, 1980.

20. Any corporate scheme to force vertically related business units to deal with each other without the benefit of open market equivalents for the purposes of transfer pricing and maintaining competitive flexibility is penalizing one party to the transaction for the sake of the other. Subsidization of uneconomic and noncompetitive business units for the sake of ephemeral corporate advantages is a strategic trap that should be carefully scrutinized. Global competition is one example where these linkages are necessary and should be sustained.

3

Methodology of the Research into Vertical-Integration Strategies

This chapter explains how the strategy framework was tested. Before describing the research process, I will restate the central hypotheses of the study because the methodology used was developed to test that particular framework.

Briefly, lower degrees of internal integration are more appropriate in environments of volatile competition than higher degrees, but firms that do not possess bargaining power over suppliers or customers will be obliged to perform several value-adding tasks internally, thereby increasing their degree, stages, and breadth of integration, as well as their risk exposure (or form). Lower degrees of internal integration are more appropriate in the earliest and latest phases of an industry's development, other things held constant.

Because the structures of industries differ, several industries were observed to isolate the structural variables that were crucial in formulating strategies for vertical integration. Because the most important of these was expected to be the relative number of ways a firm might gain advantages in competition, product differentiability was a key dimension of the sample design, as was the development of an industry infrastructure. The sample included several older industries as well as some newer ones.

Selection of the Sample

The strategy framework developed in chapter 2 argued that many traits are important to the formulation of effective strategies. However, it would have been unwieldy to encompass all of these traits in a sample design. Figure 3–1 shows the variables that were used to select industries for the field studies. These included the types of customer who purchased the product, uncertainty concerning the growth of demand, and competitive conditions. Some firms faced little uncertainty concerning future demand because their products were clearly obsolete, while others suffered uncertainty because demand for their products had not yet become large enough to be economical.

Figure 3–2 indicates the industries included in the study. These were personal microcomputers, electric-percolator coffee makers, cigars, tai-

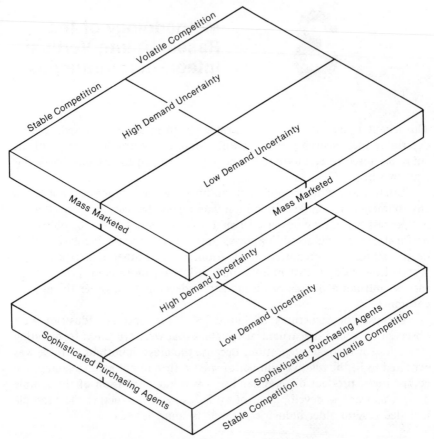

Figure 3-1. A Taxonomy for Classifying the Industries Whose Members Were Interviewed in the Study of Vertical-Integration Strategies

lored suits, petroleum refining, synthetic soda ash, ethical pharmaceuticals, electronic receiving tubes, rayon and acetate, baby foods, whiskey, residential solar heating, U.S. leather tanning, coal gasification, acetylene, and genetic engineering. As we explain below, data concerning eight of these industries came from an earlier study of declining industries and the remaining industries were selected to contrast new businesses with older ones. Figure 3-3 presents a taxonomy of these new embryonic, emerging, established, and endgame industries, grouped according to whether they produced consumer goods or goods sold to industrial customers (that is, knowledgeable buyers whose purchases are made through specialized departments). Note that the variables defining the sample taxonomies in figures 3-1 and 3-3 were observable traits, offering a tangible foundation for subsequent comparisons. The consumer products were highly differenti-

Mass-Marketed Products Sold to Unsophisticated Buyers

	Low Demand Uncertainty	High Demand Uncertainty	
	Personal Microcomputers Electric-Percolator Coffee- Makers Cigars	Rayon and Acetate Baby Foods	Volatile Competition
	Tailored Suits	Whiskey Residential Solar Heating	Stable Competition

Producer Goods Sold to Relatively Sophisticated Purchasing Agents

	Low Demand Uncertainty	High Demand Uncertainty	
	Petroleum Refining Synthetic Soda Ash	U.S. Leather Tanning	Volatile Competition
	Ethical Pharmaceuticals Electronic Receiving Tubes	Coal Gasification Acetylene Genetic Engineering	Stable Competition

Figure 3–2. A Taxonomy of the Industries Whose Members Were Included in the Study of Vertical-Integration Strategies

ated, relying primarily on nonprice attributes to gain competitive advantages. The producer goods were differentiated to sophisticated buyers, but to the undiscerning eye, competitors' products seemed similar. (Ethical pharmaceuticals, for example, were initially protected by patents, but competition among generic ethical pharmaceuticals—whether off-patent or unpatentable drugs—was primarily on the basis of price.)

Field-Research Procedure

Information concerning industry structure and firms' strategies was collected from interviews, annual reports, and other sources noted at the end of each chapter. Field data were gathered in telephone or personal interviews with firms, their suppliers, distributors, customers, and trade-

	Products Sold to Producers (Commodity Traits)	Products Sold to Consumers (Differentiable Traits)
Embryonic Industry	Coal Gasification	Residential Solar Heating
Emerging Industry	Genetic Engineering	Personal Computers
Established Industry	Ethical Pharmaceuticals	Tailored Suits
Endgame Industry	Petroleum Refining	Whiskey

Figure 3-3. A Taxonomy of Some Industries Whose Members Were Interviewed in the Study of Vertical-Integration Strategies

association representatives. Dealers and distributors also provided promotional literature.

The philosophy guiding the field-research phase was a desire to explore the variations in vertical-integration strategies from the objective perspective of a diversified parent company. Interviews were sought at several levels within firms in order to incorporate the firms' strategic considerations outside the chain of vertical businesses as well as the business managers' concerns within the vertical chain. The selective cross-corroboration procedure meant that all of the key firms in an industry did not have to be interviewed to obtain the necessary data concerning their historic behaviors, and sometimes observers or smaller competitors were interviewed but their behaviors were not reported below. Where discrepancies developed about the interpretation of competitive events, these irregularities are also reported.

In each chapter, two sections develop the industry's structure in 1981, offering a descriptive vignette and a chronology. The chronology details each industry's development from a common *base year,* 1960, up until 1981 to hold constant the exogenous effects of U.S. economic and sociopolitical factors. These data demonstrate how vertical integration developed and changed in these industries over time.[1] The merit of this method of presentation is that analysis of industry and competitor experiences can be presented separately from the data. Also, this method of exposition facilitates an unprejudiced evaluation of the hypotheses which can be gathered separately from the data to present a synthesizing chapter and subsequent statistical analysis.

A Description of the Data

The data are presented in the form of miniature industry studies. Each of the studies contains a sketch of the industry structure, a chronology of vertical-integration events, and an analysis of these data in light of the framework posited in chapter 2.

Vignettes profile each industry in 1981 in terms of the product, suppliers to the manufacturing industry, research and development needs, manufacturing processes, and customers—both intermediate and ultimate consumers. The descriptions of how products were made and marketed also suggest whether entry (or exit) was substantially affected by these attributes. The last section of each vignette sketches the major competitors (or groups of similar competitors). It explains which tasks in the vertical chain were performed internally (breadth and stages) and whether any outside contracting of these tasks was done (degree of internal integration). It also explains principal ownership forms.

The chronology notes major changes in firms' vertical integrations prior to 1960, and it details adjustments in purchasing, research, manufacturing, or distribution policies subsequent to that date, leading to the industry's 1981 structure. The major decisions include adding, buying, or selling upstream or downstream facilities. It also explains how firms gained access to markets, components, or other necessary factors; control of quality, service, and efficiency in the final product offering; and superior scanning capabilities to detect changes in technology, market attributes, or competitors' maneuvers.

The last part of each industry note assesses how well the strategy framework predicts the vertical-integration strategy undertaken. An analysis of how variations in industry structure, industry maturity, and firms' traits affected the vertical strategies is presented in which the expected strategy is contrasted with the actual outcome. Generalizations are developed from these comparisons, a separate chapter synthesizes these findings, and finally, applications of the findings are suggested.

The firms with *effective* vertical-integration strategies were those which gained stable access to materials or markets while attaining strategic objectives such as market dominance, above-average returns on invested capital, or technological leadership. Specifically, effective, vertically integrated firms earned above-average, long-term profits over the horizon period on their vertically integrated businesses, while facing few doubts concerning their abilities to continue to prosper or to dis-integrate successfully. Market-share or technological leaders were included in this group, even if their short-term profitability was not among the highest.[2]

Vertical strategies had *degree, breadth, stages* and *form*. Highly integrated firms transferred almost 100 percent of a particular material or service in-house, upstream or downstream. In constructing a ratio indicating the breadth of integration, the number of activities a firm performed was divided by the total number of activities possible to perform, and the most broadly integrated firm possessed a ratio of 1.00. *Stages* were estimated by constructing an index of upstream and downstream linkages for a particular function, multiplying the percentage of materials or services transferred at each stage by its proportion of value-added and summing each product. Form was measured by the proportion of ownership, ranging from 0 to 100 percent.

Limitations of the Data

This study examined a complex set of hypotheses concerning vertical integration by using cross-sectional field data, and its findings are subject to several qualifications because of the disparity of the industries examined. The confidences with which conclusions could be stated in this study must be reduced by the strong element of judgment needed in interpolating data and evaluating the findings as well as in describing a complex factual situation. Therefore, the data from this study should be handled with less confidence about their generalizability than those of other multiple-site, empirically based research programs.

Advantages of the Research Methodology

The medium-grained methodology[3] employed is particularly suitable for analyzing strategy-formulation issues because it retains many of the best features of single-case studies while offering the generalizability of larger data-base studies. The industry vignettes and chronologies offer the types of insights which usually would be available only using case studies. The large sample size permits generalizations to be drawn while distinguishing between the effects of important contingency variables. The multiplicity of data sources (and multiple interviews per industry) provide a greater robustness than research using single data sources. The intricate sample design facilitates the isolation of key factors hypothesized to influence choices of vertical-integration strategy for the purposes of comparison.

Notes

1. Given this sample design, observations of dis-integration strategies may be limited. The two endgame sample industries—petroleum refining and whiskey—face the beginning of declining demand conditions in the 1980s. Therefore, discussion and analysis of effective degrees, breadths, stages, and forms of vertical integration within industries facing advanced stages of declining demand will draw upon data presented in Harrigan, *Strategies for Declining Businesses* (D.C. Heath & Company, 1980). These observations are presented in chapter 4.

2. By contrast, firms with *ineffective* (or *conceptually flawed*) vertical-integration strategies were unable to obtain stable access to materials or markets, and could not attain market share, above-average returns, or technological-leadership objectives. When they tried to disintegrate linked functions, they suffered significant losses (greater than 10 percent net-earnings loss on disposal) and disrupted their other business activities significantly. They suffered below-average returns if they remained integrated and faced substantial doubts concerning their abilities to staunch their losses.

3. See Harrigan, K.R., "Research and Methodologies for Contingency Approaches to Business Strategy," *Academy of Management Review,* July 1983, forthcoming.

4 Strategies for Vertical Integration in Declining Industries

This chapter explores the hypotheses about evolution and vertical integration by examining data (detailed elsewhere[1]) on declining industries. This chapter differs from subsequent ones because either these industries no longer face viable demand, or their demand has leveled off at a significantly lower volume. The framework presented in chapter 2 predicted low internal transfers, few integrated stages, and fewer activities in such industries.

Overview of the Declining-Business Study

The declining-business research sample included more than sixty firms in eight industries, chosen to cover the broadest range of situations and to contrast three key structural traits: product differentiation, exit barriers, and concentration. The industries examined were: rayon and acetate, cigars, baby foods, electric-percolator coffee makers, electronic receiving tubes, acetylene, synthetic soda ash, and the U.S. leather-tanning industry. The method of data collection was similar to that of the vertical strategies study, and their findings are comparable.

Vignettes of Strategies for Vertical Integration in Declining Industries

This section describes briefly each of the industries with respect to factors that the vertical-integration framework has emphasized: phase of industry development, structural conditions affecting industry volatility, bargaining power, and corporate strategy. The following section discusses the strategy framework in light of these data.

Rayon and Acetate. Rayon and acetate are chemically based cellulose fibers used for textiles, tire cord, and cigarette filters. The fibers are differentiated in several ways, but were both sold by the bale or skein through direct negotiation between buyer and seller. Wood-pulp suppliers were fragmented and dependent upon the rayon and acetate plants for their sales.

Some firms were backward integrated into either wood pulp or chemicals (or both), and firms could also perform in-house research to develop new crimp-fiber designs. (Avtex, the original Courtaulds plant and first U.S. rayon firm, developed many of its machines for production out of necessity, because no supplier existed at that time.)

The tire companies which used rayon filament were concentrated, but the textile mills were fragmented. Nevertheless textiles firms were able to extract low prices, design services, and inventory financing from the rayon and acetate firms because other synthetic fibers could be substituted for rayon and acetate. Rayon staple was used for sanitary products, like diapers, as well as filters, and in 1978 only Courtaulds, the originator of rayon and the largest global textile firm, was forward integrated to manufacture textiles from its fibers. This had not always been the case.

When the first rayon and acetate plants were constructed in the United States after 1910, woolen-textile mills were unwilling to convert their assets to use the man-made fibers. Consequently firms like Courtaulds and Celanese forward integrated to textiles and garment fabrication to prove their viability. By 1930 the structure of the rayon and acetate industry was emerging, and pioneering firms disintegrated from garment production (and later from textile production also). As specialists developed, it became unnecessary for rayon and acetate firms to weave textiles. Only in markets for rayon tire filament, where firms like Industrial Rayon Corporation wove the fabric for tire carcasses from rayon, was forward integration prominent in 1968. In endgame few firms were integrated.

Except for Tennessee Eastman, most rayon and acetate firms experienced fierce price competition from each other, from substitute fibers, and from imported rayon fibers. Demand uncertainty was great because consumption fluctuated in its decline and exit barriers were high. Government regulations required costly investments in pollution-control equipment at a time when firms could ill afford to make them. In sum, this was a volatile environment that was not favorable for reinvestments of capital.

Until Avtex toppled on the brink of failure in 1976, the rayon and acetate firms had not seemed to possess bargaining power with upstream or downstream firms. Then ITT Rayonier (a supplier of wood pulp) extended substantial credit to Avtex and launched advertising campaigns to promote the use of rayon. Customers placed orders with Avtex to keep the industry giant afloat and Avtex refused to finance customers' inventories any longer.

By endgame no U.S. rayon and acetate firms were backward integrated. According to the strategy framework, low degrees of integration, few integrated stages and activities, and low ownership stakes were appropriate at this time in such a volatile environment.

Cigars. Cigars are compact rolls of tobacco for smoking. They can be differentiated in several ways, primarily in shape and quality. Many cigar makers were backward integrated to produce tobacco, but supplies were also readily available in world tobacco markets. Each cigar maker cured its own tobacco regardless of where it was purchased because curing affected the taste of cigars. Several major cigar companies produced their own versions of cigar machines and developed their own processes to supplement the machines. Culbro also created and merchandised homogenized tobacco leaf to the others.

Cigars were distributed through wholesale companies that usually possessed exclusive territories. There were many distribution companies dealing with cigar makers and Culbro purchased a major one late in endgame to obtain access to better shelf space.

The cigar industry remained fragmented until a cigar-forming machine was introduced in the 1920s. The industry began with much backward integration because tobacco leaf was specially grown for cigar production. By 1950 automated cigar-forming machines and homogenized tobacco leaf had reduced labor requirements and enabled the cigar industry to keep unit prices low. But in 1978 only a few major cigar makers grew their own tobacco and even fewer owned distribution companies.

Competition for shelf space among the lower-priced cigars was intense as demand slowly dwindled, but there was little uncertainty concerning the trend which demand would follow. Fewer cigars were being smoked. Import competition was increasing outside traditional distribution channels and the absolute number of cigar makers was declining. In sum, this was a volatile environment that was not favorable for reinvestments of capital.

The distribution companies and retailers used their bargaining power to force cigar makers to accept returns on merchandise and to grant lucrative price breaks. Upstream, the tobacco market was fragmented but subject to conditions of supply and demand.

By endgame, backward integration had been reduced and only Havatampa Cigar and Culbro were forward integrated to increase the geographic scope of the distribution companies they already controlled. The strategy framework recommended low internal integration, low ownership stakes, few integrated stages, and few integrated activities in this type of declining industry, and would *not* recommend the type of vertical-integration strategy Culbro pursued in 1978 because it amplified Culbro's exposure to the fortunes of cigars and cigar tobacco.

Baby Foods. Baby foods are commercially processed formulas and foods strained to a very fine consistency to be fed to infants. Baby foods could be differentiated by the quality of raw materials used, taste, appearance, and packaging. Grocery stores were concentrated regionally, and they possessed bargaining power because they bought large quantities of baby foods and these volumes were less than 0.5 percent of their total grocery-store purchases. Only one major baby-food firm owned farms (H.J. Heinz); other baby-food firms used contracts and agricultural-research agreements to ensure that their produce was delivered on schedule in good condition. Swift had packed baby meats since 1946 when it invented the product to fill excess-meat-packing capacity, but as demand declined Swift (Armour and Hormel) copacked baby meats for other baby-food firms.

When baby foods were first introduced around 1915 or earlier, they were sold through specialized medical outlets and as the industry's structure developed, it became evident that grocery channels were the best way to merchandise baby foods. By the 1940s, when the industry's structure was established, only Swift and Heinz were backward integrated. All of the baby-food firms employed sales representatives to ensure that grocery and convenience stores gave their brands favorable shelf space.

There was great demand uncertainty in the baby-foods industry as the number of births declined with moderate speed. The baby-food firms reacted with disbelief for almost ten years after the downward trend began, until excess capacity became so intense that price-cutting wars became savage. In the past, baby-food firms had purchased some products from outside producers that packed baby foods under contract for them. In endgame most of these contracts were terminated and products were packed in-house. This was not an environment that was favorable for reinvestments of capital.

The baby-food firms possessed bargaining power over farmers, a circumstance that enabled them to have fruits and vegetables grown to their specifications by others. Downstream, grocery outlets possessed sufficient bargaining power to prosper from the shelf-space wars among producers.

In the baby-food endgame, Swift was driven out as had been many firms in the 1940s because it did not possess the sales force and support needed to hold its position in this industry. Gerber Products diversified in a pattern of products closely related to baby foods, thereby increasing the breadth and stages of its integration in baby foods more than the strategy framework recommended.

Electric-Percolator Coffee Makers. An electric-percolator coffee maker is a pot that brews coffee using a percolating flow of heated water. Percolator coffee makers could be physically differentiated by size, materials, color, and price, and they were promoted as being part of many major small-electrical-appliance companies' lines.

The retailers who distributed percolators were most strongly influenced by cooperative advertising allowances and brand names. Price concessions were also important in competing for shelf space and retailers refused to carry some percolator models as demand declined because their turnover was too slow. As computerized-inventorying practices became widespread, the number of firms whose lines were stocked also declined. In desperation, firms slashed their percolator prices.

Early percolator firms were not integrated in 1908. Firms with raw-materials positions in metals integrated forward into percolator coffee makers at a time when a glut of metals existed. By 1950, small-housewares manufacturers produced a full line of staple electrical products (or merchandised others' products under their own labels); but by 1978, most firms simply mothballed their percolator assets and those that controlled metals used them elsewhere.

Once the automatic-drip coffee maker was introduced, there was little demand uncertainty concerning percolator coffee makers; consumption of the latter plummeted rapidly. Price-cutting was rampant and firms competed aggressively for the scarce shelf space remaining. In sum, the percolator coffee-maker industry became a volatile environment that was not favorable for reinvestments of capital.

Firms that marketed electric-percolator coffee makers promptly introduced automatic-drip coffee makers instead, when customer preferences changed. Since these firms shared their sales force with other staple housewares, their dis-integrations and subsequent exits from percolator coffee makers were executed in accordance with the strategy framework and their sales forces and other resources did not constitute exit barriers.

Electronic Receiving Tubes. A receiving tube is an active electronic component capable of transmitting, detecting, and amplifying wireless electric signals. A substantial proportion of receiving-tube producers' outputs went into their own television receivers or into those of a major customer (which also purchased private-brand, replacement (PBR) receiving tubes from them). Where economies of scale, in producing a particular type of receiving tube, were reached only at very high volumes, each receiving-tube manufacturer specialized in producing the entire industry's need for a few receiving tubes and sold them to competitors so that each firm could offer a full line of tube designs.

The first receiving-tube firms emerged in the 1920s, and early components were fabricated by the manufacturers out of necessity because there was no existing infrastructure for producing small precision-engineered components at that time. Early receiving-tube companies were also radio-set producers and there were initially few other uses for receiving tubes. The industry was taper-integrated downstream in its emerging phase, and remained so, even in endgame, due to the economies of receiving-tube manufacturing.

There was little doubt that demand was declining for receiving tubes because transistors were being used for more costly applications prior to endgame. Price levels remained stable and little rivalry disrupted the endgame. Thus it was an acceptable environment for higher degrees of internal integration, provided few firms actually did so.

The upstream, component suppliers were small and completely dependent upon the receiving-tube industry. They were not prone to exert their bargaining power, and receiving-tube manufacturers did not need to backward integrate in order to control them. Downstream firms were prone to exert their bargaining power and receiving-tube firms created arrangements to cope with this condition. Receiving-tube manufacturers advertised to and financed the inventories of independent distributors to maintain access to retailers who sold components in the replacement market.

Vertical integration was not an exit barrier in this industry because vertical arrangements were forged to sustain crucial, customer relationships without incurring undue asset risk. These arrangements included sourcing of products and changes in distribution outlets.

Vertical integration proved to be a strength in the receiving-tube industry because having access to their television unit's base of replacements sockets helped receiving-tube firms to surpass breakeven volumes and satisfy the very lucrative demand that existed. The stable and predictable rate of decline and lack of volatile competition protected this industry arrangement, unlike others studied in which industry discipline erupted into price wars and decimated profit margins. Furthermore, when internal units could purchase outsiders' tubes rather than those of sister units, firms were forced to keep their manufacturing costs among the lowest in the industry and this discipline helped firms determine when to exit.

Acetylene. Acetylene is an industrial gas which can be generated either from calcium carbide or from natural gas, and is used as a feedstock in synthesizing many organic compounds, or as a fuel with oxygen to produce a hot flame. The pattern of expansion (upstream or downstream) from acetylene differed depending upon the raw material used to generate it.

Acetylene remained an embryonic industry for almost fifty years, and its use remained low volume until the 1930s when organic chemicals were synthesized from acetylene. Acetylene sales for chemical synthesis were made on a contractual basis that included specially designed and physically interconnected units. Dis-integration could not be incremental where exit barriers were so massive, hence decisions to dis-integrate became complex where an acetylene firm supplied the gas to outside customers who did not wish to terminate their operations and use of acetylene.

The physically interconnected nature of the technology made import competition and customer switching difficult. Since most prices were stipulated by the terms of contracts, competition did not became volatile, except where lawsuits for nonperformance erupted. Dis-integration was difficult, yet it had been necessary to erect the conditions creating exit barriers when demand was healthy in order to sell acetylene.

High-integration arrangements were easier to terminate than tapered ones in acetylene due to the bargaining power of downstream firms. Tenneco Chemical and AIRCO, acetylene producers with heavy merchant positions, encountered great difficulties in terminating their gas-generating plants, in contrast to Monsanto, American Cyanamid and du Pont, which made clean exits because they were wholly contained in-house in their integrations.

Synthetic Soda Ash. Synthetic soda ash (sodium carbonate) is a granular, basic chemical produced for several manufacturing processes. It was sold by the boxcar or the bag through direct negotiation with purchasers. Glassmaking firms like PPG Industries were backward integrated to ensure that adequate supplies would be available. The raw materials required for the Solvay soda ash process—salt and limestone—were usually captively held or were easy to obtain because plants were erected near them.

Soda ash was a commodity, and only price or delivery could distinguish various firms' offerings for most industrial uses. It was only one of several chemicals that firms typically sold to outsiders, and some soda-ash suppliers were so eager to service their customers' entire chemical needs that they purchased soda-ash supplies in excess of their plant's productive capacity to resell to customers.

Firms which began as soda-ash producers acquired limestone quarries or salt supplies initially, and integrated forward in chemicals shortly thereafter. In the process of dis-integrating, firms purchased soda ash from outsiders to ship to their customers. This procedure suggested that the downstream firms possessed bargaining power over soda-ash-producing firms.

Firms incurred losses in their soda-ash ventures because they could not bring them into compliance with tightened Environmental Protection Agency (EPA) requirements regarding industrial effluents. The substitute product's ready availability speeded this process of shutdowns and dis-integrations.

Soda-ash producers recognized their need to forge ongoing purchasing relations with competitors to ensure that an adequate supply would be allotted to them (to resell) when soda ash became scarce. The only time prices could be raised was when other chlor-caustic supplies became tight, and it was generally difficult to sustain price increases for many customer applications because downstream technologies could interchange supplies of liquid or solid alkali substances. Thus firms had to reduce their integrations downstream quickly.

Leather Tanning. Tanning is the process of fixing the protein in raw hides to produce leather.[2] The raw materials used in creating leather included raw hides obtained from slaughterhouses, chemicals, dyes, and specialized equipment. Except for manufacturers of shoes, few leather tanners were linked with downstream industries during the endgame.

Early leather tanners did not own the raw hides they processed, but as the tanning industry's structure evolved, large meat packers integrated forward to process their own hides. In time, however, the advantages of linkages to tanning firms decreased for packing houses because their operations moved geographically but the assets of tanneries were inflexible and could not follow them, and an aggressive market for raw hides overseas offered better prices to packing houses than U.S. tanners could afford. The result was less integration in the tanning industry.

The tanning industry had been volatile because the small family-owned firms which comprised much of this industry were sometimes willing to price their services at a loss in order to keep their workers employed. As competitors chased after the remaining customers, many firms overextended themselves and exacerbated their losses because U.S. hides became scarce and expensive to process.

The downstream buyer that became most vital during endgame was the fashion-leather customer. To serve these very short term needs, leather tanneries had to become a part of the chaotic and rapidly changing fashion industry. The increased riskiness of this new method of competing forced tanneries' profits even lower as customers flexed their new bargaining power. Only in the case of upholstery leather was bargaining power balanced because furniture customers had fewer tanneries from which to purchase.

The strategy framework suggests that new integration in endgame would not be a profitable strategy. This warning was illustrated vividly by the example of Spencer Foods, a meat packer that created a leather-tanning subsidiary in the 1970s. Leather tanning was a sick business in the United States, and Spencer Foods exacerbated its losses by creating this linkage.

A Summary of Strategies for Vertical Integration in
Declining Businesses

Among the experiences of sixty-one firms in eight declining industries, forty-one firms had been vertically integrated at some time in their industries' histories. In endgame, only thirteen firms remained integrated. Two preliminary conclusions are suggested by these data: either vertical integration does not act as an exit barrier in declining businesses, or few firms valued vertical integration when their industries reached endgame.

The largest number of integrations in endgame, in this study, were among the cigar firms that *reduced* their degree of internal transfers of tobacco but did not totally divest their tobacco farms. The cigar industry was one that had been declining slowly for several decades and the urgency of reducing integration was less acute there. Few of the other firms in the eight sample industries studied were vertically integrated by the horizon date, 1978.

Firms who purchased many supplies from (or sold units to) sister units were expected to face high exit barriers because the pressures exerted upon firms to carry their sick business units for the sake of those upstream or downstream were expected to be great, particularly if outside markets were thin. At the end of the period studied, few firms were still vertically integrated. When the tradeoffs between sustaining an integrated structure and using outsiders was illustrated to them financially, firms frequently dis-integrated as an overture to ultimate exit from the business in question, thereby overcoming any exit barriers that their strategic linkages might have created.

Comparison of Findings in the Declining-Business Study with the Strategy Matrix's Predictions

Were the findings in the declining-business study consistent with the predictions of the vertical-strategies matrix? This section comments briefly on its major arguments.

Phase of Industry Development

As perceived riskiness increased with time, vertical integration generally decreased, except where firms served stable niches of demand that were not expected to decline as rapidly. Most industries began with an integrated structure only if it was necessary to do so (as in the case of rayon) to prove the new product's worth. The consumer-electronics firms used integration to protect their quality until substitutes became readily available. Cigar makers generally grew their own tobacco until the use of brokers made it possible to purchase the types of leaf and filler needed without owning farms. Meat packers dis-integrated when their need for tanneries subsided. As early plants became parts of viable industries, their scale increased, and as imbalances between industries upstream and downstream from these larger plants became apparent, firms embraced taper-integrated strategies which depended upon using outsiders for the excess needs. However, many of the most successful firms that were studied reduced these vertical linkages before endgame had progressed far. Thus the hypothesis suggesting that firms reduce the breadth, stages, degree, or ownership of integration in endgame seems appropriate, based on these data.

Industry Traits

The strategy framework did not recommend high degrees of integration in volatile industries because full balance between integrated operations could be difficult to sustain. Moreover, high internal transfers could blunt the competitive edge of business units because they would be isolated from outside market or technological intelligence.

In the example of receiving tubes, plants consumed sizable proportions of their total receiving-tube output and fully integrated tube makers were blinded to the potential applications of solid-state technology because of these integration policies. Managers protected the knowledge they were most accustomed to using, and thereby stultified transistor development.

In the eight declining industries studied, suppliers did not represent substantial portions of value-added, and availability was a problem in only two industries; however, it was not a problem that vertical integration could remedy. The other major motive for backward integration—that is, the need for technological coordination—was not justified in the declining industries studied. Only one firm taper-integrated upstream to acquire the knowledge to make components.

The value-added of consuming industries was high in all of the industrial products studied and some firms were forward integrated in each case to take advantage of this. Where downstream industries did not process the product further or explain its complexities to relatively uninformed consumers, however, forward integration was not necessary.

Most of the declining industries studied did not require physical interconnection, but where it was the most economic, technology firms were forward or backward integrated through interconnected plants. One pattern of manufacturing assets and endgame performance was particularly notable. In commoditylike industries characterized by high economic exit barriers, firms that recognized their decline and acted upon it *early* suffered fewer losses and made cleaner exits than those firms that could not control their endgames due to unfavorable requirements contracts with customers, insufficient provisions for laggard customers when dis-integration was executed, or unionized-labor inflexibility.

Competitors supplied products to each other to round out each other's lines without incurring costly underutilizations of redundant plants in several industries. Expectations were the competitor traits which affected industry volatility most significantly for the study of vertical integration strategies. Firms that believed demand would resuscitate and acted as though the declining demand they experienced was temporary often instigated price wars that proved painful for all competitors.

Bargaining Power

When bargaining power was strong, firms dictated prices and terms, influenced styling decisions, and forced outsiders to incur expenses for them. In declining industries, however, firms had to be wary about acting as bottlenecks because such behavior exacerbated the readiness of ultimate consumers to switch to other products.

Even in endgame, there were some market segments so specialized they needed the declining product. Firms did not need to be integrated to continue serving these customers profitably, however, and many changed their asset relationships.

In most of the declining industries studied there were alternatives for customers. Where switching costs were high, there were few painless ways to satisfy demand and the firms serving this demand did not need to be integrated to prosper.

Bargaining power regarding this attribute should most strongly favor suppliers in declining industries where customers who threatened backward integration would not be credible. The high cost of self-manufacture undertaken in endgame would create enormous exit barriers for firms undertaking it anew. Alternatively, selling assets to dependent customers could be a means of making clean exits from endgame.

If suppliers were dependent upon declining firms to purchase their outputs, they might assist them in repositioning to operate in endgame. Consequently, many firms in declining businesses were backward integrated to ensure that some of their raw-materials needs were satisfied. Downstream, several firms in declining industries were themselves ensnared by their needs for customer conduits and undertook costly services for sick customers. Notably some textile firms, leather fabricators, cigar distributors, and chemical users of acetylene won concessions from suppliers which needed their patronage. Other firms in these industries forward integrated to offset some of the bargaining power these firms possessed.

Corporate Strategy Needs

The strategy framework acknowledged that firms might digress from its recommendations if strategy needs beyond the business unit (or chain of businesses) were examined. Major strategy needs calling for higher or broader integrations included full-product-line strategies, desires for better access to customers, and synergies with nondeclining businesses.

Overview of the Industry Studies and Strategies for Vertical Integration

In the next eight chapters, vertical-integration strategies in younger industries are examined in detail to test the strategy matrix in each type of industry environment. The third section of each chapter summarizes this comparison between expected and observed integration strategies. Starting with the most mature industries (and working backward) the industries are petroleum refining, whiskey, tailored suits, ethical pharmaceuticals, genetic engineering, personal micro computers, residential solar heating, and coal gasification.

Notes

1. Harrigan, K.R., *Strategies for Declining Businesses* (Lexington, Mass.: D.C. Heath & Company, 1980). That study was interested in other strategies in addition to vertical integration, the most common being divestiture or abandonment of a declining business.

2. The details of the U.S. leather-tanning-industry endgame appear in Harrigan, K.R., *Strategies for Declining Businesses* (doctoral dissertation, Harvard University Graduate School of Business Administration, 1979) available through University Microfilms, Ann Arbor, Michigan.

5

Strategies for Vertical Integration in the Petroleum-Refining Industry

Petroleum refining is the process of boiling crude oil to separate it into useful components by upgrading and purifying hydrocarbon mixtures and blending them into salable end products. Briefly, the hydrocarbon components present in crude oil can be isolated by their boiling points and molecular weights, and separated crude oil can be refined into these components by distilling, cracking, hydrotreating, catalytic reforming, isomerization, alkylation, solvent refining, and other procedures explained below to make gasoline, petroleum feedstocks, jet fuel, heating oil and asphalt, among other products. At the end of 1981, utilization of U.S.-petroleum-refining capacity was very low (68 percent) and demand was declining. It was unclear how long demand would decline, but while the industry was in endgame, vertical-integration strategies were being reexamined and reevaluated.

A Description of the U.S. Petroleum-Refining Industry

The Product

Modern refineries in 1981 were flexible facilities for processing crude oil whose outputs could be varied (to some degree) according to seasonal demand for heating oil, gasoline, or other hydrocarbon products. Each refinery's configuration had to be planned to match the type of crude oil it was scheduled to process, and once it was set up for *sweet* crude oil, for example, a refinery was ill suited to process *sour* crude oil.

Background research was provided by Paul Gelburd, with substantial assistance from the American Petroleum Institute.

73

Crude Oil

The most important considerations in matching crude oil with a refinery to process it were its lightness (how much fuel oil it contained) and what types of impurities it contained. Sour crude oil contained sulfur, a smelly and corrosive mineral which damaged refining machinery and plugged fuel jets; it was hydrotreated (described below) to remove the sulfur. Crude oil could be light or heavy; the percentage of heavy fuel oil it contained determined its weight. Since markets for light distillate products (gasoline) were more lucrative than for the heavier naphthas and fuel oil, the refining steps after distillation (boiling) converted these other fractions also to desirable light-distillate products.

Refining Processes

In each refining step, either crude oil was cleaned or heavy fractions of crude oil were converted to light ones. Once a refinery was outfitted with these processes, it became specialized; that is, although it could refine a less-complex crude oil, the most economic use of its assets was to match it with the raw materials it was best suited to refine.

Crude distillation separated crude oil into its components by boiling range. *Cracking* units broke up hydrocarbons of heavier molecular weight into lighter hydrocarbons. *Thermal cracking* heated molecules under pressure, and *coking,* an extreme form of thermal cracking, was used to treat residual crude oil which resisted cracking by other means. *Visbreaking,* a milder form of thermal cracking, reduced the viscosity of some residual crude oils to create hydrocarbons of lower viscosity. *Catalytic cracking* heated heavier hydrocarbons in the presence of a catalytic agent which accelerated and directed the reaction. The light end products were converted to gasoline through *alkylation* (described below), and the heavy end products were treated by *hydrocracking,* a process of heating hydrocarbons under pressure in the presence of hydrogen and a catalyst.

Reforming units upgraded the commercial quality (or octane number) of gasolines by upgrading the naphtha component of the gasoline to increase its antiknock qualities. Most feedstocks for reforming were *hydrotreated* first to remove arsenic, sulfur, and nitrogen compounds which would otherwise poison the reforming catalyst. *Isomerization* processes rearranged the molecular form of a feedstock while holding down losses from cracking or condensation reactions, somewhat like catalytic reforming. The octane number of naphthas was once increased using additives such as tetraethyl lead, but in 1981 no new automobiles used leaded gasoline, hence *alkylation* units were used to increase the antiknock (octane number) qualities of motor fuel instead.

Refining Demand

The major refined-product categories were motor gasoline (unleaded and leaded), diesel fuels, aviation fuels, industrial and heating fuels, and petrochemical products. In both types of motor fuel—gasoline and diesel fuel—the use of chemical additives became more important as performance and pollution considerations were designed into their formulations. *Aviation gasolines* required particularly high quality control. Like high quality industrial oils, millions of dollars of equipment could be ruined or put out of service by a product of less-than-premium quality. The major *industrial and heating fuels* were liquified petroleum gas (LPG), distillate fuel oil, and residual fuel oil. LPG was used in ethylene production and for household and industrial fuel. *Distillate fuel oil* (numbers one, two, and four heating oils, diesel oil, and industrial distillates) was used as heating or furnace oil for domestic and small-commercial space heating, but number two fuel oil was most frequently used for these applications. *Residual fuel oil* (numbers five and six heating oils, heavy diesel, heavy industrial, and Bunker C fuel oils) were used to provide steam and heat for industry and large buildings, to generate electricity, and to power ships. By 1981, residual fuel oil represented less than 10 percent of final refining output because the price of a barrel of residual fuel oil was lower than the price of a barrel of crude oil.

Refining produced other petroleum products such as petrochemical feedstocks, lubricants, petroleum solvents, and asphalt. *Petrochemical feedstocks* such as benzene, toluene, xylene, ethane, and propane were used in many synthetic rubbers, fibers, and plastics. *Lubricants* were usually automotive oils, industrial oils, and greases. Quality control and purity were crucial in producing industrial oils, petrolatums, and greases used in food preparation. *Petroleum solvents* (mineral oils) also conformed to very rigid customer specifications in their manufacture. *Asphalts* were the oldest product of petroleum (pitch) and had many industrial uses in 1981.

Table 5-1 shows the daily production of refinery products in 1981 and previous years. The quantities produced were affected by seasonal changes in use of heating oil, motor fuel, and other products, and as greater amounts of heavy crude oil were recovered, more catalytic-cracking and hydrocracking capacity and less distillation capacity was needed. As demand remained low, the cost of holding inventory became so high that refiners tried to delay receipts of crude oil—reducing liftings where possible and slow steaming or holding tankers on station. They also sought new buyers for their crude and products in order to trim their stocks.

Total demand for gasoline in February 1981 was at a ten-year low and had been dropping at the rate of 32,000 barrels per month for the previous years; distillate demand had been falling at the rate of 21,000 barrels per month over the same period. The conservation efforts of U.S. consumers had diminished demand for refined petroleum products so drastically that

Table 5-1
Domestic Production of Refined Products
(thousands of barrels per day)

	April 2, 1982	October 2, 1981	April 3, 1981	October 3, 1980	April 4, 1980	October 4, 1979	April 5, 1979	October 5, 1978[a]
Motor gasoline (total)	5,822	6,501	5,842	6,198	6,520	6,414	6,474	7,412
Unleaded motor gasoline	3,107	3,620	3,368	3,268	3,192	2,883	2,447	2,372
Jet fuel								
Naphtha	218	201	182	179	208	173	210	199
Kerosine	941	715	774	870	937	841	839	858
Kerosine and heating oil #1	103	94	139	138	107	142	179	215
Distillate fuel oil (including #, # oil and diesel)	2,344	2,527	2,332	2,506	2,616	3,186	2,895	3,392
Residual fuel oil	1,108	1,215	1,504	1,300	1,862	1,466	1,660	3,023
Daily runs	11,240	12,167	12,379	12,679	13,869	14,395	13,688	14,655

Source: API Refinery Reports, *Oil and Gas Journal*, Penn Well Publishing Company, Oklahoma.
[a]From National Petroleum Council, *Refinery Flexibility*, December 1980.

in 1981 the need to shut down some refineries and terminate some trading relationships was inevitable. The type of refinery most likely to be shut down was one that could not process sour crude, could not use residual oil as a feedstock, and produced few light, economically valuable products.

Markets

Although some refined petroleum products were differentiable by their purity, quality, or additives, refined oil was generally indistinguishable. The principal ways to sell a firm's products were on the basis of prices and delivery. Motor fuels—leaded or unleaded—could be sold at the refinery hauled or transported by pipeline to a product terminal for sale, or distributed under arrangements stipulated in a dealer's lease. Branded sales were treated differently than unbranded sales, but there had been occasions where one product terminal supplied all of the fuel trucks in a particular region (for all of the brands marketed). Under these conditions of shared resources, any gasoline marketer that advertised special additives in its branded gasoline had to ensure that all tank cars of its product were treated as advertised. Aviation fuel was delivered right to the hangar and required special additives and care in blending to guarantee good performance. Waxes and mineral oils were very specialized markets that were less sensitive to price than other refined products. Purity and precision in product specifications were important enough to warrant an extra cent or more in pricing. Heating oil was delivered, like gasoline, from the refinery or a product terminal. Industrial grades of heating oil were sometimes transported by barge to keep costs low when customers' purchases were large. Residential heating oil was distributed in trucks to households by regional firms. Over 12 million homes used heating oil, primarily in the northeastern states, and were serviced by over 500 distributors.

Suppliers

Refiners obtained crude oil by either finding and producing their own oil, purchasing crude on the spot or futures market, exchanging crude oil with other firms, or processing crude under contract for other firms. A successful oil company was frequently also a successful explorationist because oil companies had to replenish their reserves. Table 5-2 compares the gas production of sixteen, integrated oil firms, and shows the number of years of reserves that firms would possess if they produced at their current rates. As firms drew down their crude reserves without replenishment, their ratio declined, but if improved methods of oil recovery were developed, their ratio could increase without finding new oil basins.

Table 5-2
Comparison of Selected 1979 and 1980 Data on Oil and Gas Production (Domestic Only)

Firms	1979 Reserves (MMEB)[a]	1979 Production (MEBPD)[b]	1979 R/P[c] (years)	1980 Reserves (MMEB)[a]	1980 Production (MEBPD)[b]	1980 R/P[c] (years)
Exxon	5,864	1411.5	11.3	5,635	1349.2	11.4
Mobil	1,952	659.8	8.1	1,924	643.0	8.2
Texaco	2,913	992.5	8.0	2,488	849.3	8.0
SOCAL	2,200	541.6	11.1	2,183	539.6	11.1
Gulf	1,820	698.4	7.1	1,678	665.6	6.9
Amoco	3,095	906.3	9.4	3,069	838.7	10.0
ARCO	4,814	760.3	17.3	4,817	788.7	16.7
Shell	3,390	770.7	12.1	3,466	807.7	11.8
Sun	1,199	388.7	8.5	1,322	380.8	9.5
Conoco	845	298.0	7.8	846	277.6	8.3
Phillips	1,116	441.7	6.9	1,058	427.2	6.8
Sohio	5,000	624.3	21.9	4,777	729.1	18.0
Union	1,532	380.5	11.0	1,491	367.6	10.8
Marathon	1,090	246.1	12.1	1,037	243.0	11.7
Cities Service	850	311.7	7.5	789	289.1	7.5
Getty	1,862	410.8	12.4	1,805	413.5	12.0

Source: Industry sources.
[a]MMEB stands for billions of equivalent barrels.
[b]MEBPD stands for billions of equivalent barrels per day.
[c]R/P stands for depletion of reserves by production per day.

Although refiners were frequently integrated backward into exploration, there seemed to be few new oil basins on land large enough to support their refining capacities in 1981. Offshore exploration cost between $10 and $20 million per well and there was a 90 percent probability of a dry hole. These risks were shared by joint-venture partners in a business arrangement that enabled more firms to participate in more wells and thereby to spread their risks.

On land, most exploratory drilling was done by independent firms and entry into oil exploration was relatively easy, provided a firm had land leases with good prospects. Participation in oil-exploration ventures could be obtained by passive investors seeking royalties or by refiners (or marketers) willing to pay for drilling costs in exchange for control over oil under production. Usually the passive partner wanted the right to direct the crude oil's sale to a particular refinery. When crude oil was scarce, these access agreements became commonplace until the Emergency Oil Allocation Act froze all trading relationships and made such negotiations meaningless.

Most oil producers sold their crude oil to gathering companies that represented a particular refinery. Sometimes the gathering company was employed by a refiner; otherwise it was an oil broker. Refiners also purchased oil on the spot and futures market. Since the spot market was everybody's excess production, it could be a cheaper source of raw materials, but as the 1979 cut off of Iranian oil indicated, the spot market was a very unreliable source of cheap oil. By 1981, the futures market was becoming a particularly important source of crude oil.

Exchanges of oil were frequent because the oil that firms produced may not have suited their refinery, or the firms' wells may have been far from their refineries. For example, when they were not equipped to process sour crude oil, refiners exchanged it for low-sulfur oil. Or firms with wells on the West Coast and refineries on the East Coast traded oil with refiners having opposite configurations to save on transportation costs.

Refiners purchased the services of other refineries to process their crude oil in geographic markets where they had oil and markets but no refineries, or when they underwent *turnaround* (more on this below). Some refiners' oil production exceeded their refining capacity and these firms purchased processing services from others to retain control over the higher-value refined product rather than sell their excess crude oil. Other refiners' capacities exceeded their own crude oil supplies and they processed oil for others to attain efficient levels of capacity utilization. When this occurred production companies were sometimes able to trade a barrel of crude oil for some quantity of refined product, thereby skipping a step in the chain of oil processing in order to market refined products without owning a refinery.

There was much cooperation among oil firms in pipeline ventures, and major trunklines were often jointly owned. Each firm also constructed crude-oil gathering lines and finished-product pipelines for their particular needs. No independent oil firm requesting the use of pipelines was denied access. The economics of pipeline use made shared use significantly more economic than building duplicate facilities.

In summary, there were few refiners that were self-sufficient in crude-oil production and most refiners searched aggressively for large basins of light, sweet oil. They did not necessarily consume all of the crude oil they produced internally because it might be the wrong type, in the wrong location, or they might be at full refinery capacity. A volatile spot and futures market absorbed excess crude oil and provided an alternative source of raw materials.

Manufacturing

Entry barriers: The capital costs of refining were high. The cost of building a new refinery capable of handling 125,000 barrels per day of sour, heavy crude oil in 1981 was around $1.2 billion. The cost of upgrading an old sweet refinery ranged from $5 million to nearly $1 billion, depending upon the type of upgrading and expansion undertaken. Refining assets were highly inflexible. In addition to limitations concerning the type of crude oil refineries could process, there was limited flexibility in the mix of products that could be refined at a particular site.

Most research-and-development monies in the oil industry were spent on finding oil, using seismic research, analysis of *bright spots,* etc. Most line or technical-service operations did not require large research-and-development budgets, particularly when satellite industries invented improved catalysts, superior processing equipment, or better additives for refined products. Firms did expend research-and-development monies to developed improved products, such as better lube-oil formulations, or to improve basic product quality that was protected by their gasoline brand names, however.

The minimum-efficient scale for a crude-distillation unit was 175,000 barrels per day, and the diseconomies associated with small refineries were as high as fifty cents per barrel. Refineries could operate efficiently at a lesser scale if they were located in a geographic region not served by other refineries, if cheap crude oil were available, or if they produced a very specialized output. Refineries were most efficient if operated at 85 to 90 percent of capacity. When capacity utilization fell below 50 percent it was very difficult to keep a modern refinery operating, due to some internal transfers between the catalyst and hydrogen units. Firms that tried to run large refineries at this low level had to retool them to create artificial bottlenecks in processing capacities.

The typical U.S. refinery was built to process a light, sweet crude oil, but increasingly, crude oil was sour and contained much residual oil instead. By 1981 most large refineries contained hydrotreating units to remove the sulfur, but major upgrading of the facilities to handle heavy crude were still being made. There were great advantages to physical interconnection with a chemicals plant because feedstocks like ethane, propane, naphtha, and gas oil were produced in the refining process. Moreover, gases produced in processing could be recycled back into the refinery for use in another processing step if refinery and chemicals plants were sister units connected by pipelines.

Although some refineries were shut down by 1981, many others continued to operate because they faced high exit barriers. Firms tried to sell their refineries, rather than abandon them, if they were capable of processing sour or heavy oils. Even if a refinery were mothballed, there were many necessary precautions which were costly to make so that mothballing costs were high exit barriers for some firms as well. Most refineries had little economic value except as scrap in 1981 and extensive provisions had to be made for contingent liabilities on subsequent uses of the land. The costs of actually dismantling the plant and retiring its labor force were high. Although some of the new processing equipment might be sold to other refiners, there was frequently no other use for refinery assets in 1981 when declining demand became substantial. Since so many small, inefficient, U.S. refineries had been built during the 1970s (a time when other nations' refining capacities had declined), a massive rationalization of refineries was anticipated in the 1980s.

Marketing

Downstream operations were once important as a means of disposing of abundant refined product, but the 1970s were a difficult time to enter or grow downstream because their was little refined product to sell. In 1981 the nature of downstream operations had changed and so had refiners' attitudes toward them.

There were two kinds of firms in the heating-oil business: barge buyers that purchased in lots of 750,000 gallons or more, and rack buyers that purchased in smaller quantities from the refinery or retail transshipment points. Both kinds of firms purchased directly from refiners or from independent wholesalers. Some refiners, such as Atlantic Richfield (ARCO), British Petroleum, Gulf, Mobil, Standard Oil of California (SOCAL), and

Tenneco, also engaged in the distribution of heating oil, but the integrated refiners represented less than 15 percent of the market in a field of more than 500 firms. Prior to 1981, contracts with major refineries were quite stable but they were being broken frequently in 1981. Refiners' contracts stipulated that a certain quantity of heating oil had to be taken and if their distributors were not purchasing agreed-upon volumes—if they were purchasing heating oil on the spot market, for example—refineries could cut back on the amount of heating oil they would sell to distributors.

Distributors used the vibrant futures market in heating oil to obtain the supplies they needed. Previously, the output of major refiners was a substantial portion of the volume traded among distributors, but in 1981 the spot and futures markets in heating oil represented a greater volume of total sales than refiners' direct sales. Previously, heating-oil distributors faced high switching costs in finding new suppliers because heating-oil inventories were tight, but that condition was also changing in 1981 as refiners became willing to take on new customers. Finally, the value of offering branded heating oil was slipping as distributors used the futures market to become less dependent upon specific refiners. Thus wholesaling heating oil became a more volatile business over time, and some refiners ceased supplying this product to wholesalers. Because the heating-oil firms usually had their own fleets of trucks for distributing their products, they were less dependent upon a major refiner's decision to back out of downstream operations. Gasoline retailers, by contrast frequently leased their service stations from the refiners and would have had no assets if refiners had abandoned their marketing regions and no other gasoline supplies were available.

The trend toward self-service gasoline stations reflected a change in the type of entrepreneur that managed service stations. Once repairpersons leased gasoline outlets but primarily provided repair services. When gasoline prices rose and the nature of the automobile changed from luxury to necessity, high-volume, quick-turnover operations became the key to profitability. Auto mechanics did not want to pump gas; nor did many savvy businesspersons or skilled managers. Chains of self-service stations replaced the mom-and-pop gasoline station.

First oil firms backed away from operating service stations, then they ceased building new ones. In 1981 the investment in a new service station was between $400,000 and $450,000, and the gross profit needed to justify that expenditure was substantial. But profits were poor because competition among branded gasolines became more volatile by 1981 as refiners sought to encourage more of their gasolines' consumption while many customers were conserving energy and buying on the basis of price, not brands. Brand names were still valuable among industrial users where quality differences were discernable, but the less-perceptive motorist did not notice differences among gasolines, except in a negative way. Refiners debated whether to eliminate credit cards, arguing that the cost of handling them was not justified. A few firms gave discounts for cash transactions, while others that believed credit cards brought in business for branded gasolines continued their earlier policies about the credit use.

Finally, refiners abandoned low-volume marketing regions and switched to *rack-pricing* policies. Both policies had the effect of reducing the number of firms which served some marketing areas. Rack pricing involved setting undelivered prices at each important terminal, based on transportation costs from the refinery. Prices were set lower at terminals closer to the refinery, higher at terminals farther from the refinery. At distant points, prices might be noncompetitive against another supplier, depending on the other company's pricing system and how close its terminal and refineries were to the area. The existing pricing system in 1981, by contrast, had been a delivered price with a self-hauling allowance. Its effect had been to subsidize distant customers. Under rack pricing, costs determined prices at each terminal.

As companies backed away from franchises and supply contracts, there was an opportunity for jobbers to supply refined product, and as a result, their market shares rose. The increasing use of jobbers also hastened the transition from branded to unbranded gasoline. Finally, a proposal came before Congress in 1981 to divorce all refineries from ownership of gasoline service stations. Previously, some firms had operated their own stations while others leased them to entrepreneurs under a franchise arrangement. The proposed bill would eliminate a refiners' market power to influence how business was conducted in its branded service stations.

The geographical closeness of chemical companies and their similarities in strategic posture made the marketing of commodity chemicals from refineries an efficient activity. For example, many of the privately owned pipelines in the Gulf area were interconnected, making swaps or sales of ethylene, benzene, and toluene easy to facilitate. Refiners even sold styrene monomer among themselves when their plants underwent annual maintenance or other shutdowns, in order to keep their chemical plants in operation. Thus the ready availability of other suppliers of commodity chemicals diminished each supplier's potential bargaining power in selling petrochemicals. Moreover, the physical proximity of customers to suppliers made cooperation among trading partners important in selling future products because the same trading partners negotiated deals again and again. There was some specialization among the chemical firms in making the various needed resins, but all of the natural gas or naphtha—the building-block chemicals—used for making propylene, butadiene, or ethylene came from each firm's refinery. Chemical firms preferred to be taper integrated downstream because it was not economical for one firm to make all of the needed resins; by spreading the feedstock sources among other firms, none were totally dependent on the effects of labor strikes, downtimes, or other internal imbalances at a single plant. Furthermore, it was more efficient to purchase some required chemicals in order to attain long production runs and the economies of process research than for each firm to make short runs and master the technology for making each chemical alone.

In summary, the marketing of many refined petroleum products was growing more volatile in 1981. Where previously (when supplies of crude were scarce) refiners had had some ability to stabilize contracts, in 1981 customers became less dependent upon the branded output of a single refiner and more likely to use price competition or the futures market to match consumer demands with low-cost products. The net result in the distribution of products was closer to a free market, but this also meant that less-profitable marketing regions were thinly covered as firms backed away from them in 1981.

Competition in the U.S. Refining Industry in 1981

At the end of 1981, approximately 150 firms refined crude oil. There were 10,000 exploration and production firms, 100 pipeline companies, 15,000 wholesale, refined-product distributors, and also around 300,000 retailers, making refining one of the more concentrated phases of the oil industry. The refining capacity of the top four firms—Exxon, SOCAL, Amoco and Shell—was only 29 percent of total industry capacity.

Table 5–3 lists the capacities and locations of the largest oil refineries in 1981. There were 238 refineries in 1981, a decrease from the number operating in 1978, when the small-refiner bias was still in effect; the approximate number of refineries had not changed substantially in two decades, but shakeouts were expected to reduce the industry's population significantly as the full effects of decontrol took effect.

The major refiners shown in table 5–3 were both forward and backward integrated, with the exception of Commonwealth Refining, GHR Energy, and the Energy Cooperative (which bankrupted). Southwestern Refining was affiliated with Kerr-McGee Oil, and Occidental Petroleum had no U.S. refineries. Sohio and Getty Oil possessed the highest self-sufficiency ratio, while Amerada-Hess, American Petrofina, Ashland Oil, Clark, and Mobil, among others, were significantly short of crude in the U.S.

Some firms, like ARCO, were trying to become domestically self-sufficient in oil in the 1980s. Although ARCO obtained 95 percent of its daily oil production from U.S. sources, that still left a shortfall of 31 percent at its refineries, and to fill that shortfall, ARCO fielded more seismic exploration crews than any other U.S. company.

Table 5-3
Large U.S. Refineries, 1978-1981
(barrels per day capacity)

Firm	Location	1948 Capacity (b/d)	1978 Capacity (b/d)[a]	1981 Capacity (b/d)[b]
Amoco	Wood River, IL	42,500	95,000	shut down
Amoco	Whiting, IN	145,800	380,000	380,000
Amoco	Sugar Creek, MO	31,900	107,000	104,000
Amoco	Texas City, TX	104,000	360,000	415,000
ARCO	Carson, CA	80,000	180,000	166,000
ARCO	Philadelphia, PA	112,000	185,000	125,000
ARCO	Houston, TX	73,000	222,000	222,000
ARCO	Ferndale, WA	0	106,000	115,000
Ashland Oil	Catlettsburg, KY	25,000	135,000	220,000[d]
Amerada Hess	St. Croix, VI	0	600,000	728,000
American Petrofina	Port Arthur, TX	33,000	110,000	90,000
BP Oil	Marcus Hook, PA	65,000	164,000[a]	168,000
Cities Service	Lake Charles, LA	110,000	268,000	330,000
Commonwealth	Penuelas, PR	0	161,000	161,000
Conoco	Ponca City, OK	33,000	126,000	134,000
Coastal States	Corpus Christi, TX	21,000	185,000	182,000
Crown Central	Houston, TX	24,000	100,000	100,000
Energy Cooperative	East Chicago, IL	55,000	126,000	shut down
Exxon USA	Benicia, CA	0	93,000	106,000
Exxon USA	Baton Rouge, LA	94,000	510,000	474,000
Exxon USA	Linden, NJ	135,000	290,000	265,000
Exxon USA	Baytown, TX	200,000	640,000	640,000
Getty Oil	Delaware City, DE	0	140,000	140,000
GHR Energy	Good Hope, LA	0	80,000	285,000
Gulf Oil	Belle Chasse, LA	0	195,900	198,000
Gulf Oil	Philadelphia, PA	74,700	207,600	174,100
Gulf Oil	Port Arthur, TX	206,400	334,500	335,000
Koch Refining	Rosemount, MN	0	127,300	127,300
Marathon	Robinson, IL	15,500	195,000	195,000
Marathon	Garyville, LA	0	200,000	255,000
Mobil Oil	Torrance, CA	100,000	100,000	123,500
Mobil Oil	Joliet, IL	180,000	180,000	180,000
Mobil Oil	Paulsboro, NJ	36,400	98,000	99,700
Mobil Oil	Beaumont, TX	13,500	335,000	325,000
Phillips Petroleum	Borger, TX	50,000	100,000	95,000
Phillips Petroleum	Sweeney, TX	35,000	104,000	175,000
Shell Oil	Martinez, CA	45,000	92,400	104,000

Table 5-3 continued

Firm	Location	1948 Capacity (b/d)	1978 Capacity (b/d)[a]	1981 Capacity (b/d)[b]
Shell Oil	Wilmington, CA	52,000	93,000	108,000
Shell Oil	Wood River, IL	100,000	283,000	283,000
Shell Oil	Norco, LA	3,000	230,000	257,000
SOCAL	El Segundo, CA	107,000	138,000	405,000
SOCAL	Richmond, CA	138,000	365,000	365,000
SOCAL	Wilmington, CA	59,000	108,000	shut down
SOCAL	Pascagoula, MS	0	280,000	280,000
SOCAL	Perth Amboy, NJ	15,000	168,000	168,000
Sohio	Lima, OH	18,000	168,000	168,000
Sohio	Toledo, OH	20,000	120,000	120,000
Southwestern Refining	Corpus Christi, TX	18,000	124,000	104,000
Sun Oil	Toledo, OH	35,000	125,000	125,000
Sun Oil	Marcus Hook, PA	135,000	165,000	165,000
Tenneco	Chalmette, LA	14,000	115,000	114,000
Texaco	Convent, LA	0	140,000	140,000
Texaco	Port Arthur, TX	145,000	367,000	402,000
Tosco	Martinez, CA	0	126,000	126,000
Union Oil	Lemont, IL	31,925	151,000	151,000
Union Oil	Nederland, TX	55,000	120,000	120,000
Union Pacific	Corpus Christi, TX	19,000	155,000	173,000

[a]From U.S. Department of Interior, Bureau of Mines, Petroleum Refineries, including Cracking Plants in the United States, Annual (Information Circular in years 1948–1961; Mineral Industry Surveys 1961–1977).
[b]From "Annual Refining Report," *Oil and Gas Journal,* March 22, 1982, pp. 130–151.
[c]In 1978 this refinery was owned by Sohio.
[d]Barrels per stream day (not per calendar day).

Corporate-Strategy Exit Barriers in U.S. Refining

In 1981 some refiners recognized that demand for oil would slowly decline unless major discoveries of cheap crude oil were made. The leadership of these firms was made up of oil men who remained stolidly entrenched in oil-related businesses in 1981 despite the decline. Because they were unlikely to change the nature of their businesses, the oil refiners were consolidating their assets, pruning away losing operations, and preparing for profitable endgames in 1981. Firms would never give up certain businesses—such as branded gasoline stations—and these emotional barriers kept firms in businesses that became inherently unprofitable over time. Internal vertical-integration policies sometimes exacerbated these barriers if firms did not allow their operations to use the outside market advantageously in inside versus outside purchase or distribution decisions.

Summary of Competitors in U.S. Refining

In summary, refiners differed in the degree, stages, and breadths of their forward and backward integrations. Most firms were not fully integrated with respect to crude-oil self-sufficiency and downstream businesses and some firms had to purchase their refined product just to fulfill their 1981 marketing contracts. Some firms were primarily in domestic exploration, after the many expropriations of the 1970s had occurred, while others had extensive interests in oil-producing areas other than the volatile Middle East. In joint ventures offshore, some firms were best at finding oil while others produced wells most economically. Some firms used salaried service-station operators primarily, while other firms franchised all of their service stations and brand names to be operated by outsiders. Some firms wholesaled heating oil while other firms emphasized unbranded, high-volume sales instead. Finally, some firms had invested extensively in producing chemicals beyond the commodity level of naphthas, solvents, and ethylenes in order to capture the higher value-added available from making specialized chemicals.

A Mapping of Strategic Groups in Refining

This section clusters major competitors by their breadth of forward integration in 1981. Firms were still broadly integrated in 1981 but the geographic scope of their operations had frequently been reduced. Firms were moving toward greater crude self-sufficiency in the U.S. and were eliminating refineries in uneconomic locations. The refiners could be mapped as shown in figure 5-1 to indicate whether any shared resources or linkages between important businesses existed. In 1981, SOCAL and many smaller refiners produced less than 20 percent of their U.S. crude refining capacity in the U.S., but Sohio and Getty produced more crude than they refined. Pennzoil and Tenneco produced more than 50 percent of their crude requirements but their refining capacity was less than many other refiners. For example, Exxon's Baytown, Texas refinery had a crude distillation capacity of 640,000 barrels per day in 1981. Refiners like Commonwealth and Tesoro produced substantial refined products but did not market them under their own brand names. Chemical companies like Dow and Monsanto had refining operations primarily for petrochemical purposes.

Key Events in the Refining Industry

This section traces key events in the endgame of the U.S. refining industry beginning with the 1960s. A summary of conditions before that time appears below.

Breadth of Distribution Activities (top firms for each sales category)

Degree of Upstream Integration	Gas Stations	Commodity Chemicals	Specialty Chemicals	Refined Product Sales (total)
Produced more than 50 percent crude-oil needs in U.S.	ARCO British Petroleum (Sohio) Cities Service Exxon Getty Phillips Sohio Tenneco	ARCO Cities Service Exxon Getty Pennzoil Phillips Tenneco	ARCO Cities Service Exxon	ARCO Cities Service Exxon Getty Pennzoil Phillips Sohio Tenneco
Produced less than 50 percent but more than 20 percent crude-oil needs in U.S.	Amoco Conoco Gulf Marathon Mobil Shell Sun Texaco Union	Amoco Conoco Gulf Marathon Mobil Shell Sun Texaco Union	Amoco Conoco Gulf Mobil Shell	Amoco Conoco Gulf Marathon Mobil Shell Sun Texaco Union
Produced less than 20 percent crude-oil needs in U.S.	Amerada-Hess American Petrofina Ashland Champlin Clark Coastal States Crown Central Diamond Shamrock Kerr-McGee Murphy SOCAL	Amerada-Hess Ashland Charter Coastal States Dow Chemical Koch Industries Lion Oil (Monsanto)	Ashland Koch Industries Lion Oil (Monsanto)	American Petrofina Ashland Champlin Clark Coastal States Commonwealth Diamond Shamrock Kerr-McGee Murphy SOCAL Tesoro

Figure 5-1. A Mapping of Selected Competitors in U.S. Refining, 1981

A Brief History of Refining

The oil industry began *non*-integrated around the 1850s but uncertainties in the price and quality of crude oil made the industry a risky one. The old Standard Oil Company began as a refiner, but Rockefeller and his associates, in a concerted effort to bring these uncertainties under control, created by 1981 a new concept in business structure—the vertically integrated corporation. The very last link added to Rockefeller's chain was oil production because exploration and production activities were too risky for him and Standard Oil was always quite short of crude.

Cut-rate gasoline stations first appeared in the 1930s to dispose of excess crude oil stimulated by the depletion allowance and several retailers backward integrated to obtain their own supplies. The law of capture prevailed and firms drilled shallow wells to exploit oil production rapidly in as many locations as possible. The resulting glut made crude oil very difficult to sell and motivated some producers to integrate forward into refining and marketing activities. Refining was a higher-profit operation than exploration during the 1950s because profits were taken at the refinery, and independent producers were protected from the price wars which had erupted in selling domestic crude by being vertically integrated.

1960

In the decade from 1950 to 1960, fifty refineries were constructed, but only one approached minimum-efficient scale. Thirty-five of the refineries were built by new entrants.

The Standard Oil Company of Indiana (Amoco) in 1960 had twelve refineries and produced 454 thousand barrels per day. Its domestic reserves of crude oil totalled 2.3 billion barrels, and its exploration activities were confined primarily to the Northern Hemisphere. Amoco served 27,701 retail outlets with a full line in 45 states.

Standard Oil Company of New Jersey (Exxon) in 1960 had eight U.S. refineries and its Imperial Oil Company of Canada operated ten refineries. Exxon's worldwide crude-oil reserves in 1960 were 34.8 billion barrels and it served over 23,000 U.S. service stations which were primarily operated by others under lease.

Gulf Oil Corporation in 1960 had five refineries and produced 1.6 million barrels of crude per day in the United States, other parts of the Eastern and Western Hemispheres and Kuwait. Gulf served 38 states through 1,580 bulk stations and 34,000 retail outlets.

Socony Mobil Oil Company (Mobil) in 1960 had twelve U.S. refineries and its North American crude oil production averaged 83.6 million barrels per day. Mobil owned or leased 4000 wholesale distributing plants, operated 98 retail service stations, and had 29,900 affiliated dealers in the U.S.

Shell in 1960 had six U.S. refineries and produced 325 thousand barrels per day. Shell's marketing activities were carried out through 9,500 retail service stations which Shell leased to independent retail dealers and jobbers. In addition, its products were distributed through 13,400 service stations not owned or leased by Shell.

The Standard Oil Company of California (SOCAL) in 1960 had nine refineries and produced 1.2 million barrels per day of crude in the Western Hemisphere. SOCAL's products were distributed in 29 states through 1300 wholesalers serving 14,650 retail service stations.

The Standard Oil Company of Ohio (Sohio) in 1960 had four refineries and produced 39 thousand barrels of crude per day. Sohio had 193 bulk stations (185 company-owned) and distributed through 4,756 retail outlets (1,539 company-owned).

Sun Oil in 1960 had two refineries and produced 152 thousand barrels of crude per day. Sun owned and operated 9,491 wholesale distributors of refined products, other dealer outlets, and 25 retail service stations at that time.

Texaco in 1960 had twelve refineries and produced 1.3 million barrels of crude per day. During the 1960s the path to big profits was through marketing, and a big sales network to sell big volumes of oil was easy to obtain. In this era Texaco was proud to market to 50 states, forming a network strategy which became the cornerstone of Texaco's corporate strategy. Texaco also marketed in every country of the Western Hemisphere and in West Africa. Sales in the U.S. were made through 2,500 bulk plants and terminals and over 40,500 retail service stations.

The Ohio Oil Company ("Marathon") in 1960 had three refineries and produced 101 thousand barrels of crude per day. Marathon's products were marketed through bulk plants and retail service stations in Ohio, Illinois, Michigan, Kentucky, and Indiana.

1963

From 1960 to 1963, eleven new refineries were built, but only one approached minimum-efficient scale. During this period, twenty refineries were shut down. The largest plant to be retired was a 20,000-barrel-per-day refinery.

Standard Oil (Kentucky) was acquired by SOCAL in 1961, without an antitrust challenge, because Standard Oil (Kentucky) agreed to cease marketing refined products for Exxon in the Southeast (to become a marketing arm for SOCAL), and because the merger created a giant SOCAL that was better suited to compete with Exxon. SOCAL announced it would build a refinery to support its new outlets (in Pascagoula, Mississippi), and reported itself prepared to create its own marketing channels in the Southeast.

The Atlantic-Richfield Company (ARCO) was a combination of Atlantic Refining and Richfield Oil. Atlantic marketed directly from its refineries through bulk stations, water terminals, pipelines, and service stations. Richfield Oil had a contract with Union Pacific to purchase oil produced from the Wilmington Oil Field of the Los Angeles Basin. It also marketed gasoline. A subsidiary of Cities Service and Sinclair Oil each controlled approximately 30 percent of Richfield's stock.

After selling its Corpus Christi refinery to Coastal States, Sinclair Oil had five refineries and 15,354 retail service stations, most of which were operated by others. Another 18,000 retail outlets dispensed Sinclair products, often using equipment owned by the firm.

In an effort to widen its marketing outlets, in 1963 Exxon purchased the refinery and marketing outlets of Tidewater Oil in California, Washington, Oregon, Idaho, Arizona, Nevada, and Hawaii. The acquisition included about 3,900 service stations and five supertankers. Tidewater, which was controlled by Getty Oil, had been losing market share and was selling a substantial amount of its gasoline output in the West to unbranded wholesalers. Exxon's acquisition made it a major marketer there as well as a formidable competitor for SOCAL, the dominant Western oil company.

1967

Between 1963 and 1967, eighteen refineries were built, but only one approached minimum-efficient scale. During this period twenty-seven refineries were shut down. The largest plant retired was a 56,000-barrel-per-day refinery, and all other retired plants were quite small. Several mergers of substantial size occurred during these years to create large vertically integrated oil firms which had national (rather than regional) oil interests. Ongoing oil firms continued to forward integrate in petrochemicals.

In 1967 Exxon purchased SOCAL's Signal Oil Company Division's marketing properties in four western states. The acquisition included 1500 service stations plus 150 bulk-wholesale-distribution facilities, and was made using Exxon's Humble Oil subsidiary which already marketed gasoline in four western states through about 900 stations.

In 1966 Ashland Oil & Refining Company had eight refineries—five were in operation—and it produced 68,000 barrels per day of crude oil. Its branded gasoline stations were operated by others, and Ashland's forte was chemicals.

Having been defeated by Union Oil in a bid for Pure Oil, Atlantic Refining merged in 1965 with Richfield Oil Corporation, which was partially owned by Cities Service and Sinclair Oil. Meanwhile, in its chemicals business, ARCO and Halcon formed a joint venture, Oxirane Corporation, in 1966 to build a propylene-oxide plant.

In 1966, Gulf purchased the midwest-marketing assets including retail outlets, terminals bulk plants, and other marketing facilities of Cities Service. Gulf had also planned to acquire Cities Service's 35,000-barrel-per-day refinery in Ponca City, but it was sold to Sequoia Refining instead.

In 1967, Mobil Oil put a distillation unit capable of producing 120,000 barrels per day of crude onstream at its Beaumont, Texas refinery. Modernization projects increased Mobil's refinery capacity from 220,000 barrels per day to 280,000 barrels per day.

Marathon Oil in 1967 announced its plans to upgrade and expand its plants under a ten-year-master-refining plan. It modernized the 53,000-barrel-per-day refinery at Robinson, Illinois for $100 million and began a face lift of its Detroit refinery in which a new 50,000-barrel-per-day crude distillation unit went onstream to replace two older, less economical units. It also added hydrotreating, coking, and desulfurizing flexibility there. Finally, Marathon began installing a new catalytic reformer and treating units at its 47,000-barrel-per-day refinery at Texas City to increase its ability to process higher-sulfur crudes. These expenditures were fairly typical of the upgrades many major oil companies made at this time.

1971

Between 1967 and 1971, twelve refineries were constructed. The largest of these were ARCO's Ferndale, Washington plant, Gulf's Belle Chasse, Louisiana refinery, and Exxon's Benicia, California refinery. Each of these approached efficient plant size. The other new refineries were small. Shell made major upgrades on its refineries and increased its crude-distillation capacity as well as its ability to handle heavy, sour crude. By 1971, Shell's refinery capacity had increased to 225,000 barrels per day at Houston, 240,000 barrels per day at Norco, Louisiana, and 245,000 barrels per day at Wood River, Illinois. By the end of 1969, there was considerable surplus capacity in the fertilizer business and the oil companies which had plunged into fertilizer began bailing out. Exxon began selling off its operations and Mobil disposed of all assets except its nitrogen plant. Contrary to this pattern, in 1969 Amerada Petroleum merged with Hess Oil and Chemical.

In 1969 Sinclair Oil was merged into Atlantic-Richfield and some of its major refining and marketing properties were sold to British Petroleum, giving it an entree into the U.S. market. Sinclair's 120,000-barrel-per-day refinery at Marcus Hook, Pennsylvania and ARCO's 84,000-barrel-per-day refinery at Port Arthur, Texas were sold to Sohio. Unfortunately, the Justice Department was not satisfied with the voluntary divestitures ARCO had made when it acquired Sinclair Oil in 1969 and asked ARCO to divest itself of additional properties. ARCO divested many Sinclair outlets and a 32,000-barrel-per-day refinery at Sinclair, Wyoming, but was permitted to keep Sinclair's 210,000-barrel-per-day refinery at Houston and its 135,000-barrel-per-day refinery at East Chicago. By divesting the Sinclair outlets, ARCO was permitted to retain access to some major metropolitan outlets it lacked before the merger, including Chicago, Detroit, Houston, and Dallas/Fort Worth.

In 1969 British Petroleum (BP) acquired an interest in Standard Oil of Ohio (Sohio). British Petroleum was the United Kingdom's largest corporation and it had refineries throughout Europe as well as significant interests in the Middle East. It had no U.S. properties, however, until it purchased the leftovers from various asset reconciliations which followed mergers of oil companies. After buying an interest in Sohio, the surviving company marketed in 21 states and had four refineries. Sohio gained about 10,000 Sinclair service stations in 16 Eastern states, Sinclair's 100,000-barrel-per-day refinery at Marcus Hook, Pennsylvania and ARCO's 85,000-barrel-per-day refinery at Port Arthur, Texas through the merger with BP.

In 1968 Sun and Sunray DX merged. The largest of the three Sunray DX refineries Sun gained from the merger was an 85,000-barrel-per-day refinery at Tulsa. Each firm had marketing facilities as well, but their respective territories were virtually separate before merger. By 1970 Sun Oil's merger with Sunray DX Oil had enabled it to establish a substantial petrochemical-marketing organization, and the new petrochemicals division drew its products from four Sun refineries.

In 1971 Exxon's Humble Oil & Refining subsidiary entered the private-brand-gasoline and motor-oil business on an experimental basis. Its marketing plan called for the opening of a dozen stations in New York and New Jersey and was prompted by a desire to gauge the potential of the rapidly growing market segment. Humble reported it would obtain the gasoline it marketed from non-Exxon sources.

In 1970 Ashland acquired Union Carbide's (UCC) oil and gas interests including offshore leases near Louisiana producing approximately 10,000 barrels per day. Ashland, a midwestern refiner, had been quite short of its own supply of crude oil and eager to backward integrate. The UCC acquisition, when combined with Ashland's own crude-producing leases, would yield 12 percent of its daily refinery needs. Also in 1970 Ashland acquired Northwestern Refining, a Minnesota refiner and marketer of gasoline.

In 1969 Tenneco Oil sold refining and marketing capacity when it exited operations in the western United States. Independents were receiving differ-

ent allocations of cheap foreign crude than integrated firms at this time and
this inequity made refining unprofitable for Tenneco in the West. Tenneco
Oil was a conglomerate firm in 1969 with holdings in chemical manufacturing, paperboard and packaging, real estate, banking and insurance, as well
as oil and gas production and processing. It began as the Tennessee Gas
Transmission Company, a regulated pipeline company, and entered the oil
business by acquiring two refineries and their marketing outlets. In 1969 its
Chalmette, Louisiana refinery's capacity was 77,000 barrels per day.

1972

In 1972 Mobil constructed a large refinery at Joliet, Illinois. Ten other
refineries were constructed in 1972 but they were small units, and between
1967 and 1972 thirty refineries were shut down. The largest of these was
55,000 barrels per day.

   Meenan Oil, the largest independent distributor of number two distillate (heating oil), was encountering difficulties in purchasing enough heating oil to support its rapid growth rate. It created an arrangement with an
exploration and production firm whereby it would fund drilling ventures in
exchange for the right to direct the sale of crude from the exploration firms
producing wells. (Meenan directed the crude oil to an independent refiner in
exchange for the right to purchase heating oil.)

1973

The OPEC oil embargo changed many ways of doing business. Most notably, trading relationships were frozen as they were during World War II.
Secondly, an allocation scheme was devised to compensate independent oil
companies which had access to costly foreign crude oil but not to the relatively inexpensive (and available) domestic crude. Two programs ran con-
currently, the entitlements plan (a money transaction) and barrel exchanges
under an allocation plan devised by federal planners. Major integrated oil
firms were required to spread available crude oil around among all refiners,
using entitlements as a clearing device to achieve equity. The most generous
payments went to the least-efficient refiners and the creation of this subsidy
for small refineries encouraged their proliferation.

   In 1973 Tenneco announced it would quit selling gasoline in seven
northeastern states—representing 6 to 10 percent of its revenues—because
problems in obtaining Canadian crude oil were making it difficult to continue supplying wholesale gasoline to independent retail outlets. Tenneco
had been purchasing Canadian crude for processing at a Mobil Oil refinery

in East Chicago, Indiana that Mobil was closing because its custom refining customers were short of crude.

The Emergency Oil Allocation Act retroactively froze buyer-seller relationships. That meant Meenan Oil could not divert crude oil from its drilling partner's wells to a friendly refiner to gain access to heating oil. Exploration for oil with no payoff is both risky and costly, as this independent distributor discovered during its first venture into exploration and production.

1974

The law that froze trading relationships so that refiners without crude oil were not cut off was enforced *only* by small customers. If majors happened to be selling crude oil to each other when the law passed, they did not hold each other to that relationship. Instead the integrated oil firms sought maximum flexibility to manage the allocation problems the new law had created, and some oil companies acquired upstream or downstream operations they thought would help them weather this crisis.

In 1974 Marathon acquired Bonded Oil, a marketing firm which operated 200 service stations in Ohio, Kentucky, Indiana, and West Virginia. Marathon had been Bonded's primary supplier for several years. Also in 1974, Marathon's Robinson, Illinois refinery's capacity was increased to 195,000 barrels per day.

1975

From 1972 to 1975, nineteen new refineries were constructed, but the only large one (200,000 barrels per day) was in Garyville, Louisiana. It was built by entrepreneurs that had no crude oil, and was the last refinery of minimum-efficient scale to be built before 1981. Twelve refineries were shut down between 1972 and 1975 and the largest of these was Amoco's 30,000-barrel-per-day plant in El Dorado, Arizona. The others that were retired were quite small.

1976

In April 1976, a Senate subcommittee approved a bill to force the breakup of the thirteen largest U.S. oil firms. The intent of the bill was to prevent an oil firm from being big in production if it were also big in refining or marketing, for example. In brief, it tried to legislate imbalance between the vertically related stages of oil processing and marketing. Under pressure from small refiners and Congress, the Federal Energy Administration established rules requiring an extra payment (in addition to the entitlements payment) to small refiners of up to $3 per barrel, the smaller refiners receiving larger subsidies. The regulations protected existing small refiners and encouraged new ones. Virtually all refining capacity that was added between 1976 and 1978 was in small refineries, to take advantage of the bias, and mothballed refineries sprang back to life to share in the subsidies. Some of the revived capacity had succumbed to rust and could scarcely be considered operable.

In 1977 the nearly bankrupt Commonwealth Oil Refining Corporation offered Ashland Oil preferred stock which would give it 44-percent voting shares of the firm if Ashland supplied crude oil and other raw materials to Commonwealth's 161,000-barrel-per-day refinery and petrochemical complex in Puerto Rico. Commonwealth's major trade creditors—Gulf, Exxon, and Tesoro—were apprised of the planned takeover, and they seemed particularly eager to close their books on the firm.

1978

Thirty-six facilities were built between 1975 and 1978 in response to the small-refiners-bias policies of the federal government, but none was larger than 30,000 barrels per day. Twenty refineries were shut down during these years, and the largest was a 70,000-barrel-per-day refinery. Ongoing refiners continued to expand their facilities' abilities to process more heavy and sour crude. By 1978 Exxon's Baytown, Texas refinery's capacity was 640,000 barrels per day; ARCO's Houston refinery was 322,000 barrels per day; SOCAL's El Segundo, California refinery was 405,000 barrels per day; Exxon's Linden, New Jersey refinery reached 290,000 barrels per day; Gulf's Girard Point, Pennsylvania facility was 207,600 barrels per day; and Coastal States had expanded the old Sinclair Oil refinery in Corpus Christi to a capacity of 185,000 barrels per day. But in Richmond, California, SOCAL's 365,000-barrel-per-day refinery was forced to shut down two units due to air-pollution-emissions violations. A startled SOCAL petitioned the Superior Court of California to reverse this decision in light of the energy crisis.

Finally, in 1978 the U.S. Supreme Court upheld a Maryland law that forced gasoline refiners to divest themselves of all of the gas stations they owned in that state. The decision affected Conoco and Ashland most immediately because they did not use franchised outlets in Maryland, but rather, they marketed exclusively through company-owned operations.

Early in 1978, the financially troubled Commonwealth Oil Refining (Corco) worked out an arrangement with Coastal States to assure a supply of raw materials for its huge petrochemicals complex in Puerto Rico after the Ashland arrangement fell through. Even with the new arrangement Corco finally petitioned for protection under Chapter XI of the federal bankruptcy law because it was unable to resolve its financial difficulties. The $1-billion firm's refinery and petrochemical plant continued to operate and its customers were supplied, due to a day-to-day-borrowing arrangement with a bank.

In 1978 Texaco indicated it would prune its marketing activities to emphasize profits rather than market share. With its previous fifty-state-marketing commitment, Texaco had long been ranked the number one gasoline seller. It exited from ten midwestern states, increased its exploration budget for 1978, consolidated its refining, marketing, supply, and distribution departments in Houston, and reorganized its resale and consumer divisions.

In November 1978, Ashland Oil sold its oil properties to become only a refiner and marketer (in addition to its chemical operations). The firm had always been severely short of crude. Its exploration and production operations were consuming increasing proportions of resources that Ashland preferred to devote to downstream operations (where it had strength), and under the entitlements plan imposed by the federal government, Ashland was entitled to its fair share of crude oil even if it sold off its leases.

1979

When the Ayatollah Khomeini appropriated oil firms' properties in Iran in 1979 and firms which depended upon Iranian oil could not meet their obligations, these firms could have gone to the spot market to purchase oil supplies. It quickly reflected a $10 premium per barrel after Iran fell, an amount which would have diminished the slender profit margins of unintegrated firms, especially those which had been relying heavily upon the spot market for their supplies of crude oil already. The federal government, however, obliged other firms to share their supplies of crude oil with all the refiners which had traditionally relied heavily upon the spot market as well as the firms which had lost Iranian supplies, thereby spreading the pain around and subsidizing unintegrated firms.

In 1979 Ashland disposed of its upstream operations by selling its midcontinent oil and gas properties to Tenneco Oil and Mesa Petroleum. Ashland sold its offshore Louisiana and Texas properties to Getty Oil and its Rocky Mountain, Southeast, and Southwest properties to Petro-Lewis. One year after the sale Ashland was happy with the sale of its exploration and production interests because it had received a good price for them, it still received crude oil supplies, and windfall-profit taxes were lower in 1978 than in 1979.

Gulf Oil and Mobil began to purchase oil-exploration firms with large proven reserves to offset their declining outputs of domestic petroleum. Mobil outbid Gulf for General Crude, but Gulf purchased Kewanee Industries and Amalgamated Bonanza Petroleum.

In 1979 Coastal States bought Occidental Petroleum's 100,000-barrel-per-day refinery in Antwerp. Coastal States had a history of buying refineries that others had found unprofitable and turning them around. It had purchased several of them and upgraded their capacity to process sour and heavy crudes. Coastal's refineries were heavily dependent upon foreign crude, but since the company also had one of the largest crude-trading operations in the world, it was able to get more than enough feedstock. Indeed, because Coastal was also a refiner, major international oil companies continued to sell to Coastal when they had stopped dealing with other trading companies.

In 1979 Texaco announced its plan to close 2,161 gasoline stations over the next few years. Texaco's marketing emphasis—its corporate strategy— gave it trouble now that the industry's emphasis had changed from volume to profitability. Texaco's marketing network included many small, low-volume and remote stations far from the company's refineries that were expensive to supply, and it exited completely from marketing where its market share had been less than 5 percent. Texaco's twelve U.S. refineries had met about 86 percent of the firm's needs but the Iranian oil situation was forcing refiners to allocate their home heating oil and gasoline to others. The abandoned service stations would continue to purchase from Texaco until an alternative supplier could be found.

In 1979 Clark Oil & Refining sold its entire production operation to focus on refining and marketing. Clark had never produced enough crude oil to supply its refineries, and when the switch to unleaded gas and small cars killed the premium, leaded-gas market Clark had previously focused upon, the firm sought to emphasize refinery efficiency instead. Clark also closed 400 low-volume service stations and converted the remaining 1400 to self-service outlets, some with convenience stores.

In August 1979 heavy oil prices were decontrolled to stimulate its development, and firms blessed with great reserves of heavy crude, like Belridge Oil, became very attractive targets for acquisition. In an attempt to improve its crude oil position, Crown Central, which operated a 100,000-barrel-per-day refinery in Houston, acquired 120 oil and gas wells in Oklahoma in 1979, and Tenneco purchased several midcontinent producing properties to replenish its reserves position.

In 1979 Shell acquired the sizable reserves of Belridge Oil. Although the bid seemed high at over $3.6 billion, the price Shell paid for oil reserves was less than that on the open market. Several firms sought to buy reserves rather than explore for them while oil-stock prices remained low.

In 1979, as price decontrol was phased in, the feisty independent heating-oil distributor reinvestigated its scheme to gain access to heating-oil supplies. Once again Meenan invested in an exploration firm's drilling costs in exchange for the right to direct crude oil to the refiner of its choice. (The refiner would allow Meenan to buy more heating oil in exchange for this favor.)

1980

Conservation had worked very well and demand fell while crude oil prices rose. At the beginning of 1980, sluggish petroleum markets made some refiners balk at paying ever-rising, decontrolled, crude-oil prices. In August 1980, leading oil companies lowered their gasoline prices and began a competitive scramble for gasoline sales.

In 1980 Amoco launched a major modernization program to enable its 415,000-barrel-per-day refinery at Texas City to run 200,000 barrels per day of high-sulfur, heavy crude. The upgrade also virtually eliminated residual-fuel-oil production at that refinery and boosted its yields of light products. SOCAL planned a similar upgrading for its Pascagoula, Mississippi plant.

In December 1980 Texaco discontinued marketing gasoline at 263 stations in the midwest, affecting 90 wholesalers that supplied gasoline to an undetermined number of retail outlets. Texaco gave as its reason for the withdrawal its continuing shortage of refinery capacity which forced the company to pay premium prices on the open market to meet its stations' needs. Texaco continued to sell motor oil and other products at these outlets but it helped them find other suppliers of gasoline.

Texaco invested $175 million to expand its Port Arthur, Texas refinery's capabilities to handle an additional 120,000 barrels per day of high-sulfur crude and its Convent, Louisiana refinery to handle high-sulfur, heavy crude. To gain access to crude-oil reserves, Texaco arranged a joint venture with Mesa Petroleum whereby Mesa made available 1.9 million acres of land to prospect for oil and Texaco provided the cash for development. Texaco received 25 percent of the production from this badly needed acreage.

In 1980 Tenneco acquired Houston Oil & Minerals, thereby adding 104 million proven barrels of oil and 195 billion cubic feet of gas to Tenneco's reserves. Tenneco had been acquiring exploration acreage over the years from firms like Shenandoah Oil, UV Industries, Palmer Oil & Gas, and Ashland Oil. With 8.6 million net acres of undeveloped land in the politically stable U.S., Tenneco now held the eighth largest domestic-land position in the oil industry.

In 1980 Sun purchased Seagram's Texas Pacific Oil subsidiary, defeating Mobil's bid for the properties. Sun needed the Texas Pacific properties to develop and stimulate the Ranger field, one hundred miles west of Fort Worth, using enhanced recovery techniques. In 1980 Sun's refinery system was operating at 39 percent self-sufficiency and Texas Pacific's 120-million-barrel reserves were pledged to other refiners. What Sun needed was a big oil play or to shut down or sell off some of its refineries.

In September 1980, Sun sold its 50,000-barrel-per-day refinery at Duncan, Oklahoma to Tosco Corporation, the second-largest independent refiner of gasoline in the United States that had plants in Martinez and Bakersfield, California, and El Dorado, Arkansas. The Duncan refinery could run heavy, sour crude, but Sun's major 190,000-barrel-per-day refinery at Marcus Hook, Pennsylvania could run only low-sulfur crude oil in 1980. It had not yet been modernized and the cost of doing so was over $500 million, an investment Sun could ill afford after acquiring Texas Pacific and funding an aggressive exploration program.

1981

Major oil companies were no longer forced to share their crude supplies with small refiners in January 1981, and their big refineries could finally be run at full utilization if they could find markets for their outputs. But foreign refineries, which were already adjusted to process heavy and sour crudes, were suffering even-greater excess capacity. Before long, less-costly foreign refined products, including chemicals, would be shipped to the United States from the Middle East. Thus as the United States was trying to conserve energy, each oil company wondered how to sell more gasoline to the public. In an effort to reduce costs, some integrated firms terminated deliveries to dealers that were low-volume outlets. Independent service-station owners were delighted because the gasoline glut made it easier to fill their tanks. In the summer of 1981, jobbers in the Southwest and Southeast formed buyers' co-ops to qualify for reduced prices as barge or cargo buyers.

One strong action the refiners took to control the gasoline glut was to shut down excess capacity; another step was to pull out of low-profit marketing regions. Firms that did not pull out completely continued selling refined products in weak markets but canceled their branded supply contracts.

In 1981 congressman Berkley Bedell (D Iowa) introduced a federal refiner-divorcement bill that was patterned after the Maryland law prohibiting refiners from owning gas stations. In addition to requiring that the major oil companies divest their retail stations, the bill required that retail dealers be allowed to buy the product freely from any available supplier, even while they used another firm's brand name. With such legislation pending, the value of brand names was reconsidered and several companies concluded that it was more profitable to sell nameless petroleum products at the refinery or terminal loading rack.

Also at this time, silent shutdowns and curtailments occurred among the small refiners that were built and had flourished under government subsidies, such as the entitlements program. Major refineries that had been mismatched with available crude oils were also mothballed or abandoned.

In 1981 Energy Cooperative Inc. (ECI), a 125,000-barrel-per-day refinery in Indiana, owned by eight farmer cooperatives, was one of the largest *teakettles* that failed when the entitlements program was rescinded and the small refiners' bias payments program was abolished. The farmers bought the plant from ARCO in 1976 for $80 million, and had spent $140 million in improvements, but in 1980 ECI lost a major customer and long-term contracts for crude. Since it had no crude resources of its own, the Energy Cooperative had to purchase crude on the spot market, which proved to be uneconomic.

In 1981 Exxon launched the biggest turnaround in company history at its 640,000 barrel-per-day refinery at Baytown, Texas, the world's largest refining complex. The nine-week turnaround cost $52 million and idled 250,000 barrels per day of capacity.

Slumping demand took a heavy toll on Amoco's refining and marketing operations even as the decontrol of U.S.-crude-oil prices helped its exploration and production operations, and in 1981 Amoco mothballed its 95,000-barrel-per-day refinery at Wood River, Illinois because of a continuing decline in U.S. demand for refined products. The Wood River refinery could process only low-sulfur crudes, and over half of the crude processed in the United States in 1981 was sour. Then, in an effort to generate better profits for its gasoline-marketing operations, Amoco offered discounts to retail customers paying in cash instead of using Amoco credit cards. Also, Amoco announced it would cease branded-gasoline-marketing operations in eleven states.

The move paralleled demarketing decisions by Getty, Gulf, Texaco, Mobil, Union, and Sun. By May 1981 the effects of decontrol were felt nationwide, as gluts of high-priced gasoline were not absorbed by the market, and in California, Texaco led with a rebate plan for jobbers. Soon, practically every independent was selling Texaco gasoline at prices independent refiners could not hope to match. Texaco finally raised its price a penny per gallon in July 1981 and instituted a 3-percent processing fee for credit-card transactions.

Following its strategy to reduce its refining capacity, Sun sold its 60,000-barrel-per-day refinery and petrochemical plant in Corpus Christi to

Koch Industries. Sun also tried to sell its 83,500-barrel-per-day refinery at Tulsa.

In 1981 Mobil closed its 43,000-barrel-per-day refinery at Buffalo because demand for petroleum products continued to decline. The Buffalo refinery was hampered by its inability to process heavy, high-sulfur crude oil and residual oil. It was Mobil's oldest and smallest refinery and Mobil customers were supplied from other facilities and by pipeline. Mobil also shut down crude-oil-distillation that were not needed at its Philadelphia and Houston refineries, thereby reducing capacity by 10 percent.

In 1981 Sohio purchased the assets of a major customer, Gibbs Oil, to reduce the probability that it would purchase supplies elsewhere. The Gibbs family was leaving the gasoline-marketing business and Sohio was merely guaranteeing the marketing area, comprised of 101 New England gasoline stations.

In 1981 Apex Oil purchased Clark Oil & Refining, thereby becoming a fully integrated oil company. Clark had previously divested its upstream operations, and Apex was already a shrewd competitor in whole residual oil and distillates and had a reputation as the best oil broker in the Midwest.

Demand for refined-petroleum products remained sluggish in 1982, and in February, refining output fell to an industry average of 63 percent, the lowest level in years. Foreign refiners and chemical plants, like the Kuwait National Petroleum Corporation, expanded their refining capacity dramatically and fifty to sixty U.S. refineries were closed between January 1981 and August 1982. ARCO terminated credit-card sales in April 1982, but many other major oil companies disagreed emphatically with ARCO's credit-card decision and scurried to enroll motorists in their own programs because they believed credit cards were crucial to the development of brand loyalty. But Texaco continued to levy a 3-percent processing fee for sales made on its credit card and Amoco and Exxon tested a processing fee in three cities.

The leading marketer in 1982 appeared to be Shell, an oil company that possessed the longest history of being crude-short and had created a strategy to cope with its inability to achieve a high degree of integration early. It was the first major oil firm to turn seriously to downstream operations as a source of profit, and Shell's 1982 marketing position was the envy of firms whose houses were in disorder. In July 1982 Exxon joined Amoco, Texaco, Mobil, and other refiners that tested price discounts for purchases in cash. Unlike ARCO and Pennzoil, who eliminated credit card sales, Exxon retained the cards and gave its dealers freedom to participate or not in the discounts for cash program. One observer noted that although the Exxon plan would not capture market share from other leading marketers, the discounts for cash plan might take market share from the off-brand, no-brand marketers instead.

Analysis of Strategies for Vertical Integration in Refining

Section one has described the structure of the U.S. refining industry and section two has described key events in the industry from 1960 to 1981. This section analyzes the patterns of vertical behavior sketched above and compares the predictions of the strategy framework with outcomes observed in 1981. At that time, the refining industry was in end game but the rate of decline was slow, therefore many competitors did not move immediately to respond to the declining demand for gasoline and heating oil. The industry's structure was growing increasingly volatile because branded products were valued less as consumers responded to higher gas-pump prices by purchasing unbranded, less-costly gasoline. Distributors were less dependent upon refiners as refined products became more plentiful but production companies became *more* dependent upon refiners to take their oil. Decontrol was expected to shake out inefficient refiners and ineffective marketers and therefore refiners were upgrading their plants to handle heavy oil and were testing cash incentives and other marketing changes to ascertain which strategic posture would be most profitable. Because these firms were primarily oil firms in 1981 and because their fortunes were tied to an orderly playing of the endgame, they sought to develop sizable oil reserves while avoiding gas wars downstream, hoping to delay inevitable decline.

According to the framework proposed in chapter 2, firms in declining industries could not afford to be broadly integrated into many activities, nor could their activity levels sustain many stages for each integrated activity undertaken; less internal integration would occur because a balance among the stages would become uneconomic to sustain; and firms would create business arrangements with each other to perform tasks they did previously within wholly owned subsidiaries. Although the oil industry had not progressed far enough in endgame by 1981 for these predictions to be fully tested, some facts clearly differed from the model's predictions at that time. The most significant variances were due to industry structure attributes and corporate strategy needs as firms sought greater self-sufficiency.

Phase of Industry Development

The U.S. refining business was in endgame in 1981 because unit sales of gasoline and heating oil had been declining due to conservation, fuel-efficient automobiles, and higher prices. Foreign refineries threatened to obsolete some U.S. plants. Crude-oil reserves were dwindling in 1981, relationships were terminated as marketers backed out of less-attractive markets, refiners canceled supply contracts, and oil firms terminated operations where refineries were obsolete. Government policies exacerbated uncertainty about both demand and industry structure. The industry had not always been this way. Refiners did not begin operating as integrated firms, nor did companies that began as crude-oil explorers, producers, marketers, or brokers. But starting last century in 1881, each oil firm eventually became integrated to control those risks they could not bear as their operations became more complex and the industry expanded geographically. Even after major refiners had integrated upstream and downstream, they were rarely fully integrated, because few firms could satisfy their refineries' crude requirements from their own daily crude production. Control of access to markets was originally considered more important than controlling a source of crude oil.

The introduction of the automobile changed this perspective about the need for integration from exploration down to service stations, because sales volumes increased significantly and refiners needed more crude per day to run their larger plants efficiently. But firms could not control their degree of internal integration easily as the industry matured because large exploration budgets did not guarantee success. A large outlay could mean only a few incremental barrels of crude oil for the firm's effort. Therefore firms used joint ventures and partnerships to bid for large blocks of land in offshore tracts and to unitize continuous leases onshore to spread this risk.

The industry's major structural change during the 1970s was a contrived one. U.S.-government subsidies enabled refining capacity to increase at a time when that of the rest of the non-OPEC world was decreasing. Refiners were finally unshackled in their resource-allocation decisions in 1980, when decontrol was phased in, and the industry endgame began with rounds of both rationalization and expansion. Facilities in remote locations where demand was thin were retired, and refineries that had been inflexible in their processing capabilities were upgraded if they were in prime locations. Product differentiation had been fading and customers' switching costs were decreasing. Some intermediate customers abrogated their contracts, having found cheaper sources of supply. In brief, distribution channels deteriorated at a time when government intervention sought to hasten the coming of confusion and shortages by increasing the imbalances leading to oil-supply-system decay.

Demand Uncertainty

By 1981 the forces listed above—conservation, high crude prices, foreign unrest, dwindling reserves, and government intervention—had combined to create an environment of high uncertainty about short-term demand. Long-term forecasters concurred that the industry faced decline, but disagreed on its timing. Consumers were increasingly sensitive to price increases for refined-petroleum products and were conscientiously reducing their use of gasoline and heating oil. Such uncertainty did not encourage oil firms to increase their degree of forward integration and even encouraged some companies to narrow the breadth of their forward integration by emphasizing specialty chemicals, lube oils, solvents, or other refined products where demand was less uncertain and the prospects for profitability were higher.

Endgame Industry Evolution and Vertical Integration

Because demand was declining, firms cut back on capacity and lowered their breadth of forward integration. The strategy framework suggested that decreased upstream integration was also appropriate in endgame, but the integrated oil companies tried to *increase* not decrease their degree of internal integration. As will be explained below, this significant variance from the model's predictions may be explained by oil firms' corporate strategies; even in endgame their investment decisions took a long-term perspective rather than seek the short-term profitability that might ultimately hamstring their viability. This variance may also be explained by the early phase of endgame that the industry was in. Many of the structural changes associated with declining industries had not yet occurred.

In summary, this industry's experience indicates that firms became integrated as the oil industry's structure evolved. The early integrated firms made low degrees of internal transfers and the activities they performed were not broadly integrated. The industry's degree of internal integration remained low as it matured because crude shortages kept internal transfers upstream low. In 1981 the integrated refiners were rearranging their patterns of integration by increasing their internal transfers, abandoning some activities and markets serviced previously, and relying more on outsiders for some activities they previously had done in-house.

Volatile Industry Structure

Competition was becoming volatile as weak refiners were shaken out by decontrolled prices and flexibility in trading relationships. Price-cutting erupted in late 1980 as a gasoline glut developed but gasoline prices fell below one dollar per gallon in few regions, and consumers continued to conserve gasoline while large, fuel-inefficient automobiles continued to sell poorly. Industry profits were low and several refineries were being mothballed with little hope of resuscitation in 1981, but not quickly enough to prevent a volatile competitive environment from developing.

The most flexible refineries could purify a wide variety of crude oils and thus were most highly valued. However, the willingness of inefficient competitors to serve the same market niches with undifferentiated products was a condition that made the industry more volatile.

Because crude-oil supplies had been disrupted so erratically, refiners wanted to control more of their own reserves. The diseconomies of operating refineries at a low level of capacity utilization were too great to trust the discovery and development of oil fields to outsiders in 1981. Moreover, by participating in exploration and production activities, refiners gained upstream intelligence concerning the existence of reserves, their size and flow rate, and other information useful in planning refinery upgrades, expansions, and retirements.

Motorists were less loyal to branded gasolines in 1981, after the era of gasoline lines when they discovered that the best gasoline was whichever brand was available. Refiners were changing their business practices. Rack pricing policies that made the refiner a mere distribution point became popular, and remote dealers had to pay their full shipping costs. Ultimate customers were sensitive to price changes and dealers emphasized that aspect of their product more heavily than its brand name.

Refining was the only customer of crude-oil producers; producers had no other market against which to play the refiners. There were substantially fewer refiners than there were crude-oil producers or refined-petroleum marketers. Large volumes of throughput were involved in refining and the high costs incurred with low-capacity utilization were potentially volatile since firms would take whatever actions were necessary to avoid a shutdown.

There were 150 refiners in 1981 but most of them were topping plants (or teakettles) without upstream or downstream linkages. The majority of all oil refined, however, was handled by about 30 firms, which were most likely to be forward integrated but were sometimes backward integrated as well. These two major groups had differing commitments to vertical integration and to the industry. Integrated refiners made investments to reemphasize their commitments to integrated strategic postures, even when demand seemed to be declining. Topping plants invested in a manner that could spark price competition if demand did not grow as they hoped it would.

In summary, the structure of the refining industry was potentially volatile in 1981 because there were imbalances in the chain of production—upstream as well as downstream from refining. Demand was cyclical and could become erratic due to outside forces: customer-switching costs were low in 1981 due to a glut of refined product, and maverick competitors and fringe firms used price-cutting to increase sales volumes. The strategy framework suggested that in such industry settings, high degrees of internal transfer were not expected, investments in many related activities were unlikely, and competitors were likely to share ownership risks on the most uncertain vertically related ventures.

Bargaining Power

The bargaining power of crude-oil producers over refiners was weak because there were many of them and few had large-enough crude-oil outputs to possess leverage over the refiners; sales of crude oil were frequently the producers' only sources of revenues because they were narrowly diversified firms, and few crude producers could forward integrate to refining. Downstream, refiners were losing some of their bargaining power due to the gluts of refined product. Despite the service element associated with the distribution of gasoline, heating oil, or industrial fuels, the public's perceptions of oil companies did not distinguish between independent distributors and the refiners. Thus in 1981 distributors were flexing their economic muscles and growing their marketing territories aggressively. Rather than counter their advances with costly marketing campaigns, some refiners surrendered market segments to the jobbers and reduced their involvement in those businesses they expected would become volatile. Turning their attentions to blending research, heavy-oil-processing techniques, and tertiary recovery activities, the refiners emphasized businesses where they could sustain a significant competitive advantage over the nonintegrated firms.

In summary, the strategy framework suggested firms had to commit greater ownership stakes to the linkages they could not control adequately through others, but in the oil industry few refiners invested in upgraded service stations or other distribution systems. The bulk of firms' capital expenditures went to the type of research-and-development activities that might provide more crude-oil reserves and a profitable premium-market niche for branded-product sales. Increasing volumes of unbranded refined products were sold by major refiners.

Strategy Goals

By 1981, major change in the way of thinking about refining operations had occurred. No longer was a channel used merely to dispose of excess crude oil; refineries had to balance many considerations in determining what mix of products to make with scarce crude-oil imports. The new strategy for scarce energy resources and declining demand emphasized profit at the expense of market share in many cases.

As demand declined, refiners reduced the variety of objectives they had once had. Business-unit pride in creating high-quality lube oils and high-performance gasolines proved to be a profitable policy, but marketing in fifty states was a costly policy that was abandoned once its costs were recognized. Firms concluded that market-share goals could be subordinated to capacity-utilization objectives that provided near-term profits and cash flows to fund exploration activities. Thus major asset repositionings occurred in several firms as they shut down refineries, backed away from markets, and reevaluated branded-product sales while investing heavily in refining equipment and capacity to handle the less-desirable crude oils.

In evaluating corporate objectives about cash flows and acceptable risks, a long-term perspective was needed because near-term tolerance of substandard performance somewhere in the system was necessary. Integrated firms rarely enjoyed high returns in all businesses at the same time. Oil firms were like insurance firms that evened out the risks for their total portfolio of investments, and they ultimately prospered when they concentrated on the businesses they understood.

There were abundant synergies with other energy-related businesses that could be enjoyed by retaining the vertically integrated structure even if another form of energy became dominant. Once purified and refined, the assets used to distribute new energy forms would be the same, assuming the downstream markets did not retool to use fuels other than gasoline, heating oil, bunker oil, and kerosines. If other forms of hydrocarbon could be liquified for transportation to refineries, pipeline assets would be useful.

In summary, a well-managed, vertically integrated oil firm emphasized long-range well-being even in decline, but it also kept individual business units profitable by letting them transact business with outsiders when it was mutually beneficial to do so. By cutting out opportunities for manipulative behavior, the integrated firms enjoyed stable market-share performance and acceptable returns.

The Need for Vertical Integration

There were several reasons for broad integration strategies in 1981 but fewer arguments favoring high degrees of internal transfer. There were few integration economies gained by linking activities executed in remote locations and therefore firms bought, sold, and traded to attain the balances they required for economic operations. General and administrative expenses could be pooled, however, and intelligent use of logistics could offer significant cost savings.

Vertical integration from refining to branded gasoline stations offered consumers some way of making refiners accountable for their products' quality. Without the implied warrantees of a brand name, motorists had fewer assurances that the gasoline they purchased would not damage their engines. Also, vertical integration encouraged research on gasoline additives created to differentiate one brand from another, and vertically integrated firms made expenditures that nonintegrated firms were less likely to undertake—such as pipelines or other infrastructure investments—because they took a long-term perspective regarding their activities. For example, if oil refiners ceased investments in risky exploration and production activities, the change in resource allocations would improve their earnings substantially and make them less risky, but such firms would be out of business in ten or fifteen years if crude supplies again became short. Finally, backward integration enabled firms to understand the types and quantities of crude oil available in order to match their refineries' configurations to inexpensive and relatively abundant supplies. Since refined petroleum products were commoditylike, downstream intelligence was less critical in redeploying the flow of refiners' massive investments.

Strategy Alternatives and Performance

The strategy model distinguished between ownership and the degree of internal integration firms engaged in; firms may have owned all, some, or none of the adjacent firms supplying goods and services, and transferred all, some, or none of their needs internally. Moreover firms differed in the breadth and stages of their integrations. Refiners could be backward integrated into exploration, drilling, production, gathering lines, and pipelines (as well as tankers, barges, and crude oil trucks); they could make a variety of refined products for use in their own petrochemical facilities; they could wholesale refined products, distribute them to dealers or consumers, or operate gasoline service stations. Refiners could sell branded products, or not, if these and other activities listed above were justified by firms' strategic missions and competitive strengths.

Firms strived to bring their upstream operations in line with their refining capacities in 1981, even though the industry was declining, because domestic sources of crude oil were increasingly important to refiners whose plant capacities were very large, in order to avoid uneconomic turndown rates. Also, firms that had lost access to overseas reserves wished for some security in their access to crude supplies in 1981, and exit barriers in crude-oil production were low. Although refiners aspired to be fully integrated, their inabilities to satisfy their refineries' needs for crude oil made them taper integrated at best. Nonintegrated refiners had assumed that governmental allocation schemes would again ensure they received a fair share of the available crude oil, but in 1981 the wisdom of such policies had to be questioned. Although nonintegrated refiners saved on the costs and risks of searching and drilling for oil, they had no guaranteed supplies of oil.

The number of stages of activity undertaken was determined by the products' characteristics, the nature of demand, and the mission of the refining unit relative to adjacent businesses. Since crude oils required significantly different processing (depending upon their proportions of sour impurities and heavy-fuel-oil content), and since the greatest economies were gained by matching crude oils with refineries outfitted specifically for their characteristics, it was advantageous to coordinate exploration, production, and refining facilities. Some firms with large volumes of imported crude oils also benefitted from having their own oil tankers, barges, and trucks. Pipeline ownership was unavoidable since it was the most economic way to transport crude or finished product, but larger integrated firms were more likely to invest in laying pipelines than were firms not involved in several stages of integration (due to their differing outlooks on the oil business). Similarly, the refiners that were heavily invested in production beyond the building-block-chemicals level were also more likely to undertake capital investments to improve or protect their positions in 1981.

The variety of activities undertaken was determined both by demand traits and the way firms competed. In refining, the most broadly integrated firms were also more highly integrated than many others. Briefly, Sohio used salary stations to retail its gasoline, and it received substantial oil supplies upstream, from discoveries on the Alaskan Slope. Tenneco used salary stations and had its own drilling company. With its acquisition of Houston Oil and Minerals, Tenneco's self-sufficiency ratio rose to 68 percent.

In 1981 the trend of integration was toward decreasing the breadth of operations as declining industry demand suggested contraction, and many firms were abandoning their least-promising market segments in order to concentrate on serving promising customers. No major dislocations of supply had occurred because firms had differing perceptions of which segments were attractive.

The form of vertical relationship indicated the amount of asset exposure and flexibility the venture possessed. In highly uncertain or volatile environments, where the performance of vertically integrated firms was highly sensitive to fluctuations in demand, ownership forms involving lesser amounts of asset exposure (such as quasi-integration) were used to reduce the variability of returns and increase firms' strategic flexibilities. (The generic strategy of *quasi-integration* refers to the *form* of ownership; the percentage of requirements handled through these linkages could range from small amounts to one hundred percent.) The form of integration used was determined by firms' bargaining power and their corporate-strategy objectives. The oil industry was a confusing maze of partnerships and joint ventures upstream because the risks of finding oil were high and the capital expenditures of oil exploration and pipelines were very high; by contributing to the drilling costs, construction costs or other investments in upstream activities, venture partners obtained a share of the proceeds, a right to direct the flow of product, or an opportunity to purchase crude oil. By investing in many risky projects, refiners hoped to hit at least one sizable oil field, but they invested in syndicates to reduce their exposure on one dry hole.

Although refineries were rarely owned jointly, arrangements occurred that permitted firms without refineries to hire one to process their crude oil. Also, the refiners located near each other *toll processed* for one another when annual turndowns occurred. Thus firms could control the assets of those in adjacent industries without owning them. Downstream, firms in petrochemicals frequently developed new products or tested new processes using joint ventures in order to minimize the losses of an individual firm. Frequently the feedstocks for the venture were provided by the refiner's plant and chemical firms' processes were used in production. The arrangement accelerated innovation and facilitated the testing of new materials and methods. The shared risks of these ventures enabled petrochemical firms to accommodate large write-offs if these ventures failed.

Although petroleum refining was in endgame in 1981, its structure was changing, particularly among the nonintegrated firms that had not been previously responsible for finding their own crude supplies. The firms in refining that formulated the more effective vertical-integration strategies were those that gained relatively stable access to raw materials and effective distribution while achieving their strategic objectives, including market leadership or above-average returns on invested capital.

Although Standard Oil of Indiana's cutbacks in marketing were not as severe as those of some firms, Amoco's offer of discounted prices for cash purchases was creating a stir. Its exploration arm had developed a reputation of being among the best and was successful in generating new oil reserves. Amoco had the largest acreage under lease in the Overthrust Belt (SOCAL was second) and had farmed out its acreage to independent drilling companies to participate when wildcatters found oil and to gain exclusive seismic information. With such a flurry of joint ventures going on, Amoco's upstream balance looked very promising in 1981.

Ashland Oil earned most of its revenues on marketing and transportation activities. Its exploration arm was never very large nor successful, and historically its crude sufficiency had been low. Ashland needed the entitlements and government assistance to ensure it had adequate crude reserves and when these were ended Ashland participated in wildcat drilling ventures to direct the marketing of resulting oil. Initially the stock market rewarded Ashland's grit in divesting exploration and production operations, but in 1980–1981 Ashland was whipsawed by the uneven timing of changes in refined-product and crude-oil prices. Therefore its performance looked more somber at year end.

Atlantic-Richfield had four large refineries in 1981 and emphasized refining operations that rearranged the molecular structure of longer chains of hydrocarbon into light products. Hence ARCO's refineries were highly utilized. ARCO's Alaskan reserves gave it better crude sufficiency and its marketing operations continued to emphasize branded outlets after ARCO phased out credit-card sales. ARCO seemed to be in a very strong position for continued competition in endgame because it had shifted its resources to serve the best markets and customers early.

Crown Central Petroleum had sales in excess of $1 billion and was broadly integrated in 1981. It was crude short but was buying reserves from smaller companies. It had been one of the very-profitable refining companies during the era of price controls and frozen trade relationships, and operated a petrochemical plant in Houston alongside the large, integrated refiners.

In 1981 Exxon and its affiliates operated approximately seventy refineries in thirty-seven countries. Four of its five U.S. plants were efficiently sized refineries capable of great flexibility in crude-oil processing. It had few owned service stations but Exxon was introducing prototype stations to test the motorists' reactions in Texas and discounts for cash in other markets. Unlike other leading oil firms, Exxon rarely farmed out acreage it had leased for development by others. Exxon participated in joint ventures and had the most land in the Western Hemisphere under lease, but it drilled its own prospects with great success. Exxon found reserves through its exploration ventures rather than through acquisition of proven reserves. In 1981 Exxon was approaching global crude self-sufficiency.

During the 1950s and 1960s, Mobil had emphasized its refining and marketing operations, not exploration. By 1981 however Mobil had become one of the most successful explorationists, taking its place beside Amoco and SOCAL. Like Amoco, Mobil was testing a discounts-for-cash program at its branded service stations with considerable success.

Shell was highly integrated downstream to chemicals and used leased stations, rather than salaried employees, to distribute its gasoline. Shell had made its upgrading investments and demarketing decisions early and was enjoying the benefits of these early exits in 1981.

SOCAL was a particularly successful explorationist and had been upgrading its huge refineries in 1981. SOCAL was very conservative in its capital structure and relatively undiversified beyond oil.

Sohio (the original Rockefeller oil company) had been a refiner and marketer through local service stations. Its top executives all had refining and marketing experience and they were justifiably apprehensive about finding crude reserves when it acquired British Petroleum's holdings in Alaska. When the reserves in Prudhoe Bay expired, however, the company would again be thin on good prospects. Sohio used salaried employees in its gasoline stations and would be hurt most severely if the Senate bill on marketing divorcement were enacted into law.

Sun Oil also emphasized refining and marketing historically and Sun's exploration arm had land which offered promising results. In reorganizing itself for the 1980s, Sun shut down several refineries and acquired Texas Pacific Oil in an effort to approach upstream and downstream balance.

Texaco made a most-aggressive effort to reorganize its marketing effort by backing out of unpromising markets and emphasizing exploration activities, instead. Since it had not been developing a cadre of geological stars as Amoco had done, Texaco was expected to find its resources stretched while it tried to be successful upstream and profitable downstream.

As a diversified conglomerate, Tenneco was less sensitive to the growing pains of firms like Texaco. Its exploration record was good, it had acquired Houston Oil and Minerals and sizable reserves, and Tenneco had numerous prospects to drill. Its refinery was an efficient size but had been inadequate historically to satisfy its contractual sales obligations to wholesalers and distributors. By surrendering some of those markets, Tenneco was able to bring its crude, refining, and marketing operations closer into balance.

In summary, the refiners sought to prune their downstream internal transfers while increasing their upstream internal transfers. The structure of this industry had never reached the hypothetical balance of full integration because most firms had not found enough oil to fill their efficient-sized refineries. Although demand for refined petroleum was declining and total global reserves were expected to dwindle in the coming decades, oil firms invested heavily in upstream activities to find a stable supply of crude oil. Downstream, it was not clear whether branded gasolines and heating oils would continue to be remunerative.

Selected References

Alexander, Tom. "Day of Reckoning for Oil Refiners." *Fortune,* January 12, 1981, pp. 38–41.

Alexander, Tom. "How Little Oil Hit a Gusher on Capitol Hill." *Fortune,* August 14, 1978, pp.

American Petroleum Institute. *Entry and Exit in U.S. Petroleum Refining,* 1948–1978, Washington, D.C.: American Petroleum Institute, 1981.

Berger, Bill D. and Anderson, Kenneth E. *Modern Petroleum: A Basic Primer of the Industry,* Tulsa, Oklahoma: Petroleum Publishing Company, 1978.

Bloom, John. "Old Oil: The Ranger Revival," *Texas Monthly,* February 1981, pp. 113–116, 194–198.

de Chatzeau, Melvin G. and Kahn, Alfred E. *Integration and Competition in the Petroleum Industry,* New Haven: Yale University Press, 1959.

Garrison, William G.. "Idled Refineries Require Safety Measures," *Oil and Gas Journal,* December 7, 1981, pp. 128–130.

Greening, Timothy. "Surviving the Shakeout in Refining and Marketing in the Eighties." *Oil & Gas Journal,* October 26, 1981, pp. 110–115.

McLean, John G. and Haigh, Robert W. *The Growth of Integrated Oil Companies,* Boston: Harvard University Graduate School of Business Administration, 1954.

Mitchell, Edward J., ed. *Vertical Integration in the Oil Industry,* Washington, D.C.: American Enterprise Institute for Public Policy Research, 1976.

National Petroleum Council. *Refinery Flexibility,* Washington, D.C.: Department of Energy, 1980.

Nulty, Peter. "Teakettle Refiners Scramble to Survive," *Fortune,* July 13, 1981, pp. 47–48.

"Refiner/Marketers Adjusting to Lower U.S. Products Demand," *Oil and Gas Journal,* June 1, 1981, pp. 45–49.

Skinner, Wickham and Rogers, David C.D. *Manufacturing Policy in the Oil Industry,* Homewood, Illinois: Richard D. Irwin, 1970.

Especially helpful were corporate annual reports and financial statements of the firms described in chapter 5, and conversations with representatives of twenty-three oil companies (seven nonintegrated, three partially integrated). Special acknowledgment is due to the American Petroleum Institute.

6

Strategies for Vertical Integration in the Whiskey Industry

Whiskey (if of Canadian or Scotch origin, it is spelled "whisky") is a brown alcoholic beverage distilled from a fermented mash of grain. In 1981, the leading types of whiskey were Canadian blends, Bourbon straights and blends, Scotch blends, and bonded Bourbons. Prohibition (1919-1933) virtually destroyed the U.S. whiskey industry, leaving Canadian distilleries strong enough to capture a market lead they had not relinquished by 1981. Consumer preferences had changed by that time, favoring light distilled spirits and wines (as well as bottled mineral waters), and leaving the whiskey industry a declining one with substantial excess capacity.

A Description of the Whiskey Industry

The Product

Whiskey is made from water, malt, yeast, and grain and produced by distillation. The *body* of whiskey refers to its color, flavor, and bouquet, and can be controlled by the proportion of corn to other grains used in the fermented mash and the type of vessel in which it is aged. The alcoholic content of a whiskey (*proof*) is determined by the distillation process and rectifying activities. The U.S. Bureau of Alcohol, Tobacco, and Firearms imposes very precise regulations on the contents, ages, and proofs of various whiskies.

Types of Whiskies

Bourbon is American whiskey in which the dominant grain comprised at least 51 percent of the mash. It is produced at less than 160° proof and aged in new charred-oak barrels at less than 125° proof. Bourbons can be straights, blends, or bonded whiskies. Straight whiskies are aged for at least four years and are not blended. A blend of straight Bourbon whiskies is a mixture of two or more straight whiskies. *Bonded* Bourbon is aged at least

---

Background research was provided by Kurt Feuerman and Stan Herman.

four years in a special bonded (federal) warehouse and bottled at 100° proof. Bottled-in-bond whiskies are very heavy compared with the lighter whiskies consumers preferred in 1981. Demand for bonded whiskies has declined substantially since the 1950s.

Blends are mixtures of straight whiskies and *grain neutral spirits* (alcohol). Like other whiskies they are distilled from a fermented mash and stored in oak barrels (but not necessarily new ones). In 1981 popular blended whiskies, like Seagram's 7 Crown, Hiram Walker's Imperial or Schenley Reserve, contained around 35 percent straight whiskies and 65 percent grain neutral spirits. They were bottled at roughly 86° proof.

The most popular whiskies in 1981 were the light-bodied Canadian brands, produced in Canada under Canadian regulations. These are aged at least three years in *used* oak barrels and are bottled at even lower proofs. The most-popular light-bodied Canadian brands use heavy proportions of rye with neutral spirits.

Recipes for Canadian whisky are jealously guarded secrets, as are those for other types of whiskey; it contains some heavy-bodied (imported) Bourbon, rye, and Scotch whiskies in addition to grain neutral spirits. Each distillery that blends whiskies keeps a library of master whiskies to maintain consistency in its formulas, and some of the best Canadian whiskies are blended *before* barreling, rather than after aging.

Scotch whisky is a blend of malt and grain whiskies produced in Scotland. The major grain in Scotch whisky is barley malt, and the peatiness in its flavor comes from burning peat to halt the germination of the barley as well as the vessels in which they are aged. Over thirty malt whiskies may be blended with grain whiskies to create a particular Scotch whisky. The distilleries of Scotland specialize in making specific malt whiskies that are traded (or sold) among themselves to create the mixture needed for their family recipes.

Scotch whiskey is distilled twice to eliminate heavier materials and to smooth out the taste. It mixes low-proof malt whisky with higher-proof grain whiskies to lighten the body and resulting flavor, and is usually aged in used sherry casks.

In 1981 whiskies could be sold under the brand name of a wholesaler (or second-tier distillery) when produced to order for the bottler, or when a distillery produced too much of its own branded whiskey and had to dump it as unbranded bulk whiskey at the best possible price on the spot market. Major distillers varied in their willingness to produce an off-brand whiskey to order, but distress sales of smooth premium whiskies did occur, especially in the 1970s as consumer tastes changed.

In 1981 whiskey production was highly regulated in several ways. Most importantly, whiskey was taxed when it was shipped for distribution and time limitations were imposed on the length of time a whiskey could be aged without being taxed. The distribution of whiskey was also regulated. As will be explained below, all sales of whiskey had to be made through distributors (wholesalers), except to state-controlled liquor stores. U.S. whiskies were required to carry very-detailed labeling about their grain content, years of aging in new charred-oak barrels, and proportion of straight-whiskey contents. (Whiskies imported from Canada or Scotland did not carry such labeling.) The principal purpose of such regulations was protection of U.S. consumers that had purchased raw (unaged) whiskies laced with a variety of impurities (including sulfuric acid) during Prohibition.

Sales of whiskey had declined from 63 percent of total distilled-spirits sales in 1971 to 47.9 percent in 1981. (In absolute volumes this was a reduction from 241 million gallons in 1971 to 213.6 million gallons in 1981.) Because U.S. consumers seemed to be more health conscious in 1981, absolute consumption of distilled spirits declined by one million gallons from 1980 to 1981. A preference for light spirits, white wines, and beer decreased whiskey consumption even more severely. Further, college-aged consumers had embraced other mood-changing apparatus, such as marijuana, and other amusements for their leisure hours. As table 6-1 indicates, Bourbon consumption declined 33 percent from 1971 to 1981; Bourbon blends declined 43 percent, Bourbon straights declined 19 percent, and bonded Bourbon declined 16 percent (but was a very small volume of total consumption in 1971). Scotch whisky consumption increased 9 percent from 1971 to 1981, and Canadian-whisky consumption increased 47 percent.

Every increase in whiskey taxes (or interest rates) increased the price of whiskey and drove consumers to another, less-costly alcoholic beverage. Furthermore, illegal (untaxed) whiskey was consumed in greater volume as the price of regulated whiskey was increased.

Markets

Whiskies are sold to retail stores, taverns, and restaurants. Seventeen states were controlled in 1981, which meant that all package sales of whiskey were made there by state authorities. According to wholesalers, the most difficult states to service were Pennsylvania, Michigan, and Ohio (they resist price increases), but all sales to taverns and restaurants were more difficult to service than to state-controlled retail stores.

Suppliers

Some distillers start with local water that is not specially treated, but others own reservoirs to ensure that the quality of their water is appropriate at

Table 6-1
Sales of Total Distilled Spirits
(percent)

	1971	1972	1973	1974	1975	1976	1977	1978	1979	1980	1981 (estimate)
Total Whiskey	63.0	61.7	59.2	57.3	55.3	53.5	51.9	50.7	49.6	48.5	47.9
Bourbon (American Whiskies)	39.0	36.7	33.2	31.0	29.5	27.6	26.2	24.8	23.7	22.8	22.3
Blends	18.1	16.9	15.0	13.6	12.5	11.7	10.9	9.8	9.4	8.9	8.8
Straights	19.5	18.5	17.1	16.4	16.0	15.1	14.5	14.3	13.6	13.9	13.5
Bonds	1.4	1.3	1.1	1.0	1.0	0.8	0.8	0.7	0.7	—	—
Scotch	13.9	13.9	14.2	14.3	13.6	13.7	13.4	13.5	13.5	12.9	12.9
Canadian	9.9	10.6	11.4	11.7	11.9	11.9	12.0	12.1	12.1	12.5	12.4
Other Whiskey	0.2	0.5	0.4	0.3	0.3	0.3	0.3	0.3	0.3	0.3	0.3

Source: Industry sources.

all times. In Kentucky, lakes are laced with limestone, a feature believed responsible for Bourbon whiskey's mellow taste.

The grain used in whiskey distilling is grown to the industry's specifications but not by the distillers because grain is readily available and deliveries could be easily contracted. Distilleries had once owned grain elevators for storing their corn and had engaged in grain-brokerage activities, but in 1981, only a few distillers operated grain elevators.

The yeasts used for distilling are a closely guarded family secret, and some distillers use the same yeast year after year for over a century, while others start each batch with fresh yeast. Firms can maintain their own yeasts and enzymes or they can purchase them from commercial suppliers who develop and maintain yeast cultures made to distillers' specifications.

The staves used in making new charred-oak barrels can be purchased from sawmills or brokers if distillers made their own barrels. Barrel making is not very profitable. A hand-crafted business, it does not lend itself to computerization; nor are there logistical advantages that automation might exploit. Each distiller purchases barrels from three or four cooperages and even the distillers involved in barrel-making purchase some of their requirements from outsiders in order to keep the small cooperages alive.

Distillers became barrelmakers back in the days when the federal Office of Price Administration (OPA) imposed a ceiling price on barrels of around $2.50 and nobody would sell barrels for whiskey-making to distilleries for that low a price. In order to obtain a supply of barrels, under those conditions, distillers made barrels themselves but never profited in doing so. Barrels represented over half the cost (eighty-five dollars) of making Bourbon whiskey in 1981. Used oak barrels were sold to Scotch, Canadian or other distillers (for light whiskies) which were not obliged by law to use new cooperage, and they could be reused five or six times before being discarded (over twenty years after purchase).

Most distilleries purchase glass bottles from major glass manufacturers but a few distilleries own glass-bottle subsidiaries. Because glass-bottle producers have been frequently plagued by labor strikes, multiple sources of supply are maintained at the cost of volume discounts in purchasing.

In summary, technological innovation did not occur rapidly in many upstream industries and profit margins were low in businesses like barrel making (or risky in grain brokerage). Consequently, few firms were backward integrated in 1981. This had not always been the case. After World War II many distilleries purchased barrel makers and some engaged in grain operations as well. By 1981, however, sales volumes had declined to a level where it was economically more sensible for some firms to dis-integrate and patronize those distilleries that remained backward integrated to share in scale economies.

Manufacturing

The capital costs of distilling are high. In 1971 the cost of a new distillery approached $30 million. Because different stills were needed to produce grain neutral spirits than for straight whiskies, capital costs were higher for producers of blended whiskies than for straights. Small companies in the distilling business did not own distilling equipment in some cases; rather, they leased a qualified distillery for a specific period or they purchased the precise whiskey desired on contract from an ongoing distillery.

The principal factors that affect the taste and odor of whiskey are fermentation, distillation, blending, maturing, and proof in bottling. Innovation progresses very slowly in the whiskey business because anything that is changed can affect the taste of the product adversely and distillers would not know of its effect until six years later if a production change were made.

Scale economies are available in materials handling by using methods that smaller distilleries cannot afford. Cost reductions are also available in areas such as automatic bottling, labeling, pallet packing and other logistical areas. All distilleries shut down activities temporarily in 1981 because diseconomies set in if the distillery were run at low levels of utilization. Consequently, a distillery's management ran a plant at full volume when it was operated and idled it at other times.

Grain and malt are prepared to make whiskey by grinding to a specified coarseness, and each was mixed with water to form a grain mash and a malt slurry, respectively. Malt slurry is added to the mash in the cooker where starch conversion begins. The mixture is cooled and inoculated with yeast.

When the mixture is ready for distillation, it is pumped to large distillation columns where it flows in a zigzag fashion over horizontal plates spaced evenly down the length of the still. Steam is injected near the base of the still and, as it rises and passes through small perforations in the horizontal plates, evaporates the alcohol out of the mash on each plate. The steam carries the alcoholic vapor to the top of the still where it is condensed, redistilled in other stills to remove undesirable elements, and rectified.

Distilled water is added to the high-proof mixture to lower its alcoholic content, and the colorless new whiskey is pumped to a rack-warehouse where it is tapped into charred white-oak barrels for aging. During the maturing process the whiskey attains its amber color, mellowness and additional flavor. When it is fully matured, the whiskey is pumped from the rackwarehouse to the final blending and bottling area where pure water is added to reduce the strength of the whiskey to the required proof for bottling (rectification).

In 1981 the assets used in distillery liquor were highly specific for that purpose and could not be used for any other purpose economically. Since the market for distillery assets was quite thin, many plants were simply mothballed until the market for whiskies improved. The copper pipes had some economic value but the mashing tubs and stills were useful primarily for making whiskey. In this era of excess capacity and shutdowns, distillers did not convert their assets to produce more and more grain neutral spirits for sale to others. (Quite the opposite occurred.) Instead, large firms that were already leaders in producing grain neutral spirits made them in larger volumes and merchandised them around the world in economic lot sizes. This trend toward specialization was expected to continue until firms in the U.S. made only a few whiskies or other products and purchased their remaining needs from specialists for blending purposes.

Marketing

In 1981 most distillers blended and bottled their own whiskey either under their own brand name or under the brand name owned by a customer. Private labeling occurred when a firm owned the rights to a whiskey brand but paid another to bottle the product for them. Firms' strategies regarding bulk whiskey sales varied widely.

Direct distribution of liquor by distillers was forbidden by law, although there were states where a resident distillery could sell to certain customers without going through a middleman, provided state and federal taxes were collected. Wholesalers were protected by law from any dual-distribution competition by the distilleries. Wholesaling relationships changed infrequently and there were few wholesalers to choose from, but major distillers preferred not to use the same wholesaler as did their major competitors in a particular geographic market.

Historically, exclusive distribution arrangements were used in which the wholesaler called upon every conceivable account in its territory. More recently, other wholesalers were hired as the second distributor in some territories, in an effort to squeeze out inefficient wholesalers that were not giving excellent service.

In 1981 whiskey was one of the most heavily advertised consumer products in the United States. Distillers had several sales forces (for different quality lines) and selling organizations that specialized in imported whiskies, as well. Firms that wholesaled their whiskies exacerbated their sensitivity to high-interest costs in 1981. Moreover, there were few economies available in an industry where fifty separate selling organizations had to be maintained.

In summary, whiskey marketing was quite costly because advertising costs were high, wholesalers were a fragmented and troubled industry, and interest costs were rising. Whiskey distilleries had once wholesaled their products in key markets but few did so in 1981, and dis-integration was occurring in this part of the industry.

Competition in the Whiskey Industry in 1981

In 1981 approximately forty firms distilled, rectified, or bottled whiskey. The leading brands of whiskey for the four major product categories had not changed significantly in two decades. The leading brands in each category represented a substantial portion of that category's respective total market share within a field of hundreds of whiskey brands, as table 6–2 indicates. Gins, vodkas, rums, and tequilas represented more than half of all liquor sales in 1981, but customer loyalties for leading whiskey brands were strong.

The whiskey industry was relatively concentrated in 1981 but that had not always been the case. In 1802, there were over 22,000 distilleries in the U.S.; in 1810, 14,000. There were 965 distilleries in 1899, 434 in 1914, and only 100 in 1939 after the repeal of Prohibition. Many smaller distilleries were forced out of the industry when whiskey was sold in bottles rather than in unidentified barrels. The capital costs of bottling their own branded whiskey (and the expense of promoting a major liquor brand) became too substantial for some of the smaller, less-capitalized companies to afford.

Table 6–2
Estimated 1981 Market Shares for Sales of Whiskies Numbered among the Top Fifteen Sellers of All Liquor Brands
(market shares per category of whiskey)

Bourbon	Canadian	Scotch	Blend
American Brands' Jim Beam (14%)	Seagram's V.O. (19%)	Paddington's J&B (13%)	Seagram's 7 Crown (38%)
Brown-Forman's Jack Daniels (13%)[a]	Walker's Canadian Club (17%)	Schenley's Dewar's (13%)	
	Brown-Forman's Canadian Mist (14%)		
	National's Windsor Supreme (13%)		
Total Bourbon (million gallons)	*Total Canadian (million gallons)*	*Total Scotch (million gallons)*	*Total Blend (million gallons)*
61.9	55.6	57.9	39.5

Source: Industry sources.
[a]Brown-Forman does not list its "Jack Daniels" as a Bourbon Whiskey.

Corporate Strategy Exit Barriers in Whiskey

In 1981 the narrowly diversified firms possessed exit barriers resulting from the strategy they had pursued in the past, and these barriers could make dis-integration difficult for them to accept. Although the industry seemed to become more specialized in 1981, there were certain whiskey products distillers would never subcontract because distillers would not trust the formulas of their leading brands to outsiders. Too much historical pride in their products would have to be overcome for that form of dis-integration to occur.

Summary of Competitors in Whiskey

In summary, whiskey distillers could differ in the breadth of their diversifications as well as whether they manufactured *and* marketed whiskies (or only marketed them). By 1981 all whiskey companies relied almost exclusively upon independent wholesalers to distribute their whiskies and other alcoholic beverages. Since physical interconnection did not appear to be necessary in grain storage and brokerage, aging and warehousing, bottling and labeling, or distribution operations, high degrees of internal integration did not appear to be necessary in 1981.

A Mapping of Strategic Groups in Whiskey

This section groups major competitors by their breadth of vertical integration in 1981. Firms were less broadly integrated than they had been in the past, and where an integrated relationship remained, it tended to be tapered rather than full integration. The whiskey distillers could be mapped as shown in figure 6–1 to indicate whether any shared resources or linkages between important businesses existed.

In 1981 Norton Simon, Paddington, and Heublein marketed whiskies produced by others. (Glenmore and Heublein bottled bulk whiskies.) Most distillers rounded out their lines by importing Scotch whisky or other alcoholic beverages, but used independent wholesalers to market their lines. Only Hiram Walker, Publicker, Seagram, and Schenley had operated company-owned wholesaling subsidiaries (and these were protected in 1981 by grandfather clauses). Generally, distillers were not allowed to distribute their products in 1981, but they were permitted to deploy sales forces to assist exclusive or dual wholesalers.

Seagram developed grains, operated a fleet of grain hopper cars and grain elevators, and engaged in brokerage activities. Hiram Walker had been both a grain broker and a whiskey broker at one time. Norton Simon and Hiram Walker produced glass containers and Publicker produced bulk whiskies. Barrels had once been made by Brown-Forman, Glenmore, Hiram

Breadth of Nondistribution Activities

Breadth of Distribution Activities	Bottles/ Sells Whiskies Produced by Others	Distilling	Cooperage	Glass Containers	Grain Brokerage
Outside Distributors & Wholesalers	NS HBLN PAD GLEN	BEAM PUB STD SEA BF SCHN HW GLEN NATL	BF SCHN GLEN (HW) (NATL) (PUB) SEA	HW NS	(HW) SEA
Sells Bulk Whiskey to Other Distillers, Brokers, Blenders or Bottlers		PUB	(PUB)		
Company-Owned Wholesaling Subsidiary		HW SEA PUB SCHN	SCHN (HW) SEA (PUB)		(HW) SEA
Distributor of Imported Whiskies	PAD NS	SCHN HW SEA	SCHN (HW) SEA	NS HW	(HW) SEA
Merchandises Whiskies Produced by Others	HBLN GLEN	GLEN	GLEN		

Key:

BEAM	= James B. Beam	NATL	= National Distilleries & Chemical
BF	= Brown-Forman	NS	= Somerset Importers (Nortin Simon)
GLEN	= Glenmore Distillers	PUB	= Publicker Industries
HW	= Hiram Walker-Gooderham & Worts	SEA	= Seagram
HBLN	= Heublein	SCHN	= Schenley (Rapid American)
PAD	= Paddington (Liggett Group)	STD	= Fleischmann's (Standard Brands)

Note: Parentheses indicate a former activity that was inactive in 1981.

Figure 6–1. A Mapping of Competitors in Whiskey, 1981

Walker, Publicker, National Distillers, Schenley, and Seagram, but in 1981 only Brown-Forman, Schenley, Glenmore, and Seagram both made and used white-oak barrels. Other distillers purchased barrels from them and from a handful of surviving independent barrel makers.

Key Events in the Whiskey Industry

This section traces key elements in the endgame of the whiskey industry, beginning with the 1960s. A summary of conditions before that time appears below.

A Brief History of Whiskey

The manufacture of distilled liquor was first a domestic handicraft like weaving or candlemaking; then it became a small-scale vocation, usually associated with grain milling and farming. During the nineteenth century the distilling industry was surrounded by many scandals, and speculation in whiskey became a big business. Initially, the distillers themselves kept aloof from the quarrels and venality associated with marketing their products by simply selling warehouse receipts to rectifiers, who did as they pleased with the unidentified barrels of whiskey. When the distillers realized they could capture more value-added by becoming rectifiers and bottlers themselves, the era of brand-name reputations, national advertising, and modern whiskey marketing began.

During Prohibition bootleggers taught a generation to drink gin instead of whiskey, but an enormous marketing effort was undertaken to reinstate whiskey as the nation's favorite drink after 1934. One of the major tactics the Post-Prohibition whiskey distillers used to bring consumers back to whiskey was *quality,* and Seagram was a leader in blending. Rather than sell freshly distilled, unmixed liquors like Bourbon or straight rye, the new Seagram brands were well aged and carefully blended.

By 1960, consumers' tastes in whiskey were changing. During World War II and the immediate postwar era, straight rye and Bourbon whiskies almost disappeared from the market. Almost every distiller was obliged to market increasing quantities of blended whiskies in order to conserve rapidly dwindling stocks of straight ryes and Bourbons. Demand for straights was increasing and this trend benefited the firms whose market images had been built on straight Bourbon, rye, or Tennessee whiskies.

1960

By 1960 less than ten distillers promoted their own branded whiskies. Many others bottled and branded bulk whiskies provided by other distilleries, and importers distributed Scotch whisky and specialties. All of the leading distillers had created wide product lines by distributing the products of other wineries, distilleries, and sometimes of breweries as well as their own.

In 1933 the largest liquor producer in the world had been Distillers Company Ltd. of Edinburgh, Scotland (DCL), a trust comprised of six Scottish distilleries controlling famous Scotch brands like Dewar, Johnny Walker, Black & White, and John Haig. During the years of U.S. Prohibition, DCL of Edinburgh and the Bronfman brothers of DCL-Seagram had earned high profits through shipping operations in Halifax. In 1933 Seagram distilled, blended, and bottled Scotch-type whisky under contract with DCL, but the two firms did not invest in each other's markets. Traditionally, DCL licensed sales agents rather than enter the United States itself, and in 1960 each of its leading brands was imported and distributed by a separate organization.

James B. Beam Distilling Company made whiskey in Claremont, Kentucky in 1960 and owned twenty-five bonded warehouses and two water reservoirs located on sites totaling 700 acres. The trend toward straight whiskies helped "Jim Beam," its leading Kentucky Straight Bourbon brand.

Brown Forman's Louisville, Kentucky, distilling business was founded in 1870. In 1940 Brown-Forman acquired the Old Kentucky distillery in Shively, Kentucky, and the stocks of a Frankfort, Kentucky, distillery. It purchased sixteen acres of land and a woodworking plant in Kentucky to form the Blue Grass Cooperage, and it manufactured staves and heads for whiskey barrels in West Virginia. By 1960 Brown-Forman's principal distillery in Louisville had been matched by the Lynchburg, Tennessee, distilleries of Jack Daniel that were acquired in 1956, and it had four distilleries in total. "Jack Daniel Tennessee Sippin' Whiskey" was helped by the trend toward straight-whiskey consumption.

Glenmore Distilleries was a major company in 1933 and its relatively inexpensive Kentucky Tavern brand Bourbon was of high quality. The Thompson family did not put much effort into merchandising it, but the brand sold well without a marketing campaign. Glenmore operated distilleries at Owensboro and Shively, Kentucky, and its Bourbon Cooperage Company operated in Campberville, Kentucky, with subsidiary stave operations in Daviess County, stave mills in Pennsylvania and West Virginia, and timber land in five eastern states. Glenmore's subsidiary, Yellowstone, Inc., distilled and sold bulk whiskey to distributors from its Shively, Kentucky distillery and whiskies were aged in Glenmore's warehouse in Owensboro, Kentucky in 1960.

Hiram Walker was founded by a miller and grain merchant who began distilling as a means of capturing more value-added. The Walkerville plant covered nineteen acres and was both broadly and fully integrated. In 1927 Hiram Walker acquired the older Gooderham & Worts distilling business (1833) with a plant in Toronto, Ontario. It had begun the Great Western distillery in Peoria, Illinois, in 1919 but mothballed its construction until after repeal of Prohibition. The Peoria plant was the largest distillery in the world, and it made barrels, glass containers, and handled grain in its elevators.

In 1950 Hiram Walker subsidiaries included five sales organizations, one grain dealer, three grain elevators, several bonded warehouses, six distilleries, one barrel maker, and two whiskey merchants and importing organizations. By 1960 Hiram Walker had also acquired a Scottish maltster and grain-merchant organization, two more Scotch distilleries, additional warehouses, and it had five major distilleries.

National Distillers and Chemical began as a whiskey distiller, formed by reorganization in 1906. With Prohibition upon them, National made medicinal alchohol and packed maraschino cherries. It also purchased whiskey in bond from bankrupt distilleries and warehouses until National owned 40 percent of all stocks of bonded U.S. Bourbon (9.4 million gallons were available in 1933.) One of its earliest arrangements in preparing for the ratification of the repeal of Prohibition was a sale of 40,000 shares of stock to Owens-Illinois, the largest U.S. bottle maker. Another was a joint venture with U.S. Industrial Alcohol, Penn-Maryland, Inc. to make blended whiskey (by mixing National Distillers' seventeen-year-old whiskey with grain neutral spirits).

By 1940 National had seven major distilleries and had acquired 51 percent of Chickasaw Wood Products in 1934 to ensure an uninterrupted delivery of barrels made at four locations. By 1950 National was selling straight whiskies under the same labels as its blended whiskies and building inventories at such an accelerated pace, National's cooperages ran full out. At the same time, less-efficient distilleries at Bardstown, Kentucky, and Vincennes, Indiana, were sold or shut down. But by 1952, shipments of whiskey had declined and National shut down all distilleries until spring 1953 to balance inventories with anticipated demand. National sold its distilleries in Scotland at this time and entered into a distribution agreement with DCL instead. Finally in 1955, National's interest in four other distilleries was sold. In 1960 National operated five distilleries in Kentucky, a grain-neutral-spirits distillery in Cincinnati and a cooperage in Memphis. It had mothballed but not sold two distilleries in Kentucky and Illinois, respectively, and had diversified well beyond whiskies.

Publicker Industries was formed in 1913, and after Prohibition it advertised a whiskey that had been aged artificially (using heat and agitation). By 1960 Publicker owned three distilleries and four selling organizations. It had a government contract to produce butadiene and was heavily involved in the production of industrial alcohol.

Although Schenley was incorporated in 1933, its leadership had grown up in the whiskey industry and had been accumulating aged whiskies during Prohibition until it controlled 25 percent of U.S. whiskey stocks in 1934. Schenley acquired five distilleries and purchased the brands, trademarks, and whiskey stocks of other distillers. Schenley became DCL's U.S. distributor of John Dewar & Son Scotch whisky and importer of several other alcoholic beverages. It acquired Louisville Cooperage, and by 1950, Schenley had distilling and bottling plants in twenty-two locations. Acquisition in 1957 gave Schenley two additional distilleries in Indiana, five more Kentucky distilleries, two Maryland distilleries, plus plants in Missouri, Tennessee, Vancouver, and the United Kingdom in 1960.

Seagram was created in 1928 by acquiring the Montreal Distillers Corporation Ltd. operations and the Joseph E. Seagram & Sons Ltd. operation in Waterloo, Ontario. Bottling arrangements with Distillers Company Ltd. of Edinburgh, Scotland (DCL), gave Seagram access to several fine Scotch whiskies. The Seagram plant in Montreal consisted of a Kentucky Bourbon plant, American and Canadian Rye Plants, and a Scotch-type grain whisky plant. Tariff barriers made exported Canadian whisky more costly than American whiskey, so Seagram acquired a 130-year-old distillery in Lawrenceburg, Indiana, the Calvert distillery in Baltimore, Maryland, and marketing arrangements with other U.S. companies. By 1960 Seagram owned sixteen distilleries and nine additional bottling and rectifying houses. In 1934 Seagram imported aged Canadian whisky to use with its vast supplies of rye and Bourbon whiskies to create the high quality, blended American whiskies, Five Crown and Seven Crown. Their introduction represented a major milestone in the industry's development. Seagram's experience with DCL blending procedures had enabled it to create a product that countered the so-called rotgut image ascribed to the industry's pre-Prohibition years.

1962

The distilling industry began to enjoy better times in the 1960s. Computerized order filling enabled them to give liquor dealers faster service. Scotch whisky was selling well and consumption of distilled liquors in all categories was increasing. The liquor importers seemed especially profitable.

In 1962 Schenley purchased majority interest in a Scottish firm which produced a blended Scotch and a single-malt Scotch whisky. This acquisition made Schenley one of the three only integrated Scotch firms on the islands—firms whose various whiskies could be blended to create the final consumer product without having to purchase from outsiders. In 1963 Schenley acquired a Scottish firm of whisky blenders and importers, Stanley Holt & Son. The deal was made by Schenley's Long John Distilleries Ltd., which produced around four million gallons of Scotch per year.

In September 1962 National took an important step forward into marketing by acquiring Peel Richards, Ltd., a company responsible for the distribution in New York City of all of National's liquor brands (except "Old Crow"). The acquisition opened the way for National's efforts to create a greater sales effort in the retail trade.

In 1962 Seagram expanded its Strathisla-Glenlivet distillery and built a second Scotch distillery, the Glen Keith-Glenlivet distillery. Seagram had acquired its own Scotch-whisky assets during the 1930s when it purchased Robert Brown Ltd., the Glenlivet distillery, and Chivas Brothers Ltd. In Scotland, each distiller produced a whisky not only for in-house needs, but also with the understanding that some outside distillers would purchase a portion of the output. In the trading of Scotch, procedures had been so formalized that whisky brokers made it possible to buy or sell whiskies on contract.

In the United States, Seagram manufactured its own barrels in three cooperages that employed over 300 skilled coopers and other craftsmen and satisfied all of Seagram's needs for new charred-oak barrels in 1962. Seagram elevators in Lawrenceburg, Indiana and elsewhere in the U.S. corn belt were procured to maintain control over grain quality. Seagram operated its own fleet of grain hopper cars to ensure no leftover materials were mixed with the grain used in its whiskies.

1963

Consumer preferences for Canadian and Scotch whisky became more apparent in 1963 as domestic (U.S.) whiskey's share of the market dropped from 68.9 percent in 1955 to 56.3 percent in 1962. Of particular interest was the trend away from blends, as straights became available. The leading liquor brands at the beginning of 1963 were, in order of popularity: Seagram 7 Crown (7.4 million cases), Seagram's V.O. (2.5 milionl cases), Walker's Canadian Club (2.3 million cases), National's Old Crow and Walker's Imperial, a tie (2.2 million cases each). Heublein's Smirnoff vodka was the sixth most popular liquor in 1963.

In 1963 Glenmore entered into a contract to import and sell The Real MacKenzie Scotch whisky. Through its acquisition of Columbia Distilling, Glenmore gained a plant in Illinois as well as bottling lines to increase its whisky production.

1964

In 1964 National acquired Alberta Distillers Ltd., a Canadian firm that produced bulk Canadian whisky. With National's assistance, Alberta Distillers' brands were expected to gain market share in the United States. The acquisition gave National two Canadian distilleries.

1968

U.S. light whiskies were legalized by a change in the Department of Treasury regulations that authorized U.S. distillers to make and market (after July 1, 1972) a new higher-proof product distilled in seasoned rather than new charred-oak barrels. Distillers began production to distill and age the light whiskey for at least four years before its introduction. Preparing to beat that market introduction, Brown Forman readied a white dry whiskey which was not subject to Treasury regulations regarding marketing.

In 1968 Seagram announced its first Bourbon whiskey, Benchmark Bourbon, a premium, or high-priced Bourbon. This was a category that was experiencing a big rise in sales.

In 1969 Schenley explored the possibility of selling its partial interest in Buckingham Corporation, an import company that distributed Cutty Sark Scotch whisky. Between them the firms controlled 20 percent of the Scotch-whisky market. After studying the problem, Schenley elected to acquire the remaining shares in Buckingham and to merge it into existing import operations.

1970

In 1970, Publicker Industries depended upon alcoholic beverages for 76 percent of its sales and two of its bottling plants were for sale. In Linfield, Pennsylvania, its distillery was inactive; in St. Louis, Missouri, Publicker's barrel plant was inactive. Distribution of Publicker products at the wholesale level was performed in three major cities by wholly owned subsidiaries, and only its whisky complex in Scotland seemed to be financially healthy.

1972

In 1971 Northwest Industries purchased Buckingham Corporation, importer of Cutty Sark, from Schenley. The sales contract provided for the sale of certain cases of Buckingham products Schenley held over the next five years. At this time Schenley had ten inactive plants, some of which had distilling equipment and two had cooperage facilities.

In 1971 Brown-Forman bought a Canadian whisky business, including a brand, Canadian Mist, a distillery and warehouse in Ontario, and Canadian whisky inventories.

In 1972 Joseph E. Seagram & Sons acquired Old Bushmills Distillery Company and 15 percent of Irish Distillers Group. The acquisition gave Seagram global distribution of the Old Bushmills brand. The purchase of Irish Distillers gave Seagram marketing organizations for five whiskies and one liqueur.

In 1972 Hiram Walker's new distillery in the Okanagan Valley, British Columbia was brought into production. The plant cost more than $30 million and was built to service the western areas of Canada, the United States, and the East. A major expansion program was also undertaken at the Walkersville site. Hiram Walker was affiliated at this time with a distiller of wholesale whiskies and industrial alcohol called Corby Distilleries Ltd. which was, in turn, affiliated with a distilling company in Scotland. Corby marketed few of its own whisky brands.

1974

In 1974 vodka was becoming the most popular U.S. drink and tequila was close on its heels. Liquor advertising was banned (as cigarette ads had been) on television, and some outdoor billboard advertising drew criticism as well. Finally, the younger generation did not embrace whiskies as their parents had done. Although vodka supplanted demand for whiskies, premium brands were affected less adversely than others. For example, Seagrams's Chivas Regal Scotch and V.O Canadian whisky did not seem to be suffering declining sales volumes. Since most major distillers produced or imported both the popular white liquors and whiskies that were losing sales, they simply mothballed their whiskey distilleries and waited for the market to improve.

In 1975 National resumed distilling activities at its Bourbon plants. However, its profit margins had fallen from the levels enjoyed in 1973 when its distilleries were mothballed.

1976

In 1976 Heublein announced a $26-million liquor plant in Paducah, Kentucky, which would bottle several imported liquors, including Canadian whisky. (Heublein made no whiskies of its own.)

Although overall consumption of Bourbon declined in 1976 by 2 percent, Beam Bourbon increased its unit sales and thereby enlarged its share of the market. Demand for used cooperage continued to be slow and the market price for dried grain, a by-product of the distilling process, also continued to be low.

In 1977 Publicker reshaped its distribution network and upgraded its sales force. It discontinued its company-owned distribution operations in New York and Chicago, and a cost control program in manufacturing buttressed Publickers efforts to make its whiskey operations profitable.

In addition to changes in its marketing arm, Publicker sold its barrel-making facility at Marcus Hook, Pennsylvania, in 1977 and its bottling facility at Lemont, Illinois. All operations at the Lemont plant were terminated and arrangements were made with another distiller to bottle

Publicker's brands for distribution in the midwest and west-coast areas. Publicker, in turn, bottled this distiller's brands for distribution in east coast areas, using its Linfield, Pennsylvania, bottling facility.

1978

In 1978 the five leading liquor brands in case sales were Smirnoff vodka (6.2 million), Bacardi rum (5.6 million), 7 Crown blended whiskey (5.6 million), Canadian Club whisky (3.9 million) and Jim Beam Bourbon (3.4 million). In 1978 James B. Beam Distilling reduced to one the number of Scotch-whisky brands it distributed, in light of depressed Scotch sales.

In 1979 the brand of liquor that made the greatest case-volume increase in sales was Heublein's Popov vodka. A lower-priced liquor, it increased volume 24 percent from 1978 to 1979. The second-greatest volume improvement was made by Brown-Forman's Jack Daniels Tennessee whiskey, which increased case sales 15.5 percent. The top-brand ranking was unchanged from that of 1978, but case sales decreased for 7 Crown and Canadian Club by 4.1 and 1.4 percent, respectively.

In 1979 Brown-Forman acquired Southern Comfort Corporation and associated companies for $89 million. The 1978 sales of Southern Comfort specialty whiskey were 1.6 million cases (a 14 percent increase over the previous year's volume).

In 1979 Publicker agreed to sell its Inver House Scotch whisky, a liqueur, and related inventories to Standard Brands. At the time of sale, U.S. liquor operations represented 41 percent of Publicker's revenues, they had a $6.6 million loss, and they had not been profitable in the prior four years. In August 1979 Publicker sold virtually all of its domestic inventories of distilled spirits, related inventory items and trademarks, and a portion of the whisky inventories located in the United Kingdom that would be aged over the following four years, to Medley Distilling Company. In the United Kingdom, Publicker shifted its emphasis from cased-goods marketing (which offered lower profit margins) to export and bulk-whiskey marketing.

In 1979 Hiram Walker began construction of a $63 million plant for bottling Scotch whisky at Dunbarton, Scotland, to complement a recently contructed blending, barrel dumping, and filling facility at that location. The bottling plant would enable Hiram Walker to reduce its dependence on outside bottlers. Also in 1979 Hiram Walker announced the shutdown of its huge Peoria, Illinois, distillery. Operations were scheduled to be terminated by 1982 (or sooner if a purchaser were found). At the same time Walker announced it was building a plant in Fort Smith, Arkansas, to produce cordials at a cost of $37 million.

1980

Consumption of distilled liquors in the United States was flat in 1980, although its population was growing older. Consumers seemed to prefer white wines, mineral waters, and imported beers. American whiskey suffered the steepest decline; Scotch and Canadian whisky sales increased slightly. White goods (gin, vodka, tequila, and rum) accounted for more than half of all distilled liquor sales for the first time in 1980.

In May 1980 Hiram Walker sold the distillery portion of the fully integrated facility at Peoria, Illinois. As a result of the sale, Hiram Walker no longer distilled in the United States. Rather, it contracted with independent distillers for the distillation and aging of Bourbon and American blended whiskies made according to Hiram Walker's specifications. The sale of its enormous Peoria facilities represented the end of an era for Hiram Walker. Once it had been a grain trader (like Cargill, but on a smaller scale) with several grain elevators, but when enormous international grain deals became commonplace, Walker began purchasing for its own account alone. Similarly Walker's barrel-making establishment had been economical to operate in the early sixties when demand for Bourbon was high, but Canadian Club whisky did not need costly new white-oak barrels. By 1980 only Brown-Forman's Blue Grass Cooperage (and Seagram's in-house Tennessee cooperage) were operating regularly. Ten years earlier, whiskey firms operated cooperages employing hundreds of craftsmen to produce their own staves and barrel headers rather than purchase them. But during the 1960s and 1970s, firms quietly dis-integrated these stages of barrel production and then shut down their barrel-making plants. Finally Walker had made amber glass bottles in the Hillsboro Glass plant which was acquired in 1961 from the Ball Brothers Glass Company of Illinois. There was a limited market for these specialized assets and Hiram Walker did not sell them.

In 1980 National Distillers put two inactive Bourbon distilleries into service, making alcohol for gasohol. It planned to spend $5 million in renovations to convert the plants that had been idle since 1972 because of declining demand. Earlier in 1980 National Distillers had announced the conversion of a Lexington, Kentucky, Bourbon distillery for the same purpose.

In 1980 Schenley retired its cooperage plant and purchased staves and headers from outsiders. Schenley continued to produce the barrels it needed without operating the sawmills and other machinery used in roughcutting oak wood thereafter. Also in 1980 Schenley sold its Massachusetts liquor-and-wine distribution company to former employees. It operated nine distilleries and had four inactive plants in 1980, including a cooperage facility.

1981

In 1981 the five leading liquor brands (in case sales) were Bacardi rum (7.8 million), Smirnoff vodka (6.0 million), Seagram's 7 Crown (5.7 million), Seagram's V.O. Canadian whisky (3.7 million) and Walker's Canadian Club (3.5 million). All of these (except Bacardi) suffered declines in the volumes sold from 1980 to 1981.

The Canadians

In 1981 The Seagram Company Ltd. specialized in spirit blends and marketed little or no straight or bond whiskey. It produced and marketed over 150 brands of distilled spirits and 300 brands of wines, champagnes, brandies, ports, and sherries in over 175 countries. It also marketed the brands of others in certain markets. Of the top thirty-five brands of liquor, Seagram had the leading Canadian and the three top blends.

Seagram was both broadly and highly integrated. It developed grains, owned a fleet of grain hopper cars, and operated grain elevators; it manufactured white-oak barrels, and it had several tiers of company-owned wholesalers for its several tiers of brands in addition to over 500 independent wholesalers. By 1981 only 52 percent of Seagram's revenues were generated by distilled liquors and wines. Its assets in 1981 were $2.8 billion and it was number one in sales volume.

The other major Canadian distiller that dominated the U.S. market in 1981 was Hiram Walker-Gooderham & Worts, Ltd. Walker emphasized Canadian whisky and marketed over 100 of its own brands and also acted as sole marketing agent for numerous other brands of distilled liquors throughout the world. Of the top thirty-five brands of whiskey, Walker's Canadian whisky ranked second (close behind Seagram's), its Bourbon ranked fourth, and its blended whisky ranked fourth in that category. Seagram and Walker seemed to be competitors in many ways but Walker was the more profitable.

Hiram Walker was broadly and highly integrated, but less so than it had been. Both Walker and Seagram were concentrating their marketing efforts on fewer brands, less advertising, and rationalization of whisky distilling operations, with favorable results in 1981. Walker ranked fourth in distilled liquor sales but it was one of the most profitable whisky firms overall, because its profits relied heavily on sales of Canadian whisky.

The U.S. Firms

Although National began as a whiskey company, it was a major chemical firm in 1981. It made every type of whiskey and other alcoholic drink, but its mainstay was and had been Bourbon whiskey. National's Bourbon ranked fifth among Bourbons in 1981, and its Canadian ranked fourth. National Distillers was less integrated than its Canadian rivals and had terminated sales of bulk whiskey years earlier. National did not emphasize international markets as did Seagram and Walker, and ranked seventh in distilled-liquor sales. In 1981 National shut down its barrel-making business and entered into an arrangement with Seagram to acquire the barrels it needed. National had been manufacturing barrels in a highly automated plant which was far too large for its consumption rate in 1981, and had made the staves and headers as well as assembled the barrels. The shutdown left National with over $5 million in stave stock, which it stored. By cooperating with Seagram, both firms enjoyed lower barrel costs because Seagram's cooperage enjoyed a higher level of capacity utilization.

Schenley was incorporated as U.S. Prohibition was repealed and had acquired more than thirty distilleries. Roughly 55 percent of its distilled-liquor sales were brown goods, and its Scotch ranked number one; its Bourbon ranked number three in 1981. Schenley owned Louisville Cooperage Company, the world's largest barrelmaker and used company-owned wholesalers, in addition to independents in key markets. The number of brands it imported exceeded the number of distilled-liquor brands it produced, and it did not emphasize branded sales overseas. Rather, Schenley licensed its trademark to customers that bottled Schenley's bulk whiskey overseas. Schenley owned an advertising agency and heavily emphasized promotional activities, but it lagged behind the rest of the industry in profits in 1981, when Schenley announced the sale of its Canadian subsidiary. Schenley's Canadian whisky was its third largest selling brand in 1981. The principal motive for the sale appeared to be to generate cash for its parent, Rapid American.

In 1981 Brown-Forman specialized in Tennessee whiskey, Bourbon, and Bourbon specialties. Its Jack Daniels Tennessee whiskey ranked sixth among all distilled liquors in sales in 1981 and was the largest-selling Tennessee whiskey. Its Bourbon ranked number two and its Canadian was number three in their respective product categories. Brown-Forman's Southern Comfort specialty liquor ranked number thirty-one among all distilled liquors in 1981. The company marketed only twenty products and was remarkably profitable.

Brown-Forman owned Blue Grass Cooperage Company which produced all the barrels needed to age the Tennessee and Bourbon whiskies of the company as well as those of several other distillers. It heavily advertised its leading brands and concentrated on gaining market share for established brands rather than introducing new products. Its heavy reliance on Bourbon and other full-bodied whiskies was contrary to market trends, and yet Brown-Forman was very successful in doing so. It was narrowly diversified beyond whiskey.

James B. Beam Distilling Company produced Jim Beam Kentucky straight Bourbon whiskey, which was the world's number-one selling Bourbon in 1981. It concentrated upon full-bodied whiskies and had emphasized its Bourbons in defiance of market trends. (Bourbons represented 78 percent of sales and 86 percent of company profits.) American Brands acquired Beam in 1967 and, with a strong advertising campaign to back Jim Beam, catapulted its Bourbon to an undisputed market lead. James B. Beam Distilling did not manufacture its own barrels in 1981, but it made its own ceramic containers for specialty promotions of Jim Beam Bourbon. In 1981 James B. Beam marketed four of its nationally advertised Bourbon brands as well as a line of other distilled liquors, but had discontinued many other whiskey products.

Publicker produced and sold distilled liquors, industrial alcohol, and chemicals in 1981. During the 1970s Publicker had been one of the largest industrial-alcohol firms and one of the top-ten distillers in the United States. Although it marketed many brands of Bourbon, blended whiskies, Scotch, and other whiskies, as well as other alcoholic beverages, none of its whiskey brands ranked in the top five of their respective product categories. Publicker sold bulk whiskies for bottling by others. It had previously produced its own barrels and used company-owned wholesaling subsidiaries to supplement independent wholesale operations. In 1981 it continued to supply bulk whiskies in the United States and the United Kingdom, but it left the marketing of whiskey to others.

In 1981 Glenmore Distilleries was narrowly diversified. It produced Bourbon whiskey and bottled Scotch and Canadian whisky sold in bulk by others. Glenmore had no brands that were leaders in any whiskey categories and it operated a barrel-making plant that provided white-oak barrels for itself and other distillers.

The era beginning after World War II to 1973 was a period of uninterrupted growth in the distilled-liquors industry. It was one, long, drawn-out honeymoon and it affected managers' thinking about the industry. These managers never knew a period of hardship in the distilled liquors industry and had great difficulty recognizing the upheaval that occurred in 1981 when it became necessary to back out of unprofitable businesses and disintegrate some relationships.

Analysis of Strategies for Vertical Integration in the Whiskey Industry

The first section described the structure of the whiskey industry and the second described key events in the industry from 1960 to 1981. This section analyzes the patterns of vertical behavior sketched above and compares the predictions of the strategy framework with the outcomes observed in 1981.

In 1981 the whiskey industry was in endgame, but many competitors did not acknowledge that demand was falling. The industry's structure was potentially quite volatile, and according to the framework proposed in chapter 2, the declining sales volumes suggested that first, firms could not afford to be broadly integrated into many activities, nor could they sustain many stages of integration for each activity undertaken; second, less internal integration would occur than previously because firms' sales could no longer absorb entire plants' outputs; and third, firms would create business arrangements with each other to perform tasks they did previously in wholly owned subsidiaries. The experiences of the whiskey-distilling industry matched the predictions better than did those of the oil-refining industry.

Phase of Industry Development

The whiskey industry was in endgame in 1981 because unit sales were declining and acceptable substitutes existed. Firms were beginning to recognize that the old rules of competition had become inadequate to cope with declining demand, structural relationships were dissolving, and instability was exacerbated by governmental policies (excise taxes, antitrust, and advertising bans, among others). Although there was still considerable uncertainty concerning the rate of decline, it was clear that whiskey consumption was falling.

When whiskey distilling was an embryonic industry, firms did not need upstream or downstream integration to obtain access to raw materials or customers. Research expenditures were low because firms feared to tamper with a proven recipe for success and the quality image of the product was low. Initially there was no compelling need to control quality or take risks on integration, and the advantages of doing so did not seem to justify the high perceived risks.

After Prohibition was repealed firms integrated forward to influence customers and integrated backward due to price controls. Integration was undertaken as the industry's structure emerged in a way that firms like Seagram saw as disadvantageous. By forging closer links with distributors and by controlling the quality of raw materials these firms sought to differentiate their products' attributes, particularly with respect to quality. Thus, integration did not occur in the embryonic phase; it occurred later.

As demand declined in 1981, firms began terminating activities they had previously performed in-house. Divestiture of barrel-making in particular, occurred as firms joined together to produce their combined requirements in a single, economically sized plant.

By 1981 demand for whiskey was declining and lower-priced whiskies were especially sensitive to the effects of increases in excise taxes. Demand for premium brands was less sensitive to price or the economy but was sensitive to changing tastes—it was more fashionable to serve rum-or-vodka-based drinks when entertaining. Uncertainty regarding how long whiskey would be unfashionable was high, hence conditions did not favor much internal integration.

Because demand was declining firms reduced their integrated activities and created policies to obtain the grain supplies, barrels, or water they required. Superior quality-control techniques enabled them to achieve the integrity they had previously had to integrate to achieve. Thus upstream integrations were less imperative in endgame.

In summary, this industry's experience indicates that firms did not integrate until they were forced to do so by the federal Office of Price Administration (OPA) discrepancies or when they saw an advantage in creating perceived quality by doing so. The founders of distilling firms knew little about the businesses beyond liquors and reinvested in businesses they understood until 1981 when they were forced to reevaluate their earlier vertical arrangements and reduce ownership stakes, do less in-house, and rely more on outsiders for a portion of their needs.

Volatile Industry Structure

Competition was becoming more volatile in the lower-priced whiskey markets and even among the premium brands, absolute sales volumes (in cases) were shrinking as the drinking population increased. Although competition using technological innovation was not likely to make this industry volatile, advertising and promotional tactics could erode profit margins as demand continued to drift downward. At worst, industry discipline could erupt into price-cutting and destroy profits for all.

The quality of whiskey seemed most sensitive to differentiation in 1981, and yet it was not clear that firms had to be integrated to achieve the differentiation they desired. Although the process of distilling was complex and manufacturing had to be precise, integration was not mandatory for barrels, grain, bottles, and water. All of these could be readily purchased and made to firms' specifications by outsiders.

Grain was readily available from outsiders and contamination could be controlled by the purchasing distiller. The research-and-development requirements to improve glass bottles were too high for most distillers' sales volumes to justify making their own glass. Grain elevators were too speculative in the high-interest-rate environment of the 1980s and larger players overshadowed the deals distillers might make. Even in Scotland, where a formal market for blending whiskies existed, there were few requirements for a firm to own whisky brokers as well as a distillery. Business custom reduced the need for high ownership stakes in controlling trading relationships.

Legal barriers prevented the distillers from forward integrating when it might have been most advantageous to do so in distribution activities. Whiskey distillers once forward integrated to give special attention to markets they considered most crucial to their success, because outside wholesaling firms did not guarantee adequate attention for their lines. With time liquor wholesalers became primarily order takers and deliverymen, and firms' own sales forces performed the detail work needed at individual retail outlets. Thus, in 1981 little advantage seemed apparent in having a special wholesaling sales force, and these organizations became more like sales representatives as the industry evolved.

The technology of producing whiskey enabled firms to distill it at one location, age it at a second location, and bottle it elsewhere. The marketers of whiskey need not have produced it themselves and as the industry evolved, firms that were better distillers than marketers specialized in producing bulk whiskies rather than performing the blending, bottling, and marketing tasks in-house.

Whiskey distillers were dissimilar in their pattern of vertical integration, their strategic posture, and their parents' corporate strategies; yet they were all competing for the same scarce shelf space. Firms competing at the bottom of the line were likely to use price competition or other tactics which threatened to erode profitability. In particular, the specialization of grain-neutral-spirits production by firms outside the traditional whiskey industry threatened to squeeze out marginal firms or relegate them to blending and rectifying operations.

In summary, the structure of the whiskey industry was potentially volatile in 1981 because uncertainty regarding future demand was creating chaos in the industry, customer-switching costs among brands were low, fringe firms were using price-cutting, and cut-rate wholesalers were exacerbating this trend. Firms were expected to dis-integrate by reducing their ownership stakes, shutting down oversized facilities, and buying more of their requirements from outsiders to escape harm from excess capacity in adjacent units, and many did so.

Bargaining Power

In 1981 sick barrel makers had bargaining power over whiskey firms because they consciously purchased a portion of their requirements from nonaffiliated cooperages to keep them in business. In brief, even backward-integrated distillers wanted an alternative source of barrels. The down-stream bargaining power of wholesalers over whiskey distillers was bilateral because distillers needed them to provide access to customers, but whole-salers needed name brand whiskies in order to sell their full product lines. Wholesalers acted as though they believed that whiskey distillers could easily replace them. Nevertheless, wholesalers had less time to set up dis-plays or give their lines much attention, particularly if they did not have an exclusive distribution territory, and whiskey distillers granted dual distri-bution rights to rival wholesalers to spur a less-effective wholesaler to im-proved performance.

In summary, the phase of industry development and industry structure did not argue for broad or high degrees of integration. If demand continued to be stagnant or declining, it would be advantageous for those firms affected most severely to be less integated and less exposed to the damage created by exit barriers, and their bargaining power was usually adequate for them to do so.

Strategy Goals

In 1981 firms were dis-integrating vertical relationships and dismantling the structures created earlier because they were uneconomic and they no longer provided competitive advantages. Firms that had previously created com-pany-owned wholesaling units were no longer using them to prod outsiders to work harder at selling their brands. Firms that made barrels were shut-ting down their cooperages. Grain elevators sat vacant and warehouses sat idle. Several inactive plants and cooperages were for sale.

Producers of leading whiskies were proud of their distilling abilities. Vodka and gin were too easy to make, they felt, and this tunnel vision con-tributed to some firms' reluctance to turn their backs on their mother busi-ness and dis-integrate as demand fell. Market-share and technological-leadership goals—the types of goals such attitudes engendered—were un-justified in the whiskey industry in 1981 as were broad or high degrees of integration. Profitability (focus) goals suggested lesser degrees and breadth of integration were needed, and as demand declined several firms reduced the varieties of liquor they carried and rationalized their plants to become more profitable. Uneconomic activities were abandoned, as the strategy framework predicted.

Depending on their objectives, parent firms could enhance or discour-age vertical relationships among business units in the distilled-liquor indus-try. Since demand for whiskey was declining and capital expenditures for whiskey facilities had been halted perhaps ten years earlier, the cash flows and return on their whiskey businesses were good, particularly for Canadian whisky. Thus when Rapid-American needed cash and received a lucrative offer, it sold its Canadian whisky business.

There were few synergies with other businesses besides distilled liquors except in unique situations. The assets used to make grain neutral spirits and industrial alcohol were similar but were not used interchangeably. The wholesaling channels primarily handled alcoholic beverages. Thus the relationships, skills, and assets used to distill, age, bottle, and market whiskey did not offer many opportunities for synergy beyond liquor.

In summary, parent firms were more reluctant to subsidize losing units and had fewer emotional attachments to whiskey (exit barriers) than did their business units. Although the whiskey-distilling unit may have preferred to control upstream and downstream operations through a corporate relationship, the uneconomic nature of those times made them less valuable in 1981.

The Need for Vertical Integration

By 1981 there were fewer reasons for high internal integration in the whiskey business. Grain, water, glassware, and barrels were available elsewhere. The processes of manufacture did not require physical interconnection nor technological coordination. The long gestation periods associated with aging whiskey increased the costliness of heavy investments in this industry. Suppliers could produce to firms' specifications.

During the rough years after Prohibition when whiskey carried an image of low quality, vertical integration had been used effectively to create product differentiation by ensuring whiskey quality. Except where firms' volumes were large enough to justify continued use of in-house units to provide the services or products in question, the costs of underutilization could erode any profits which might have been available. Moreover, firms risked being linked to a sick business, when they could purchase the same services in arm's-length transactions without degrading quality.

Strategy Alternatives and Performance

The strategy model distinguished between ownership and the degree of internal integration firms engaged in; firms may have owned all, some, or none of the adjacent firms supplying goods and services, and transferred all, some, or none of their needs internally. Moreover firms differed in the breadth of their integrations. In whiskey, firms could be backward integrated into grain elevators, malting, barrels, bottles, water reservoirs, or brokerage services (grain or bulk whiskey); they could sell bulk whiskey to rectifiers and bottlers, use company-owned wholesalers to supplement their marketing campaigns, or bottle whiskey under contract for others, if these activities were justified by firms' strategic missions and competitive strengths.

Firms that used high degrees of internal integration in the whiskey industry did so because it was most economic to do so. Their sales volumes justified the use of entire plants' outputs in-house, and when their inventories became unbalanced with consumption rates, firms shut down their distilleries or barrel factories and waited for conditions to improve. Taper integration was used primarily downstream where whiskey distillers fretted that independent wholesalers would not try hard enough to sell their brands, and little taper integration remained in endgame because it was usually not cost effective to maintain it. Thus ownership became too risky, the need for full integration had passed and acceptable suppliers were waiting to fill whiskey firms' needs in 1981.

The number of stages of activity undertaken was determined by the product's characteristics, the nature of demand, and the mission of the whiskey-distilling unit relative to adjacent business. Seagram engaged in the greatest number of stages in 1981 and Hiram Walker had also once been engaged in wood processing, glass-bottle production, and other upstream activities that supported whiskey distilling. For both firms the motivations were desires to control the supplies used in distilling, and conservative diversification policies that led firms to invest surplus funds in familiar (or seemingly familiar) businesses. Like petroleum-refining firms, the whiskey distillers faced declining demand that was unlikely to resuscitate with time, and their recognition that sales volumes could not support integration into many unrelated stages of production led some firms to reduce the breadth of their activities, as the strategy framework suggested.

The breadth of integration—the number of different activities which were integrated—was determined by demand traits and the nature of competition. Although broadly integrated firms need not also be highly integrated ones, in whiskey Seagram was one of the most highly and broadly integrated firms. Seagram made barrels, barrel staves, and headers, and once owned timber land as well. Seagram developed hybrid grains, shipped grains in its hopper cars, and stored grain in its elevators. Although Seagram may have engaged in brokerage activities from time to time, it primarily satisfied its own vast needs for barrels and grain. Downstream, Seagram and other distillers including Schenley, Publicker, Standard Brands (Fleischmann), and Hiram Walker employed wholesalers in key whiskey markets.

By 1981 Seagram was still broadly integrated, although the extent of its barrel operations had been reduced, and Seagram was selling its excess barrels to other distillers. Its basic strategy of broad integration had not changed, however, because its sales volumes had not yet been affected so adversely that change was required and it still valued its control over productive resources.

There were few joint ventures in this industry because most materials, supplies, or services needed in distilling whiskey could be purchased readily without penalties to quality or market position, each firm preferred that its supplies and activities be identified with it alone, and legal restrictions limited the opportunities for a whiskey distiller and a wholesaling firm like Glazer or McKesson to create a venture to brand and market whiskey. Customary trade relationships which were not even formalized by contracts were the principal form of quasi-integration in the Scotch-whiskey business. In 1981 whiskey firms were engaged in a form of quasi-integration to ensure that an adequate supply of inexpensive, good quality barrels were available. By pooling their needs, the whiskey distillers hoped to enjoy scale economies in production. After Prohibition was repealed, joint ventures were used to reach customers efficiently where firms had no previous experience in the market. Such arrangements were abandoned long before 1981, however, and few arrangements of this nature offered value to prospective partners.

The most effective vertical-integration strategies in the whiskey-distilling industry were those that gained relatively stable access to raw materials and distribution while also achieving strategic objectives, including market dominance, above-average returns on invested capital, or quality leadership. Although whiskey was in endgame in 1981 its structure was still changing, and for some firms only half of the whiskey products' life had yet expired. Their brands were still prosperous.

Jim Beam Bourbon increased its sales when other Bourbons were declining and Beam's profit margin has been good (around 13 percent). Beam was not broadly integrated and its vertical strategy was appropriate for 1981.

Brown-Forman has contradicted traditional product behavior with the success of Jack Daniels Tennessee Sippin' Whiskey and Southern Comfort specialty liquor. It also contradicted vertical-integration wisdom by operating the largest barrel factory in 1981. Brown-Forman did cease milling the staves and headers, but continued to attain scale economies by virtue of its highly utilized barrel operations. With its successful brands and position as a supplier of barrels, Brown-Forman earned a before-tax return on assets of 25 percent.

Glenmore's strategic posture changed with time from a seller of bulk whiskies to a bottler of bulk whiskies. In 1981 it continued to produce white-oak barrels, although it no longer milled staves and headers as it did before. Its branded whiskies were not as successful as Glenmore might have hoped; its 1981 pretax return on assets was only 3.7 percent.

Although Walker had once been a grain broker, a malter, a whisky broker (in Scotland), and a producer of barrels, it had dis-integrated from malting, cooperage activities, and grain elevators. In 1981 Walker continued to produce its amber glass bottles for Canadian Club and broker whisky in Scotland. Much of Walker's success in achieving a 21-percent pretax return on assets must be attributed to the popularity of its whiskey, but the strategy framework also suggested that, in endgame, less-integrated firms would be more profitable than broadly and highly integrated firms.

By 1981 Publicker had sold its U.S. marketing operations and became a manufacturer of bulk whiskies. Although its Scottish operations did well enough, Publicker had been unable to develop whiskey products that proved popular in the U.S. market. Publicker retired its barrel plant and dismantled its wholesale organization before selling its brands to other distilleries. In 1981 it showed a loss before extraordinary items.

Schenley's branded products were largely Bourbons and Schenley retired its private-label business, suspended barrel operations, and dis-integrated as the strategy matrix suggested. Nevertheless Rapid American had proposed to sell Schenley and when it failed to do so, it began selling Schenley's most-profitable operations.

Seagram Company, the world's largest distiller, was more highly and broadly integrated than the strategy framework suggested for reasons discussed above. With its large throughput, Seagram could support more integration than other distillers. The Seagram pretax return on assets was around 6 percent, reflecting its emphasis upon market-share leadership and long-term-wealth maximization.

In summary, less ownership investment and narrower integration seemed preferable in this declining business. Uncertainty was high about when and whether consumers would again prefer whiskies over white liquors. Given industry practices of mothballing distilleries until demand revitalized or inventories were brought in balance with anticipated demand, it is clear that whiskey distillers could cope with vertical integration in an environment of declining demand. Whether they would be profitable in doing so was unclear.

References

"Demand for Liquor Leveling." *Standard & Poor's Industry Surveys,* March 27, 1980, pp. B72–B75.

Joseph E. Seagram and Sons, Inc. and the House of Seagram, Inc. *vs.* Hawaiian Oke and Liquors, Ltd., 416 Fed. 2nd 71 (1969).

Newman, Peter C. *King of the Castle: The Making of a Dynasty—Sea-*

gram's and the Bronfman Empire. New York: Atheneum, 1979, especially chapter 5.

"Why Spirits Sales are Slipping a Bit." *Business Week,* May 17, 1982, pp. 141–143.

Also helpful were corporate annual reports and financial statements of the firms described in chapter 6 and conversations with five whiskey distillers and two liquor wholesalers.

7 Strategies for Vertical Integration in the Tailored-Suits Industry

Tailored suits are hand- or machine-sewn garments purchased off the rack (ready-to-wear) or custom-fitted. The jacket and trousers (or skirt) can be of matching or contrasting fabrics and the suit may include a vest.

A Description of the Tailored-Suits Industry

The Product

Tailored suits can be differentiated by price, colors, and quality. The quality of a suit is determined by fabrics, style, comfort or fit, and tailoring. The term tailored once referred only to a custom-fitted, hand-sewn garment, and the highest-quality suits in 1981 continued to be those that had the greatest proportion of handwork. In 1981 garments were graded to designate the relative amount of handwork they contained, and table 7-1 lists suit brands by grade. A number-six-quality suit was almost completely hand tailored; the second-highest grade was a number four. A number-two-quality suit was the least-expensive *branded* grade; X-quality suits had no handwork and were not branded. Hand-tailored garments were expensive (over $500 at retail) and represented only a small portion of the total market for suits. The largest volumes of suits sold were number-two- and X-quality grades. Brand names were very important in differentiating suits because much of the hand-tailored work that gave a suit its quality could not be seen from the outside. Another way of differentiating one's suits was to offer them in fabrics that no other manufacturer was using. The finest suits were of 100 percent worsted wool or woolen textiles. Style changes also were an important part of competing in the tailored-suit industry. Examples of style changes included the continental cut which hugged the torso, the change from narrow to wide lapels, and the change back to narrow lapels.

As the price of labor rose so did the prices of tailored suits, until some parts of the market began to wear sports jackets and unmatched trousers instead of suits. In 1980 14.5 million suits of all prices were shipped compared with 15.9 million units in 1979 and 17.5 million units in 1978. Twenty

---

Background research was provided by Kris Ishibashi and Stan Herman.

Table 7–1
Suit Brands by Estimated-Quality Grades, 1981

Number 6 Quality Brands

Chester Barrie	Hickey Freeman	Oxxford
Louis Roth	Walter-Morton	

Number 4 Quality Brands

Austin Reed	Greif (private brands primarily)	Pierre Cardin Couture
Bloomingdale's		Saks Fifth Avenue
Botany 500 (in 1972)	Hart, Schaffner & Marx	J. Schoeneman (private brands)
Brooks Brothers	H. Freeman	
Christian Dior by HSM		

Number 2 Quality Brands

Bond Stores	Jonathon Weitz	Palm Beach
Botany 500 (in 1981)	Johnny Carson	Phoenix (private brands primarily)
Chaps by Ralph Lauren	Joseph & Feiss (private brands primarily)	Pierre Cardin
Christian Dior Monsieur		Yves St. Laurent
Cricketeer	Levi Strauss	
Evan-Picone	Oxford (Sears)	

Number X Quality Brands

These were nonbranded but included some suits sold by Bond Stores and Robert Hall.

Source: Industry sources.

years earlier, in 1960, 18.8 million units were shipped. The declining demand for tailored suits was attributable to price as well as increasingly casual lifestyles during the 1970s and to a decline in the number of twenty-eight-to-thirty-five-year-olds, a key age for first-time purchases. The energy crisis of the 1970s could also be blamed in part for reinforcing the stagnant demand for tailored suits because dress attire became more casual when thermostats went up during hot summers of energy conservation.

Historically, tailored suits were manufactured primarily as business attire for men, but by 1981 a substantial number of women also purchased business suits retailing above $300. In theory, the same firms skilled in manufacturing and merchandising men's tailored suits should have been able to satisfy this new demand for tailored garments as well. In fact, union rules and preconceived notions about competition kept some firms from participating in this new market for suits.

Markets

The ultimate consumers of suits were men and women who required professional-looking clothes for work, a smart-looking outfit for formal occasions, or somewhat-formal leisure wear. They were usually over the age of twenty-five and working (especially true for women). Serving the women's-wear market risked creating conditions which made competition more volatile because that market traditionally changed styles faster and more severely, thereby creating the need to inventory more patterns and colors in an era of high interest rates. Moreover, manufacturers risked being stuck with unsaleable merchandise. There were two major seasons per year for men's suits—fall and spring. By contrast, women's wear had five to seven seasons annually, plus mini-events that justified new shipments every few weeks. Men's-suit manufacturers owned their factories, but women's-wear production was usually subcontracted. Consequently men's-wear plants planned for a very stable, conservative volume of outputs well in advance of each season, but women's-wear producers tried to respond to the vicissitudes of fashion.

Tailored suits were sold to consumers through specialty stores, department stores, chains, mail-order houses, and discount houses. Approximately 60 percent of the suits manufactured were sold under the manufacturers' brand names, and as department stores became important customers of the manufacturers, they sold suits made for sale under their names as well as the regular branded lines of suit manufacturers. The number-six-quality suit could be sold only in limited volumes (usually in a downtown headquarters store), but number-four- and number-two-quality suits were more-widely available and sold in greater volumes.

Some manufacturers of tailored suits owned retail outlets, but most firms did not. Dual distribution had not been as advantageous as tailored-suit manufacturers had hoped, in part because of the declining importance of specialty-apparel stores. Department stores and chains accounted for an increasing percentage of apparel sales, and discount chains became important outlets as lower-priced suits grew in importance.

Suppliers

The styling silhouettes of men's tailored suits did not change nearly so much as the patterns and other attributes of textiles changed, and the attention devoted to the details of these changes was immense. The hue, the tint, and the weight of successful fabrics was changed from season to season, but only incrementally. In addition to past successes, tailored-suit manufacturers could choose their textiles from hundreds of new designs offered by leading manufacturers in the United States or abroad.

In the United States the leading suppliers of textiles to the manufacturers of tailored suits were Burlington and Worsted-Tex. Each of the leading producers of worsteds and woolens produced an open line which they would sell in pieces to any manufacturer. If a firm ordered between 2,000 and 3,000 yards per pattern and per color, they could purchase a confined line that was created exclusively for their use. (Overseas textile mills were willing to run confined lines at even-lower minimum volumes.)

When styling new patterns, fabric designers conferred with suit manufacturers and retailers to ascertain whether colors were going from a deeper or darker hue to lighter hues and shades, whether to drab out a color that was popular the previous season or sharpen it, and whether to make incremental changes from a hard deco (decoration and color) to a soft deco. Left on their own, manufacturing companies were very risk-averse and unwilling to change designs significantly. Therefore, styling decisions for most fabrics were made by the textile manufacturers.

Few suit makers were linked with textile firms because the cost of entering textile production could be substantial—for example, one specialized loom cost $100,000 and a different setup was needed for each worsted or woolen line. Furthermore, the outlooks of the two types of firms were very different. Textile companies sought long production runs to obtain low production costs, but suit manufacturers wanted as many varieties of patterns and colors as possible to choose from. Moreover, any firm producing suits would have to consume all of its textile output in-house, because competitors would be unwilling to share their ideas and thus they would be handicapped in responding to fashion changes because they would be cut off from access to others' viewpoints.

In summary, suit makers saw few advantages to in-house textile production as long as the existing suppliers offered good service. The balance between textile outputs and manufacturers' needs would force backward integrated suit makers to sell many of their textiles to other types of customers, given the design secrecy among competing suit manufacturers prevailing in 1981, and doing so would have put them into a business they may not have desired to enter—one that was cyclical and low profit in 1981.

Manufacturing

The entry barriers in suit production were low and some firms operated without their own factories, as did Yves St. Laurent (YSL), a French firm that had no factory of its own. (YSL designed the garments sold under its name, styled the textiles, and contracted for the manufacture of them from one of the many factories which operated on a cut-make-and-trim (CMT) basis.) Men's-suit manufacturers usually operated their own factories, but entry barriers were low in suit manufacturing because much second-hand equipment was available. The scarcest resources were tailors who were needed to perform the handwork on higher-quality lines. Consequently, entry occurred most frequently in the lower quality number-two and X lines. The volatility of the industry was also a significant barrier to entry. The industry was very competitive and many number-four- and number-six-quality suit makers had gone bankrupt in previous decades.

Tailoring was an art which had enjoyed improved tools over the centuries but used the same work methods. Some innovation in technology had occurred, however. If apparel makers could not afford automation, their factories were frequently overseas where labor costs were lower.

The minimum-efficient scale of suit-manufacturing was small (less than 1000 suits per week for a contract manufacturer), but it was one of the most labor-intensive industries in the United States. Automation was limited by materials-handling capabilities because cloth was soft and pliable. Therefore the cost of garments requiring handwork would continue to rise dramatically because there were few ways to speed up the process of hand sewing.

The major tasks in suit making were designing, cutting, sewing, pressing, and examining. The sewing of a jacket could be broken down into approximately 150 separate operations. The cost of the garment (its quality) determined how many inspections and how stringent the standards were.

Men's suit manufacturers were *inside houses* that rarely sent out sewing to be completed or finished by others. (The exception to this was where regular manufacturing capacity could not accommodate the construction of fad garments like leisure suits or Nehru jackets because it was difficult to make capacity adjustments quickly within an inside house.) Established suit makers rarely manufactured for each other but they would produce suits on contract to the specifications of retailers. Generally, each factory specialized in making one particular quality grade because their work methods were geared to the economics of making garments of a certain cost.

Disposing of suit-making assets could be difficult in depressed times. There were no buyers for the suit-making assets of manufacturers like Robert Hall (X-quality garments), Curlee (number-four-quality-private-label garments), Grossman (number-four-quality suits), or Kuppenheimer (a venerated number-six-quality line) for a long time after these firms failed. Hammonton Park, Eagle Manufacturers, and Botany sold their brand names but their other assets were difficult to salvage. The Multi-Employer Pension Act of 1980 which required employers with union-shop pension plans to be fully vested before exiting was a significant barrier. Consequently these firms which could neither exit nor compete effectively resorted to price competition, and their presence made the industry more volatile and profits lower.

Marketing

Selling to thousands of specialty stores was more difficult and costlier than selling to chains and large retailers because it required more attention to detail and more service. It protected suit manufacturers from some of the demands of large retailers, however, because the specialty stores were small and unlikely individually to charge penalties for early or late delivery of goods, as the large retailers routinely did. Big retailers used their purchasing power to demand faster production times, more inventorying services and longer payment terms from smaller manufacturers, and sometimes a large chain refused to accept delivery of merchandise for several weeks (or months), forcing suppliers to finance this inventory.

Firms needed strong brand images to defend themselves against strong retailers, and as the importance of specialty stores as distribution channels faded and department stores became important, the value of a strong brand became even more pronounced. Table 7–2, which matches brand names with manufacturers, suggests which firms were strongest in various quality grades. Most major suit manufacturers employed their own sales forces because an effective representative was also a professional intelligence system which helped each retailer choose appropriate branded merchandise and reported back to manufacturers about fashion trends, competitors' designs, and merchandising patterns. Dual distribution (selling part or total output to one's own stores) was a way of ensuring some basic volume of sales would be made, but suit makers that sold *all* of their output in-house risked the loss of competitive vitality.

In summary, profit margins were squeezed for many suit manufacturers in 1981 because large retailers, that possessed bargaining power by virtue of their sizable purchases, forced the manufacturers to bear inventory costs and provide other costly services to them. A strong brand name in the high-quality lines was the most important attribute needed for effective distribution through specialty retail outlets.

Competition in the Tailored-Suits Industry in 1981

In 1981 less than 300 firms manufactured tailored suits, down from 450 in 1960. The largest manufacturer of men's tailored suits was Hart, Schaffner, & Marx; the second largest was Rapid American, with Palm Beach in third place. Rapid American's brands included Botany, Cross Country, MacGregor, and Donovan (number-two- and X-quality brand names). Palm Beach sold the famous summerweight suits plus a full line of men's suits and Evan-Picone ladies' sportswear separates. The top of the line

Table 7–2
Branded Suits and Manufacturing Firms

Manufacturer	Number Six	Number Four	Number Two
Bond			Bond
(Botany Industries) bankrupt		Botany 500	(Botany 500—under new ownership
Brooks Brothers		Brooks Brothers (contract manufactured)	
Cluett, Peabody		Bloomingdales Saks Fifth Avenue Schoeneman (private brands)	
Genesco		Greif (private brands mostly)	Chaps by Ralph Lauren Phoenix (private brands)
Hart, Schaffner & Marx	Hickey-Freeman Chester Barrie Walter-Morton	Austin Reed Christian Dior by Hart, Schaffner & Marx Hart, Schaffner & Marx H. Freeman Pierre Cardin Couture	Christian Dior Monsieur Johnny Carson Pierre Cardin
Levi Strauss	Oxxford		Levi Strauss
Louis Roth	Louis Roth		
Oxford			Oxford (Sears)
Palm Beach			Palm Beach Evan-Picone Johnathon Weitz
Phillips-Van Heusen			Cricketeer Joseph & Feiss (private brands)
Private Hand-Tailoring	Chipp, Dunhill, and other small entrepreneurs		
Yves St. Laurent			Yves St. Laurent

Source: Industry sources.

(number-six quality) included Hickey-Freeman, Oxxford (Levi Strauss), and the privately owned Louis Roth. A more-expensive, custom-tailored suit could be obtained at Saville Row in the United Kingdom, in New York City, Hong Kong, or Beverly Hills for between $600 and $800 in 1981.

The fastest-growing market was the machine-sewn (number-two-quality) $150-to-$250-price range that was dominated by Palm Beach and Phillips-Van Heusen's Cricketeer. Levi Strauss and Hart, Schaffner & Marx had recently entered that popularly priced segment with new labels, and

Levi Strauss had sold X-quality separates that could be worn like a suit for approximately $100 in the past. Genesco's Greif and Phoenix divisions, which had made private-label number-four- and number-two-quality suits, respectively, emphasized *branded* suits such as Lanvin, Chaps by Ralph Lauren, and Oleg Cassini under licensing arrangements in 1981. Although many suit manufacturers had been forward integrated in 1970, few remained so by 1981 and those that were did not sell substantial proportions of their own products through their stores.

Corporate Strategy Exit Barriers in Tailored-Suit Manufacturing

Strategic exit barriers were low for some firms in the tailored-suit business because firms were diversified and tailored suits were no longer their base business. For hundreds of other small manufacturers, however, tailored suits were still their base business and this condition made competition in the tailored-suits industry especially likely to erupt into price-cutting in the lower-quality segments where large retailers could easily pressure small manufacturers.

Summary of Competitors in Tailored Suits

In summary, suit manufacturers differed in their breadth of integration downstream, but no manufacturer was backward integrated to textiles in 1981. They differed in their degree of integration because many firms that were forward integrated to retailing supplied only a small portion of the suits their specialty stores sold, but others supplied all of the tailored suits to that outlet. Richman Brothers, the Bond Stores, and Robert Hall were among those that supplied 100 percent of their stores' tailored-suit needs.

A Mapping of Strategic Groups in Tailored Suits

This section groups major competitors by their breadth of forward integration in 1981. Since no major competitor was backward integrated, they have been segmented by quality grades. The suit makers had backed away from retailing, except for Hart, Schaffner & Marx which expanded the number of stores in its specialty-outlet chains and enjoyed substantial success as a dual distributor. The suit makers could be mapped as shown in figure 7-1 to indicate where shared resources or linkages existed. The X-quality manufacturers that were privately held are not mapped.

In 1981 Palm Beach had no specialty retail outlets but it did have factory outlet stores. Phillips-Van Heusen and Hart, Schaffner & Marx were successful in their retailing ventures, but Genesco and Cluett, Peabody were less sanguine about the attractiveness of forward integration after their

Breadth of Distribution Activities	Quality of Branded or Private Label Lines			
	X-Quality	Number 2 Quality	Number 4 Quality	Number 6 Quality
Owned Fifty or More Specialty Retail Stores	(Bond Stores) Richman Bros.	(Bond Stores) Hart, Schaffner & Marx	Brooks Brothers Hart, Schaffner & Marx	Hart, Schaffner & Marx
Owned Less than Fifty Retail Stores		Phillips-Van Heusen	Cluett, Peabody Genesco	Custom Tailoring Establishments
Owned No Specialty Retail Stores	Rapid-American	Oxford (Sears) Palm Beach Rapid-American Yves St. Laurent		Louis Roth Oxxford (Levi Strauss)

Figure 7-1. A Mapping of Selected Competitors in Tailored Suits, 1981

experiences. Demand for tailored suits was reviving slowly in the 1980s after a catastrophic drop in the 1970s. Unless a retail outlet was inherently profitable on its own, 1981 was not a good time to be forward integrated.

Key Events in the Tailored-Suits Industry

This section traces key events in the tailored-suits industry, beginning with the 1960s. The structure of the industry was well-established and had been for several years. A brief summary of conditions before 1960 appears below.

A Brief History of Tailored Suits

Tailored suits were originally custom-made for each customer and ready-to-wear suits were poorly fitting and poor-quality garments that tailors made from excess materials during their slow seasons. Initially, jobbers procured textiles from the United Kingdom, wholesaled them, sold textiles to suit manufacturers, procured ready-to-wear suits from these manufacturers, wholesaled suits, and distributed them for sale through retail outlets. By the 1920s the national market was served by retailers like Richman Brothers and Bond Stores that manufactured their own tailored apparel. Other manufacturers, such as Hart, Schaffner & Marx, Cohen, Goldman & Company and L. Greif & Brothers, acquired their best retail customers. By 1960 demand for tailored suits was fairly stable and prosperous. The industry was not particularly attuned to changes in fashion and it was male-oriented.

In 1960 Bond was primarily a retailer of men's and ladies' ready-to-wear garments. It manufactured men's two-trouser suits until the government suspended their manufacture during World War II. Its suits were number-two and X-quality and were all produced in-house.

Botany Worsted Mills was incorporated in 1889 to manufacture fine worsted yarns and goods. Botany began to manufacture worsted menswear in the 1930s, and its Botany 500 line was of number-four quality.

Originally a shirt maker, Cluett, Peabody & Company, Inc., acquired J. Schoeneman, Inc., a leading manufacturer of number-four-quality, private-label men's suits, in 1955. This acquisition gave Cluett, Peabody a manufacturer of a complete line of men's suits, sport jackets and slacks that were sold to leading department stores throughout the country.

Genesco acquired L. Greif & Company, a private-label manufacturer of number-four-quality suits in 1959. Genesco (General Shoe Company) was forced to diversify into suits by an antitrust consent decree forbidding it to buy any more shoe companies.

Hart, Schaffner & Marx began in 1876 as a retail business, but its was incorporated in 1887 as a manufacturer and wholesaler of men's tailored suits. It had purchased several major menswear specialty stores since the 1920s and had introduced a major innovation in the marketing of men's tailored suits—the all-woolen product—which guaranteed the fiber quality of ready-to-wear apparel at a time when the business suffered from the use of poor-quality fibers by some companies.

Palm Beach began in 1931 as a privately owned maker of Palm Beach suits—a lightweight summer suit made from Palm Beach cloth provided by its parent firm, Goodall-Sanford, Inc. The Palm Beach textile plant made worsted fabric, but production of the suits was initially contracted out.

In 1960 Richman Brothers owned the Anderson, Little retail-clothing chain in New England, as well as other stores located throughout the United States. Richman Brothers remained a retailer that produced its own X-quality suits for sale in-house. The price of Richman Bros.' original $22.50 suit had increased, but the spirit of popular-priced merchandising was the same.

United Merchants & Manufacturers began as Cohn-Hall-Marx in 1912, and its operations were limited to fabric conversion. Mergers with several yarn-spinning plants and fabric-weaving mills in 1928 created United Merchants & Manufacturers, a vertically integrated textile company that opened its first Robert Hall retail outlet in the 1940s. United Merchants & Manufacturers merchandised and marketed woolen and worsted fabrics in 1960 but did not weave them. Its Robert Hall Clothes, Inc. subsidiary had 297 stores and it manufactured some of the X-quality clothes it sold.

1961

In 1961 many owners of specialty and men's clothing stores were unwilling or unable to expand their operations and some were selling their stores. Larger corporations, including manufacturers of tailored suits, began to acquire them, infuse them with capital and expand their geographic operations. The 1960s were prosperous and suit manufacturers historically had made acquisitions during good times. Cluett and Botany acquired several stores and expanded their sites geographically.

1962

In 1962 the success of Evan-Picone's line of women's tailored suits caught the eye of Charles Revson and Revlon acquired the line. Evan-Picone made its customs-made-look suits in volume, using section-shop assembly methods, interspersed with handwork, and sold them at lower prices than designer labels. Revlon sold the line to nearly 5000 retailers.

1964

In 1964 Hart, Schaffner & Marx acquired Hickey-Freeman, a manufacturer of premium (number-six-quality) men's clothing whose line was priced substantially above the 1964 Hart, Schaffner & Marx clothing lines. In addition to gaining a top-of-the-line-suit manufacturer, Hart, Schaffner & Marx also gained Hickey-Freeman's premium retail outlets.

1965

In 1965 Hart, Schaffner & Marx acquired six more retail specialty stores, and Phillips-Van Heusen, a shirt maker, acquired a chain of New England and Florida apparel stores through its Kennedy's Inc. clothing-store subsidiary. Rapid-American purchased Joseph H. Cohen & Sons, Inc., a privately held manufacturer of men's apparel, and thereby began to build its MacGregor menswear division.

1966

By 1966 a trend toward dual distribution had become apparent. Suit manufacturers owned retail outlets that competed with independent merchants in selling their products. In this environment Joseph & Feiss, a large clothing manufacturer, was merged into Phillips-Van Heusen, Genesco purchased Roos/Atkins, Inc., a large northern-California men's-specialty chain, Botany Industries opened thirteen new stores in 1966, and Hart, Schaffner & Marx expected to add ten stores—through acquisitions or openings. The Joseph & Feiss acquisition (with brand names Joseph & Feiss, Cricketeer, and Tempo) enabled Phillips-Van Heusen to fill a substantial portion of its thirty-nine Kennedy's stores (and other outlets Phillips-Van Heusen might open) using internal sources of merchandise.

1967

In 1966 Hart, Schaffner & Marx had acquired five stores (for a total of 140 stores), while Cluett, Peabody had fifty-eight stores representing ten retailing companies. Four major firms were selling number-four-quality suits— Genesco (through L. Greif), Cluett (through J. Schoeneman), Botany (through Botany 500) and Hart, Schaffner & Marx. The market was moderately competitive but not yet particularly attuned to fashion merchandising or high fashion in the styling of suits.

In 1967 Hart, Schaffner & Marx leased eighteen new stores in shopping centers and had increased the number of retail stores it operated to one hundred seventy-five. Hart, Schaffner & Marx began to produce the Austin Reed line in its plants to sell in Hart, Schaffner & Marx stores. (Hart, Schaffner & Marx had acquired an 11 percent interest in the British Austin Reed, Ltd. company, a manufacturer and retailer in its home markets.) Hart, Schaffner & Marx's major lines were Austin Reed ($85 to $100 for suits), Hart, Schaffner & Marx ($95 to $175), Society ($100 to $175), and Hickey-Freeman ($165 to $270).

1968

In 1968 Hart, Schaffner & Marx acquired ten specialty-clothing stores, while two firms that dominated the number-two-quality market acquired additional suit manufacturers and their labels. Phillips-Van Heusen and Brookfield Industries, a maker of men's apparel, agreed to merge. Rapid-American acquired Cross Country, also a manufacturer of men's clothing.

In 1968 Botany acquired Fashion Park, a Rochester, New York manufacturer of men's tailored clothing including the number-six-grade labels of Fashion Park and Stein Bloch. (Botany's other men's clothing brands, Botany 500 and Worsted-Tex, were number-four-grade suits in 1968.) Fashion Park merchandise was sold in many of the one hundred men's-specialty stores owned by Botany.

In November, 1968 the Justice Department filed a lawsuit against Hart, Schaffner & Marx seeking an injunction of further store acquisitions and a divestiture of everything acquired after 1966. Since its program of acquisitions did not appear to damage competition in the number-two-quality market, where Hart, Schaffner & Marx was a minor factor, the firm contested the lawsuit. In 1969 Hart, Schaffner & Marx operated 206 men's clothing stores in seven metropolitan areas.

1970

Sales volumes for men's tailored suits peaked in 1969. Then economic and demographic factors combined with sociological changes (increased informality) to depress demand for tailored attire. The major change in business in 1970 was the introduction of the continental or European cut, a slimmer and more fitted look. Botany was hurt most badly by this development. It held a large inventory of the older styles which it could not dispose of.

In 1970 Hart, Schaffner & Marx agreed with the Justice Department on a consent decree that provided for the sale of thirty men's-clothing stores owned by Hart, Schaffner & Marx, court-and-Justice-Department approval for any acquisition of men's-clothing stores for the next five years, and court approval for the subsequent five years (ending in 1980) for acquiring existing men's-clothing stores. The consent decree did not enjoin the opening of new men's specialty clothing stores in new locations.

1971

By 1971 several firms were experiencing losses, including Bond, Robert Hall, and Botany. Their stores had not kept pace with fashion changes in men's wear, and stores were located in dying communities and out-of-the-way locations, not in shopping malls. By the time top management noticed their stores had missed the movement into malls, it was too late.

Botany's sales were off 37 percent ($25 million) in 1971 and its net loss was $23.5 million. Botany discontinued the manufacturing operations of two subsidiaries, closed the plant of another and moved its operations to another subsidiary's plant. Botany also sold its retail stores located in Southern California and tried to sell the balance of its retail stores.

Genesco's acquisition campaign continued, however, and by 1971, its financial statements listed several stores that had been acquired since the Department-of-Justice suit against Hart, Schaffner & Marx.

In 1971 Phillips-Van Heusen purchased thirty-one Harris & Frank stores from Botany Industries. Two stores in Nevada and the others in Southern California were acquired for around $10 million in cash.

1972

By 1972 most menswear manufacturers had stopped acquiring menswear stores and Genesco began to digest what it had acquired. Hart, Schaffner & Marx found that selling retail stores was not easy in this economic climate and disposed of only three stores in 1972.

In 1972 Botany and its subsidiary, H. Daroff, filed under Chapter XI of the Federal Bankruptcy Act. Botany's problems centered around the losses incurred by its 104 retail outlets that Botany had aggressively acquired around 1961 when dual distribution was moving towards a peak among menswear producers. Although some of its retail outlets were profitable, others were a drag on earnings and consistently lost money. They distributed Botany's suits but were not inherently profitable.

1973

In late October, 1973 Botany was declared bankrupt and ordered liquidated by a federal judge. There were several offers to purchase the Botany 500 brand name; in particular Rapid-American's Joseph H. Cohen & Sons division offered to purchase the inventories and following tradenames: Botany 500, Tailored by Daroff, Worsted-Tex, Stein Bloch, and Fashion Park. When the acquisition was completed, the Cohen division manufactured a new line of men's clothing under the Botany labels.

In 1973 Palm Beach acquired Evan-Picone, a manufacturer of tailored suits for women, and converted two of its underutilized men's-suit plants to manufacturers of the Evan-Picone women's-suit line. The same fabrics were used as for men's suits and the prices were lower than designer-label suits for women.

1974

By 1974 Hart, Schaffner & Marx was able to comply with part of the Department of Justice's decree that twenty-five stores representing forty-two menswear-outlet locations had to be divested. Hart, Schaffner & Marx sold twenty-four stores to Hughes & Hatcher of Detroit. Hart, Schaffner & Marx sold an additional eight stores to individual proprietors but it was not easy to do so. By 1974 the market for specialty retail outlets had become quite soft. Hart, Schaffner & Marx's stores were all profitable at this time, however, which made it easier to sell them.

In 1974 Bond posted a loss of $1.2 million on sales of $93.4 million in 1973, and a loss of $1.5 million for the first nine months of 1974 on sales of $73.2 million. Private investors purchased and closed thirty Bond Stores and converted other locations to youth-oriented outlets offering blue jeans, flashy T-shirts and mod suits. The new owners hired a Phillips-Van Heusen retailing executive to dispose of Bond's less-profitable units, including factories.

At the height of the retail slump in 1974, Cluett examined its acquisitions and began to divest those stores that did not yield a satisfactory return.

In 1974, Phillips-Van Heusen reported a loss. Its campaign to rectify this problem included eliminating unprofitable areas, reducing capital requirements, and reducing overhead and operating expenses. One of the casualties of this program was Phillips-Van Heusen'srecently acquired manufacturing arm, Brookfield Industries.

Declining sales, management shakeups, and conflicts between manufacturing and marketing policies combined in 1974 to produce poor morale in the S. Schoeneman division. Company policies to reduce expenses were implemented by cutting corners and producing defective and inferior merchandise. As a result Genesco's sales declined even further.

1975

In 1975 Genesco began to rationalize its many apparel businesses by trimming the West-Coast Roos/Atkins men's-apparel chain from fifty-five to twelve stores, but the retail chain was still unprofitable as were Genesco's other menswear stores. In Genesco's manufacturing division, new management sought to improve production quality and launch the firm into branded products. A former Greif designer was hired to improve the patterns used in cutting the suits and brands such as Donald Brooks, Lanvin, Chaps by Ralph Lauren, Guy La Roche, and Kilgore, French & Stanbury were introduced.

In 1975 United Merchants & Manufacturers began closing its geographically isolated and low-volume Robert Hall stores as quickly as possible. Some stores were locked into long-term leases with penalties for early termination that would be more costly to United Merchants & Manufacturers than continuing to operate losing stores, however.

1976

In 1976 Brooks Brothers announced an end to custom tailoring, a service it had offered since 1818. The decision was attributed to the difficulty of getting qualified tailors and a decline in demand for the service.

In 1976 United Merchants & Manufacturers announced its second consecutive loss, blamed primarily on the inventory writedowns at United Merchants & Manufacturers' 357-store Robert Hall Clothing chain. (One retailing transgression attributed to the Robert Hall management was returning clothes that did not sell to Robert Hall warehouses. Management hoped to sell them the following year rather than take markdowns and move them out.) In its efforts to save the firm, United Merchants & Manufacturers closed eighty-five freestanding Robert Hall stores and invested millions in turning around Robert Hall.

In 1976 L. Greif & Company finally became more than just a manufacturer for private-label men's tailored suits. It introduced its first season of a new branded line, Chaps by Ralph Lauren, which was accepted enthusiastically by consumers.

1977

The resurgence in demand for tailored clothing was expected to continue in 1977. But consumers were choosing basic colors and natural fibers, thereby shrinking the diversity and size of their wardrobes by choosing fewer items.

In June 1977, after a long series of losses and other problems, United Merchants & Manufacturers filed for reorganization under Chapter XI of the Federal Bankruptcy Act. After seeing it amass widening losses and lenders pressuring it in other operations, United Merchants & Manufacturers' management finally announced it would phase out Robert Hall. Inventories of $125 million in clothing were liquidated separately from the 366 stores' leases and fixed assets, and unions filed charges with the National Labor Relations Board (NLRB) because United Merchants & Manufacturers did not notify the union of the shutdown.

1978

In 1978 retailers bought apparel closer to their actual selling season and asked manufacturers to space out deliveries to suit the stores' sales forecasts. In the past orders were usually booked months in advance of specified shipping dates so manufacturers could better plan production. The change in retailer behavior made the apparel business even more risky as manufacturers produced in anticipation of orders. This change also forced apparel manufacturers to incur the costs of carrying inventory and the risks of style changes.

In 1978 the widely known menswear manufacturers Michaels Stern (Rochester), Middishade (Philadelphia), and Sussex Clothes (New York) shifted from supplying other retailers to selling directly to consumers at lower prices than they would pay in stores. Eagle Clothes, an old, established menswear producer in New York was in Chapter XI bankruptcy proceedings and GGG Clothes, a producer of premium-quality suits in New York, closed after more than six decades in business. More men were buying their suits at warehouselike manufacturers' retail lofts, off-price urban retailers with low-overhead, or at suburban factory outlets teeming with pipe racks. These discounters represented 10 percent of the U.S. menswear market in 1978 and were gaining share. Suit manufacturers such as St. Laurie Ltd. and Sussex Clothes sold directly to consumers from Manhattan lofts as manufacturers' retail outlets.

In 1978 Hart, Schaffner & Marx had 249 men's stores that operated with great autonomy because there was no requirement to purchase a certain amount of goods from its manufacturing divisions and Hart, Schaffner & Marx's stores were not operated for the purpose of providing distribution for its manufacturing divisions. Rather, the stores purchased from Hart, Schaffner & Marx factories only to the extent that it was profitable for them to do so.

In 1978 United Merchants & Manufacturers emerged from bankruptcy proceedings to begin repaying its debtors. Robert Hall, which had been a great success in a depression economy, was a bitter memory and United Merchants & Manufacturers vowed never to enter retailing again.

In 1978 Palm Beach introduced Evan-Picone—for Men, a line of custom-made-look sportswear separates for men and used the underutilized plants of other apparel companies it had acquired to turn out these garments. Association with the women's-wear business taught Palm Beach the value of shorter production cycles in knowing what the market truly desires. The faster pace of production enabled Palm Beach to minimize inventories and lower overhead costs.

Consistent with the trend toward designer labels to supplement traditional tailored-suit offerings, Phillips-Van Heusen introduced Geoffrey Beene, as its newest label. The garments were licensed from the designer and produced by Joseph & Feiss in 1978. Phillips-Van Heusen had been watching the success of the Evan-Picone products carefully and decided to introduce its own line of branded tailored suits for working women, Cricketeer Tailored Woman.

1979

Suit sales declined from 17.5 million units in 1978 to 15.9 million in 1979, as lapels became narrower, colors and patterns were more subdued, and shoulder padding was removed. Cluett, Peabody acquired Merit Clothing Company, a Montreal-based manufacturer of suits, sport coats, and trousers, and Genesco continued to shut down retail outlets that were losing money, including menswear stores such as Roos/Atkins, Burkhardts, and Baron's.

In 1979 Levi Strauss acquired Koracorp, a women's-sportswear maker that owned Oxxford, the producer of number-six-quality men's suits. Paradoxically, Levi Strauss' invasion of Hart, Shaffner & Marx's home territory came at a time when Hart, Schaffner & Marx was entering Levi Strauss' low-priced-suit markets.

Hart, Schaffner & Marx introduced a new line of Playboy-brand suits retailing for $115 to $155, a market representing one-third of all men's-suit sales in 1979. Hart, Schaffner & Marx's major opponent in the X-quality, branded-suit business was Levi Strauss. Also in 1979 Hart, Schaffner & Marx acquired Intercontinental Apparel, Inc., the U.S. licensee for Pierre Cardin men's suits, slacks, and rainwear. Hart, Schaffner & Marx's retail specialty stores had been carrying Intercontinental's merchandise with great success for several years.

In 1979 Palm Beach acquired Haspel Brothers of New Orleans, a manufacturer of men's clothing, and Gant Inc., a shirt maker. One year earlier Palm Beach had acquired Eagle Shirtmakers when it was in financial difficulty.

In 1979 Phillips-Van Heusen sold back its twenty-one Redwood & Ross clothing stores to their former owner. The midwestern menswear chain was acquired by Phillips-Van Heusen in 1968. Also in 1979 Phillips-Van Heusen concluded that Cricketeer Tailored Woman was not a profitable line and sold it.

1980

Although Hart, Schaffner & Marx had acquired one retail firm in Salem, Oregon, it concluded in 1980 that few specialty stores were profitable enough to buy. It was so difficult to sell manufacturing assets that nobody purchased Robert Hall's factories long after its demise, and Kuppenheimer of Chicago and Grossman of New York, number-six- and number-four-quality suitmakers, respectively, had problems finding buyers for their assets. Hammonton Park's plants were liquidated after selling Palm Beach its brand names, as were Eagle Shirtmakers'.

Cluett reduced its retail operations from sixty to twenty-six stores in 1980 by disposing of five chains. Its private label business, J. Schoeneman, reported better performance than Cluett's designer label, Halston for Men.

In 1980 Genesco again announced that certain menswear retail outlets were for sale. Genesco had great difficulty selling its Roos/Atkins line, and offered to sell three very profitable chains, in addition to several others. Genesco had to shut down the chains it could not sell including many Roos/Atkins units.

Depressed by sluggish sales, Palm Beach temporarily mothballed some menswear factories in 1980 because they were running 25 to 30 percent below capacity. Meanwhile Palm Beach's Evan-Picone sales did very well, suggesting Palm Beach might switch more menswear factories to the construction of tailored women's wear.

1981

In 1981 the principal brands of Hart, Schaffner & Marx included Hart, Schaffner & Marx, Hickey-Freeman, Walter-Morton, Chester-Barrie, Society Brand, Austin Reed of Regent Street, Graham & Gunn, and Johnny Carson, with the following designer labels: Christian Dior, Pierre Cardin, Nino Cerruti, and Cesarani. Its three manufacturing divisions were Hickey-Freeman (number-six quality), Hart, Schaffner & Marx (number-four quality) and M. Wile (number-two quality). Hart, Schaffner & Marx served a well-established quality market through both its retailing and manufacturing divisions, composed largely of business and professional men rather than blue-collar consumers. The company was proud of its vertical integration, and it had argued that vertical integration dampened the impact on the company of economic swings because they affected retailing and manufacturing differently and at different times.

In 1981 Genesco's principal brand names included Lanvin, Donald Brooks, Chaps by Ralph Lauren, Colours by Alexander Julian, Phoenix, Hardy Amies, Aquascutum, Kilgour, Oleg Cassini, and French & Stanbury. Its private label company, Greif, produced number-four-quality suits, but in lesser quantities, as Genesco shifted its emphasis to selling branded suits. (Eighty percent of its sales were branded products.) Genesco was no longer in menswear retailing except for seven stores located in southern Florida which it was also likely to sell.

Although Palm Beach had no specialty retail outlets, it was the first suit manufacturer to have a factory outlet store open to the public. Its principal brand names were Palm Beach, John Weitz, Gianni Versace, and Evan-Picone, and 55 percent of the firm's sales went to specialty retailers, 45 percent to department stores.

Phillips-Van Heusen's principal brands included Cricketeer and Geoffrey Beene, and Joseph & Feiss was its private-brand manufacturing arm. Phillips-Van Heusen had several retail chains throughout the country in 1981.

In 1981 Oxford Industries, a traditional supplier of medium-priced, number-two-quality apparel to retailers like Sears, Roebuck and J.C. Penney's, introduced its first designer-apparel line—Ralph Lauren's Polo sportswear. By broadening its customer base, Oxford hoped to participate in the lucrative upscale market some manufacturers were predicting.

In 1981 Rapid-American's principal brands included MacGregor, Botany, Botany 500, 500, Cartier, Worsted-Tex, Fashion Park, Stein Bloch, Broadstreets, and Coat Tails. Its major manufacturing division was MacGregor, and Rapid-American was not affiliated with any men's-clothing retailer.

In 1981 Richman Brothers was owned by Woolworth's and distributed products through its Anderson, Little-menswear retail chain and made private brands for other stores it did not own. Richman Brothers used outside suppliers for some of its needs and many of their products were sold through factory outlet stores.

In 1981 Cluett, Peabody's private-brand manufacturer, J. Schoeneman, produced number-four-quality suits for leading retailers, and Cluett owned several menswear retail chains.

At the end of 1981 fewer suits were sold through small specialty stores and more through chains and large department stores. A major change in merchandising policies was precipitated by high interest rates—retailers would not accept shipment until they were ready to display garments. Manufacturers were thus obliged to bear those costs or else change their manufacturing policies to be less working capital intensive. Consumers seemed unaware of the differences between various quality grades beyond fabric and price, and some retailers resisted price increases by switching to suits containing less hand tailoring to compensate for the effects of rising manufacturing costs.

Analysis of Strategies for Vertical Integration in Tailored Suits

Section one described the structure of the tailored-suits industry and section two described key events in the industry from 1960 to 1981. This section analyzes the patterns of vertical behavior sketched above and compares the predictions of the strategy framework with the outcomes observed in 1981 when customers abandoned fashion for basic value, and firms retrenched to accommodate these new buying patterns. The industry's structure was volatile in the lower-priced segments where most sales occurred, but not in higher-priced markets where higher-quality brands commanded such strong customer loyalties that some retailers could not avoid ordering them each season. Specialty stores which had sold 69 percent of the suits in the 1960s sold only 44 percent by 1981, and some suit makers had divested their stores because they were both less important as market conduits and were not profitable.

According to the framework proposed in chapter 2, firms could undertake many functions within an established industry structure, for example, high degrees of internal transfer could be undertaken if the environment were not too volatile, as well as greater proportions of ownership. In tailored suits, however, the economic balance between textiles and suits was unfavorable unless, as in the case of United Merchants & Manufacturers, the firm were primarily in some other business. This meant, first, that the greater bargaining power of downstream parties made it unnecessary for suit makers to produce textiles or for retail specialty outlets to make their own garments. Instead textile firms wooed apparel makers who, in turn, courted retailers. Secondly, the industry became so volatile that high degrees of internal transfer became unwise and led to disaster, especially in the lower-priced markets.

Phase of Industry Development

Tailored suits were a mature industry, but demand was declining during the 1970s. The decline was part of a large cycle the industry had passed through several times due to demographic, economic, and sociological changes. Demand for number-six- and number-four-quality suits was more stable than for lower-quality suits since the higher costs of 100-percent-wool textiles and hand tailoring could be passed on with greater ease. There had been little vertical integration in tailored suits early in the industry's development, when firms contracted for many necessary supplies and services and did not commit heavy investments to factories. In 1981 there were no manufacturing secrets to protect and quality concerns did not dictate forward integration either, unless the decision was an economic one rather than a strategic one.

In summary, the integration patterns observed in this industry were temporary arrangements that were discontinued when they became uneconomic. Retailers who backward integrated to manufacture suits for their owned retail outlets and sold 100 percent of their tailored suits in-house, tended to emphasize inexpensive suit qualities.

A policy of full in-house manufacturing and retailing worked best for short periods in the lower-priced market segments where price was the dominant means of competing and marketing intelligence was less important, but in the long run, integrated stores benefited from some access to the ideas of others. Since demand fluctuated and was characterized by fashion cycles, high degrees of integration were unwise.

Firms that owned healthy retail outlets in 1981 and let them operate autonomously enjoyed the benefits of market scanning and some increased sales volumes without limiting themselves to a narrow range of retailing channels. Each year successful firms shut down or sold defunct store locations and replaced them with new ones to ensure that the retail outlets they held were the very best stores available in that region. Less successful firms, by contrast, kept their store locations frozen and used them to buy retail distribution.

In summary, suit manufacturers tried a variety of integrated relationships over time. (The same firms did not try all of them. Rather an unsuccessful firm from an earlier era was purchased, or its brands were acquired, by subsequent entrants or by competitors.) In this mature industry, firms were not uniformly integrated upstream or downstream. Nor were their degrees of internal transfer the same. Since there were several segments to the market this industry served, there could be several approaches to vertical integration that were effective for the particular firms in question.

Volatile Industry Structure

Demand slumped during the 1970s, forcing marginal competitors to cut prices or exit, and new distribution channels segmented the market more finely as menswear marketing became more volatile—more like women's wear. Competition also became more volatile in the number-two-quality markets as the former value of some manufacturers' brand names were eroded by price-cutting.

Brand names were important and insulated some tailored-suit manufacturers from the volatile price-cutting of less-prestigious brands and lower quality. In 1981 a major threat to profitability was the rising cost of labor which came at a time when consumers grew less discriminating in demanding garments with hand tailoring.

A large portion of the seasonal variations in suit styles was due to differences in textile styling, not in the cut of the garment. Consequently textile suppliers contributed significantly to the value-added and differentiation of tailored suits. The services textile houses provided were so complete that suit manufacturers did not have to backward integrate to control the diferentiability of their products. Also backward integration would be an impairment to strategic flexibility in suit manufacturing because competitors would not purchase the excess capacity of a backward integrated suit maker; thus the firm would be limited in its styling options since it would have to take much of its textile output from upstream. A firm would not get many ideas from outsiders if it were locked into transactions with its own supplier firm, and in an industry like suit manufacturing, where access to new styles, colors, textiles, and ideas is of paramount importance in maintaining product differentiation, such competitive inflexibility can not be tolerated.

Similarly it was important to maintain channels of communication with customers to determine where fashion was going and what consumers wanted. Textile houses consulted leading retailers and so did effective suit manufacturers. Thus the most responsive suit manufacturers were those that did not force their product line on owned retailers, but rather used their stores as listening posts that purchased garments from their sister manufacturing units when products suited the market but spurned their designs when they did not. Thus if suit manufacturers acquired stores that mirrored the images they hoped to create and considered their advice concerning styling, they were brought closer to the ultimate consumer and better able to compete in the volatile tailored-suit market. If instead suit manufacturers acquired stores merely to have assured distribution outlets to keep their factories operating, they were likely to create unstylish and undesirable products.

Firms that were skilled at producing a particular quality grade could produce private-brand suits for retailers to fill their factories, but by 1981 firms that had once been content to be primarily private-brand manufacturers, like Genesco or Oxford, had introduced designer-brand apparel in order to penetrate the branded market quickly. Licensing designers' names added only $1.50 to $2.00 to the cost of manufacturing a garment and made it both more acceptable to the ultimate consumer and more profitable to manufacturers and retailers.

Although the number-six- and number-four-quality manufacturers had seen the demise or downgrading of labels like Fashion Park, Stein Bloch, Kuppenheimer, GGG, Botany 500 and others, their market was not nearly so volatile as the lower-priced, high-volume market for tailored suits. Committed apparel manufacturers had always found a way to compete, but by 1981 they increasingly used price competition to achieve what a strong brand name could not give them. Some manufacturers acquired retail outlets to gain distribution for products that did not have strong consumer loyalties on the basis of their labels alone. Although this strategy was a near-term means of keeping a plant utilized, it was not a good long-term strategy if it meant isolating retailers from the market.

In summary, competition in the tailored-suit industry was growing more volatile because: (1) the multiple seasons, short production runs, and other policies used by ladies'-wear producers were being adopted by firms that serviced large retail chains; (2) uncertainty concerning future demand was leading firms to prepare differently for the coming decade, with the effect that some firms that had never been competitors previously were preparing to invade each others' markets; (3) fringe firms were using price-cutting to stay in business; (4) the development of merchandisers such as discounters, manufacturers' lofts, and factory outlets exacerbated the trend toward low industry profits; (5) customers grew increasingly sensitive to higher prices created by higher labor costs but less sensitive to quality differences; and (6) retail specialists were becoming less important as a distribution channel for popularly priced suits.

Bargaining Power

The textile suppliers and suit manufacturers possessed bilateral market power because textile houses provided significant differentiating services that could raise a suit maker's dependence on a supplier, and an individual manufacturer's purchases were not significant to many of the large broad-line textile firms; but suit manufacturers represented the major purchasers of woolen and worsted textiles, and they were free to shop around to select the best fabrics and patterns from suppliers who incurred expenses in design and market research to satisfy them. Downstream, the bargaining relationship varied by quality grade and type of distribution channel. Although large retail chains and department stores were the largest customers of tailored suits, they rarely purchased number-six- or number-four-quality suits that were either branded or private label. Consequently most of the price reductions and other services demanded by them affected the manufacturers of number-two- and X-quality suits that enjoyed less consumer loyalty for their brand names and exhibited a greater willingness to shade prices to buy retail distribution. Manufacturers of number-six- and number-four-quality suits operated in an environment where retailers and suit makers had bilateral bargaining power because the specialty retailers needed these most-popular branded products and manufacturers needed the high-quality retailers as distribution outlets. The types of stores that these suit manufacturers were more likely to own were those stores that reflected the high-quality image of their high-grade garments.

In summary, the low bargaining power of lower-priced-suit manufacturers suggested a need for upstream or downstream integration to obtain the services they could not extract as economically in other ways. But the costs of entering textile production, and scale of operations required, foreclosed that investment for most firms, and downstream integration would have been fruitless for them in many cases because competition was quite volatile.

Strategy Goals

In 1981 firms were selling or closing their retail stores, creating designer labels, or returning to a basic line of products. Many firms that had previously produced suits primarily for sale within their retail outlets were bankrupt, and there was excess capacity in textile production. The assets of former suit manufacturers went unsold, and several stores were on the auction block.

One of the principal problems with some integrated firms' performance was their unwillingness to permit suit makers or retail stores to operate as autonomous, strategic business units. There was a great opportunity to force manufactured products into owned retail outlets and many firms did so, even where it penalized the profits of the stores. Requiring downstream units to purchase suits only from sister units may have given upstream units low manufacturing costs but it also stultified the variety of offerings available downstream. Hence long-term competitive viability downstream was sacrificed for near-term, illusory profits upstream.

Profitability goals suggested a focus strategy in which something less than full integration was appropriate, unless technological, differentiation, or market-share objectives dictated more integration, as would be appropriate. In tailored suits there were no technological secrets to guard and differentiation was not enhanced by high internal transfers. The most widely recognized brand name in men's tailored suits, Hart, Schaffner & Marx, was sold through 275 owned outlets as well as through hundreds of independent retailers; Hart, Schaffner & Marx was only taper integrated such that 40 percent of its output was sold through owned stores, but this represented less than 20 percent of each store's annual sales volume.

Depending upon their objectives, parent firms could enhance or discourage vertical relationships among business units in the tailored-suit business. When firms let their business units trade autonomously in tailored suits, relatively low internal transfers resulted.

The competitive advantage of owning both suit-manufacturing units and retail outlets was improved intelligence in recognizing changes in consumers' tastes and reporting them to their manufacturing units quickly. This was a linkage of greatest advantage to firms in high-fashion businesses, not those serving traditional and conservative tastes. Firms like Phillips-Van Heusen, for example, that competed in the number-two-quality market could take the greatest advantage of these synergies.

In summary, some parent firms created inconsistencies in suit manufacturing by forcing sister units to trade, even when the transactions were less profitable and created myopic visions of the market for tailored apparel. Enforcing these relationships meant they subsidized losers initially and created substantial exit barriers later by delaying the divestiture of unprofitable and unsalable business units. There were no dominant strategic needs served by maintaining high vertical integration between these adjacent businesses and the principal advantage firms seemed to enjoy from owning stores was high profits from inherently profitable properties. Thus by 1981 vertical integration was of less value for most firms.

The Need for Vertical Integration

By 1981 the volatile market for tailored suits had minimized many potential advantages of vertical integration. There were no shortages of raw materials and the manufacturing process required neither physical interconnection nor any owned factory. The major advantages many firms saw in vertical integrations were intelligence related. Using firms' sales representatives to gather impressions about which hues and patterns were preferred, how freely consumers were spending, and whether fashion ideas were becoming incorporated into the styling of traditional tailored suits, enabled firms to maximize the benefits of style and fabric discussions between upstream and downstream units. Earlier decisions on colors and patterns enabled firms to create textile exclusives sooner and exploit other bargaining advantages associated with leadership. Again the major danger in integration was a loss of fashion sense, strategic flexibility, and competitive edge which came from too much internal transfer and too little outside scanning.

Strategy Alternatives and Performance

The strategy model distinguished between ownership and the degree of internal integration firms engaged in; firms could own all, some, or none of the adjacent firms supplying goods and services, and transfer all, some, or none of their needs internally. Moreover firms differed in the breadth of their integrations. In tailored suits, firms were once backward integrated into textiles as well as forward integrated into retailing if these activities were justified by firms' strategic missions and competitive strengths.

The firms that used high degrees of internal integration—Bond, Robert Hall, Botany, and Richman—did so because of historical origins in retailing. These firms sought to sell low-priced tailored suits to the masses. Their $22.50 suits were a marketing success in the 1920s but the justification for these policies was gone by 1981, when these customers demanded fashionable styling in their apparel. Failure to notice this change in consumer attitudes left firms like Robert Hall with obsolete merchandise. In 1980 the more-successful, forward-integrated manufacturers were taper integrated, selling less than 20 percent of their sister units' output.

The number of stages of activity undertaken was determined by the products' characteristics, the nature of demand, and the mission of the tailored-suit unit relative to adjacent businesses. The nature of the raw materials (textiles) made upstream integration difficult for most firms (due to the large scale of production required). Automation of suit construction was difficult due to the pliable nature of cloth, making subcontracting feasible at several points in the manufacturing process. Yet most tailored-suit firms performed all tailoring in-house (except for seasonal or fad items). Few of them were successful in operating retail specialty outlets that featured their suits because quality mismatches (between tailoring quality and store clienteles) occurred so frequently that few firms could enjoy synergies from retailing operations.

The breadth of integration—the number of different activities which were integrated—was determined by demand traits and the way firms competed. Few suit manufacturers found broad integration useful. In tailored suits, United Merchants & Manufacturers had been the most highly and broadly integrated firm before its Robert Hall unit went bankrupt in 1975. United Merchants & Manufacturers spun fiber into yarn, wove yarn into textiles, sewed textiles into suits, and sold its tailored suits through its retailing subsidiary. Palm Beach had originally been a textile firm before becoming a suit manufacturer; it once made Palm Beach cloth. Hart, Schaffner & Marx had once left merchandising to concentrate on manufacturing when the suits made to its specifications in the 1890s offered a better commercial opportunity than retailing. Hart, Schaffner & Marx returned to retailing by acquiring premier menswear stores during the 1920s.

The form of vertical relationship indicated the amount of asset exposure and flexibility the venture possessed. In highly uncertain and volatile environments where the performance of vertically integrated firms was highly sensitive to fluctuations in demand, ownership forms involving lesser amounts of asset exposure (such as subcontracting) were used to reduce the variabilities of returns and increase firms' strategic flexibilities. The form of integration used was determined by firms' bargaining power and their corporate-strategy objectives.

There were few joint ventures in this industry because most materials and services needed could be purchased readily without penalties to quality or market position, suit manufacturers guarded their ideas jealously and preferred their products to be identified with them exclusively, and the industry changed too quickly for firms to be bound by trade relationships that extended more than a season. Joint ventures would have impeded these firms' abilities to shift resources quickly in response to changes in demand.

Many tailored-suit firms subcontracted for parts of their suits' construction (for example, vests) if they anticipated demand would be temporary. The advantages of doing so included lower asset inflexibility, lower overhead, and breakeven volumes, and no need to undertake design or market-research activities in-house.

Tailored suits was a mature industry in 1981, but its structure was still changing because it had become evident that companies that produced tailored suits solely for sale in their company stores performed poorly. The manufacturers that formulated the more-effective vertical-integration strategies were those that gained relatively stable access to textiles and widespread distribution while also achieving their parent firms' strategic objectives, including market dominance, above-average returns on invested capital or leadership (fashion).

For years Oxford Industries enjoyed steady but modest earnings as a supplier of Sears, Roebuck and J.S. Penney Company. It shifted from this quasi-integrated form of distribution to selling to outsiders like Bloomingdale's and Neiman-Marcus when it branched into designer label apparel. Keeping its stable base but adding this risky, nonintegrated business substantially boosted Oxford's near-term profitability.

When Palm Beach was Goodall Worsted in 1925, it manufactured cloth, made summerweight suits and distributed them to retail specialty outlets. It was able to plan its mill runs to almost 100-percent-capacity utilization because it had national distribution and a virtual monopoly in Palm Beach cloth. Since its line changed style little (and the fabric rarely changed) there were fewer risks to pyramiding a textile business atop an apparel and retailing business. In 1981 these stable conditions no longer existed and Palm Beach had no stores and no textile plants.

Hart, Schaffner & Marx had more stores and more labels than any other suit producer. Although Hart, Schaffner & Marx had been strongest in the conservative upscale markets where its number-six- and number-four-quality suits were popular, the firm had ventured into the number-two-quality market successfully and was battling Levi Strauss for leadership of the branded X-quality market where no manufacturer's brand had attained dominance.

Hart, Schaffner & Marx enjoyed several advantages by being both a retailer and a manufacturer. Its manufacturing divisions were confident of a substantial amount of business that gave them the opportunity to make early production plans and to smooth out production levels. Its retailing divisions provided expert fashion guidance to the manufacturing divisions in terms of early sales advice on colors, models, and fabrics. The constant dialogue between retailers and manufacturers worked to their mutual advantage.

United Merchants & Manufacturers was very integrated in textiles—spinning, weaving, conversion to greige goods, and fabrication into finished fabrics for apparel or home furnishings—but when it extended its successful policies of vertical integration to its Robert Hall subsidiary to make attire for sale in these stores, United Merchants & Manufacturers did not recognize market changes because it was insulated from outside inputs.

In summary, forward taper integration was more advantageous than full integration as well as no integration at all in this mature business because the nature of demand was so uncertain and competition so volatile. Each firm performed the fashioning, cutting, sewing, finishing, packaging, and shipping tasks in-house, except where particularly volatile markets led some firms to subcontract their production needs to reduce their asset inflexibility. Future demand for tailored garments was uncertain, most particularly in the lower-priced markets where buyers were price sensitive. There was no advantage to backward integration in 1981, but many firms saw an advantage to some form of forward integration.

References

"Apparel's Last Stand." *Business Week,* May 14, 1979, pp. 60–70.

Cobrin, Harry A. *The Men's Clothing Industry: Colonial Through Modern Times.* New York: Fairchild Publications, 1970.

Davis, H.S., Taylor, G.W., Balderson, C.C., and Bezanson, A. *Vertical Integration in the Textile Industries.* Philadelphia: Wharton School of Finance and Commerce, 1938.

"Designer Names." *Stores,* October 1977, pp. 22–23, 63.

Feldman, E. *Fit for Men: A Study of New York's Clothing Trade.* Washington, D.C.: Public Affairs Press, 1960.

Kasten, Matthew. "Computer Systems Getting Firm Mold in Apparel Industry." *Daily News Record,* September 19, 1978, pp. 1, 19.

Koshetz, Herbert. "Human Hands Are Garments' Backbone." *New York Times,* September 27, 1975, p. 37.

Morris, H. *The Story of Men's Clothes.* Rochester, New York: Hickey-Freeman Company, 1929.

"Separate Approach." *Stores,* October 1977, pp. 30–32.

Sturm, Paul W. "Men's Fashions: Off the Peg Profits." *Forbes,* June 26, 1978, pp. 84–88.

Yarger, Deborah Sue. "Apparel Makers Face Consolidation as Stores Stiffen Delivery Terms." *Wall Street Journal,* February 5, 1978, p. 1.

Also helpful were corporate annual reports and financial statements of the firms described in chapter 7 and conversations with three tailored-suits manufacturers, two textile companies, and three retail specialty stores.

8

Strategies for Vertical Integration in the Ethical-Pharmaceuticals Industry

Ethical pharmaceuticals are drugs primarily advertised only to the medical profession and available only on prescription. (Proprietary drugs are advertised to the general public and available over the counter.) The efficacy of ethical pharmaceuticals for a particular *indication* is substantiated only after meticulous clinical testing, and the Food and Drug Administration (FDA) permits ethical pharmaceuticals to be marketed *only* for those uses that have been properly tested and validated. Although the industry structure had been relatively stable for over thirty years, changes in the importance of wholesalers and licensing arrangements indicated it was changeable. By 1981 the ethical pharmaceuticals industry was a truly global one because shipping bulk products from chemical plants to tableting facilities throughout the world was economical. U.S. demand for ethical pharmaceuticals was slowing, making it an established industry.

A Description of the Ethical-Pharmaceuticals Industry

The Product

Ethical pharmaceuticals are highly pure chemicals or biological products for human consumption, and many types of drugs are capable of treating an illness such as an infection. In 1981, the U.S. Census of Manufactures listed three major subsets to the pharmaceuticals industry and nine major product-use categories as shown in table 8–1. *Biological* products included vaccines, allergenic extracts, serums, plasmas, and other blood derivatives. *Medicinal chemicals and botanicals* included bulk botanical drugs, herbs, and basic vitamins. *Pharmaceutical preparations* were chemical synthesis products, fermented antibiotics, and drugs placed in final-dosage form. Major use categories included analgesics, antibiotics, cardiovascular agents, hormones, nonsteroidal anti-inflammatory agents, oral contraceptives, psychotherapeutics, respiratory agents, and calcium blockers.

The key to successful new pharmaceutical products is research, and as soon as a drug is developed and taken into clinical testing, research on its

Background research was provided by Stan Herman.

Table 8-1
Major Categories of Ethical-Pharmaceutical Uses and Example Brands

Product Category	Major Use	Example Brands
Analgesics	Reduce pain sensation without losing consciousness. Can be narcotic or nonnarcotic.	Darvon, Demerol
Antibiotics	Arrest the growth of and destroy microorganisms such as bacteria, viruses, and fungi. Includes tetracyclines, erythromycins and other broad- or medium-spectrum drugs as well as penicillins and cephalosporins.	Keflex, Vibramycin, V-Cillin
Cardiovascular agents	Includes hypotensives, coronary vasodilators, and other cardiovasculars.	Inderal, Aldomet, Dyazide
Hormones	Chemical substances produced in the endocrine system and carried through bloodstream to exert physiological effects at sites remote from origin, includes corticoids.	Medrol, Decadron, Aristocort
Nonsteroidal anti-inflammatory agents	Ease pain, swelling, and tenderness.	Motrin, Clinoril, Indocin, Feldene
Oral contraceptives	Hormones to control ovulation and prevent pregnancies.	Ortho-Novum, Ovulen, Norinyl
Psychotherapeutics	Moderate, treat or tranquilize nervousness or excitement, anxiety, depression and schizophrenia.	Valium, Thorazine, Elavil, Sinequan
Respiratory agents	Bronchial remedies, antihistamines.	Benylin, Benadryl, Chlor-Trimeton (all OTC)
Calcium blockers	Expand coronary blood vessels by preventing calcium from entering those muscle sheaths which create angina.	Isoptin, Procardia, Cardiem
H_2 receptor antagonists	Treatment of ulcers	Tagamet

Source: *U.S. Census of Manufacturers* and industry sources.

next generation can occur. Soon after the perfection of a new drug, nearly identical chemical structures (analogues) are often synthesized by competitors. The next generation of a drug—frequently synthesized by using the old drug as a starting material—often results in fewer side effects than the previous generations. Research on dosages, delivery systems, and other clinical testing is sizable even for off-patent (generic) drugs.

Generic drugs are ethical pharmaceuticals which went off patent. (Generic drugs can be over-the-counter drugs too.) Although many physicians continue to prescribe drugs by brand name after their patents expired, state laws on generic-drug substitution permit a pharmacist to decide which manufacturer's equivalent drug to use in filling a prescription if physicians indicated substitution was acceptable.

When a drug goes off patent, other drug companies can obtain FDA approval to sell the equivalent drug formulation. Although some generic marketers produce their own bulk pharmaceuticals (active ingredients), others sometimes purchase their active ingredients from the original manufacturer of the off-patent drug or from Italy, Poland, Hungary, or other places where bulk active ingredients are readily available because patents are unavailable or ineffective.

Although a drug patent can expire, trademark protection does not. The original branded version of a generic drug often retains a sizable market share after patents expire. Some manufacturers of patented drugs also sell a line of branded generic drugs because they lack enough new products from their own laboratories. Alternatively, these firms license new Japanese or European drugs to broaden and rejuvenate their product lines.

It is not unusual for a pharmaceutical manufacturer to purchase generic products from another drug firm (or purchase the right to process a patented drug from bulk chemicals) to fill out its product line. Some drug firms sell their own branded, patented drugs as well as some generic drugs (usually antibiotics) sold to pharmacies at substantially lower prices. If an ethical pharmaceutical is not strategically important to the firm—if it is merely a filler—an outside source is sometimes used to obtain active ingredients.

Demand for ethical pharmaceuticals increased in dollar volume by approximately 10 percent annually from 1971 to 1981. Most of this growth was due to inflation. According to the *U.S. Census of Manufacturers,* group sales were largest in 1981 for central-nervous-system disorders (23.5 percent), parasitic and infective diseases (19.2 percent), metabolic and neoplasm products (15.6 percent), cardiovascular agents (14.8 percent), prescription vitamins (13.2 percent), and digestive and genito-urinary products (6.6 percent). Antibiotics (11 percent) and cardiovascular agents (8 percent) led worldwide demand for ethical pharmaceuticals, and generic prescription drugs were becoming a larger portion of sales. Their dollar volume increased from 10 percent in 1978 to 15 percent in 1979 while the unit volume for original drugs plus generic drugs increased from 18 to 22 percent.

Markets

Ethical pharmaceuticals are sold to hospitals and pharmacies through wholesalers or directly by the manufacturer. The major decision makers affecting demand for particular drugs are physicians, but most do not purchase the drugs themselves.

Physicians frequently prescribe drugs by brand names rather than by chemical compound or generic names, but prescriptions are based primarily upon the efficacy of the drug, side effects that patients might incur, and alternative drug and nondrug therapies. Physicians obtain their knowledge about prescription drugs primarily from literature provided by manufacturers' sales representatives, but they were also sensitive to cost-containment pressures.

Pharmacists decide which generically equivalent drugs patients will receive in states that have generic-drug-substitution laws, unless physicians explicitly indicate that the brand name drug is required. Once pharmacists had compounded drugs, but by 1981 virtually all drugs were obtained in finished-dosage forms that pharmacists merely repackaged for sale. Dispensing pharmaceuticals was profitable in 1981, and pharmacies found themselves in competition with hospitals that were seeking to expand their domains by dispensing prescription drugs to outpatients.

Hospital accounts are very cost conscious and purchase generic drugs wherever they are available (rather than branded drugs). Hospitals participate in buying groups to gain quantity discounts in drug purchases and some belong to several buying groups for competitive bid contracts. This arrangement allows them to take the prices they prefer for each item on their shopping lists. Large hospitals usually purchase directly from manufacturers unless a drug firm sells only through wholesalers, and they prefer unit-dose packaging, which is less costly for them than the labor needed to package pharmaceuticals in-house in individual doses. Prior to 1981, hospitals called upon wholesalers for those emergency drug needs that were expensive to supply but had not used wholesalers for most of their pharmaceuticals needs. By 1981, however, order automation and other services wholesalers supplied began to be attractive enough for some hospitals to pay wholesalers for them.

Many of the details of servicing pharmacies, hospitals, government agencies, and other health centers are undertaken by drug wholesalers. They usually receive a discount from direct-account drug prices for these services and purchase in large volumes to exploit additional quantity discounts. Wholesalers break down large shipments into smaller lots and monitor pharmacists' inventories. They offer merchandising services and handle product returns if drugs or their packaging are faulty. In 1981 wholesalers were the least-cost distribution channel for several customer types, largely due to their computerized stockkeeping services and the high cost of holding inventory. Before these services became significant the drug wholesaling business was floundering as more and more sales were shipped direct to customers. By 1981 this trend had reversed itself.

Suppliers

The raw materials needed to make ethical pharmaceuticals vary from drug to drug, but active ingredients are usually synthesized from bulk chemicals (except where the raw materials are biological). Bulk pharmaceuticals (active ingredients) can be shipped economically throughout the world because their value per kilogram is high, and they can be mixed with inert ingredients locally to produce friable tablets, capsules, syrups, ointments, suppositories, serums, or other dosage forms. A variety of licensing and sourcing arrangements are possible, and most major firms produce their own bulk pharmaceuticals, but only occasionally their raw chemicals; however, most of the several hundred small firms in this industry are involved primarily in tableting and labeling operations and purchase their active ingredients from other firms.

There are four major steps in developing patentable drugs which firms can perform in-house or purchase from others: (1) basic research on chemical or biological substances, (2) process research to develop desired products, (3) animal clinical research to test a product's safety and determine the probable dosage range for human consumption, and (4) human clinical research to test the safety and efficacy of a drug and its dosage on human beings (an Investigational New Drug Application (IND) is needed to progress to the fourth stage of product research). Few companies directly perform their own human clinical research, but pharmaceutical companies usually write the protocols specifying the tests they want performed by hospitals, universities, or individual physicians that test their new drugs. Animal research is often done by outside laboratories, but after several animal-testing houses were found falsifying or keeping incomplete test results, many firms perform their animal clinical tests in-house. Moreover, the Good Manufacturing Practices and Good Laboratory Practices Regulations have made outside laboratories as expensive as operating internal laboratories, and this regulatory change accelerated the move to in-house testing. Most major research firms have developed customary testing and consultation relationships with teaching hospitals or research institutes to obtain access to scarce personnel, such as trained pharmacologists. Hoffman-LaRoche, Lilly, and Upjohn had established their own pharmacology laboratories early in the industry's history.

Pharmaceutical firms can contract for the animal-testing phase of product development and many firms once preferred to do so because animal research was expensive and the necessary capacity often varied from year to year. Preclinical facilities were idle at some times of the year, yet pathologists and other costly experts had to be retained during these periods of low utilization since they were difficult to rehire. Basic-product or developmental research can also be purchased from outsiders like Alza, and toxicology can be farmed out to firms like Hazeltine.

Pharmaceutical firms race against each other to authenticate drugs that could possess rival therapeutic values, and the first drug on the market frequently claims the largest market share because it is perceived by physicians as being the pioneering drug. Thus, in 1981, some firms preferred to be backward integrated in all phases of research because they desired secrecy.

Basic research leading to new products had been the most important activity in building pharmaceutical firms' futures for half a century, but firms like Marion Laboratories recently publicized a diametrically opposite strategy. Refusing to do any basic research, they reviewed medical journals and other product literature and licensed products from Japanese firms, small European firms, or others that had difficulty gaining a toehold in the U.S. market. Because these firms were proficient in passing products through FDA certification procedures and marketing them, these firms have a broad line of products, but only in the United States.

The active ingredients used in compounding bulk drugs are made from raw materials and intermediate chemicals. For example, manufacturing chloramphenicol (an anti-infective agent) might require the following bulk chemicals: acetic anhydride, benzaldehyde, dichloromethyl acetate, dimethylamine, formaldehyde, hexamethylene tetramine, and methyldichloroacetate, among others. Suppliers of these chemicals in 1981 included American Cyanamid, Dow Chemical, du Pont, and Eastman Kodak.

Bulk chemicals are a step below the elements—the air, earth, fire, and water level of chemistry—but for the purposes of pharmaceutical production, fine-quality chemicals are also building blocks. For example, barbiturates—drugs in their own right—are starting materials to make several other pharmaceuticals. Similarly, aspirin and other drugs like penicillin are bulk chemicals to some firms.

Few pharmaceutical houses are associated with manufacturers of bulk chemicals because they need such small quantities that chemical manufacturers can not afford to rely on them as customers for their outputs. Most pharmaceutical houses purchase their small lots of bulk chemicals as needed from nearby suppliers. Pharmaceutical firms prefer to have several sources for their ingredients, the opportunity to shop for the best prices, and an uninterrupted supply. Thus few pharmaceutical firms purchase bulk chemicals from sister units.

Bulk pharmaceuticals are fine chemicals (also called active ingredients), and by 1981 major research firms produced their own. They are made in small volumes under highly controlled processes involving many production steps. For a regular chemical company, outputs of 99-percent purity are acceptable, but for pharmaceutical companies output has to be 99.9-percent pure. Often there are processing techniques that give firms better yields which are not reported as part of their patent applications, and in 1981 firms integrated backward to keep these processes a secret.

Pharmaceutical firms tend to control the bulk products associated with making their patented pharmaceutical products since they have the best understanding of how to make active ingredients in the least-costly way and are most likely to purchase the bulk products of other off-patent drugs from original patent holders or from foreign suppliers. Sometimes a pharmaceutical producer makes reagents or chemical intermediates in-house because no other firm offers them as cheaply or makes them as finely as the firm can make them. In general, easy-to-synthesize compounds are made in-house, as are very-complex, sophisticated, or secret processed ingredients. Pharmaceutical firms make their own active ingredients to maintain product quality and keep a secure supply of raw materials, even if outsiders can provide some chemicals more cheaply.

Dosage operations put active pharmaceutical ingredients into the tablets, capsules, or other forms for human consumption. Many smaller pharmaceutical firms are engaged primarily in this part of production, and they purchase active ingredients from others, although sometimes a tableting and labeling firm is hired to place the bulk pharmaceuticals of a larger firm into dosage form on an emergency basis. Most of these firms are either marketers of generic drugs or marketers of licensed drugs from foreign firms.

It is possible (and often economic) to have many services and materials provided by others in the pharmaceuticals industry, particularly when a pharmaceutical manufacturer can obtain better labeling (range of indications) through a marketing contract. (Bad labeling results in poor or weak claims for drugs. Many drugs are better than their FDA label indicates, but because firms can not authenticate their claims in effective clinical tests, they are not permitted to put the full range of indications on the label.) In 1981 major pharmaceutical firms were committed to licensing products to introduce new drugs faster than their labs could produce them. Usually, cross-licensing arrangements with firms like Fujisawa, Glaxo, Organon, or Astra, that had little U.S. presence, stipulated a quid pro quo license of U.S. products in their home markets. Marion Laboratories, whose forte was U.S. marketing, had no products of its own to cross-license, and therefore in 1981 had no market presence outside the United States nor any foreign subsidiaries.

Products can be cross-licensed from U.S. manufacturers but most firms are reluctant to cross-license except when the patented drug has very specialized indications (for example, for ophthalmic care) and is licensed to a firm that specializes in marketing those types of products, or when the patented drug has several diverse indications and dosage forms and is cross-licensed to get different marketing presentations for each indication. Cross-licensing brings strong competitors into markets where they might otherwise not have entered. For example, when one of Schering-Plough's antibiotics was about to go off patent, it offered to cross-license and supply bulks to other companies to keep its plant fully utilized. Their offer brought Upjohn into the market and may have resulted in a faster decay to the price-reduction curve than is usually the case for off-patent, single-source drugs, even in the hospital market.

No drug firm sets out to be a supplier of bulk products but sometimes it is necessary to do so to attain economic volumes, even if that means serving competitors. As excess capacity for older drugs sets in, some pharmaceutical houses become bulk suppliers while others arrange for outsiders to supply their bulk needs (and competitors' needs), thereby freeing plant space to produce new drugs, to research new processes, or to build new facilities. Sourcing arrangements are also used to procure small volumes of needed chemicals or to permit firms to specialize. For example, some firms have customarily agreed to provide one another with active ingredients that both firms need for their respective products. These arrangements sometimes require firms to share information they would otherwise have kept proprietary, but it is justified for them because they avoid having to build a specialized plant or to learn to operate a process that has many bugs in it for newcomers. Make-or-buy decisions are germane for almost every substance or service firms make or perform in-house. Decisions turn on capacity difficulties, skills in handling hazardous materials, or special synthesis requirements. Any sourcing arrangement has to be approved by the FDA to ensure that good manufacturing practices, adequate facilities, and quality-control standards are maintained, and firms often consider sourcing arrangements worthwhile if they avoid the red tape, the need to gear up to learn how to do something that would represent a low-volume activity, or the need to build costly, separate buildings, perhaps in distant locations.

Manufacturing

Capital costs in the ethical-pharmaceuticals industry increased in 1981 due to increased regulations about laboratory procedures. Prior to 1981, a moderate-sized organic-synthesis plant cost $50 million, and a tableting and labeling plant cost as little as $1 million. The ability to persuade the FDA and medical-opinion leaders about a product's efficacy represented a substantial entry barrier, as did product differentiation. The expertise needed to manufacture ethical pharmaceuticals was not readily available, and many pharmaceuticals were not simple to produce. Moreover, pioneer drugs were extremely costly to invent, making new-product development the most costly barrier to entry of all. Creating multiple-dosage forms was an important aspect of this barrier because if a pharmaceutical company offered the same drug in a variety of forms, companies wanting to offer generic versions of the pharmaceutical would also wish to offer these different multiple-dosage forms or delivery systems. This would force generic-drug companies to do some extra research that they would not ordinarily perform.

Introducing a new drug in the United States and meeting all FDA requirements took an average of ten years and cost $60 million or more in 1981. Research was a very risky part of the ethical pharmaceuticals business for several reasons: it is very costly, most candidates fail to live up to their early promise and are dropped, competitors may introduce a similar product sooner and capture the lion's share of the market, and the drug might show unexpected side effects despite chemical testing and be withdrawn from the market after sizable development expenses has been incurred. The key to successful product development is to introduce superior products first.

In 1981 there were few manufacturing economies for batch processes when the pharmaceutical being synthesized changed with each run, but continuous-chemical-synthesis technologies and long production runs offered more opportunities for economies. There were experience-curve economies for complex syntheses. For this reason, some steps in the production process—ones requiring expertise in bromine chemisty, for example—were contracted out to specialist firms. The volume required to break even on a particular drug depended on its price. Firms producing generic drugs had to keep their assets more fully utilized than did firms selling premium-priced products. The minimum-efficient scale of a plant depended primarily on its use and technology—that is, fermentation, organic, chemical synthesis, or filling operations. Excess capacity was unavoidable because a variety of pots, kettles, tubing, and tanks was needed to make the many different therapeutic classes of pharmaceuticals that some firms offered, and some portion of them was always underutilized because they were not needed for a particular run.

The assets of ethical pharmaceutical firms were most flexible if used in chemical synthesis because these pot-and-kettle operations could be modified by adding or subtracting some machinery from the chain of equipment set up to make a particular active ingredient. Typically, production capacity was brought onstream to manufacture a particular active ingredient in pilot-plant scale-up volumes during clinical testing, until the product attained FDA approval and commercial acceptance. Then production went to a larger facility that was dedicated to the manufacture of that ingredient at a capacity that would suffice until rising demand forced a make-or-buy decision about the need for more bulk-pharmaceutical capacity. If the active ingredient were readily available analysis might recommend purchasing bulk active ingredients or intermediates rather than expanding incremental production capacity.

Much of the production of pharmaceutical products was done in one shift to leave capacity available to process rush orders, to balance capital costs (inventory) with scale economies that would be attained by running large, economic lot sizes, and to complete perishable products like ointments or creams. Production planners tried to schedule loadings to maximize the utilization of the largest portion of expensive assets for as long as possible. Each pharmaceutical was made separately and precautions against cross-contamination were taken. In each batch process, chemical synthesis progressed in steps, varying temperature, pressure, time, stirring, and the adding of reagents, all done in very clean surroundings.

Exit barriers were low in the ethical pharmaceutical industry in 1981 because assets were flexible for other uses and outside suppliers could satisfy the demand of remaining customers. Since firms invested heavily in research-and-development cross-licensing, and acquisitions of smaller firms, there were few examples where firms sought to exit and encountered difficulties in doing so. Ciba—Geigy, for example, exited from production of sterile injectables, after FDA requirements about packaging became too costly to satisfy, and instead contracted to purchase them without difficulty.

Marketing

Whether pharmaceutical firms used wholesalers or not, in 1981 all firms maintained sales forces to educate physicians and promote their firms' products. Advertisements in medical journals, direct mailings, and other promotional techniques were not believed to be as effective as their detail services in persuading physicians to prescribe certain drugs.

In 1981 a medical-detail sales force cost over $50,000 per person (at least 100 detail persons were needed), and their most important task was to transfer knowledge about new drugs, and new indications for existing drugs, to physicians. Physicians monitoring clinical tests of new drugs also frequently spread the word about particularly effective drugs, and scientific researchers studying new drugs as parts of concurrent testing programs published articles in medical journals about their results with the new drugs. By the time the FDA approved new drugs, their sales forces had placed them on the shelves of pharmacies where they were most likely to be prescribed. During the countdown to FDA approval, the marketing departments of drug firms prepared aggressively to promote their products as soon as approval was given, and the race to the market was often quite competitive.

Virtually all (if not all) firms tightly controlled their sales forces by producing printed materials and sales aids specially designed for the types of physicians being called upon. Research on prescribing behavior indicated that although physicians had a wide range of drugs to prescribe from, their choice of product was influenced by the effectiveness of pharmaceutical detail men's presentations. All physicians also had access to a desk reference book containing indications and contraindications, dosage, etc., for each drug manufactured, by company, name, and therapeutic category (not by price).

Wholesalers do not call on physicians; wholesalers take orders from pharmacies, hospitals, or other customers. Although the detail men of some pharmaceutical firms call upon pharmacists to arrange inventories, take back returns, and discuss new products and special offers, wholesalers usually handle returned merchandise for their clients. Wholesalers also provide retail credit, warehouse drugs, remove dated materials from pharmacists' shelves, process returned merchandise, and provide twenty-four-hour-delivery service on any out-of-stock drug. By 1981 major wholesalers like McKesson-Robbins offered computerized inventory control, automatic shipments, records of patients' prescriptions, and flags warning of dangerous interactions or overdosages. Firms differed in their use of wholesalers. Eli Lilly used wholesalers exclusively (except in government sales), and American Hoescht, which had few products, also used wholesalers heavily. By contrast, Upjohn and Merck generally sold directly to pharmacies and offered wholesalers no discounts for the services they rendered in 1981.

Marketing to pharmacies is hotly competitive whether drug firms use their own sales forces or wholesalers to promote ethical pharmaceuticals. In 1981, all kinds of price breaks and deals were offered to fill pharmacists' shelves with certain brands, particularly of generic drugs. Wholesalers could be persuaded to do more than take orders if a pharmaceutical house was important to them. Sometimes wholesalers ran special promotions for manufacturers or provided special attention to their lines if firms possessed bargaining power. If they were not powerful or important, drug firms could acquire the service needed by paying higher commissions.

Some firms also had strong over-the-counter drug lines and needed continuing contact with each pharmacist to garner sales of these lines based on the advice of the pharmacist. Branded generic marketers also needed close contact with pharmacists to ensure that their brands were stocked and dispensed. Pharmaceutical firms often sold directly to hospitals, which purchased many products on the basis of price rather than other attributes. One service hospitals valued was the prepackaged unit doses some drug firms made primarily for them.

In summary, the power of the independent pharmacist was small compared with the buying power of hospitals' buying groups and large drugstore chains. Hospitals and drugstore chains extracted the greatest price breaks and special services directly from some pharmaceutical manufacturers (except those pharmaceutical firms that sold only through wholesalers).

Table 8–2
Selected Leading Pharmaceutical Companies by Therapeutic Areas in the United States

Therapeutic Areas	Pharmaceutical Companies
Analgesics	Johnson & Johnson, Lilly, and Sterling
Antibiotics	Lilly, Beecham, Merck, Schering-Plough, Squibb, Pfizer, Bristol, and Upjohn
Cardiovascular agents	Merck, Ciba-Geigy, Ayerst, Squibb, Pfizer, U.S. Vitamin, Searle, SmithKline, and Hoechst
Hormones	Merck, Schering-Plough, Upjohn, Syntex, and Squibb
Nonsteroidal anti-inflammantory agents	Merck, Upjohn, Lilly, Johnson & Johnson, Syntex, and Ciba-Geigy
Oral contraceptives	Ortho (Johnson & Johnson), Wyeth, Syntex, and Searle
Psychotherapeutics	Merck, Hoffman-LaRoche, Abbott, Squibb, Pfizer, Sandoz, and Ciba-Geigy
Respiratory agents	Key, Ciba-Geigy, Parke-Davis, and Breon
Vitamins (mostly OTC)	Lederle, Squibb, A.H. Robbins, Parke-Davis, and Upjohn

Source: Industry sources.

Competition in the Ethical-Pharmaceutical
Industry in 1981

There were over 1,000 ethical-pharmaceutical companies in 1981, and the largest of these represented only 5 percent of sales of all prescription bulk, proprietary, and over-the-counter drugs, or 7 percent of the ethicals. Table 8-2 indicates which firms led in major therapeutic categories. Direct comparisons among these firms were difficult because they did not specialize in the same product groups but in 1981 more of them were broadening their product lines through licensing arrangements.

In 1981 major research firms in ethical pharmaceuticals saw their industry as a booming one filled with great technological opportunities to exploit new products in the cardiovascular, antispasmodic, antiarthritic, and antibiotic areas (among others) as well as opportunities for new research approaches like genetic engineering. Firms leading in research and new-product development were most firmly entrenched in this industry, and there was also a second tier of firms selling specialized ethical pharmaceuticals, such as dermatological products. Both the first-tier firms, which had huge research-and-development efforts, and the second-tier firms, which had protected niches in their specialty markets, had high strategic exit barriers. The great middle part of the ethical pharmaceuticals industry was represented by affiliates of European companies (such as Organon or

Glaxo) and by smaller U.S. firms like Richardson-Merrill, Rorer, or Carter-Wallace. This group also included firms that licensed another firm's products and took them to FDA approval, such as Marion Laboratories. Finally there were the generic companies that produced ethical pharmaceuticals but did not have significant sales forces or promotional efforts. This group performed no research and development and developed no new drugs. Wholesalers like McKesson-Robbins and drugstore chains like Rexall Drug also packaged and promoted ethical pharmaceuticals. This group had the lowest overhead invested in ethical pharmaceuticals and would face the lowest strategic exit barriers in moving from their current positions.

Competitors in the pharmaceuticals industry can be described by their research efforts. One group manufactures its own drugs and is backward integrated to bulk products for the pharmaceutical products they pioneered. The others purchase bulk pharmaceuticals from Italy, Poland, Hungary, or other places and file for a quick FDA registration after a drug goes off patent in the United States. Most frequently, this latter group sells its drugs to hospitals or other customers seeking low prices.

This section groups major competitors by their breadth of vertical integration in 1981. It indicates which firms sold raw materials and how they distributed their ethical drugs. The drug manufacturers could be mapped as shown in figure 8–1 to indicate shared resources or linkages between important businesses. Merck, American Hoechst, Pfizer, Hoffman-LaRoche and American Cyanamid provided both medicinal chemicals and botanical substances for use in preparing bulk pharmaceuticals. Some firms whose products had gone off patent also sold finished pharmaceutical bulks. Lilly and Parke-Davis made gelatin capsules for the rest of the industry and firms with large sales volumes like Merck, Lilly, SmithKline, Roche, and Upjohn made their own plastic containers. In 1981 most pharmaceutical firms used a mixture of wholesaler and direct selling to distribute their products. Even a firm like Upjohn, which was very strongly entrenched in direct selling, used wholesalers to distribute approximately 20 percent of its sales volume in different markets and for emergency purposes.

Key Events in the Pharmaceuticals Industry

This section traces key events in the ethical-pharmaceutical industry, beginning with the 1960s. A summary of conditions before that time appears in the paragraphs below.

The U.S. pharmaceutical industry of the nineteenth century depended heavily upon European suppliers. Although native herbs were compounded into remedies domestically, synthesized drugs were imported. A large drug wholesaling network to import them developed early in the United States.

Breadth of Nondistribution Activities

Distribution Activities	Pharmaceutical Preparations	Medicinal Chemicals	Biologicals
Direct Distribution Primarily	Bristol Labs (Bristol Myers) Abbott Labs Cutter Wyeth Squibb Parke-Davis Upjohn Ciba	Abbott Labs Wyeth Upjohn Squibb	Cutter (Parke-Davis)
Combination Wholesale and Direct Distribution to Pharmacies	Syntex Merck Marion Labs Mead, Johnson (Bristol Myers) Schering-Plough American Cyanamid Pfizer A.H. Robins G.D. Searle Rorer	Syntex Merck American Cyanamid Pfizer	Syntex Merck Schering-Plough American Cyanamid Pfizer
Wholesale Distribution Primarily to Pharmacies	NcNeil SmithKline Sandoz American Hoechst Hoffman-LaRoche Eli Lilly Winthrop Labs Geigy Ayerst Labs	SmithKline American Hoechst Eli Lilly Hoffman-LaRoche	American Hoechst Ayerst Labs Hoffman-LaRoche

Figure 8–1. A Mapping of Selected Firms in the Ethical-Pharmaceuticals Industry, 1981

U.S. companies put drugs in medicinal form or merely resold European products until World War I, when German drug companies, which had kept their formulations and processes a secret and had exported bulk medicinals into the United States for domestic tableting and labeling operations, were cut off and U.S. subsidiaries were expropriated. U.S. companies learned to produce their own synthetic drugs when this traditional source was cut off, and thus began the massive research tradition of ethical-pharmaceutical firms.

Brand names became important after World War II when synthetic penicillins, steroids, minor tranquilizers, vaccines, and sulfanamides were discovered in rapid succession in rival laboratories and each producer strived to persuade and inform physicians of the value of their discoveries. Pfizer, which had previously been only a producer of fine chemicals, became a major pharmaceutical firm during this era.

Abbott was an early researcher in alkaloidal chemicals whose acquisitions gave it distribution companies and manufacturing capabilities. Thirty-four foreign subsidiaries sold Abbott products globally through its international distribution company, and Abbott emphasized direct selling in the United States.

In 1960 Lederle Laboratories, acquired in 1929, was one of the major producers of broad-spectrum antibiotics, vaccines, antitoxins, and serums. In 1951 American Cyanamid acquired the patent rights to an automatic gelatin-encapsulating process and machine. American Cyanamid was a manufacturer of fine chemicals, bulk chemicals, and small plastic containers. In 1960 it was one of the most highly integrated pharmaceutical firms because it supplied some chemical requirements entirely from in-house output. Downstream it was taper integrated, using both wholesalers and its own distributors.

Eli Lilly was founded in 1876 when Colonel Lilly manufactured medicines to sell through his wholesale channels. In 1960 it was the dominant supplier of insulin to diabetics. Except for veterinary products, Lilly was undiversified, but it had forged strong ties with the medical school of Indiana University in its headquarters city and launched a massive research effort there. Lilly sold exclusively through wholesalers and spent substantial sums on maintaining excellent public relations. Its sales force attended to all returns of product from pharmacies so that the wholesalers' sales representatives never were troubled by Lilly products.

Merck, Sharp & Dohme, Inc. was a combination of Merck—a manufacturer of specialty chemicals including citric acid, B_{12}, some pharmaceutical preparations, and many raw materials needed to formulate other pharmaceuticals—and of Sharp & Dohme, a manufacturing chemists establishment that had a pharmacy, some tableting and labeling operations, a research-and-development laboratory, and a field sales force calling on physicians and pharmacies. Their merger created a huge research-and-development organization and made Merck a market leader. Merck used dual distribution channels, but in 1960 relied mainly on direct sales.

Prior to 1950 Chas. Pfizer & Co., Inc. was a manufacturer and dealer in fine chemicals as Merck was, and it possessed great fermentation skills in citric acid, which enabled it to commercialize a deep-tank-fermentation process to make penicillin during World War II. Prior to this success, the firm had manufactured chemicals and sold them in bulk to processors and packagers whose labels went on the finished product. In 1950 FDA approved Pfizer's patent on Terramycin, and rather than sell it through other drug companies, Pfizer entered the pharmaceutical business itself. Pfizer primarily used wholesale distribution but made direct sales to large customers.

In 1960 Schering and Plough had not yet combined their assets. Schering was the U.S. heir of a German company, Schering A.G., whose assets were seized during World War II. Plough was a diversified drug manufacturer in 1960, operating from Memphis, Tennessee with six retail drug stores.

In 1960 Smith, Kline & French Laboratories manufactured pharmaceuticals and medical specialties. SmithKline had an aggressive direct-sales policy but occasionally used wholesalers to distribute its products.

E.R. Squibb & Sons was a part of Olin-Matheison in 1960. It produced antibiotics under its own label and sold them in bulk. Squibb had been a manufacturing chemist in 1905 and was highly integrated downstream.

The Upjohn Company produced antibiotics, steroids, nutritional, and other pharmacological products in 1960. Upjohn began as a manufacturer of patent medicine. It sold products directly to pharmacies, hospitals, and other customers and offered wholesalers no discounts from its retail prices.

It became increasingly important in the 1960s to market the drugs that were patented in previous years. Major firms developed their sales forces and diversified their product mixes as patented drugs were cross-licensed or their patents expired. The heavy emphasis on market penetration diverted funds from research and development and firms sought wider product lines through acquisition.

1962

In 1962 Lilly and Syntex extended a marketing accord about hormone products that Lilly distributed for Syntex. In their ongoing agreement Lilly contributed research funding to obtain marketing rights from Syntex, one of the newest firms to enter the pharmaceuticals business. Syntex, a Panamanian firm, was founded on the research of an eccentric scientist with knowledge about the synthesis of progesterone.

1965

The thalidomide tragedy that resulted from the drug's distribution from 1958 to 1961 had one beneficial effect on pharmaceutical research. The efficacy of all new drugs had to be tested on assorted animals at various stages of pregnancy to ensure that deformed offspring were not produced by them, and to prove the drug worked.

1966

Pharmaceutical firms acquired research laboratories, wholesaling companies, and other businesses to consolidate their positions. Research efforts had not been as productive during the 1960s and new products were needed faster than firms could produce them. Although pharmaceutical firms could not force the rate of their laboratories' success, they could diversify by acquiring firms producing other medical products.

In 1966 Schering Corporation announced a marketing arrangement with Bayer A.G., a West German-pharmaceutical firm, in which Schering would market Bayer products in the United States. The arrangement would provide a large outlet for products other than Bayer aspirin, which was purchased by Sterling Drug from the Alien Property Custodian shortly after World War I.

1968

As pharmaceutical firms continued their efforts to create new products, acquisitions of research facilities continued. McKesson-Robbins acquired Hamilton-Schmidt, a small surgical firm, Upjohn purchased Laboratory Procedures, and Abbott bought Courtland Labs in 1968. These acquisitions were part of a trend for pharmaceutical manufacturers to acquire laboratories, service firms, and makers of related health-care products.

In 1968 Olin-Matheison spun off Squibb from direct corporate supervision and prepared to merge it with Beech-Nut Life Savers, Inc. Olin Matheison, a chemicals firm, did not supply Squibb with sizable amounts of bulk or fine chemicals for pharmaceutical preparations.

1970

In 1970 Schering Corporation and Plough, Inc. agreed to merge. Schering's major pharmaceutical business was concentrated in prescription drugs, including antibiotics, and Plough's main emphasis was on nonprescription drugs, cosmetics, and household products. Their combination created a diversified firm which earned approximately 69 percent of its revenues from pharmaceutical products.

1974

Many important patents expired in the early 1970s, and the consumerist movement increased pressures for physicians to prescribe generic drugs rather than specify a particular manufacturer's products. These factors made the market chaotic and consumed cash that could have been used in research. When firms suffered excess plant capacity, they often filled it by producing other types of drug products whose patents had expired. Thus the market's structure changed from one of specialized firms serving medical niches of the market to broad-line firms seeking to serve many therapeutic markets.

In 1974 Merck announced plans to construct a methyldopa facility in Pennsylvania. Methyldopa was the active ingredient in aldomet, a Merck antihypertensive drug prescribed to treat high blood pressure. SmithKline had also started a joint venture to make methyldopa to meet its chemical needs, but in 1972 its intended partner dropped out, leaving SmithKline to find a new one. A.H. Robbins offered to purchase SmithKline's participation in 1974.

1976

In 1976 Merck and Alza Corporation agreed to a program of joint research on new cardiovascular and anti-inflammatory pharmaceuticals The resulting products were to be marketed by Merck under worldwide royalty licenses from Alza. The arrangement also provided for Merck to purchase 3.5 percent of Alza's common stock.

In November 1976 SmithKline's Tagamet ulcer medicine was introduced. The drug healed peptic ulcers, making surgery unnecessary in many cases, and it became one of the most stunningly successful products in the history of U.S. business. Prior to the introduction of Tagamet, SmithKline had been a sluggish innovator; its laboratories were almost bereft of new products in the late 1960s. Tagamet was so successful initially that SmithKline's manufacturing capacity was inadequate to accommodate demand. Much of the manufacturing had to be farmed out to other chemical companies. To penetrate Japan, SmithKline arranged a joint venture with Fujisawa Pharmaceutical in which its partner manufactured and marketed Tagamet.

1977

In 1977 Lilly began construction of a $24 million parenteral plant to manufacture insulin, anticancer drugs, and several of the firm's other injectable products including antibiotics. The new facility was built in compliance with federal regulations concerning sterile block compounds and included barriers between levels of sterility, as had been suggested by researchers at recent conferences about safety procedures in microorganic research. The FDA's manufacturing-practice guidelines were costing other pharmaceutical firms millions of dollars to comply. Lilly's new complex went beyond these new federal rules.

In 1977 Abbott and Takeda Chemical Industries of Japan formed a joint venture to develop and market new pharmaceuticals in the United States and Canada. Early research projects included antibiotics, sedatives, and antihypertensives that had been already introduced in Japan and other markets.

Britain's top retail drug chain and major pharmaceutical manufacturer, Boots Company, Ltd., sought a foothold in the U.S. market by purchasing Riker. Previously, Boots' antirheumatic drug Ibupiotin had been marketed there with great success by Upjohn. Antimonopoly laws prevented Boots from building a chain of drug stores like the 1,250 retail outlets it had in the United Kingdom, and Boots was seeking growth opportunities. It used price-cutting to capture shelf space.

In 1977 Ciba-Geigy acquired Alza Corporation, and the two firms formed product-development and marketing agreements. Alza had limited penetration of its products in the United States, and Ciba-Geigy agreed to market drugs for it there. Alza had developed two drug-delivery systems that could be used under the terms of the acquisition to place many Ciba-Geigy products in the market. One such delivery system was a flexible-membrane unit placed under the eyelid and programmed to continuously release a precise dose of medication for the treatment of glaucoma. The other delivery system was a similar unit placed in the uterus for birth-control purposes.

In 1978 Squibb announced its Squibb Pharmachoice line of high-quality generic products. The original four products were offered in a variety of formulations and were priced below many branded generics. Squibb offered pharmacists guaranteed prices throughout 1978, a liberal returns policy, and dependable sales-force service.

1979

In 1979 Squibb formed a new chemical division to supply raw materials, intermediates, and finished chemicals to the pharmaceutical plants of Squibb's worldwide operations. The new division marketed any excess chemical capacity and coordinated with other Squibb divisions to sell or exchange chemical expertise.

In 1979 SmithKline sued Premo Pharmaceutical Laboratories, a manufacturer of generic drugs, for patent infringement on a diuretic and hypertension product, Dyazide, whose patent did not expire until March 1980.

Premo was charged with marketing a substance in capsules that was extremely similar to the drug protected by SmithKline's patent.

1980

In 1980 SmithKline acquired Humphrey Instruments and Allergan Pharmaceuticals. Allergan produced drugs and solutions used in treating eye ailments, and Humphrey made instruments for ophthalmologists and optometrists. SmithKline licensed a cephalosporin from Fujisawa to introduce in the United States. It also expected to file a New Drug Application (NDA) for its oral antirheumatic gold compound.

In 1980 Premo Pharmaceutical Laboratories sought a buyer for its five-week-old-chlorpropamide new drug application because it was prevented by Pfizer from marketing it. In addition to the patent challenge that the Premo-Pfizer consent decree made moot, there was the issue of look-alike formulations that resembled other firms' branded products. Newark's federal court ordered Premo not to market its product in a dosage form that might deceive customers into concluding that the drug was Pfizer's.

In 1980 Premo Pharmaceutical Laboratories was prohibited from producing, advertising, selling, or offering to sell any product containing the active ingredient Libfax, which was patented and produced by Hoffman-LaRoche. Moreover the court ordered Premo not to copy Roche's Librax trademark or make other unprivileged imitations of the physical appearance of Roche's drug. Premo liquidated its assets in 1981.

In 1980 Key Pharmaceuticals was one of the tiniest drug companies and had a narrowly focused strategy. Key never took on the expense of developing new pharmaceuticals. Rather, Key emphasized research on delivering existing drugs to the body more effectively. Key Pharmaceuticals was licensing large pharmaceutical firms to market its products because it recognized that the expense of launching its own sales force was too much for such a small firm to undertake. Mitsubishi Chemical provided funding for product development in exchange for 10 percent of Key's common stock. They also agreed to joint research efforts in which Key would sell (or license) their drugs in the West and Mitsubishi would sell them in Asia.

1981

In May 1981 the FDA enacted a new policy intended to speed the introduction of cheap copies of drugs developed by research companies when it approved the sale of three generic drugs. Until this decision, firms seeking to introduce copies of drugs developed by others had to repeat costly research on animals and humans to prove their formulations' efficacy before obtaining FDA approval.

In 1981 Ciba-Geigy of Basel, Switzerland sold pharmaceuticals produced on the firm's three properties in Switzerland. Its joint ventures included Toms River Chemical (with Sandoz) and several in veterinary products and research. In April 1981 Ciba-Geigy bought Sandoz's interest in the Toms River Chemical venture and agreed to supply Sandoz's needs for the next three years. Both companies reported that this new arrangement ensured more flexible use of their U.S. production capacity. Ciba-Geigy transferred production of its sterile-injectable products to contractors in 1981. New FDA requirements about processing of these products made their in-house production too costly for Ciba-Geigy to justify.

In 1981 Dow acquired Merrell Pharmaceuticals from Richardson-Merrell. Dow produced a line of ethical pharmaceuticals and biologicals, but it was primarily known as a producer of bulk chemicals. Dow's pharmaceutical preparations were tableted, packaged, and labeled by its customers in the United States.

In 1981 E.I. du Pont de Nemours made both chemical and pharmaceutical bulk products and was trying to enter the pharmaceuticals business as a broadly integrated firm. Du Pont had excellent lab facilities and research capabilities. It possessed excellent toxicology resources to track the effects of its drugs. Du Pont had purchased firms that brought it closer to pharmaceutical marketing, such as Indo and supplier firms like New England Nuclear, and it constructed a large life-sciences-research facility.

In 1981 Roche postponed building a chemical-intermediates plant in Freeport, Texas because its forecast of medium-term demand could be met more cheaply at current interest rates by enlarging existing plants. Hoffman-LaRoche had preferred to use direct distribution channels for its U.S. pharmaceutical products until computerized-pharmacy-inventory systems became more sophisticated. By the end of 1981 Roche had changed its distribution system to wholesalers only. Consistent with this change in marketing policy, Hoffman-LaRoche formed a new marketing unit to consolidate and streamline its five existing marketing factions. Roche was also working with Genentech on the production of human interferon using recombinant-DNA techniques.

In 1981 Lilly undertook a larger clinical effort than some of its competitors had done. It maintained its own assay facilities, a very cumbersome process of substantiating the therapeutic validity of a particular product, and it forged a relationship with a teaching hospital which permitted Lilly to do its own clinical testing. Replicating that advantage in 1981, had another company attempted to do so, would have been costly and difficult in most geographic locations.

In 1981 Merck entered a research-and-marketing agreement with Astra,

Sweden's largest pharmaceutical firm in 1981. Under this arrangement, Merck developed a number of drugs discovered by Astra for the United States market. Although Merck would market the drug initially, a specially formed and jointly owned firm was expected to assume marketing duties after about ten years.

Novo Laboratories was the U.S. subsidiary of Novo Industri of Denmark, a prominent producer of insulin and industrial enzymes. In the U.S. enzymes were 50 percent of Novo's total revenues, and insulin was 75 percent of Novo's pharmaceutical sales. Although Novo used its huge fermenters in North Carolina to produce industrial enzymes most of the time, it could make antibiotics in them when enzyme demand was low. As the leading biotechnology firm in the world, Novo was particularly well-suited to commercialize production of genetically engineered products. In 1981 Novo formed an arrangement with Squibb, the second largest U.S. marketer of insulin, that helped it penetrate the U.S. market. Novo produced the insulin crystals marketed in parenteral solution by Squibb, and it marketed an insulin of even-higher purity under its own brand name, representing five percent of the U.S. market.

In 1981 Pfizer expanded its major research facility in Groton for the discovery and development of new drugs and work in biotechnology. One of its major growth targets was cardiovascular products, and Pfizer licensed drugs developed overseas to enlarge its product mix. For example, Cefobid, a cephalosporin antibiotic, was developed in Japan and Procardice, for angina pectoris, was licensed from Bayer A.G. of West Germany for four years.

In 1981 SmithKline had joint ventures with Fujisawa Pharmaceutical of Japan and with Alza to develop systems of drug administration that were rate controlled. SmithKline was funding the research and marketing the output. In May 1981 SmithKline made a licensing-and-supply agreement with Key Pharmaceuticals, obtained worldwide marketing rights for an Italian drug to treat congestive heart problems, and a license from Toyama Chemical to produce an antispasmodic drug. In July 1981 SmithKline and Fujisawa formed a joint venture to test-market pharmaceutical products in the United States. SmithKline's 1981 research venture with Allergan subsidiary included a project to apply histamine-blocker knowledge, gained from Tagamet's development, to applications in eye disease. Allergan had purchased Tubi Lux, an Italian ophthalmic firm, in 1980 to supplement its mix of eye products and strengthen its distribution system.

In 1981 SmithKline merged with Beckman Instruments, a firm that made medical diagnostics and instruments used by chemical and pharmaceutical companies to perform genetic engineering and other molecular-biology research. These instruments included an amino-acid analyzer, peptide synthesizer and sequencer, but not the so-called gene machine that routinized the synthesis of oligonucleotides. (See chapter 9.)

In 1981 Upjohn manufactured the pharmaceutical chemicals needed for its own products and sold some bulk chemicals and active ingredients to others. Although Upjohn mounted a massive research effort in-house, it also licensed new products developed by others.

At the end of 1981, competition from nondrug companies, such as Dow Chemical, E.I. du Pont de Nemours, and Monsanto, loomed on the horizon. Each had acquired a minority interest in genetic-engineering firms. Although the cost of developing marketing channels and credibility in the medical community was substantial, firms like these were more likely to become pharmaceutical firms if they had a way to make superior products. In 1982 Proctor & Gamble acquired Norwich-Eaton, the maker of prescription and over-the-counter-drug products. Norwich's ethical-pharmaceuticals line was not impressive but the entry of Proctor & Gamble could be a significant change in the industry.

Analysis of Strategies for Vertical Integration in Pharmaceuticals

Section one described the structure of the ethical-pharmaceuticals industry and section two described key events in the industry from 1960 to 1981. This section analyzes the patterns of vertical behavior sketched above and compares the predictions of the strategy framework with the outcomes observed in 1981. The structure of the ethical-pharmaceuticals industry was established, but changes were occurring to make the industry's structure potentially more volatile than it had been in the past. Changes in the registration requirements for off-patent drugs by new firms had been simplified, cross-licensing arrangements with overseas firms had increased competition where it had formerly been tranquil, and the rate of technological change seemed to be accelerating. According to the framework proposed in chapter 2, in this industry the steady demand and rising population suggested that firms could afford to be as broadly integrated as their individual sales volumes justified and that they could sustain many stages per integrated activity; high degrees of internal integration would occur upstream, where it seemed crucial to be so integrated while patents were in force, and downstream to direct selling outlets as needed to ensure firms' products received aggressive promotion and frequent consideration; however, joint ventures or other leveraging business arrangements would be less likely to occur in areas of strategic importance to firms.

Phase of Industry Development

The structure of the ethical pharmaceuticals industry was well-established by 1981 and few firms entered except through cross-licensing arrangements. Upstream vertical integration was high in 1981, but the industry did not begin either broadly or highly integrated. When the U.S. ethical-pharmaceuticals industry was embryonic, pharmaceutical activities were limited to tableting and labeling. The principal move to vertically integrate structures came with the synthesis of penicillin and subsequent sulfa drugs after World War II. This was when the industry's structure became more integrated upstream and downstream because research and development and communication with physicians were so important to drug firms' corporate strategies that they could not be entrusted to outsiders.

There were elements of great risk in the ethical pharmaceuticals industry, nevertheless, demand for ethical pharmaceuticals was clearly established and was increasing, especially as medication became a viable alternative to surgery. Greater degrees of internal integration could be tolerated because demand was not sensitive to disposable income, penalties for excess capacity were not high, and demand was not markedly cyclical.

Because demand was stable and drugs were a necessity, the ethical-pharmaceuticals industry could undertake as much vertical integration as firms deemed necessary. New, patentable drugs were needed at a rate faster than most firms' laboratories could satisfy; hence cross-licensing arrangements and formal joint ventures were undertaken to increase the rate of technological change. In this industry, firms integrated late, often defensively, and as a natural progression of business activities. Other firms were often willing to perform the needed tasks, firms did not need to reach ultimate consumers (only their physicians), and absolute manufacturing-cost advantages were not relevant in an industry such as this one where research-and-development expenses represented the greatest cost of operations. The chief reason for firms' early integrations was to improve product quality by making the pharmaceuticals they wholesaled that had previously been supplied by others.

Volatile Industry Structure

Major ethical pharmaceuticals firms raced each other to bring new drugs to FDA approval first, and competition was on the basis of product innovation. Among the tableting and labeling firms, price competition was fierce because their products were commodities, but many firms were vertically integrated in both groups.

The most important attributes of ethical pharmaceuticals were their established therapeutic values and their side effects. Physicians were highly sensitive to these differences and made purchase decisions for patients who were less sophisticated about ethical drugs. In addition to being highly differentiated, the active ingredients in ethical pharmaceuticals were very complex to synthesize. Several trade secrets were used in synthesizing active ingredients that were not articulated in their patents. Given the meticulous precision of manufacturing and rapid rate of product innovation required to compete effectively, ethical pharmaceutical firms needed control over upstream, bulk pharmaceutical production.

Ethical-pharmaceutical firms traditionally synthesized the active ingredients needed in their patented drugs, and less frequently made their bulk chemicals, because they could not consume the entire output of a bulk chemicals plant. It was very attractive to chemical firms to be forward integrated from bulk chemicals to pharmaceuticals, however, because pharmaceutical formulation added great value to their chemicals. Hence firms like Dow Chemical and du Pont were eager to enter the ethical pharmaceuticals business.

Once prescribed, customer-switching barriers for a particular ethical pharmaceutical were high. Moreover, busy physicians were likely to remember and prescribe the first pharmaceutical of a particular therapeutic class, unless subsequent drugs possessed noteworthy attributes. Firms that had generic drug lines or over-the-counter products to sell, as well as patented drugs, often kept direct contact with drugstores to improve their line's likelihood of being used for generic prescription purposes. Firms without generic lines were more likely to use wholesalers unless their lines were quite wide.

The efficient scale of pharmaceutical-bulk and dosage-formulation plants was substantially lower than for upstream chemical plants, and interconnection did not occur. Active ingredients could often be purchased on the open market or from overseas producers, and local dosage-formulation firms could prepare tablets, capsules, or other pharmaceutical forms for a manufacturer that was short of its own tableting capacity. Vertical control of outsiders' production facilities was practical and made economic sense where secrecy was not a concern. But sometimes firms would *not* sell their excess bulk capacity to competitors when patents had expired because the knowledge of how to synthesize their active ingredients effectively and the experience-curve economies they enjoyed in making them were the only significant entry barriers that existed in this portion of the industry.

The research portion of the ethical-pharmaceuticals industry was not volatile in 1981 because there was no price-cutting and profits were not low. Firms had adequate access to physicians in a stable environment, making success easier to achieve for them. Product differentiation was enhanced by this vertical control. Downstream, the wholesaling versus direct-sales decision was influenced by the breadth of a firm's product line and the types of physicians it had to contact in promoting its drugs. In the generic portion of the ethical-pharmaceuticals business, prices fluctuated as firms tried to buy distribution, and profits were low. Their products were commodities and offered few dimensions for promoting them, except twenty-four-hour delivery, packaging, and other services. These firms tended not to be backward integrated as was fitting because their environments were more volatile.

Bargaining Power

Ethical-pharmaceutical manufacturers controlled the most important activities connected with their operations in-house, because they believed these activities were too sensitive to entrust to outsiders. Firms used their in-house medical-detail-sales forces to obtain market intelligence about therapeutic problems with their drugs. In summary, research-oriented pharmaceutical houses used outsiders for tasks that were less critical to their operations, when suppliers or distributors were readily available and eager to serve, and when a substantial educational effort was not needed. Patents gave the pharmaceutical houses power over fine-chemical and pharmaceutical-bulk producers that they did not exert except in emergencies. Brand names gave their patented drugs bargaining power among retailers because physicians preferred certain drugs over others. Yet pharmaceutical firms were highly integrated upstream and downstream in their contacts with physicians because it was most appropriate to their corporate strategies to do so.

Strategy Goals

In 1981 pharmaceutical firms were spending massive sums on research, creating joint ventures and licensing arrangements, and using other methods to extend their therapeutic categories and accelerate their rates of product introductions. Among research firms, this activity was crucial to future well-being because their patents gave them quasi-monopolies of limited durations and price levels in the generic-drug market were dropping quickly.

   Among the research-oriented firms, near-term profitability was less crucial than long-term product development. The drug firms were very conservative in asserting their claims for the hopes of a new technology and emphasized the need for careful testing and consideration of economics before introducing new drugs. By contrast, near-term profitability was a goal the tableting and labeling firms had to heed very carefully because they had

no long-term security in their 1981 strategic postures and could only formulate the older pharmaceutical products. According to the strategy
framework, firms seeking technological leadership would seek integration
in the functions most critical to their long-term success, but tableting and
labeling firms would not.

Depending upon their objectives, parent firms could enhance or discourage vertical relationships among business units in the ethical-
pharmaceutical industry. In this industry high degrees of internal integration were encouraged and corporations were willing to invest in drug
research and to tolerate high degrees of excess capacity upstream in vertically linked units.

Many corporations that were in the ethical-pharmaceuticals business
were also in the nonprescription-drug, hospital-supply, veterinary, and
other health-care businesses. Synergies in product development and toxicology were substantial between these related businesses. Pharmaceutical
houses also exploited synergies between product research and cosmetics to
develop skin-care products with greater efficacy than simple lubricants and
colored waxes. Where firms maintained a sizable research effort with in-
house pharmacologists, toxicologists, and other specialized personnel, these
other businesses presented projects for scientists to undertake when ethical-
pharmaceutical volume was low. The capability to produce active ingredients in-house and formulate them into ointments or other dosage forms
also created synergies in gearing up to production in these other businesses,
since the parent corporation gained a knowledge of manufacturing complexities (and their solutions) from its in-house scientific and manufacturing experts.

In summary, parent corporations were willing to subsidize pharmaceutical projects and encourage intrafirm trading because the outlook
for the ethical pharmaceuticals business looked good. Moreover, high
degrees of internal integration were needed to achieve their business units'
objectives of therapeutic leadership.

The Need for Vertical Integration

By 1981 the principal advantages of vertical integration were competitive
rather than economic. The nature of ethical-pharmaceutical production
reduced opportunities for cost savings because ingredients were sent from
plant to plant (sometimes even out to subcontractors for a processing step
and then back again). The most significant advantage to vertical integration
in the ethical-pharmaceuticals industry was in product differentiation.
Being forward and backward integrated enabled firms to exploit technological changes in this industry faster. They could control product quality

and material flows better, in order to create more value for the bulk chemicals they purchased and to rearrange their assets when a different research thrust was needed.

Nonmultinational manufacturers of generic pharmaceuticals found backward integration costly to achieve, however. Generic firms' costs of manufacturing and quality assurance were being squeezed on one side, while their prices were being eroded on the other side. The net effect was lower profits for generic firms and reduced competitive vitality for firms that could not generate enough cash for new pharmaceutical products. Thus, as pharmaceutical firms' patents expired and their mix of products increasingly became generic, lesser degrees of internal integration were appropriate.

Strategy Alternatives and Performance

The strategy model distinguished between ownership and the degree of internal integration firms engaged in; firms may have owned all, some, or none of the adjacent firms supplying goods and services, and transferred all, some, or none of their needs internally. Moreover, firms differed in the breadth and stages of their integrations. In ethical pharmaceuticals, firms could be backward integrated to produce bulk pharmaceuticals, intermediate chemicals, and bulk chemicals. They could also make plastic bottles or gelatin capsules. They could supply active ingredients to other firms, or they could tablet and label pharmaceuticals under contract or for their own account. Downstream, firms with patented drugs could employ medical-detail-sales representatives, a sales force to contact hospitals and pharmacies, and wholesalers. They could market drugs developed by others under a marketing agreement, or they could license others to market their products.

Many firms were fully integrated with regard to research, development and clinical testing, bulk pharmaceuticals, and medical-sales representatives. They provided most of their requirements for materials and services in-house, because they desired to protect their proprietary processes from espionage and required tight quality control at all stages. Full integration was acceptable in this industry because price competition was not fierce and diseconomies were not significant if adjacent stages were unbalanced.

Some firms used taper integration to obtain off-patent bulk ingredients and distribute their ethical pharmaceuticals because the raw materials and wholesaler services they needed were cheap and abundant. It was more convenient to use outsiders than to build or invest in the additional capacity that would be required if outsiders were not used when the ingredients or services in question were not central to firms' corporate strategies. Finally, using outsiders' research and development to supplement in-house activities was appropriate when firms were not adequately productive in-house.

The number of stages of activity undertaken was determined by the product's characteristics, the nature of demand, and the mission of the ethical-pharmaceutical unit relative to adjacent businesses. American Cyanamid, du Pont, and Dow were chemical firms that could supply commodity chemicals, intermediates, fine chemicals, and pharmaceutical bulks, if shipping costs were favorable. Frequently the building-block chemicals used to synthesize pharmaceutical bulks were purchased from nearby vendors instead because very-small volumes were needed to make pharmaceuticals. Firms valued their upstream linkages, however, and during the period under observation Schering-Plough acquired the capabilities to become more basic in the chemicals it prepared. (Schering-Plough was also preparing to build a fermentation capability for its interferon research described in the following chapter.)

The breadth of integration—the number of different activities which were integrated—was determined by demand traits and how firms competed. In ethical pharmaceuticals, Merck and Lilly were among the most broadly integrated firms. They made fine chemicals, bulk pharmaceuticals, dosage-form pharmaceuticals and plastic bottles. (Lilly made gelatin capsules for the rest of the industry, as well.) Parke-Davis, Pfizer, Abbott, Lederle, and SmithKline offered generic pharmaceuticals in addition to their patented-pharmaceutical lines.

The form of vertical relationship indicated the amount of asset exposure and flexibility the venture possessed. In highly uncertain or volatile environments, where the performance of vertically integrated firms was highly sensitive to fluctuations in demand, ownership forms involving lesser amounts of asset exposure (such as forms of quasi-integration) were used to reduce the variability of returns and increase firms' strategic flexibilities. The form of integration used was determined by firms' bargaining power and their corporate-strategy objectives.

Several joint ventures and licensing arrangements existed in the ethical-pharmaceuticals industry in order to extend product lines and achieve entry in new markets. Astra and Organon, from Europe, had marketing agreements with U.S. firms. Marion Laboratories had licenses to develop a Japanese anti-ulcer medicine and a calcium blocker. Upjohn licensed Japanese antibiotics (as did Pfizer, Abbott, and Lederle). SmithKline formed a joint-venture company. (Fujisawa-SmithKline marketed the antibiotics Cefizox, Ancef, and Kefzol. These last two antibiotics were also licensed by Fujisawa Pharmaceutical to Lilly.) Warner-Lambert licensed an antiasthmatic and Lilly licensed an additional antibiotic from Shionogi.

Several pharmaceutical companies had either equity investments or marketing arrangements with genetic-engineering firms to exploit any breakthroughs made using recombinant-DNA techniques as a tool. These firms included Abbott, Johnson & Johnson, Schering-Plough, Novo, Alza, Lilly, Hoffman-LaRoche, Bristol-Myers, and American Cyanamid. As was the case with the cross-licensing arrangements listed above, pharmaceutical firms intended to exploit their medical-detail-sales forces' access to 450,000 to 500,000 U.S. physicians.

Ethical pharmaceuticals was a vibrant industry in 1981 and its structure was still evolving as new medical discoveries spurred firms to deliver improved pharmaceutical products in more-efficient ways. Although the industry's structure was still mutable, it was more established than others where vertical integration was less uniformly in use. A discussion of these highly integrated firms is germane because they obtained relatively stable access to raw materials and distribution while achieving their objectives in technological leadership and high profit margins. Ethical pharmaceuticals was one of the most broadly and highly integrated industries studied; it was also one of the most profitable.

Tableting and labeling firms, like Premo Pharmaceuticals, Bolar Pharmaceuticals, and Elkins-Sinn, were not backward integrated to raw materials because bulk pharmaceuticals could be purchased and formulated easier than producing small quantities of the many active ingredients needed in-house. At their smaller investment levels, many tableting and labeling firms performed well.

In 1979 the following firms obtained more than 50 percent of their revenues from off-patent drugs: Parke-Davis, Abbott, Squibb, Wyeth, Pfizer, Burroughs-Wellcome, and Ciba-Geigy. Of these, Pfizer was most broadly integrated; it pursued a generic-line strategy and was quite successful overseas. Burroughs-Wellcome and Ciba-Geigy imported their bulk pharmaceuticals from their overseas plants, and several firms sought to improve their cash flows and balance of patented to nonpatented sales by licensing products from Japanese firms. They recognized a need to replenish their arsenals of patented drugs in 1981.

In 1979 the following firms obtained most of their revenues from patented drugs: Hoffman-LaRoche, Merck, Upjohn, Ayerst, Schering-Plough, and SmithKline. This group led in antibiotics, cardiovascular agents, hormones, nonsteroidal anti-inflammatory agents, and psychotherapeutics. Merck was most broadly integrated and enjoyed the largest pharmaceutical-sales volumes. Upjohn enjoyed the highest return on assets, and this group's five-year-average return on assets was slightly higher than the lower-innovation group's return.

In summary, broad and high degrees of integration could be advantageous within the ethical-pharmaceuticals industry, but there did not seem to be much advantage to being vertically integrated in generic-pharmaceutical manufacture because the bulk chemicals and pharmaceuticals could be produced more cheaply overseas. Firms varied in the direction of their historical movement to a vertically integrated structure. Dr. Upjohn began as a producer of patent medicines and Colonel Lilly began by formulating dosage pharmaceuticals for wholesaling. Pfizer began as a fermentation specialist, moving downstream like the European-pharmaceutical firms. McKesson-Robbins, the wholesaler, formulated pharmaceuticals to capture more value-added for its private line of branded generic drugs. All of these firms moved successfully into vertically integrated structures.

References

Bureau of the Census, U.S. Department of Commerce. *Current Industrial Reports*. MA-Z8G (80)-1 "Pharmaceutical preparations, except biologicals." 1980, pp. 2-6.

"Innovative Japanese Drugs Move into the U.S." *Business Week,* May 10, 1982, pp. 150-155.

King, Donald C. *Marketing Prescription Drugs.* Ann Arbor: University of Michigan, Bureau of Business Research, no. 56, 1968.

Magnet, Myron. "The Scramble for the Next Superdrug." *Fortune,* October 19, 1981, pp. 94-112.

Mahoney, Tom. *The Merchants of Life: An Account of the American Pharmaceutical Industry.* New York: Harper & Row, 1959.

"Pharmaceutical Manufacturers Consider Promoting Brand Name Prescription Drugs to Patients as Well as Physicians." *American Drug,* April, 1981, pp. 13, 96 + .

Schwartz, Harry. "Medical Costs and the Drug Industry." *Wall Street Journal,* April 21, 1980, p. 23.

"Segmented Marketing Approach Spells Lower Promotional Costs, Increased Market Share for Abbott Laboratories' Pharmaceutical Products Division." *Product Marketing,* December, 1977, pp. 1, 26 + .

Urbanski, Al. "New Era in Drug Marketing." *Sales and Marketing Management,* March 15, 1982, pp. 37-40.

Walker, Hugh D. *Market Power and Price Levels in the Ethical Drug Industry.* Bloomington, Indiana: Indiana University Press, 1971.

Wiener, Harr., M.D. *Generic Drugs: Safety and Effectiveness.* New York: Pfizer Inc., 1973.

Also helpful were corporate annual reports and financial statements of the firms described in chapter 8 and conversations with nine ethical-pharmaceutical firms, one drug wholesaler, and one chemical firm.

9

Strategies for Vertical Integration in Genetic Engineering

Recombinant-DNA technology (genetic engineering) is a generic technology that can be applied to the development of many product lines in diverse industrial settings. It is used to modify microorganisms already capable of forming commercially desirable products or to design microorganisms that normally would not form desired products, such as vaccines and hormones. The technology was extremely young in 1981, but it had already become a favorite of the stock market, and for a brief period corporate sponsors, venture capitalists, and private backers were all eager to invest in the scientific breakthroughs that they assumed were very near. Some observers likened the technology's potential for revolutionizing industries to that of the microprocessor (see chapter 10).

By late 1981 the industry was chaotic. Over 150 genetic engineering firms had been formed; another 300 to 400 firms had introduced products directly related to the industry. *Yet there were no commercial products.* Many firms were expected to fall by the wayside and investors were growing impatient for quick results in an industry where years of research were needed. Although the rules of competition were not yet clear, some strategies appeared to be better suited for commerical success than others as embryonic firms set out to create their niches in an industry that would someday be overrun by large chemical and pharmaceutical firms.

A Description of Genetic Engineering

The Product

In 1981, genetic engineering was a tool used in the laboratory to synthesize improved versions of existing products, to synthesize more rapidly products that normally had long gestation periods, and to synthesize substances in such limited supply that their attributes could not be fully studied. Ultimately, it would be used to make existing products using a technology that some day would be cheaper than current methods. Commercial applications

Background research was provided by Stan Herman with special assistance from F. Eberstadt & Co., Inc. of New York.

seemed years away in 1981, and although biomedical applications, such as the creation of interferon in the laboratory, were in the limelight then, the most immediate applications of genetic engineering would occur in the agriculture and chemicals industries in costly products such as insulin and proteins. Genetic engineering would not be used to make products that could be made more cheaply using current processes.

Genetic engineering (or gene splicing) is used to alter the genes of living things by transferring them from one organism—an animal or plant— to a much-simpler organism (a bacterium or yeast) and persuading it to produce a specific protein. Like other operations involving industrial enzymes, after the gene transfer is achieved, the resulting organism has to be manufactured (usually in large-scale-fermentation processes) and the desired product has to be recovered from the fermented broth. This manufacturing process had not been perfected in 1981 and was very expensive due to the highly sterile conditions required in the factory. The product in genetic engineering is a chemical—either simple or very complex—and genetic engineering enables scientists to create products that would be impossible to synthesize or produce using other biotechnology processes.

Basis for Product Differentiation

Firms that can both cause laboratory specimens to express a desired product and manufacture sizable quantities of it at lower costs than current methods possess a very-desirable expertise. Few firms had made the transition from laboratory to factory in 1981. The principal means of product differentiation was the development of patentable products and processes. Trade secrets were also keys to technological differentiation.

Producing an organism discovered in the laboratory was very expensive in 1981. Fermentation incurred high inventorying costs, and distillation of the last ten percent of liquid in a broth, for example, required a large amount of heat. Therefore the recovery process had to be economical or the product of genetic engineering could not be commercialized. Therefore, fermentation and recovery skills were also ways to differentiate one firm from another.

Markets

When genetic engineering became economically feasible as a technology, it had applications in pharmaceutical, agricultural, food processing, energy, and chemical markets. Expensive proteins would be among the first products synthesized. In the pharmaceutical industry, the major project categories included vitamins, steroid hormones, peptide hormones (for control of metabolic disorders—for example, insulin and human-growth hormone), other proteins (therapeutics—for example, interferon and human serum albumin), and gene preparations (for control of hereditary disorders—for example, sickle-cell anemia). In agriculture, the major product categories that could use genetic-engineering technology included vitamins (feed additives) and peptide hormones (growth promoters—for example, bovine-growth hormone).

In 1981 genetic engineering was a powerful biological tool for the researcher but there were no factories for manufacturing genetically engineered products. The only products commercially available in 1981 were a European vaccine against diarrhea in piglets and a human insulin that was subject to approval by the FDA. (Traditional production costs for insulin were $125 per kilogram in 1981.) Interferon could also be a promising product for genetic-engineering techniques. Made from human blood, interferon had previously been too expensive to test for effectiveness in treating cancer. Using genetic-engineering techniques to produce it in volume, researchers discovered there were at least thirteen different types of interferon, each requiring further study to ascertain whether any of them was effective against cancer.

In agriculture, genetic engineering could enable scientists to develop seeds faster than traditional hybrid techniques, when the technology was perfected. Researchers also hoped to introduce genetic variability into crops so that they were disease resistant, without decreasing their yields. This attribute was ten years away from commericalization in 1981, however, because the new seeds required field testing before farmers—who tend to be very conservative—would purchase them.

In the chemicals industry, two scenarios were feasible, depending on the nature of future investments in genetic-engineering applications: one, the industry could develop a subgroup whose structure was like that of the specialty-chemicals business, or two, genetic engineering could lead to a commercializable process that offered lower production costs for many basic as well as specialty chemicals. In the latter scenario, the energy-intensive, multistep reactions used in the capital-intensive chemicals industry of 1981 could give way to a new synthetic-plastics industry, for example, that was not based on petroleum.

In summary, many applications for genetic-engineering techniques could exist. In most cases, the key to commercializing new processes was their need to be significantly better than existing methods.

Suppliers

Manufacturing genetically engineered products was expensive and materials intensive. The gestation periods required in fermentation made capital costs substantial, as well. The principal raw materials were enzymes and nucleic acids used to manipulate pieces of DNA, food for the microorganisms, and mechanical devices (or gene machines). Furthermore, the gene-transfer laboratory required a substantial investment in scientific personnel.

Enzymes are complex-natural-protein triggers, or catalysts, that cells manufacture to set chemical reactions in motion. Restriction enzymes (which act like a chemical scissors) are a specialty enzyme product purchased in small volumes on the basis of quality rather than price. The purchase decision is made by scientists at their benches in most cases. Other times enzymes are made in-house. The raw materials that genetic-engineering firms produced in-house in 1981 were essentially standardized materials that were not high in value-added. With time, genetic-engineering firms hoped these standardized enzymes and biologicals could be sold by others, leaving their laboratories free to synthesize materials that were more complex and offered higher value-added.

In 1981, restriction enzymes were supplied by several firms, including New England Bio Labs, Bethesda Research Laboratories, Biotec, Calbiochem-Behring (American Hoechst), and Enzo Biochem. The leading producers of industrial enzymes included Novo Industri, Miles Laboratories, G.B. Fermentation Industries, and twenty-four others, and their operations were geared to carload quantities. Thus, some raw materials were not available commerically and had to be made in-house. Cetus, for example, once considered marketing the enzymes it had developed for its own use, but found it was the world's largest user of them.

The media for enzyme fermentation are carbohydrates or proteins. Waste molasses obtained from harvesting Caribbean sugar cane is one inexpensive source of feed.

DNA sequencers and gene synthesizers (gene machines) provide solid supports on which the growing stands of DNA are deposited, followed by attachment of the first nucleotides of the desired sequence. (At this point the chain is very sticky and a protective group is added to prevent undesired reactions—something like putting corks on the ends of a pocket full of fish hooks to prevent them from being tangled.) Controlled by a computer program, the machine pumps the correct sequence of chemically modified nucleotides onto the support, where it is linked to the previous group, and the protecting group is removed, forming the correct DNA strand. Biochemists are needed to purify the completed DNA from DNA pieces (which is not an easy task), but during synthesis, gene machines act as biochemists' lab technicians, leaving them more time for the conceptual work that is crucial to the development of new substances. Priced between $19,000 and $49,500 in 1981, the sequencers and synthesizers enable many small firms to enter the research segment of genetic engineering.

The leading suppliers of these machines in 1981 were Vega Biotechnologies and BioLogicals, but any firms with skills in making liquid-chromatography instruments could make the machines and their manufacture was subject to a steep experience curve. Firms like BioLogicals sold reagents and custom-synthesis services in addition to machines; indeed, there was more money to be made by selling these products than the machines. Manufacturers of the DNA sequencers and gene synthesizers also offered custom synthesis of nucleotides where the synthesis was a particularly difficult one that was time-consuming or posed a stiff technological problem.

Most fermentation is a batch process whereby holding tanks are filled with broth. It requires special glassware to avoid contamination and vacuum-sealed chambers. The leading U.S. supplier of fermentation equipment in 1981 was New Brunswick Scientific, and most fermenters were produced by northern European or Japanese firms. Because bioseparation techniques were frequently a problem for firms new to fermentation, suppliers of the equipment also provided consulting services. Separation media were supplied by firms like Millipore or Osmonics, and other equipment was similar to that used in chemical laboratories, such as filter presses, ion exchange columns, centrifuges, and other recovery devices. The fermenters used for genetic engineering were smaller than many fermenters used in 1981, and had to be custom designed.

Although successful genetic-engineering firms received an average of 100 resumes per week, there were shortages of certain skilled personnel, such as biochemical engineers, fermentation engineers, plant geneticists, and microbiophysiologists. The high service complement of the genetic-engineering industry made the shortages of microbiophysiologists particularly acute because these so-called bug doctors, who could assess why a microorganism was sick and suggest how to improve the microorganism's health, were not graduated in large numbers. It was important to have *name* scientists who would attract investors to a project (and junior scientists to the lab), and it was possible to lure relatively underpaid professors with formidable scientific reputations—both tenured and untenured—away from prestigious academic institutions to lead research efforts in 1981.

In summary, although it was not clear in 1981 that being integrated upstream was an advantage, some firms believed they could commercialize products better with an enhanced knowledge of technological processes. These firms included Bethesda Research Laboratories, Biotech, BioLogicals, Enzo Biochem, Collaborative Research, Vega Biotechnologies, New Brunswick Scientific and many others. In 1981 Rohm & Haas sold its enzyme business to Corning Glass Works, a leading producer of laboratory glassware and glass media supports for recombinant-DNA processes, and Corning was expected to launch its own genetic-engineering venture. Some major users of enzymes sold their excess capacity to other firms, and many effective oligonucleotide sequencers performed custom syntheses for less-skilled firms.

Manufacturing

Given the low cost of raw materials and equipment, the principal entry barrier for genetic engineering was a means of commercializing discoveries. In general, the personnel barrier was low in 1981 and thus many genetic-research companies were formed. Commercialization was more expensive; a fermentation process was estimated to cost between $50 and $100 million with a minimum-efficient-plant scale of less than 50 million gallons per year.

The half-life of a discovery in genetic engineering was very short. For example, Genentech's process for making insulin (announced in 1979 for commercialization by 1983 at the earliest) was already made obsolete in 1982 by subsequent discoveries. Genetic-engineering firms had to improve their abilities continually to respond to others' innovations by creating new products and new processes for making their improved products more inexpensively.

Genetic-engineering firms had initially licensed production rights or sold the marketing rights to their discoveries in exchange for research funding, because research-and-development costs were substantial. Genetic-engineering firms worked feverishly to develop their own patents because they would serve as an umbrella under which a small company could develop. Moreover, patents could also become bargaining chips that allowed small companies to function even if giant pharmaceutical and chemical companies came to dominate the field.

Biotechnology techniques were subject to a very-steep learning curve, and various types of microorganisms required different amounts of time to develop. Most fermentation was a batch process in 1981 whereby holding tanks were filled with the broth and held for the gestation period. This process incurred large capital costs compared with in-line chemical processes, because its inventory sat in fermentation for several hours. The distilling process during recovery was very energy intensive, making fermentation processes *more* expensive than traditional manufacturing technologies in 1981. As long as biotechnology relied on batch-fermentation processes, it would be difficult to compete economically with the lower unit costs obtained from continuous chemical processes.

The most commonly used enzyme in genetic engineering was *E. Coli,* a starting material that was cultured in a fermenter after the gene transfer was accomplished. DNA, which contains the genetic information of a living organism, was cut into defined pieces, and when it was reassembled, a piece of the DNA from another plant or animal cell was inserted in place of one of the original DNA pieces. When the microorganism divided, it replicated and retained the attributes of the transplanted DNA piece. Once the difficult and time-consuming procedure of growing altered bacteria had been mastered, the desired protein product had to be extracted and purified.

The altered cells were crushed, or lysed, with ultrasound. Primary separation could involve many cycles of ultrafiltration, and purification involved meticulous care if the substance recovered was to be administered to patients parenterally or by injection. Some firms were researching membrane technology to develop an alternate (and less costly) method of recovering the desired products. It appeared that gene transfer was the easiest part of using biotechnology in 1981.

In 1981 mobility barriers seemed to be more significant than exit barriers. The genetic-engineering laboratories contained equipment that could be used readily for other scientific purposes. Few scale-up plants existed, and none were physically integrated processes. The scientific personnel could find academic positions or join other laboratories if their firm dissolved, and therefore the barriers that might prevent a firm from exiting were primarily those that prevented privately held, single-business firms from acknowledging that they had little promise of earning an acceptable level of profits; they were strategic, not economic barriers.

Ongoing chemical firms could face mobility barriers in using genetic-engineering technology. Although the transition from chemical-reaction assets to those of a fermentation process would not be extremely costly, the mental leap for some workers was analogous to asking vacuum-tube assemblers to produce transistors, instead.

Marketing

Access to the market was a significant barrier in 1981. In addition to having no manufacturing facilities, the stand-alone genetic-engineering firms had no distribution channels in most cases and no marketing expertise. (This was not the case for the established and integrated industrial companies that were pursuing genetic engineering in-house for defensive reasons, or because they foresaw long-term competitive advantages from the creation of new manufacturing processes.) Stand-alone genetic-engineering firms hoped to progress from contract research to earn revenues to fund additional research-and-product development, to licensure or outright sale of products that were developed, then to joint ventures with outsiders to bring the genetically engineered product to the marketplace, and finally to stand-alone plants financed primarily by the genetic-engineering firm itself, using public funding or privately placed debentures. Their relationships with outside firms were as research extensions of other firms that were minority investors, suppliers of licensed technology (production licenses), suppliers of products the outsider marketed (marketing rights), ouside consultants (contract research), or partners in joint ventures in 1981.

Stand-alone firms first undertook contract research until they found a product or process that was either lower-cost or substantially more effective than existing products or processes. In this phase, entrepreneurs worked outrageous hours for low pay, and showed low or negative profits because they funneled all cash back into their own research until a breakthrough was achieved. The entrepreneurial firms were able to take tremendous risks to prove their ideas and were frequently on the cutting edge of technology.

Research contracts frequently developed into pilot plants or licenses. When genetic-engineering firms licensed their sponsors, they were at a terrible disadvantage in cutting a deal, and firms tried to write the best contracts they could without giving away their birthrights. That is why genetic-engineering firms tried to develop their own products to license. When genetic-engineering firms lacked the capital and wherewithal to market their products to customers on a large scale, they combined their strength in basic research with those of major corporations possessing development and marketing skills, and both parties benefited from such associations. For example, many genetic-engineering firms working in the area of pharmaceuticals had marketing agreements with leading firms whereby the pharmaceutical house performed clinical testing, guided the product through FDA approval, and marketed the resulting drug.

There were two situations in which a genetic-engineering firm could hope to market its own innovations: agricultural researchers that already owned seed companies, and markets so specialized that only five or six customers existed. Seed companies tended to be small and regional, and genetic-engineering firms could use acquisitions to expand marketing operations geographically. Specialized markets could be served with a limited sales force, much like the specialty-chemicals industry where products were developed sometimes on a one-on-one basis, almost like a research contract, until more firms begin to use the product, and customers valued these suppliers because the specialists developed products more effectively than customers could in-house. Like the small catalyst companies that served the oil industry, genetic-engineering firms could specialize in selling to a narrow market and renewing their competitive vigor with ongoing basic research.

Competition in the Genetic-Engineering Industry

In 1981 approximately 150 firms developed or marketed products through genetic engineering, or performed such research on contract. Approximately twenty-five firms provided apparatus or instrumentation, and some performed in-house research on genetic engineering as well. Sixty publicly traded corporations were known to have equity investments in genetic-engineering ventures, and five venture-capital organizations that invested primarily in biotechnology had been identified. In addition to these, major firms in pharmaceuticals, chemicals, energy, food processing, and agribusiness had in-house-research units studying genetic engineering, but they were extremely secretive about their activities. Table 9-1 lists the stand-alone firms, ranked according to their absolute and relative number of doctorates, and table 9-2 lists major corporate equity investments in, and research contracts with, selected genetic-engineering firms.

Large corporations made defensive investments in genetic engineering despite manpower shortages and an anti-big-business bias that permeated academic laboratories in the early 1980s. These firms included Atlantic-Richfield, Royal Dutch-Shell, AMOCO, Monsanto, Allied, du Pont, Eli Lilly, Schering-Plough, Hoffman-LaRoche, Lubrizol, National Distillers and Chemicals, and Pfizer. The antibiotics firms and enzyme firms (such as Novo Laboratories, Gist-Brocades NV, and KabiGen) were expected to be particularly skilled in producing genetically engineered substances because they possessed fermentation experience.

Ongoing corporations frequently sought defensive toehold investments in genetic engineering by purchasing minority ownership in entrepreneurial firms before undertaking genetic-engineering experiments in-house. Whether or not this business fit well in the portfolio of projects that firms managed often determined management's attitudes about the treatment of diversification. For some, it was a quasi-integration; for others it was primarily speculation. Many observers doubted that genetic-engineering firms could survive independently. They were expected to be absorbed by larger firms or driven to failure as the technology became better understood.

Corporate-Strategy Exit Barriers in Genetic Engineering

In 1981 the stand-alone genetic-engineering firms were undiversified and not attentive to market pressures. As long as they could raise venture capital, the scientists persevered in their search for genetically improved substances. Since the stand-alone firms did not possess the channels needed to market their products, their competition would be based upon efforts to create new products and processes, not price competition.

Summary of Competitors in Genetic Engineering

In summary, the firms developing synthetic genetic products and processes differed in their strategic postures according to whether they possessed:

Table 9-1
A Ranking of Genetic-Engineering Firms, December 1981

Ranking by Number of Doctorates Firm	Number	Areas of Specialization
1. Novo Industri	100	Industrial enzymes, insulin
2. Genentech	75	Varied projects
3. Bethesda Research Laboratories	65	Research products, diagnostics
4. International Plant Research Institute	55	Research in plants
5. Biogen (Swiss)	45	Research
6. Cetus	45	Research, especially large market products
7. Genex	45	Research, especially enzymes, amino acids
8. Agrigenetics	40	Seeds, soil bacteria, plant sciences
9. Applied Molecular Genetics	30	Research, especially human health
10. Biogen USA	30	Research

Ranking by Doctorates Relative to Total Employees		
Firm	Ratio	Annual Revenues (millions of dollars)
1. ARMOS (South San Francisco, CA)	.48	0
2. Applied Molecular Genetics (Newbury Park, CA)	.47	0
3. Molecular Genetics (Minnetonka, MN)	.40	1.0[a]
4. BioLogicals (Toronto, ON)	.39	0.2
5. Biogen (Geneva, SWZ)	.80	1.9[a]
6. International Plant Research Institute (San Carlos, CA)	.34	3.0[a]
7. Biotech (Madison, WI)	.33	0.5[a]
8. Collaborative Research (Waltham, MA)	.29	3.4
9. Native Plants (Salt Lake City, UT)	.29	2.6[a]
10. Enzo Biochem (New York, NY)	.26	0.2
11. New England Bio Labs (Beverly, MA)	.26	3.0[a]
12. Genentech (South San Francisco, CA)	.25	6.5
13. Genex (Rockville, MD)	.23	5.0[a]
14. Biotech Research Laboratories (Bethesda, MD)	.20	1.2
15. Bethesda Research Laboratories (Bethesda, MD)	.19	11.0[a]
16. Hybritech (La Jolla, CA)	.14	0.1
17. Cetus (San Francisco)	.12	9.9
18. Novo Industri (Denmark)	.03	262.4

Source: Industry sources.

Note: Several firms appearing in first list were so diversified that the density of their genetic engineering effort cannot be ascertained.

[a] Estimate.

Table 9–2
Equity Investments or Marketing Rights (MR) in Selected Genetic-Engineering Firms, December 1981

Firm	Business	Corporate Investor	Estimated Investment
Advanced Genetic Sciences	Research in plant genetics and agricultural projects	Cardo (Sweden) Rohm & Haas	19% 19%
Applied Molecular Genetics	Research, especially human health (Research, oil recovery)	Abbott Labs Tosco	13.5% 9.5%
BioLogicals	Instrumentation, fermentation organisms (Health care products)	Allied Johnson & Johnson	8.9% 8.9%
Biogen	Research, pollution control, mineral extraction Research (right of first refusal) (for animal growth hormone)	INCO Monsanto Schering-Plough International Minerals & Chemicals	19.0% 12.3% 12.4% MR
Biogen USA	Research, interferon and others	Biogen	100%
Biotech	Research	Dennison	—
Biotech Research	Research, especially cell science	Ethyl	1.8%
Calgene	Research in plant genetics, fertilizer	Allied	20%
Cetus	Research, especially large market products, including antibiotics, interferon, industrial and agricultural applications (for interferon)	National Distillers & Chemicals Standard Oil (California) Standard Oil (Indiana) Shell	11% 17.3% 21.3% MR
Collaborative Research	Research, especially growth factors, health care, agricultural products, industrial catalysts	Dow Chemical Green Cross (Japan)	4.7% 0.9%
Collagen Corp.	Collagen for medical and lab uses	Monsanto	24%

Table 9-2 continued

Firm	Business	Corporate Investor	Estimated Investment
DNA Plant Technology	Research, plant genetics	Campbell Soup	30%
DNAX Institute	Research, especially human health	Alza	option
Engenics	Process development	Bendix	5.8%
	Process development	Koppers	5.8%
	Process development	Mead	5.8%
	Process development	General Foods	4.5%
Genentech	Various projects, including interferon, human growth factor, insulin, and animal growth factor	Fluor	20%
		Lubrizol	2%
		Monsanto	MR
	(for insulin)	Eli Lilly	MR
	(for interferon)	Hoffman-LaRoche	MR
	(for hoof and mouth vaccine, exclusive)	International Minerals & Chemicals	
Genex	Research, especially enzymes, amino acids	Koppers	45%
	Research, especially enzymes, amino acids	Monsanto	10.25%
	(for interferon)	Bristol-Myers	MR
Hybritech	Hybridomas	Mitsubishi (Japan)	—
Molecular Genetics	Research, agricultural, animal health	American Cyanamid	20%
Salk Institute Biotech./ Industrial Assoc.	Research	Phillips Petroleum	37%

Source: Industry sources.

(1) marketing channels, (2) fermentation-technology experience, or (3) whether they manufactured genetically engineered products in-house or subcontracted their production. Firms also differed in the type of genetic-engineering research undertaken and in how they obtained the strains for their pilot plants. For example, Eli Lilly maintained both an in-house-research effort and a licensed process for synthesizing insulin that it marketed through its existing channels. Although capital costs were not high in the research phase of product development, they were very high where firms had not previously used fermentation technology. Commercialization was particularly costly for the clinical-testing procedures required for new drug approval, yet a substantial proportion of 1981 research efforts were dedicated to such health-care products. This was due to the pharmaceutical industry's willingness to make higher research-and-development expenditures—due to the higher prices of pharmaceutical products—than those in other industries where genetic-engineering techniques might be applied.

A Mapping of Strategic Groups in Genetic Engineering

This section groups major competitors by their breadth of vertical integration in 1981. Few stand-alone firms were backward integrated from genetic engineering to restriction enzymes, genetic synthesizers, industrial enzymes, or fermentation capability, and only those firms owning seed companies were forward integrated. Firms could be mapped as shown in figure 9–1 to indicate whether any shared resources or linkages with other business units existed.

In 1981 firms developing genetically improved products performed contract research, used outside marketers to distribute their products in joint ventures, shared research results with corporate minority shareholders, or used their existing distribution channels. Some of the genetic-synthesis researchers also produced enzymes or instrumentation, but many were completely nonintegrated.

The genetic-engineering industry was young, and uncertainty regarding commercial success was high because the technology was relatively new to industry participants, economics justifying pilot or scale-up plants were not expected to be good, approval to sell genetically engineered products in regulated markets could be withheld, secrecy among competing laboratories had become increasingly high, and there was a risk that the technology of gene transfer could not be adequately controlled in marginal laboratories. Few firms reported profits in 1981, but this poor performance may have been due to practices by genetic-engineering firms of spending heavily on research for future products and foregoing current profits. Whatever the reasons for poor profitability, stand-alone-genetic-engineering firms were

Breadth of Nondistribution Activities

Distribution Activities	Recombinant DNA Only	Fine Restriction Enzymes	Gene Synthesis Machines and Instrumentation	Enzymes	Fermentation Capability
Existing Channels of Distribution	Agrigenetics ARCO-Desert Seed		Beckman Instruments	Corning Glass Works Novo Industri Gist Brocades Miles Laboratories Beckman Instruments	Gist Brocades Miles Laboratories National Distillers & Chemicals Dow Chemical Eli Lilly Upjohn Schering-Plough Hoffman-LaRoche
Equity Investment with Rights to Reserve Findings for Sponsors	Advanced Genetic Research Applied Molecular Genetics Biogen Calgene Cetus Genex Molecular Genetics	Biotec	BioLogicals	BioLogicals	
Joint Ventures	Biogen Cetus Collaborative Research Genentech AMOCO Royal Dutch-Shell SOCAL Kabi				Dow Chemical Hoffman-LaRoche Eli Lilly Schering-Plough Upjohn
Contract Research	Biogen Cetus Calgene Genex Genentech IPRI Molecular Genetics	Bethesda Research Laboratories Biotec Enzyme Center New England Biolabs	BioLogicals Bio Response Vega Biotechnologies	Enzo Biochem Genzyme BioLogicals	

Figure 9-1. A Mapping of Selected Competitors in Genetic Engineering, 1981

not likely to exit until they had exhausted their sources of financing, and corporate-genetic-engineering projects were unlikely to be commercialized until profit margins had improved.

Key Events in Genetic Engineering

Genetic engineering was a very-young industry that may be explained using the following metaphor. Genetics was a language that Watson and Crick taught scientists to read in 1953. Khorana taught them how to write that language in the 1960s through research using gene-synthesis techniques. The development of the mechanical gene synthesizer (metaphorically, a typewriter) enabled scientists to edit the language. The next milestone occurred when the first recombinant-DNA product was proven in a laboratory by Jackson and Berg in 1972. Their publication on studies of the SV40 virus was followed by other discoveries, and in 1975 a conference was called by scientists in Asilomar, California to assess the field and agree upon standards of conduct. At this scientific conference, information was shared readily, and the knowledge needed to recombine genetic matter spread quickly. Public outcries (based on unfounded fears of a Frankenstein's monster or Andromeda strain) delayed the entry of some large firms into genetic engineering, thereby giving some small firms a chance to become established. In 1981 genetic-engineering firms of all types were progressing toward a kind of *creative writing,* the ability to compose substances for a particular purpose that may not appear in nature.

In 1972 General Electric applied for a patent on behalf of a researcher, Ananda Chakrabarty, for a laboratory-produced life form. (The Supreme Court ruled in 1980 that life forms could be patented.) The patent legitimized the industry and set off a race to win other patents.

A Brief History of the Genetic-Engineering Industry

Early stand-alone entrants included instrumentation firms such as New Brunswick Scientific (founded in 1954), Dynatech (1961), and Flow General (1971); research firms such as Cetus (1971), Bio Response (1972), Biotech Research Laboratories (1973), Native Plants (1973), New England Biolabs (1974), Agrigenetics (1975), Bethesda Research Laboratories (1975), Ecoenergetics (1975), and Enzo Biochem (1976); and enzyme and fermentation specialists such as Novo Laboratories (1973) and Gist-Brocades (1976). In 1976 Genentech was founded by a venture capitalist and a scientist, and it announced the first commercializable product of genetic engineering the following year.

Cetus was backed primarily by Standard Oil of Indiana (AMOCO) initially and had formed a joint venture with Royal Dutch-Shell to develop interferon (for which Shell received marketing rights). SmithKline was marketing an animal vaccine for the firm, and two of Cetus's sponsors (AMOCO and SOCAL) were interested in applying recombinant-DNA techniques to the production of alkene oxides. National Distillers and Chemicals was studying gasohol with Cetus, and both AMOCO and National Distillers operated pilot-stage, continuous-fermentation processes in-house.

Cetus had remained essentially a research company; it had no commercializable products to sell. Moreover, it had not articulated a strategy for doing so. Cetus tried to remain up-to-date on technological breakthroughs by recruiting scientists proven as leaders in their fields, taking joint ventures with universities to gain access to theoretical inquiries, and forming a council of advisors comprised of corporate representatives who discussed the commercial applications of their laboratory research in genetic engineering. Cetus had also established a series of satellite subsidiaries to protect the integrity of the original Cetus corporation while offering scientists it hoped to recruit a piece of the action in the subsidiary that they would affect most directly. This scheme enabled new scientists to share in Cetus's successes, but did not allow them to participate in the appreciation of capital stock that was risked in 1971.

Standard Oil of Indiana had acted as a type of white knight to Cetus and pursued several recombinant-DNA ventures both with Cetus and for its own account. Cetus research for AMOCO included a project to upgrade oil biologically. AMOCO's in-house research included a biological process to make less-expensive antifreeze and other projects involving alkene oxides.

Agrigenetics engaged in research to develop genetically improved seeds and to grow along the steep learning curve of biotechnology by creating better agricultural products. It reached that market by acquiring twelve seed companies. Agrigenetics was a private company that did *not* perform research for outsiders. Its capital needs were met by selling limited, five-year research-and-development partnerships to investors and by obtaining private-equity placements. It was affiliated with the University of Wisconsin at Madison, with facilities in Denver and Hollister, California as well.

Novo Laboratories was the U.S. subsidiary of Novo Industri, a Danish producer of insulin and industrial enzymes as well as other pharmaceuticals. It was the leading biotechnology firm in the world and was particularly well-suited to scale up fermentation facilities for producing genetically engineered substances. Indeed the geneticists and enzymatologists were integrated in the same research group at Novo, and the firm was genetically developing an insulin to rival Eli Lilly's human insulin (which was also developed genetically).

Genentech was backed by Lubrizol, INCO (a venture capital consortium), Monsanto, and Fluor, as well as its partners in joint ventures. Genentech preferred to develop products for its own account that were low volume but high margin. In this way Genentech hoped to use its own sales force to market its products. Virtually all of Genentech's revenues were from contract research, but royalty income was anticipated from its joint ventures to make commercializable hormones. Genentech had filed over two hundred patent applications and hoped to establish protection in the area of basic patents on processes with wide availability. This meant that many of Genentech's basic organisms might be used for advanced genetic-engineering research, and it might serve as an additional source of revenues if the patents were upheld and Genentech's ownership of them were protected.

1977

In 1977 Genex was founded as a private firm with venture capital from Innoven (a venture of Monsanto and Emerson Electric) and a corporate investment from Koppers. Genex specialized in chemical products but performed contract research in pharmaceuticals to help companies develop superior products or processes. Genex had identified the biomass market as one of its targets, as well as other specialized niches where few customers existed. In this manner Genex hoped to market its own products.

Genex had developed one product, aspartic acid, which it manufactured in-house. This had been an important learning experience that prepared the firm for future commercialization of additional products. Sales of contract research services accounted for 99 percent of Genex's revenues, but 50 percent of its research expenditures were made for its in-house accounts. Genex hired excellent researchers as they became available, thereby preempting other maverick firms (or large corporations) from hiring them, and this practice improved its ability to investigate the *hard* applications of genetic engineering. Genex had possessed no special competitive advantage over other genetic-engineering firms in 1977, but by moving quickly to hire its staff, it had gained a formidable strength.

In 1977 Genentech announced it had produced somatostatin, an organism that inhibited the activity of other hormones such as insulin and growth hormone. Although somatostatin was of clinical interest for certain disorders, it did not appear to offer sufficient commercial promise for Genentech to begin clinical testing alone.

In 1977 Cetus and National Distillers and Chemicals formed an investment-and-advisory relationship by which Cetus avoided acquisition by other corporate suitors and maintained its autonomy to develop products

for its own account. Thereafter, Cetus undertook a series of research contracts for royalties and joint ventures, in order to obtain security in financing of its projects, but one of its first research contracts was with Schering.
(It studied the use of microorganisms to enhance antibiotic yields.) A
similar arrangement with Roussel-Uclaf (to improve the productivity of
vitamin B-12 processes) also provided Cetus with royalty revenues.

Upjohn, the pharmaceutical house, began its own genetic-transplant-
research program in 1977. Its experiments included exploring the feasibility
of inducing a bacterium to produce ovalbumin, the main protein of common egg white. The research was intended to aid Upjohn in serum-albumin
and interferon production.

1978

In 1978 International Plant Research Institute (IPRI), Biogen SA, Hybritech, and Bio Chem Technology were founded. IPRI was backed by private
investors and researched agricultural applications for genetic engineering.
Biogen SA, a Netherland Antilles corporation with a laboratory in Switzerland, brought together ten top university scientists and INCO (a venture
capital consortium). Hybritech was backed by the same venture-capital firm
that launched Genentech, and it researched antibodies. Bio Chem Technology researched pilot and scale-up fermentation technology.

IPRI was considered one of the top agricultural-genetic-engineering
firms and was funded by corporate investors such as Atlantic-Richfield and
Eli Lilly. The combination of expertise in molecular biology and
agricultural skills was sufficiently uncommon that IPRI did not face many
independent competitors.

Biogen SA, located in Geneva, brought together ten scientists from
leading universities as consultants by offering them each a free grant of 3
percent ownership, generous research contracts to compensate the scientists
and schools for the time they would be spending on Biogen's projects, and
other bonuses for important discoveries. Biogen's major U.S. support came
from INCO and Monsanto, and one of its first discoveries was a formulation of interferon.

In 1978 Standard Oil of California purchased 25 percent equity in
Cetus. SOCAL was interested in the enhanced production of alcohol for use
in gasohol, in a cost-saving method for producing large-scale industrial
chemicals, and in a microorganism for improved oil recovery from heavy-
oil fields. (Much of SOCAL's domestic acreage contained heavy oil, as
chapter 5 explains.)

In 1978 Genentech constructed bacteria that produced human insulin.
Eli Lilly, which had been experimenting with its own recombinant-DNA

processes to create human insulin, licensed the Genentech process to build a pilot plant and commence clinical testing of the product. Also in 1978 Hoffman-LaRoche and Genentech began a collaboration to synthesize interferon. Hoffman-LaRoche received marketing rights from the joint venture, should any commercializable product result.

Lilly had been doing in-house recombinant-DNA research on insulin for several years because a widening gap was forecast between the number of diabetics requiring insulin and the volume of cattle or pork that was being produced. (The pancreas glands of slaughtered animals had to be specifically prepared to maximize insulin outputs.) The biosynthetic-insulin formulation Lilly was testing was *human* insulin (as compared with the insulin commonly marketed which was bovine or porcine in origin), and it was licensed from Genentech. As Lilly guided this formulation through clinical tests to FDA approval, it continued to research other formulations of genetically developed insulin.

The Roche Institute of Molecular Biology had sponsored studies to isolate interferon for over ten years, and Roche collaborated with Genentech to produce genetically engineered interferon. It had a similar research agreement with Takada Chemical Industries of Japan.

1979

Several genetic-engineering firms were formed in 1979, including Advanced Genetic Sciences, BioLogicals, Biotechnologies, Collaborative Genetics, and Molecular Genetics. Advanced Genetic Sciences was backed by private investors, including Rohm & Haas, and performed research in agriculture. Molecular Genetics was backed by venture capital from American Cyanamid as well as from several other funds. Collaborative Genetics was a wholly owned subsidiary of Collaborative Research. BioLogicals, a producer of genetic synthesizers, was backed by Johnson & Johnson and the Canadian government.

In addition to selling genetic synthesizers (gene machines), BioLogicals also sold reagents and custom-synthesis services. Because it had worked with the gene synthesizer longer than the machine was commercially available to customers, BioLogicals offered greater depth of staff and knowledge concerning synthesis than many smaller customers possessed. BioLogicals performed contract research (and research on its own account) as well as research for Johnson & Johnson.

An important milestone occurred in the development of the genetic-engineering industry when Genentech announced it had produced somatotropin (human-growth hormone), a drug used to treat hypopituitary dwarfism. In 1979 the principal treatment for this rare form of dwarfism was with human-growth hormone extracted from human corpses. The raw materials were rare, the extraction procedure difficult, and the hormone expensive. Genentech arranged for KabiGen AB of Sweden, then the world's largest supplier of human growth hormone, to manufacture the product for Genentech. Both KabiGen and Genentech intended to market the product. Also in 1979 Genentech constructed bacteria that produced thymosin alpha-1, a protein affecting cellular immunities.

In 1979 Cetus announced a joint venture with Standard Oil of California (SOCAL) to develop a less-costly process for producing fructose from corn starch that coproduced alkene oxides, thereby giving SOCAL an entree into the markets for ethylene oxide and propylene oxide.

In June 1979 Schering-Plough announced it had agreed to acquire a minority interest in Biogen NV for $8 million, giving it right of first refusal for any health-care products developed by Biogen. The two firms were expected to form a joint venture to investigate the production of interferon. (Schering-Plough maintained a parallel, in-house-research facility and in 1982 it began building a plant to ferment and purify interferon.)

1980

By 1980 several more genetic engineering firms had been founded and stock-market fever became contagious as Genentech became the first of the prominent genetic-engineering firms to make a public stock offering. Among the many new entrants were Applied Molecular Genetics (backed by Abbott, Syntex, and Tosco), Armos, Calgene (Allied), and Biotech (Dennison). Armos became the first, second-generation genetic-engineering company because it was founded by former employees of Genentech.

In June 1980 the Supreme Court decided that new, laboratory-produced forms of life could be patented. The patent request under question was filed in 1972 by General Electric for an oil-sludge-consuming microorganism created in its laboratories.

In early 1980 Biogen and Schering-Plough announced a human-interferon gene that expressed interferon. Interest in genetic engineering rose substantially when this announcement occurred, but it cooled when scientists revealed there were many different forms of interferon, each requiring individual research and clinical testing to assess their therapeutic value. Later in 1980 Monsanto purchased $20 million of Biogen preferred stock to gain access to its research expertise.

In 1980 Agrigenetics announced its purchase of the Jacques Seed Company, which specialized in hybrid seed corn and had been purchased by Union Carbide in 1977 as a part of a larger acquisition. Union Carbide had been one of the leading investigators of enzyme modification in the early 1970s.

In 1980 Allied Corporation acquired an equity interest in BioLogicals and indicated it would fund research involving the use of biotechnology to diversify into high-technology products. Allied did not have an in-house genetic-engineering-research effort at that time.

In 1980 Dow Chemical entered a $5 million agreement with Collaborative Research to generate fundamental genetic-engineering techniques. The contract gave Dow rights to products and processes through a series of features that made the firm virtually a research arm of Dow Chemical.

In 1980 Bristol-Myers purchased exclusive rights to manufacture and sell the interferon formulation Genex was working on. Unlike the Biogen process that recreated interferon only in bacteria, Genex used yeast in a process that had fewer pathogenic properties.

In 1980 Genentech announced that it had constructed bacteria that expressed human proinsulin and several human interferons. Under the terms of a joint venture with Hoffman-LaRoche, both Genentech and Roche could manufacture the interferon but Roche would be responsible for marketing the product. In October 1980, when Genentech offered its stock to the public, its shares shot up as high as eighty-eight dollars on the first morning of trading after being offered at thirty-five dollars.

In December 1980, Cetus prepared to register an initial stock offering with the Securities and Exchange Commission. Cetus ownership at this time was: SOCAL (25 percent), AMOCO (28 percent), National Distillers & Chemicals (16 percent), and its founders and private investors (31 percent).

1981

As the stock market awaited Cetus' stock offering, sharing of research findings in matters of genetic engineering became increasingly rare. A basic gene-cloning patent was issued to Stanford University in December 1980, and over fifty firms were licensed to use it.

The fourth milestone in the genetic-engineering industry occurred when Cetus stock sold out in one day. It gave the industry considerable glamour, and other genetic-engineering firms benefited in their fund-raising efforts from Cetus's halo effect. New Cetus products included a pig-and-cow anti-diarrheal vaccine marketed for Cetus by Norden Laboratories and a joint venture with Royal Dutch-Shell to produce human interferon. In July 1981, Cetus received permission from the National Institute of Health to scale up production of human interferon to above the ten-liter-per-batch limit. The funding for the Shell/Cetus research-and-development agreement was used to begin construction of a large-scale, $10-million facility in Emeryville, California to produce the interferon. The first products for testing were expected early in 1982.

These arrangements indicated Cetus' approach to product development, whereby it intended to fund research and development for early phases of product development internally and sell commercial development to corporate partners later. In the past, Cetus had funded its activities through research contracts and licensing of its products. In the future, Cetus considered royalty agreements only when there were compelling business reasons not to establish joint ventures or to retain full ownership.

Shell viewed the development of human interferon as its opportunity to enter the health-care field as a specialty-pharmaceutical firm. Shell anticipated that several years of difficult research lay ahead in developing recombinant-DNA products, and it suggested also that construction on Shell's own facility for such research could commence in 1982.

Late in 1980 Fluor Corporation, an engineering-and-construction-services concern, signed an agreement with Genentech to explore the design and construction of large-scale, industrial facilities for the production of substances based on Genentech's genetic-engineering technology. In January 1981, Genentech interferon and human-growth hormone began clinical testing. In June, Genentech announced the manufacture by genetic-engineering techniques of a foot-and-mouth-disease vaccine developed for International Minerals and Chemicals. In September 1981, Genentech revealed that a group of Japanese financial institutions and a Japanese academic institution had purchased an equity interest in it. The transaction did not involve a transfer of commercial rights to products or technology. Table 9-3 lists some of the other joint ventures and licensing agreements between U.S. and Japanese firms at that time.

Engenics was established as a research organization to investigate fermentation and other production processes used to commercialize genetic-engineering techniques. Its sponsors included the University of California at Berkeley and Stanford University, as well as Bendix, Koppers, Maclaren Power and Paper, Mead, Elf Technologies, and General Foods; and it was founded to improve knowledge of continuous-fermentation technology by designing-and marketing super efficient bioreactors, bundles of tiny, hollow-fiber tubes of membranes with pores that let nutrients and products flow through but were too small for bacteria.

In 1981 Agrigenetics acquired McCurdy Seed and Supply and Keystone Seed Company in its continuing effort to expand its marketing system geographically. Agrigenetics maintained an integrated effort—from seed-storage proteins to plant tissues to plants—in its approach to evolutionary biology and plant development.

In 1981 Biogen NV established a U.S. subsidiary in the Boston area. Walter Gilbert, a Harvard University professor, took a leave of absence to become chief executive officer of Biogen NV, the parent of Biogen USA.

In 1981 Eli Lilly annnounced a long-term agreement with IPRI in which Lilly hoped to enter the agricultural field. The agreement called for IPRI to conduct research for Lilly to improve crop yields.

Table 9-3
Joint-Venture Involvement of Japanese Firms in U.S. Biotechnology

Firm	Partner	Business
Daiichi Seiyaku	Genentech	Marketing rights for interferon development
Green Cross	Collaborative Research	Joint-research agreement and equity investor
	Genex	Joint-research agreement
	Biogen	License to produce hepatis B vaccine
Mitsubishi Chemical	Hybritech	Marketing rights for monocloned antibodies
Mitsui Toatsu Chemical	Genex	Research contract to produce urokinase
Nissho-Iwai	Cetus	Equity investor
Takeda Chemical	Hoffman-LaRoche	License to produce interferon
Toray Industries	Genentech	Marketing rights for interferon development

In 1981 Corning Glass arranged to purchase Rohm & Haas' enzyme-manufacturing business as part of its efforts to backward integrate and strengthen its biotechnology position. Prior to its acquisition, Corning Glass purchased the enzymes from Rohm & Haas for implantation in its immobilized-enzyme glassware. Corning Glass intended to build a plant to produce enzymes by fermentation soon after the acquisition.

In 1981 National Distillers & Chemicals began construction on a continuous-process facility to make alcohol via a genetically engineered yeast developed by Cetus. At year end, National Distillers & Chemicals was awarded a patent for its continuous-fermentation process for producing ethanol.

In November 1981 SmithKline acquired Beckman Instruments, a leading producer of diagnostic instruments and supplier to biotechnology labs which also produced synthetic peptides. SmithKline's new $20-million facility for molecular-biology research was expected to aid the merged firms' entry into genetic engineering to develop related products.

After 1981 firms relied on outsiders, as well as funding in-house research, to leverage their abilities to develop new products using biotechnology. Capital was becoming so scarce for genetic-engineering firms in 1982 that industry observers predicted second-tier firms would soon be acquired by larger firms or fail. For example, Bethesda Research Laboratories (BRL) had built up a staff of 460 in anticipation of going public, but the sour market and overspending by BRL forced it to abandon those plans and cut back its personnel by 30 percent to preserve its capital.

In June 1982 Standard Oil of California pulled out of the fructose joint venture with Cetus, dealing a substantial blow to Cetus's research-and-development revenues. Cetus had announced plans to build a $100-million fructose plant with SOCAL in September 1980, and it tried to market the fructose venture to existing manufacturers after SOCAL terminated the partnership. SOCAL cited technical problems as its principal motive for stopping the project, but industry observers commented that it might have encountered difficulties in marketing its fructose—even in bulk form—since it had no previously established distribution channels in the sweetener markets.

Analysis of Strategies for Vertical Integration in Genetic Engineering

Section one described the structure of the genetic-engineering industry in 1981 and section two described key events in the industry leading to its 1981 structure. This section analyzes the patterns of vertical behavior sketched above and compares the predictions of the strategy framework with the outcomes observed in 1981. The structure of the genetic-engineering industry was emerging in 1981 but was still highly chaotic because there were few products to sell and only pilot facilities in operation. Nevertheless, the contract-research portion of the industry had flourished for a decade, and in 1981 many firms had made marketing arrangements, constructed pilot plants, and built preliminary infrastructures for coping with technological change and customer needs. Although the riskiness of investing in genetic engineering was still high, it was less so than earlier because some products existed, were being tested, and would soon be commercialized. According to the strategy framework proposed in chapter 2, in this industry firms would strive to reach the ultimate consumer to prove their products but would not be broadly integrated nor involved in many stages for each integrated activity, they would not be highly integrated internally, and would keep their ownership stakes in the industry low until uncertainties concerning industry viability were relieved. Firms would use forms of quasi-integration wherever possible to reduce their riskiness, but as they grew more certain of their strategies, firms would seek more control over their ventures.

Phase of Industry Development

The genetic-engineering industry was emerging in 1981 because trade secrets were best protected against competitors by performing research and development internally, firms were using more of their excess capacity (scientists and technicians) to pursue their own projects while backing away from outside contracts, pilot plants were under construction, and trading relationships were becoming defined. Some clear patterns of competition were beginning to emerge, but the industry's structure could change, depending upon FDA actions. More vertical integration was occurring and an economic-experience-curve effect had become apparent for some applications. Innovators were developing patentable, continuous-fermentation processes, but secrecy was the principal way to protect ideas. Some firms obtained windows on their competitors' ideas by custom-synthesizing difficult nucleotide chains for them, but information was diffused more slowly as time passed, and the rate of innovation began to slow as firms hoarded their ideas and data. As a consequence, uncertainty concerning the viability of products continued to be high, and faster improvements in products and processes did not occur as the industry began to have a discernable structure. The principal barrier to entry became access to the market. Large-scale fermentation-and-recovery processes were also difficulties that had to be hurdled, but the finite number of market conduits foreclosed access to aspiring entrants that forward integrated late.

Demand was sensitive to economic fluctuations because the corporations that funded contract research were affected by economic downturns. The stock market became skeptical and genetic engineering firms did not receive the high prices desired for their initial equity offerings. Bethesda Research Laboratories was one of the first firms to discover there were limits to corporate patrons' patience and indulgence for genetic engineering. In 1981 no genetically engineered product was available commercially. The first project approved would bear the burden of setting precedent by satisfying all possible FDA objections and inquiries, and uncertainties about its success were high.

Given the uncertainties of technology, government regulations, and customer skepticism, low degrees of integration were anticipated. Upstream firms that provided glassware, enzymes, and gene synthesizers, among other supplies, forward integrated to perform contract research, but few firms were backward integrating in 1981; their attentions were devoted to downstream activities, including scale-up fermentation technology, recovery-and-delivery problems, and to proving their products' commercial viability.

In summary, although many fledgling genetic-engineering firms desired forward integration for reasons suggested by the strategy framework, they could not muster the required capital without giving away control of their activities. Moreover, the established and diversified firms, which were studying the applications of genetic engineering to their existing product lines, saw no need to risk their capital yet, given that entrepreneurial firms would take risks for them. Until some event forced these established firms to bind their genetic-engineering ventures more closely to them, quasi-integrations were sufficient to achieve their purposes, given the condition of the industry's development.

Volatile Industry Structure

In 1981 the industry's structure could change rapidly because conditions were so fluid, but the increasing secrecy that was developing retarded the rate at which these changes occurred. Entry was easy as was exit, and until sponsors tightened their reins, firms could continue to address questions of basic research. Depending upon how the industry developed, it could become a hospitable environment for broad and high integration.

If significant differentiation of firms' research services and products could be attained, high degrees of internal integration would be justified because customers were very sensitive to the differences between products and frequently required special services or customized designs, the product was very complex and its integrity had to be ensured through tight quality control, and trade secrets were the most effective way to protect innovations in 1981. All of these factors argued for the high control provided by internal transfers and broad integration. Unlike the pharmaceutical industry, where patents were effective as protection (hence certain steps of the production process could be subcontracted if necessary), genetically engineered bacterial strains could be copied simply by adding an extra amino acid somewhere in the chain. Only the most mundane tasks could be subcontracted if secrecy were to be maintained.

Suppliers of gene synthesizers offered value-adding potential but the suppliers of enzymes did not. Relatively little raw material was purchased. In 1981 the attributes of these materials did not suggest that backward integration was necessary, because the minimum-efficient scale of plants supplying raw materials to the genetic-engineering industry was substantially larger than the needs of that group. Upstream scanning did not seem crucial in 1981 because product modifications were infrequent and coordination with downstream activities could occur without being integrated.

Forward integration to consumers did seem necessary in 1981, but the stand-alone firms could not afford to do so unless they confined their product mix to substances valued by a few specialized users. Larger diversified firms possessed the necessary access to sell genetically engineered substances as they would sell substitute products. If demonstrations, explanations, or other servicing were necessary, they were likely to be provided by the same types of seed-sales respresentatives, detail persons, and marketers that had done so historically. Because customer acceptance was the key to repurchases, nonintegrated genetic-engineering firms formed and market agreements with firms possessing this infrastructure. Where distribution had to be relatively exclusive to enhance product reputations or exert control over their uses, some genetic-engineering firms contemplated forward integration.

Developing low-cost-manufacturing processes was costly, frequently more costly than a stand-alone genetic-engineering firm could afford. Consequently, production was either subcontracted or licensed to firms that could bring the product from pilot plant to commercial quantities. Upstream, the synthesis of certain nucleotides was neither so sensitive nor so difficult that subcontractors were unwarranted, and by 1981 many firms desired to purchase this service rather than use their scarce laboratory space to do it in-house. Many firms operated research laboratories but few had progressed to scale-up capacity. Yet if stand-alone firms subcontracted their manufacturing tasks and had little market presence, these firms ultimately offered little beyond their initial scientific breakthroughs.

In 1981 the genetic-engineering industry was fragmented and a shake-out seemed inevitable because investors were becoming wary of funding vast research projects without seeing results. Competitors possessed very dissimilar outlooks and dissimilar commitments to vertical integration. By 1981 some form of linkage was crucial in the health-care markets where joint ventures were formed with ongoing firms to manage the clinical testing and marketing of new products. Few stand-alone firms appeared to be capable of forward integration in 1981.

In summary, genetic engineering was a potentially volatile industry where the industry could stabilize and innovation could continue to progress if stand-alone firms could take positions as highly specialized manufacturers of customized products. But if the smaller genetic-engineering firms tried to penetrate the larger firms' markets, broad and high degrees of integration would have disastrous results for them.

Bargaining Power

Genetic-engineering firms possessed little bargaining power—upstream or downstream—if they were stand-alone firms. Upstream, their purchases were small and of relatively little consequence to industrial-enzyme or instrumentation firms. Downstream firms needed the genetic-engineering firms' products as badly as the genetic-engineering firms needed market access to some industries in 1981. This bilateral bargaining power could be observed in the plants constructed on behalf of the genetic-engineering firms.

In summary, backward integration was not necessary to counteract the bargaining power suppliers exerted, but forward integraton could be. Among established firms using in-house channels for research and development and marketing, access to technological innovation was ensured by research grants to academic institutions that would offer royalty-free licenses to these sponsors, as well as some guarantee that projects that interested them were more likely to be explored than others.

Strategy Goals

In 1981 the firms that sought technological leadership seemed best justified in pursuing broad or high degrees of integration. Where a firm's interest was primarily defensive, low integration (to attain a window on the technology but no internal transfers) sufficed until genetic-engineering techniques had proven themselves.

Whether genetic-engineering projects were undertaken in-house or by outsiders, the enthusiasm of the managers and scientists associated with genetic-engineering projects was strong. Given the fragmented structure of this industry, however, market-leadership goals were unrealistic unless firms were first to commercialize a lowest-cost technology. The technological content of the products that genetic-engineering produced was high, as was the value-added of this activity. When this venture was primarily experimental for firms, quasi-integration forms of ownership seemed to suffice.

Genetic-engineering research was frequently supported by top management because they hoped the long-term well-being of the firm could be enhanced by high degrees of internal integration. To that end, parent firms subsidized research and encouraged transfers of knowledge to the various businesses that might exploit genetic engineering. Initial research contracts or minority investments in stand-alone genetic-engineering firms were pioneered by top management, and maintenance of these investments was frequently placed in an internal venturing department or office of special projects until pilot plants were constructed and operative, or until results from outside research could be diffused to operating departments.

In many cases parent firms hoped to foster synergies between business units such that they could continue to utilize their distinctive competences. In many cases this meant high degrees of internal integration because firms' marketing skills were particularly vital, and batch-unit outputs were small enough for all to be absorbed in-house.

In summary, large firms frequently possessed the crucial skills needed to commericalize the products of genetic engineering, and they were willing to subsidize the necessary start-up costs. If damage was caused to competitive vitality by forcing sister units to work with this foreign technology, it was not evident in 1981. But stand-alone firms sought strategic postures requiring a breadth of integration they could not attain in 1981.

The Need for Vertical Integration

Although there were few economies of integration in 1981 from joining production stages involved in genetic engineering, there were ample competitive-scanning reasons to be integrated if a firm wished to be more than a supplier of research to other firms. Being forward integrated improved firms' understanding of the user markets and the existing products that genetically engineered substances had to supersede in order to be successful.

In summary, firms sought vertical integration to create credibility in penetrating new markets and to capture more value-added. The form used most frequently was the joint venture in which the firm that marketed during this era would keep customers' loyalties after the venture dissolved, unless the other firm created its own sales force. These arrangements limited each stand-alone firm to one corporate partner for each market application, but large firms could form partnerships or buy marketing rights from as many small genetic-engineering firms as they wished.

Strategy Alternatives and Performance

The strategy model distinguished between ownership and the degree of internal integration firms engaged in; firms may have owned all, some, or none of the adjacent firms supplying goods and services, and transferred all, some, or none of its needs internally. Moreover, firms differed in the breadth of their integrations. In genetic engineering, firms could be backward integrated into fine restriction enzymes, instrumentation, or other services that were needed to perform genetic-engineering research and synthesis; they could reach the market using contract research, joint ventures, or their ongoing channels of distribution if these were justified by firms' strategic missions and competitive strengths. The leading stand-alone genetic-engineering firms recognized that their partners possessed knowledge of fermentation or marketing that constituted advantages in negotiating with them. Consequently the stand-alone firms were eager to find projects in which they could exert more control.

In genetic engineering, firms perceived their projects to be so risky that they wanted to exert close control over as much of each project as they could. Full integration would be effective in protecting the integrity of firms' products as well as their proprietary knowledge, but research contracts with outsiders could supplement the internal flow of products and activities surrounding genetic engineering. Hence, the isolation that frequently accompanies full integration was a less-weighty factor in this industry, and some firms made particularly skillful use of contracts, instead of internal integration. Agrigenetics used limited, five-year research partnerships to raise venture capital, and others used contracts to dispose of their excess synthesizing capacity, to market products, to manufacture products for other firms to market, and to perform research on behalf of another.

The number of stages of activity undertaken was determined by the product's characteristics, the nature of demand, and the mission of the genetic-engineering unit relative to adjacent businesses. Unlike the refining, whiskey-distilling, tailored-suits, and ethical-pharmaceutical industries discussed in previous chapters, genetic engineering was not a mature business and its infrastructure was one of the least developed because it promised to be a new type of industry with new, single-business firms as participants. Consequently, new firms would be less likely to have experience in more than one stage of potentially integrated activity. Most of the stand-alone genetic-engineering firms had no marketing capabilities in 1981, and many had no fermentation expertise. Two firms were backward integrated to supply oligonucleotide synthesizers, but few stages of integration were undertaken by most new firms in this business.

The ongoing pharmaceutical, chemical, or oil companies that launched genetic-engineering ventures often had well-established marketing channels for the applications they would pursue using recombinant-DNA technology. Many were also accomplished at using this technology for fermentation and recovery techniques for commercial production and could undertake more integrated stages successfully.

The breadth of integration—the number of activities undertaken—was determined by demand traits and how firms competed. Since genetic-engineering techniques had not yet produced commercial products in 1981, it is not surprising that few firms undertook activities that were not part of their ongoing business activities. Thus fermentation firms were often skilled in enzyme synthesis and marketing, but they did not provide the instrumentation needed. Gene-synthesizing specialists could provide customized oligonucleotides but not raw materials or equipment. By 1981 downstream linkages became very important and the ongoing chemical, pharmaceutical, or oil companies that had created subsidiaries or quasi-integrated ventures in genetic engineering seemed to be in the most advantageous positions. The highly prolific, stand-alone genetic-engineering firms aspired to perform more activities themselves but had not yet made the transition to become broadly integrated competitors.

The form of vertical-integration relationship indicated the amount of asset exposure and flexibility the venture possessed. Joint ventures were popular in genetic engineering because stand-alone firms lacked the requisite capital to experiment and develop genetically engineered products themselves, and ongoing firms could better leverage their in-house genetic-engineering efforts if they monitored multiple projects or used the stimulus of the outside venture to vitalize their own ventures. There were also many minority equity investments without projects, or research contracts with licensing provisions and other rights, assigned to the investigating firms.

The quasi-integration form was advantageous because it lowered the entry costs for most firms, and it reduced their asset exposure should genetic engineering prove noncommercializable in the near term. Two problems inherent in quasi-integration arrangements had become apparent by 1981: (1) firms like Cetus recognized their growing dependence on larger firms and balked because they wanted more autonomy and wanted to capture more value-added themselves, and (2) marketers possessed inherent bargaining power in the quasi-integration arrangements, which they were beginning to exert. These problems—an inflexible identification with partners and an impeded ability to shift resources in the desired manner—were recognized and reacted to by industry participants in 1981.

The genetic-engineering industry was emerging in 1981, hence evaluation of firms' vertical strategies must be tempered by a recognition that if the technology were proved more effective or lower in cost, demand for genetic-engineering and fermentation products could take off, and the industry's structure could change. However, for the purposes of this research, firms that formulated the more-effective vertical-integration strategies were those that gained relatively stable access to raw materials and markets while also achieving market dominance, above-average returns on invested capital, or technological leadership.

Many stand-alone firms had links to major corporations that marketed their products, constructed their plants, or developed commercializable fermentation processes for manufacturing. Their successes should be considered in light of the products they sought to commercialize as well as the consistency of their strategies.

Genentech was moving to become a vertically integrated pharmaceutical house. Hence its Genencor venture (with Corning) to produce enzymes, its use of KabiGen and Hoffman-LaRoche as its agents, and the licensing arrangement with Eli Lilly were all decisions intended to maximize the success of its projects. Genentech was using joint ventures initially because it lacked the capital and wherewithal to satisfy all of its needs internally.

Cetus's signals about integration were contradictory in 1981 because it appeared to be interested in controlling more of the value-adding activities itself, yet the cancellation of SOCAL's project created a sizable shortfall in its research monies at a time when Cetus was seeking to become autonomous in selecting the projects it would research. Since Cetus did not possess its own links to the marketplace, its decision to procure sponsorship *after* products were formulated (rather than responding to outsiders' requests for products they believed were saleable) seemed risky.

As an instrumentation supplier that also custom-synthesized proteins for customers, BioLogicals was in an excellent position to prosper from the upsurge in genetic-engineering activity in 1981. Unfortunately, its supplier status would be limited after firms had purchased gene synthesizers and could fashion their own oligonucleotides. BioLogicals' strategy seemed oriented to short-term success because it was without commercializable genetically engineered products in 1981.

In 1981 Agrigenetics was broadly integrated from laboratory to regional seed companies and had a steady stream of cash from acquired seed operations as well as private venture capitalists. It seemed to be in a strong position to exploit its laboratory research and the distribution of products it might develop. Agrigenetics had made skillful use of limited, five-year research-and-development partnerships and wisely avoided contract research that might divert it from the vision of agribusiness projects it hoped to pursue.

In summary, embryonic genetic-engineering firms viewed contract research as a less-desirable activity as they developed their own products; yet excluding their partners risked insularity from the market's needs and a realistic understanding of competitive cost structures. In 1981 the stand-alone genetic-engineering firms could not afford to perform the necessary market research and cost studies many of them needed to make informed choices about which substances to synthesize. For this reason (and others), many firms used industrial councils as sounding boards as they struggled to become true stand-alone companies.

Many corporations formed joint ventures, bought minority-ownership stakes, or let research contracts while operating parallel laboratories, in order to exploit the know-how of the genetic-engineering firms while controlling the technology themselves. The small firms offered an entrepreneurial vigor larger firms could rarely capture without using unorthodox control devices.

As the leading manufacturer and marketer of insulin, Lilly's license for the Genentech strain of insulin-producing bacteria enabled it to exploit the advantages of using recombinant-DNA techniques in making and testing pharmaceuticals in the exhaustive clinical testing needed to earn FDA approval. Lilly maintained a pilot plant to test each generation of insulin formulated by its labs (or by Genentech's) in order to remain on the cutting edge of insulin technology. A kilogram of insulin was very expensive, hence highly suited to a process that promised lower costs.

Schering-Plough had been an aggressive supporter of genetic engineering as a means of leveraging its new-product development and had first explored the use of fermentation processes around the time that Cetus was founded. Schering-Plough was a relatively early user of Cetus research contracts and an equity investor in the formidable Biogen NV consortium of scientists. Its interferon plant (announced in 1982) was not a joint venture with other firms, however.

Shell enjoyed two advantages from its affiliation with Cetus: an early understanding of fermentation technology, and access to new products that could constitute significant diversifications for Shell. During 1981 Shell had been signaling that it sought to enter the research-intensive pharmaceutical industry through its interferon venture. Shell was one of the few nondrug corporations that possessed the staying power needed to successfully market pharmaceuticals.

Monsanto was also interested in entering pharmaceuticals and held equity in Biogen NV, Collagen, Genentech, and Genex. From these quasi-integrations, Monsanto planned to develop new products in the areas of animal health and human-tissue replacement.

In its efforts to develop a niche in genetic engineering, Corning Glass acquired an enzyme company and formed a joint venture with Genentech to construct a supplier relationship to the industry at large. The enzyme venture was compatible with the ongoing delivery systems for immobilized-enzyme glassware that Corning currently marketed to users of fermentation technology. Since enzyme manufacturing was an inherently profitable business that offered an opportunity to erect high customer-switching-cost barriers (through development of customized products) Corning Glass' vertigal strategy seemed to be particularly appropriate.

References

Aunstrup, Knud, Andresen, Otto, Falch, Edvard A., and Nielsen, Tage Kjaer. "Production of Microbial Enzymes." In Peppler, H.J. and Perlman, D., eds. *Microbial Technology.* 2nd Edition, Volume I, New York: Academic Press, Inc., 1979, pp. 281–309.

"Biotechnology—Seeking the Right Corporate Combinations." *Chemical Week,* September 30, 1981, pp. 36–40.

"Biotechnology Tax Shelter." *Genetic Engineering News,* September-October 1981, pp. 1, 21.

Bylinsky, Gene. "DNA Can Build Companies, Too." *Fortune,* June 16, 1980, pp. 144–154.

Fox, Jeffrey L., "Can Academia Adapt to Biotechnology's Lure?" *Chemical Engineering News,* October 12, 1981, pp. 39–44.

Fudenberg, H.H., ed. *Biomedical Institutions, Biomedical Funding and Public Policy.* New York: Plenum Press, 1982.

"Gene Machines Will Add Players to the DNA Game." *Chemical Week,* February 4, 1981, p. 52.

Jackson, David A. and Stich, Stephan P., eds. *The Recombinant DNA Debate.* Englewood Cliffs, N.J.: Prentice-Hall, 1979.

Steinhart, Peter. "The Second Green Revolution." *New York Times Magazine,* October 25, 1981, pp. 47–64.

Also helpful were corporate annual reports and financial statements of the firms described in chapter 9 and conversations with twelve producers of genetic engineering services, two suppliers of enzymes and instrumentation, and two industry observers.

10 Strategies for Vertical Integration in the Personal Microcomputer Industry

Personal computers are microcomputers that are cheap enough for individuals to buy and simple enough for a lay person to operate. They include not only the microprocessor chip and other components that go into the logic, or computing power, of a machine, but also a variety of peripheral devices. The most important attribute of any personal computer is its ability to do the particular tasks a user desires (systems). In older and larger computers, independent software determined a system's capabilities, but by 1981 much of this information could be inscribed on a microprocessor chip, the heart of a personal computer. Before 1981, demand exceeded firms' abilities to satisfy customers, but by the end of 1981 pressures to cut prices were strong. Some firms emphasized features such as greater computing speed and user friendliness, but access to distribution and good software appeared to be the crucial strengths needed for survival.

A Description of the Personal Microcomputer Industry

The Product

A personal computer contains a tiny microprocessor (or computer-on-a-chip) surrounded by other miniature components and a keyboard for entering information. By adding a monitor (a TV set) and a way to load programs into the computer (a cassette tape recorder), the system's capabilities are enhanced. By adding a printer, typed letters are produced, and computers may receive stored data over telephone lines by attaching a modem. The usefulness of the microcomputer is determined by its software, which tells the microcomputer whether it is processing a letter, controlling inventory, or playing Space Invaders. Without software, however, microcomputers are just electronic boxes.

The brain of a personal computer is the microprocessor, a fifth-generation integrated circuit made of silicon that is smaller than a thumbnail. The more binary digits (bits) it can process per second, the faster the microprocessor. Each microprocessor design is unique and is often produced by

Background research was provided by Mary Ellen Waller and Paul Gelburd.

specialized firms in relatively small volumes (compared to RAMs and ROMs, which are explained below). In 1981 the three most-popular micro-computers used eight-bit logic chips, but the introduction of IBM's six-teen-bit machines forced competitors serving business users to design faster machines.

A microprocessor needs a printed circuit board full of support chips to control its operations and to store information. While there are many semi-conductor chips on the circuit board, the integrated circuits that determine a microcomputer's capacity are random access memories (RAMs). Like a telephone exchange, each cell in a RAM can be contacted individually and is capable of storing a binary digit (bit) of information. (A byte contains eight bits.) Microcomputers with larger memories (64-kilobyte RAM, for exam-ple) can process tasks faster because more information can be addressed by the brain at any time. RAMs are commoditylike and are produced in huge batches. In 1981, U.S. and Japanese producers were battling for leadership of the 64K RAM market and many semiconductor firms were also working on 256K RAM devices at year end. RAMs can be erased and recoded, but the information inscribed on ROMs (read-only memories) is permanent in each cell. Permanent instructions (such as operating systems) are placed in personal computers using ROMs.

The power-transformer module is unique to each microcomputer design and is the second-most-costly component. It provides the continuous power supply to the circuit board and logic chip of the computer.

Every microcomputer uses a keyboard (attached by an umbilical cord to the processing unit) to input data. Information can also be stored on tape cassettes, floppy disks, or rigid disks. Depending upon the type of storage media employed, microcomputers are connected to various disk-drive devices.

The screen (or monitor) that displays information differs in the quality of its resolution, depending on whether it contains a forty- or eighty-column character display. Although either display can offer color graphics, an eighty-character display is usually preferred for word-processing applica-tions. Television set makers, among others, possess video-display-produc-tion capabilities.

Printers (containing daisy-wheel or symbol-ball elements, for example) are used to produce typed output for microcomputers. Although manufac-turers of office equipment were capable of producing printers for personal computers, an entire segment of this industry developed during the 1970s that specialized in making these output devices for microcomputers.

When microcomputers were used in business offices, interconnection with sister units within the building was frequently desirable. Local networks could link microcomputers without using high-distortion tele-phone lines. Most desirable was a compatible link to join personal computers not only with one another, but also with other types of computers within a building.

Every microcomputer has an operating system (OS) that instructs it about how to perform tasks that other programs would describe. Software packages can be very expensive if written for a single user, but mass-produced software makes instructions for the microcomputer less costly. Because the usefulness of a microcomputer depends on the variety of software that will operate on it, access to larger customer segments becomes available if a computer uses the same operating system as others. Early personal-computer manufacturers wrote their own operating systems, and each tried to make theirs the industry standard. Each major microcomputer firm's operating system had outside programs written for it, and in 1981 some firms offered devices that made their microcomputers compatible with CP/M, the operating system that was adopted as standard, thereby making vast libraries of existing software available to their users. Each microcomputer also needed a language in which users could program their unique instructions. BASIC was the most widely offered programming-language capability, although some machines also offered FORTRAN, COBOL, or PASCAL programming-language capabilities.

Basis for Product Differentiation

Personal-computer users frequently do not wish to understand *how* or *why* a microcomputer runs; they are interested only in *what* a computer will do for them. The personal computer industry boomed when *computer illiteracy* no longer deterred laymen from purchasing microcomputers. By using *friendly* programs, that were similar to English, and highly readable instruction manuals, computer firms enticed increasing numbers of consumers to buy their product, rather like automobile makers who have sold cars to a public that cannot understand or repair their products. Personal computers could be differentiated on the basis of speed (microprocessors) and memory capacity (RAMs), but increasing numbers of first time purchasers chose their systems on the basis of user friendliness, a quality determined by how simple to understand the instructions for using the computer seemed to be. Friendly software explained any errors (or *bugs*) in the user's instructions in thoroughly understandable language. Some operating systems offered a "Help!" button users could push any time they became confused (even in the middle of a program subroutine) without loss of data or processing steps created by the interruption. Because friendliness was an attribute each manufacturer could control, substantial attention was devoted to creating a wide variety of software in easy-to-understand terms for their unique machine configurations. Software was expected to be the major attribute that distinguished U.S. microcomputers from others because Japanese microcomputers used existing, compatible programs rather than create new software for the U.S. market.

Users were also interested in the availability of support services, especially repairs. Brand names were valued if manufacturers possessed good reputations for supporting their products. Otherwise computer specialty stores provided the repairs, education, and software assistance needed by microcomputer users. (Clubs that shared advice—and pirated software—sprang up in many locations to assist the layman. Computer magazines were more formidable sources of information because they relied heavily upon the jargon of *computer freaks,* engineers who preferred to talk only to the initiated.)

Demand for Personal Computers

The demand for microcomputers grew rapidly from 1974, when the first personal computer, a bag of unassembled components, was offered in kit form by MITS/Altair. The number of units installed in 1981 was more than double the number installed one year earlier, as table 10-1 indicates. The market for personal computers differed in many ways from that for minicomputers. Substitutes for the microcomputer varied, depending upon the type of user—small businesses, hobbyists, or educational institutions. Their low price made them cheap enough to use at home.

Markets

The products offered by microcomputer makers became more sophisticated as various markets developed. Initially, products were low in sophistication

Table 10-1
Estimated Installed Base of Personal Computers, December 1981

	Units	Cumulative
1974–1978	250,000	250,000
1979	59,000	309,000
1980	327,000	636,000
1981	755,000	1,391,000

Source: Industry sources.

and appealed to hobbyists possessing considerable electronics expertise who assembled the kits, devised ways to input data and receive outputs, and programmed the homemade microcomputers themselves. Early products offered by Tandy/Radio Shack and Commodore International were for this hobbyist market. When Tandy/Radio Shack discovered that microcomputers were being purchased by small-business owners rather than by homemakers, it began to offer disk storage, word-processing capability, compatibility with large computers, leasing options and extended-service contracts to satisfy this user group. Other personal-computer makers also redesigned their offerings and introduced second- (or third-)generation machines for business users.

Since 1979 (and until 1982) the largest- and fastest-growing market had been small businesses. Although word-processing capability for this market did not require much memory (RAM), disk space or speed, other business software required substantial on-line disk handling, storage capacity, and speed. The educational market was also important because schools frequently had six or seven personal computers apiece in 1981, and ambitious parents purchased the same models to develop computer literacy in their children at home. The educational market was best served by the less-costly personal computers offering superior software and documentation. The hobbyist, or home market, was the most fragmented, least developed, and slowest growing in 1981, but it exploded into the most rapidly growing and most highly competitive market in autumn 1982. Much of the hobbyist demand was satisfied by microcomputers that emphasized games, personal-financial services, and programming education. Competition stressed reliability, price, and user friendliness initially, but as sales volumes increased, price competition became increasingly important. Home computers were expected to become as ubiquitous as portable televisions and extension telephones, and their sales volumes doubled every six months.

Software sales were a key determinant of vendor success and were expected to exceed the value of personal-computer-hardware sales after 1984. Retail estimates of software sales in 1981 ($600 million) did not include software copied illegally, and as electronic protection was added to foil copying, software sales began to increase sharply. Few manufacturers compiled their own libraries of programming; instead they used outside programmers to write software for their microcomputers.

Suppliers

By 1981, more than twenty-five firms made integrated circuits. The likelihood that an unintegrated personal-computer maker would backward integrate was low because the production of semiconductor devices was very capital intensive and a new plant cost $50 million in 1981. Moreover, global demand for integrated circuits was depressed, and existing firms were likely to retaliate fiercely if entry were attempted. RAMs were subject to substantial experience-curve economies, and only Texas Instruments and Motorola were able to carve out substantial shares of this market. Dominance of the market for lower-capacity memory chips had been surrendered to the Japanese years earlier, but because the electronic-component business was a technology-driven one, many electronics firms hoping to participate in the next generation of integrated circuits had to compete in the current one or suffer competitive disadvantages later.

RAM chips were commodities that could be purchased from outsiders, but firms that designed truly unique microcomputer systems made their own logic chips (microprocessors). Logic chips were not subject to as steep an experience curve because their manufacturing process involved designing, writing, and testing software and their volumes were much smaller. If firms wanted unique designs for their microcomputer units but did not wish to integrate backward, firms such as Texas Instruments, Motorola, or Intel, for example, would custom-build logic chips for these customers. (This business practice was called the "silicon foundry" concept, an arrangement whereby customer firms designed hardware circuits for microprocessors and the foundry firms acted as subcontractors in manufacturing them. The silicon foundry was increasing in popularity in 1981 because it took advantage of efficiencies in production that only these manufacturing leaders could attain.) In most cases, custom logic chips were not necessary in 1981 because microcomputer users had not yet demanded high levels of sophistication in the number of functions available or in faster computing speeds. Standard (or *off-the-shelf*) logic chips were adequate for most uses. Buyers insisted that good microprocessor designs be cross-licensed to ensure they would not be cut off from a supply of the chip that their computer was built upon, and cross-licensing increased the rate of technological change in the microcomputer industry. When photomasks, templates used in etching circuits onto silicon substrates, and production details were exchanged, both firms better understood how to improve their productivity in making microprocessor chips.

Any semiconductor firm that made microprocessors was capable of producing microcomputers as well. Texas Instruments, MOS Technology (Commodore), Motorola, Hitachi, and Intel were all forward integrated to microcomputers. Japanese firms were highly integrated to ensure secure supplies of their components and to capture value-added, but most other firms purchased only 30 percent of their requirements from their in-house unit to safeguard efficiency. Japanese firms had great patience in developing a product line, such as semiconductor products, where no expertise previously existed, and their patient shareholders allowed Japanese consumer-electronics firms to carry costly amounts of excess capacity in their vertically integrated postures when demand became depressed. Their greater concern with longer-term, strategic-posture advantages permitted Japanese semiconductor firms to earn lower reported profits without being forced to exit from a line of business due to vertical integration. U.S. electronic-components manufacturers readily recognized there were disadvantages to such vertical integration, such as obsolescence if the downstream unit did not possess the autonomy to purchase components from outsiders, and sizable diseconomies during periods when demand for certain RAM and logic chips was depressed. Nevertheless some electronics firms followed their Japanese counterparts in this strategy and featured vertical integration prominently as a prized attribute in their financial reports.

Two types of software-supply problems plagued all microcomputer makers—software for the microprocessor chips and software for programs that could be sold independently of their machines. Japanese and U.S. firms suffering software disadvantages in microprocessor production entered joint ventures with—or acquired—small firms that were particularly adept at designing custom-logic chips or writing software. Japanese firms used mass-produced, *semi-custom* chips to remedy a portion of their software disadvantage and to gain production economies.

Applications software was needed in such great volumes that firms used contract labor and joint ventures to stimulate concentrated-software-writing efforts, and to supplement the stables of programmers each firm maintained. Control over outside programmers was exerted by writing the operating-system packages for a particular task (*kernels*) in-house and by writing the manuals for each program to ensure that the end product would be sufficiently easy to understand. Microprocessor firms usually specified the tasks the software must perform and designed the display that users would see during processing to control how their product would be presented. In 1981 microcomputer vendors were scrambling to strengthen their competitive positions in software by recruiting outsiders to write programs that would run on their machines—and *not* on those of their competitors. Generous licensing agreements were offered as personal-computer firms strived to become the marketing agents for promising software houses.

Backward integration from personal computers to peripherals, such as disk drives or printers, seemed unwise in 1981 because capital requirements were high and diseconomies from excess capacity were significant. The leading manufacturers of disk drives in 1981 were Seagate Technology, Siemens, Tandon, MPI, and Shugart Associates (owned by Xerox), and the leading manufacturers of printers were Diablo (Xerox) and Qume. Recently, Ricoh became a major supplier of printers to Tandy, and Epson supplied printers for the IBM personal computer. Other suppliers included CPT, Nippon Electric (NEC), Itoh, and Fujitsu.

In summary, technological change occurred rapidly in the industries supplying the personal-computer makers, and backward integration could be very costly. Instead of doing so, many firms purchased their requirements from suppliers whose business strategies depended upon the existence of an outside market for their excess production.

Manufacturing

Although patents protected electronic components and copyrights protected software, neither acted as entry barriers for the production of personal computers. All components could be purchased from outsiders and assembled in-house. Osborne Computer, for example, bragged that its assembly operations required only forty screws and sixty-eight minutes to produce an Osborne 1, and Sinclair's entire production was subcontracted to Timex.

The computer industry is a technology-driven industry subject to short product cycles, rapid obsolescence, and heavy research-and-development outlays. The cost of white-collar labor made vertical integration particularly costly in this environment. Consequently, some personal-computer firms purchased the best pieces of a system from diverse suppliers to exploit innovations, and assembled these pieces in-house. Truly proprietary processes in the manufacturing of components were protected by trade secrets in cases where disclosing production details in a patent would make it too easy for unlicensed firms to copy them. Nevertheless, small firms did pirate ideas, designs, and people from larger firms, expecting perhaps that they were too small to be sued.

Laborers tended not be unionized in the personal-computer industry, but the high cost of engineers made wages and salaries often as much as 60 percent of the cost of production. Automation offered cost advantages, even in assembly operations where firms used insertion equipment to place electronic components on printed circuit boards. Minimum-efficient plant size was trivial because units could be assembled in garages and a minimal plant cost only $100,000. It was possible, moreover to specialize in a portion of the operations for producing finished microcomputers and purchase other services. As consumers became more sophisticated in their ability to discriminate among vendors, they forced personal-computer firms to spend greater amounts on quality-control assurance. Such expenditures also reduced opportunities for production economies.

Although production of electronic components was highly automated, assembly of the components and pieces that comprised a personal-computer system was not necessarily automated in 1981. Because the electronic components represented high value-added per ounce, they were frequently shipped from one site to another for stages in the assembly and testing process. Because firms varied substantially in their proportions of in-house production (and because steps in the process did not have to be physically proximate), it is difficult to generalize about the steps each firm elected to perform in-house.

The cost of physical assets was of minor importance in evaluating exit decisions. If a product were discontinued, the engineers would be transferred to another project (or laid off). Asset inflexibility was not a significant problem because the technology was general purpose in 1981 and standardized parts were produced. Although technology was changing rapidly and making product designs obsolete, the personal-computer markets did not demand product updates as rapidly. Therefore firms committed to particular technological configurations did not face insurmountable exit barriers in easing out of their product designs.

Marketing

The major problem *all* microcomputer makers faced was access to their ultimate customers. Marketing expenses included instructional efforts, demonstrations and sales aids, advertising, setting up dealers and financing customer purchases, and maintenance and service personnel. Some of these expenses were borne by outsiders that distributed personal computers for the manufacturers, such as both independent and chain, specialty computer retailers, department and discount retail stores, company-franchised retail outlets, company-owned retail stores, mail-order and catalogue-sales outlets, and company sales forces calling on national accounts.

Computer stores were an over-the-counter business and microcomputers competed for shelf space using whatever means their manufacturers believed would entice a retailer to carry their particular brand of computer. One of the most important attributes to retailers was market success. Therefore, firms that entered the personal-computer industry *early* had the advantage of large installed bases that gave them customer credibility. Recognized brand names and reputations for quality in other markets that could carry over to the microcomputer market were also assets in capturing retailer shelf space. Early retail outlets were mom-and-pop stores patronized by electronics buffs, and their capitalization was as low as $50,000 for some chain stores. By 1981 small shops run by inarticulate technological wizards were made obsolete by slick and well-trained, business-savvy personnel who could communicate with and sell complex systems to computer-illiterate customers, and the capitalization of a new computer store approached $160,000.

As the market grew larger and more firms introduced personal computers, distributors grew stronger and forced manufacturers to offer them better support, faster service, and better profit margins. This meant that some firms absorbed price cuts, although retail prices appeared unchanged. Computer makers also offered financial support and personnel instruction to dealers that possessed the power to attain this assistance. Seeing their margins shrink and desiring more control over the distribution of their microcomputers, some manufacturers also began distributing personal computers through their own stores. Tandy was the 1981 leader in merchandising computers and had initially offered personal computers produced by several firms through their stores. As personal computers increased in popularity, Tandy specialized in its own branded machines, and began opening specialty computer stores in key, business-user markets. Although all 8,000 Radio Shack stores continued to stock personal-computer products, the higher end of the Radio Shack line was displayed most completely in its 225 specialized computer stores by 1981. Other personal-computer firms that had computer stores included IBM, Digital Equipment, Xerox, Commodore, Zenith, and Texas Instruments (TI). (By 1981, TI had closed its stores or converted them to Learning Centers.)

Japanese microcomputers were expected to encounter some difficulty in attaining shelf space in computer-specialty chains where they lacked brand loyalty and user software. Hitachi had been selling machines to chains for private branding. Under this arrangement, store personnel provided the software Hitachi needed to interface with other competitive programs, and retailers enjoyed higher profit margins. Private-brand shelf space was limited, however, and some Japanese firms would be unwilling to lose the advantages of brand recognition by selling in this manner.

In summary, personal-computer makers competed for shelf space through many retail outlets in 1981. Because user service was becoming very important in this industry, many manufacturers were forward integrating or increasing their control over distributors of microcomputer products.

Competition in the Personal-Computer Industry in 1981

In 1981 approximately ninety firms manufactured personal computers, which were merchandised through over 1,500 computer-specialty stores, countless department and discount stores, and increasing numbers of owned retail outlets. Market shares changed daily; table 10–2 is merely a snapshot of an arena where competitors rose and fell. It does not show leaders for the three major user groups, nor does it reflect the take off in sales among home computers (Texas Instruments, Atari, etc.) in 1982.

The assemblers—Apple, Tandy, Sinclair, Osborne, and Atari, among others—enjoyed some early, spectacular successes in marketing by offering microcomputers at popular prices, with popular software, easy-to-understand documentation, and desirable features. Among the assemblers, Tandy

Table 10–2
Measures of Competitive Performance among Selected Personal-Computer Firms, December 1981

	Market Share of 1981 Retail Sales	
	Millions of Dollars	Percent
1. Apple	506	23
2. Tandy/Radio Shack	506	23
3. Commodore (International sales)	220	10
4. Nippon Electric Co.	154	7
5. Hewlett-Packard	110	5
6. IBM (U.S. sales only)	88	4
7. Others (Xerox, Digital Equipment, Zenith, Texas Instruments)	616	28
Total	2,200	100

	Market Share of Unit Sales			
	1981		1980	
	Thousands	Percent	Thousands	Percent
1. Apple	180	24	79.5	24
2. Tandy/Radio Shack	170	23	99.3	30
3. Commodore	150	20	41.4	13
4. IBM	40	5	0	0
5. Texas Instruments	30	4	8.1	3
6. Atari	30	4	17.0	5
7. Hewlett-Packard	25	3	11.3	3
8. Others (Digital Equipment, Xerox, Data General, Zenith, Nippon Electric)	129	17	70.5	22
Total	755	100	327.1	100

	Market Share of Cumulative Installed Base, 1981	
	Thousands	Percent
1. Tandy/Radio Shack	400	29
2. Apple	350	25
3. Commodore	300	22
4. Texas Instruments	45	3
5. Atari	40	3
6. IBM	40	3
7. Hewlett-Packard	36	2
8. Others (Digital Equipment, Xerox, Data General, Zenith, Nippon Electric)	180	13
Total	1,391	100

Source: Industry Sources.

and Apple, the market leaders, were pursuing the business-user market most aggressively in 1981 with large advertising outlays and newly designed products. Between them, Tandy and Apple accounted for over half of all installed microcomputers in 1981, but there was one significant difference between them. Tandy controlled its shelf space, maintained its own service personnel, and offered a local-network-communications link for business users. Apple and the other nonintegrated assemblers could not offer repair services nor the other business-user support that Tandy possessed. Consequently, they relied heavily on their distributors to provide the user assistance they could not furnish internally.

Because microcomputer customers were relatively unsophisticated in 1981, firms could purchase logic chips from outsiders and build a machine around them that was sufficiently sophisticated for the home-user market, but eventually the business-user market would demand features that some firms believed would require custom logic chips. In 1981 the following firms were producing microprocessors designed for personal computers: Intel, MOS Technology (Commodore), Motorola, Sharp, Hitachi, NEC, Texas Instruments and Zilog (among others). Other computer firms that could manufacture microprocessors if their volume became economic, or some technological advantage could be gained by doing so, included Digital Equipment, National Cash Register (NCR), Hewlett-Packard, and IBM.

Corporate Strategy Exit Barriers in Personal Computers

In 1981 many small microcomputer makers were undiversified firms that could exit easily because they assembled their systems, but were likely instead to use price-cutting to recover sales volumes because they were computer wizards rather than business persons and were willing to eke out a modest salary. For them, strategic exit barriers could be high until they lost sizable sums. The *mainframe* computer makers and office-equipment firms were unlikely to exit from personal computers because the microcomputer was becoming a necessity in well-run offices and could easily supplant the larger, minicomputer systems currently under lease if connected with a local-networking-communications link. Microcomputer sales were too close to the central strategy of IBM, Digital Equipment, and other computer makers to be surrendered without a fight in 1981.

Summary of Competitors in Personal Computers

In summary, the personal-computer firms could differ in the user market they served—small businesses, educational, home-hobbyist, or scientific, whether or not they were backward integrated, and where they sold their microcomputers. By 1981, software and access to good distribution channels were the keys to larger sales volumes, and firms that could not command the best shelf space often wrote very-friendly software, permitting their personal computers to demonstrate themselves to browsing customers in unorthodox retail outlets.

Broad integration (from microprocessors and peripherals to stores) was very capital intensive, and the salaries paid to stables of white-collar programmers, engineers, and designers added to the capital costs that raised their breakeven points. Competitors that made their own microprocessors, RAMs and ROMs, and sold these components to other firms as well as to sister units, enjoyed economies from scale, experience, and vertical-integration effects. When prices fell in the microcomputer market, integrated firms would have the lowest manufacturing costs.

A Mapping of Strategic Groups in Personal Computers

This section groups major competitors by their breadth of vertical integration in 1981. Some firms were fully integrated with respect to keyboards, disk drives, or other components produced in-house, while others sold the greatest proportion of their output to other firms. They could be mapped as shown in figure 10–1 to indicate whether any shared resources or linkages between important businesses existed.

In 1981 many personal-computer firms used several distribution channels, including their own stores. Firms such as IBM, Xerox, and Zenith trained their repair forces to service personal computers, and assemblers arranged service contracts with distributors. Financing arrangements were designed to convince dealers to allocate certain machines better shelf space, and software packages were developed exclusively for specific machines to persuade consumers to purchase them. In 1981 demand was increasing fast enough to accommodate many firms that were largely assemblers.

Key Events in the Personal Microcomputer Industry

This section traces key events leading to the 1981 industry structure. The microprocessor—Central Processor Unit (CPU) and memory-on-a-chip—was first invented in 1971 by Texas Instruments (TI), and the first single-chip microcomputer was demonstrated by TI shortly thereafter. Intel concentrated its efforts on developing microcomputer chips, while TI emphasized calculator microprocessors. Neither firm commercialized microcomputers at this time, and without software, input-output devices, or other infrastructure, the microprocessor was a high-technology gadget for engineers and hobbyists. The early microcomputer firms did not foresee which markets would eventually embrace the microprocessor nor how much support the product needed before it became a computer for the masses.

Breadth of Nondistribution Activities

Distribution Activities	Primarily Assembly	Micro- pro- cessors	Printers or Disk Drives	Displays and Power Supplies	Circuit Boards	Local- Network- Communi- cations Links	Key- boards
Company-Owned Retail Outlets	TRS	COM (IBM)	COM XEROX	ZDS	(TRS) COM IBM XEROX ZDS	TRS (DEC) (XEROX)	IBM
Company- Controlled Wholesalers	APPLE						
National Accounts (Direct)	APPLE TRS	(IBM) (DEC)			TRS IBM DEC ZDS	(DEC) (XEROX) TRS	IBM
Mail Order	APPLE SIN			ZDS	ZDS		
Company- Franchised Retail Outlets	APPLE TRS				(TRS)	TRS	
Multibrand Specialty Computer Retail Outlets	ATARI APPLE OSB	COM (IBM) SHARP NEC TI	COM TI XEROX	ZDS	COM IBM TI XEROX ZDS HP	(DEC) (XEROX)	IBM TI
Department Stores	ATARI	COM (IBM) TI	COM TI		COM (IBM) TI		IBM TI
Private Label		NEC HIT TI	TI		SHARP HIT TI		TI

Key to corporations:

APPLE	Apple	OSB	Osborne Computer
ATARI	Atari	TRS	Radio Shack (Tandy)
COM	Commodore International	SHARP	Sharp
DEC	Digital Equipment	SIN	Sinclair
HIT	Hitachi	TI	Texas Instruments
HP	Hewlett-Packard	XEROX	Xerox
IBM	International Business Machines	ZDS	Zenith Data Systems
NEC	Nippon Electric		

Figure 10-1. A Mapping of Firms in Personal Computers, 1981

1974

The first microcomputers available commercially were offered by obscure firms like MITS/Altair, and Imsai. They had peripherals and were merchandised through publications like *Popular Electronics* in an unassembled form. MOS Technology offered KIM, a circuit board containing a microprocessor, ROMs, RAMs, and an input-output device in 1974. With little display and keyboard, KIM could be hooked up to a cassette tape recorder to receive programming, and was sold aggressively to the educational market, especially to universities that wanted to teach microprocessor theory.

1975

In 1975 Texas Instruments engineers demonstrated a sixteen-bit microcomputer that was brilliant but premature. It was based on a TI9900 microprocessor chip, and TI also produced many of the other electronic components it needed. The TI 99/7 market forecasts were wildly optimistic.

In semiconductor devices, Texas Instruments was backward integrated to silicon raw materials, photomasks, and process equipment. It strongly believed in the long-term benefits of vertical integration and used its integrated posture to leverage market advantages it had attained. A very important part of its corporate strategy was the protection of its technology, and TI used full (100 percent) ownership of worldwide operations, trade secrets, patents, and vertical integration to do so. Like its Japanese competitors, this meant TI was willing to live with the imbalances that sometimes resulted from using vertical integration to stake out a position of uniqueness in the market early.

1976

In 1976 the microprocessor was packaged and sold as a complete microcomputer laboratory—microprocessor, board, memories and other necessary peripheral devices, testing and debugging programs, documentation and schematics, software, and microcomputer dictionary. The new product received a huge response—mostly from engineers.

In 1976 MOS Technology built the first true personal computer—the PET—containing its 6502 microprocessor, a RAM and ROM, and an input-output device. The PET had a true keyboard and display, and it was programmable using BASIC. In November 1976, Commodore acquired MOS Technology and applied its knowledge of retailing consumer products to the PET. Commodore's first microcomputers were created for the home-hobbyist market, but many of them were used in small-business offices.

MOS Technology's 6502-microprocessor design was cross-licensed to other manufacturers and the firm produced storage devices for its personal computer, but it farmed out much of the software development to contract programmers. Commodore purchased video displays, some subassemblies, and many of the low-technology components needed in order to reserve its plant space for the manufacture of high-technology components used in its personal computers and those of other customers. (Only 25 percent of its microprocessor output was consumed in-house, and Commodore's manufacturing costs were lower than Apple's and Atari's, two other users of its 6502-chip design.)

Commodore valued its backward integration, believing it allowed the firm to control its costs better and to obtain insights about technological change. By picking and choosing which components to produce in-house and which components to source, Commodore maximized the advantages of its systems capability. Because its research and tooling-up expenses could be amortized over high-output volumes, Commodore enjoyed research-and-development economies of scale as well as of integration. Because it had cross-licensed the 6502 chip, Commodore's microcomputer division could find several sources of emerging supply for this crucial component, and MOS Technology was able to operate as an autonomous supplier to downstream industries, thereby alleviating some of the riskiness associated with depending on few customers for the consumption of its chips.

Commodore's personal computers were distributed through department stores, specialty computer stores and company-owned stores in the Silicon Valley area. Its chief competitive advantage was its low price, but marketing and distribution were not Commodore's strengths. Historically, its dealer relationships had been poor and its advertising budgets were meager.

In 1976 two former design engineers in Silicon Valley founded Apple Computer to create a computer that would be accessible to everyone. Because Apple was neither forward nor backward integrated, Apple relied heavily upon the mom-and-pop computer stores to merchandise its microcomputers initially. Many of these early dealers owed their success to Apple and were loyal to the company even after Apple's dealer support deteriorated.

1977

The microcomputer market began to develop when the CP/M program was created in 1977, because this operating system permitted software writers to program more applications for microcomputers. Another crucial change that enlarged the personal-computer market was the packaging of machines in less formidable forms. Early firms, such as Vector Graphic, Ohio Scientific and Processor Technology, grew with startling speed due to these changes.

Apple, the firm that had been started by two, young, college dropouts, sold $100,000 worth of microcomputers in 1976 and earned a 20 percent pretax profit. Quickly the firm introduced its product in Europe, where ITT was so impressed by the Apple II that it agreed to market the microcomputer for Apple. In 1977, 500 retailers sold the Apple, and its distribution network was expanding rapidly.

In 1977 a Radio Shack employee rigged a crude microcomputer from components sold in the Radio Shack stores and proposed that the stores merchandise assembled personal computers. The amused management authorized an initial order of microcomputers—enough for each Radio Shack store to use the machine for in-house-inventory record-keeping, in case the units did not sell. The new personal-computer systems sold faster than they could be assembled, and Tandy started building its own microcomputers by purchasing printed circuit boards and electronic components that they assembled to form the CPU and memory devices. Tandy purchased its sixty-four- and eighty-character video displays from Taiwanese television firms, its printers from a Japanese vendor, and its Z-80 microprocessor chips from Zilog. It purchased its keyboards, floppy discs, input-output circuitry and power supply from outsiders, and little research and development was invested in the Tandy/Radio Shack product because users wrote software and traded programs for it.

1978

In 1978 specialized, Radio Shack Computer Stores deleted the personal-computer products of other vendors and concentrated exclusively on their own products. Regular Radio Shack stores continued to devote a niche of floor space to the lower end of the Tandy computer line—the hobbyist products—although demand was clearly segmented into home-entertainment and business-user markets. When Radio Shack did some research about who purchased their product in 1978, it discovered that its customer was actually the businessperson who could not afford a larger IBM-minicomputer installation, and this discovery resulted in a change in the products being offered as well as the type of software being merchandised. The Model II memory was increased to a 64-K RAM, and the Model III was placed between Model I and Model II in its capabilities. The limiting factor in Tandy's growth became software.

In April 1978, Commodore acquired the Mr. Calculator group of retail stores. These were later converted to retail outlets for its microcomputers.

In 1979 IBM opened a series of nationwide Business Computer Centers to sell its minicomputer to groups of potential customers. The stores were part of an IBM experiment with mass-merchandising techniques to reduce the cost of selling its lower-end office products.

1979

At the end of 1978, fewer than 250,000 cumulative personal-computer units had been sold. Radio Shack sold 100,000 units in 1978, Commodore sold 25,000 Pets, and Apple sold 20,000 units. Although 1979 was expected to be a year when large volumes of personal computers would be sold, these forecasts did not materialize, due to a shortage of chips.

In 1979, VisiCalc was developed and marketed by Personal Software, Inc. Initially the software ran only on Apple machines, and its popularity gave Apple an enormous lead over other personal computers.

In 1979 Exxon's Zilog introduced the MCZ-1 microcomputer based on its Z-80 microprocessor. Zilog had become a major force in microprocessors with Exxon's backing. In 1979 its sales volume of $25 million doubled that of a previous year.

In June 1979, TI introduced the 99/4, a personal computer that included a video monitor and keyboard console that accepted programs for education, games, and home finance. The 99/4 was a home-entertainment computer, but now the market seemed to be going in the opposite direction. The leaders in microcomputers—Tandy, Apple, and Commodore—had shifted their emphasis to systems designed for the very-small-business person, but Texas Instruments chose a focused market that most firms were ignoring in 1979. Like the Sinclair ZX-81, the TI99/4 home computer was user friendly and easy to use. It offered a forty-character, color screen and a substantial library of games and programming aids (BASIC), but electronic hobbyists found the TI99/4 difficult to program for business applications and little TI business software had been written.

Texas Instruments sold its home computer through its own consumer-electronics stores, computer-specialty stores, department stores, catalogue showrooms, and discount stores (like K-Mart) where the product needed little explanation from sales personnel. The TI99/4 was not a favorite in computer-specialty stores, however, because its margins were thin, and Texas Instruments did not scramble to follow the market as other computer firms did. Texas Instruments seemed content to stay in the home or schools where it hoped the TI99/4 would become as ubiquitous as the Texas Instruments calculator.

In October 1979, Zenith acquired the HeathKit business from Schlumberger Limited. This acquisition gave Zenith two personal computers—the HeathKit and the Zenith microcomputer. Zenith also acquired a library of programs, a base for training microcomputer technicians, and a network of HeathKit stores. In 1979, HeathKit had a 90 percent share of the kit business and its educational products were among the best on microprocessors.

In 1979 Xerox introduced Ethernet, an intra-office-communications system for connecting free-standing, electronic, information-processing machines. Ethernet was designed to be compatible with any computer. Other networks available at that time included DECnet (Digital Equipment) and ARCnet (by Datapoint).

1980

By 1980 the personal-computer market that grew most rapidly was clearly the business-user one, but high interest rates and a sagging economy discouraged some purchases. Nevertheless, firms continued to introduce new computers, investments in research and development to develop more powerful microcomputers continued, and new software was written as the year progressed.

In 1980 Apple's distribution system changed when Apple terminated independent distributors and established company-owned, regional-support centers. This distribution restructuring was intended to provide better support for Apple's 850 domestic dealers, and as Apple became increasingly interested in the business-user market, it was moving further away from its founders' original desire to make computers accessible to everyone. In 1980 the Apple III was launched. It was intended to appeal to the management and professional business-user market, but it encountered significant manufacturing problems for over six weeks after its introduction, and those units that were sold had to be repaired in the field. At this time, Apple had no sales force of its own and its credibility was undermined by this embarrassing product recall. After the Apple III died in the market from a premature birth in 1980, Apple scrambled to soothe its retailers and organized regional dealer-support centers to assist them in the better servicing of Apple equipment.

After acquiring HeathKit, Zenith split it into two pieces. One half continued to sell computer kits through the seventy retail stores nationwide. The other half, Zenith Data Services, sold a small HeathKit computer system—the Z89, based on Zilog's Z-80 microprocessor—to business customers. As part of Zenith's marketing efforts, it arranged for dealers to finance their purchases of the Zenith personal computer with Zenith itself paying the interest. It also offered dealers demonstration packets of software at substantially reduced prices. Zenith employed two types of wholesale distributors to market its personal computers. One type specialized in sales to schools and for scientific applications, the other sold microcomputers to retail outlets such as ComputerLand.

Zenith personal computers were marketed to the rapidly growing business-user group by writing very explicit documentation. (It read like a HeathKit book). By making a very reliable product supported by non-threatening user information, Zenith appealed to the relatively unsophisticated manager who desired results and did not care about what was inside the black box.

In 1980 Texas Instruments encountered trouble in microcomputers. Its 99/4 had been designed for Mr. and Mrs. America, and was the least-threatening computer available in 1980. Unfortunately the 99/4 was too expensive for the household market ($1400 compared with $595 for Commodore) yet too simple for the business market. Furthermore, users found it difficult to write software for the 99/4 and its library of software was small. In response to market dissatisfaction, Texas Instruments discounted the 99/4 heavily and marketed it through channels such as K-Mart. In November, Texas Instruments introduced a rebate program followed by a price cut of 30 percent on its microcomputer to make it competitive with the Apple and Commodore machines. Then it introduced the TI99/4A, a talkative microcomputer that demonstrated itself.

Although Radio Shack was still the market leader in June 1980, it expected that Apple would soon become a challenge. Tandy introduced computers for the small-computers market and a desktop model to rival Hewlett-Packard's HP-85. Tandy maintained a team of software programmers to develop applications for its personal computers, and its machines ran VisiCalc. Moreover, Tandy encouraged independent software writers to bring their TRS-80 programs into the firm's marketing system, and it formed a joint venture with Datapoint to develop an interoffice-network communications link.

Like its major competitor, Apple Computer, Tandy marketed aggressively to the small-business-user market, the segment that seemed to be growing most rapidly in 1980. Unfortunately, Tandy had an image problem. The media were fond of reminding consumers that Radio Shack stores were dowdy and cluttered, true to Tandy's history of offering decent quality, low-priced, and mundane merchandise, and that these were scarcely appropriate outlets to woo the business-user market and sell ARCnet-data communications links. To reach the market more effectively, Tandy created specialized computer stores where its full line of personal computers could be displayed, but its top-of-the-line microcomputers were emphasized. The slick displays and polished Tandy employees in these outlets were better suited to their fashionable locations and blue-chip clientele. Radio Shack stores soon numbered 6,000 in the United States with fifty-seven Radio Shack computer stores and an additional 100 stores specializing in computer products. In 1980 Radio Shack entered a marketing arrangement with Random House publishers for the educational market, and its services were enlarged when Tandy introduced the Videotex, a device the converted users' telephones and televisions in an output display device for accessing the CompuServ network and several databases. In November 1980, Tandy acquired Lika, a printed-circuit-board manufacturer. Only 25 percent of

Lika's output was consumed internally for the TRS-80 personal computer, but the purchase represented Tandy's first step toward backward integration in a product line representing 12.7 percent of its 1980 sales.

In April 1980, Xerox opened its first retail outlet in Dallas. The office-equipment store carried Xerox-brand products as well as those of other vendors, including an Apple computer and Hewlett-Packard calculator. Xerox hired a team of former Radio Shack store managers to keep the project from failing, as so many other computer stores had done.

In its efforts to penetrate the U.S. market, Commodore had eliminated independent distributors and established seven regional distribution centers that would also be dealer-support centers. When Commodore established company-owned stores in 1980, these dealers complained loudly that the new dedicated outlets would cannibalize their sales. Unlike IBM, Commodore stores carried other firms' computers and peripherals as well as Commodore-brand office-equipment products.

1981

Computer stores sprang up in 1981 to sell personal-computer products, and even traditional retailers like Sears, Roebuck and Montgomery Ward experimented with them. At the start of 1981, the leading sellers for the home-computer market were Radio Shack, Commodore, and Apple.

In April 1981, Xerox introduced its personal computer, the 820, which offered more features at a price equivalent to the Apple II or the Radio Shack TRS-80 III. The Xerox desktop microcomputer could use over 2,000 independently written applications programs currently for sale because it used the CP/M operating-system software, and it could interface with large, mainframe computers as an intelligent terminal. In its effort to sell microcomputers, Xerox signed on fifty-five independent dealers and distributors to supplement the Office Product Division's own 500-person sales force and Xerox's twenty-five owned retail stores. The Xerox 820 microcomputer was largely assembled from components purchased from outsiders (for example, the microprocessor was a Z-80 from Zilog), but Xerox subsidiaries provided disk drives (Shugart) and printers (Diablo Systems). Its Ethernet local communications network was already in widespread use and the Xerox personal computer was also compatible for interconnection.

In February 1981, IBM announced the creation of a wholly owned subsidiary to finance installment-payment agreements with U.S. customers. It centralized this function for its four divisions that all needed customer financing. In March 1981, Matsushita indicated IBM had contacted it about buying some low-priced microcomputers. (The rumor was credible because IBM had recently sourced low-end copiers from Japanese suppliers). These rumors had been circulating for over one year and Matsushita, which had been making computers for the past two years to sell in Europe and wanted to enter the U.S. market, did not deny them.

In August 1981, the microcomputer industry came of age as IBM announced its first personal computer. It created a substantial stir because the IBM personal computer offered features unmatched by existing products. Its sixteen-bit microprocessor made it faster and more powerful; it had a larger memory capacity (up to 256K), links to outside databases and popular software (VisiCalc, Easy Writer, Microsoft Adventure, and other self-diagnostics that made the machine easier to run).

Historically IBM had been broadly integrated and satisfied roughly 75 percent (or more) of its in-house needs for semiconductors, keyboards, and other peripherals, but in the case of microcomputers, IBM departed substantially from its traditional policies. The sixteen-bit microprocessor (the 8088) was purchased from Intel, the floppy disks (and disk drives) were from Tandon Magnetics, the printer was from Epson, and much of the software to be offered was purchased from or marketed for independent software houses that would earn royalties from IBM's sales of their programs. (Individual programmers were also encouraged to submit their work for licensing.) This was the first time IBM used outside software houses, and it represented a sizable change from the many programmers maintained to write software for other IBM systems. In a further departure from tradition, IBM marketed the personal computer through Sears specialty computer stores, computer-specialty chain stores, like ComputerLand, its own retail outlets, and through the IBM sales force.

The IBM personal computer was an instant best-seller and captured 4 percent of the market in the few months following its introduction in 1981. Competitors believed that IBM's entry made the industry more credible to users and discounted predictions that IBM's personal computer would capture a substantial share of the business-user market. Apple (which had a market share of 23 percent before IBM's entry) seemed most vulnerable to the effects of IBM's entry. Retailers complained that their margins on Apple products were too low.

When IBM entered, Hewlett-Packard was beginning a campaign to penetrate the business-user market. Hewlett-Packard specialized in microcomputers for the scientific and analytical, professional-user groups. It did not market its personal computer to small-business users initially, because that market wanted low prices and much follow-up support, but its Model 83, 85, and 86 were geared to business users. Hewlett-Packard produced some solid-state components for in-house use and purchased others to capture the benefits of larger firms' scale economies. Its line of electronic-data products included business, scientific, and desktop computers. Thus, Hewlett-Packard possessed the capability to design and produce very-sophisticated microcomputer components if it found it advantageous to do so.

In 1981 Hewlett-Packard sold its personal computers through an independent-dealer market and had no plans to open its own computer stores. Personal computers represented 12 percent of group revenues in 1981, after IBM entered.

In October Digital Equipment announced its entry into personal computers. Rather than introduce a new machine, Digital Equipment offered a device that converted its VT-100 computer terminals into personal computers (an existing base of 250,000). The attachments would be sold in Digital Equipment's twenty-five retail stores and through direct telephone orders.

In December 1981, the Apple III desktop microcomputer was reintroduced. The redesigned model offered more software applications, expanded data-storage capacity, and a lower price. Following an idea from Commodore's emulator, the new Apple III was designed to emulate the IBM program library by adding an accessory microprocessor to the basic machine. Apple also hinted that a new Apple IV (code named "Lisa"), possessing remarkable graphics and editing capabilities, was in the works and would be offered to the office market soon, in addition to a local communications network for its personal computers. When it was unveiled, Lisa proved to be innovative in software, but it used traditional personal computer hardware.

In an effort to prevent mail-order houses from undercutting the prices of authorized Apple dealers, Apple refused to allow telephone and mail-order sales of its products in 1981. Apple's dealers had been educating the customers who then purchased the machine elsewhere. Controversy concerning the new policy was strong because mail-order sales had increased Apple's share of the market substantially.

Two of the least-expensive systems that captured the fancy of microcomputer buffs were assembled in environments of very low overhead in 1981. The Sinclair Research ZX-81 computer was created to teach programming, and was the smallest and cheapest personal computer. It was distributed by mail, to reduce distribution costs, and was available in kit form. The Sinclair microcomputer was based on a Zilog Z-80 microprocessor, and all manufacturing was performed by Timex in a factory in Scotland. Its lowest-priced microcomputer in 1981 cost ninety-nine dollars.

Osborne Computer was similarly nonintegrated, limiting manufacturing activities to simple assembly and testing operations. Its self-contained system cost $1,795. Osborne's healthy margins of 41 percent ensured that dealers would stock the machines, and Osborne's policies regarding software helped to sell the microcomputer to business professionals. Although Osborne Computer employed no programmers, the firm offered users a package of software worth $1,500 by forming a joint venture with four software suppliers willing to take Osborne stock for their equity participations.

Although Atari was best known for its video games, top-of-the-line

Atari machines were actually microcomputers capable of programming in BASIC. The Atari 8000 used the 6502 microprocessor as did Apple and Commodore, but few business users took their Atari's to the office.

In 1981 NEC Information Systems had a market share of 2.5 percent of microcomputer unit sales. Industry observers expected Matsushita to also become a dominant force in the U.S.-microcomputer market. Most Japanese companies already produced some of the components that comprised a microcomputer system, including microprocessors, and they were CP/M compatible so that existing software could be used with them. NEC, Panasonic, Camm, and Hitachi were among the microcomputer firms already private branding or otherwise selling in the United States. Toshiba, Casio, and others were about to enter.

In 1982 the rate of technological change accelerated, price-cutting became a significant means of competing, and the low-priced, home-user market grew more rapidly than the rest of the microcomputer industry. The 1981 market leaders in under-$1,000 microcomputers were Atari and Commodore (25 percent each), Texas Instruments (11 percent), Sinclair (15 percent), Tandy/Radio Shack (19 percent), and all others (5 percent). In 1982, Texas Instruments, Radio Shack, and Commodore each slashed prices to capture greater sales. Even Hewlett-Packard introduced a model priced at $995. The TI99/4A cost $199, the TRS-Color Computer cost $299, and the Commodore VIC 20 cost just under $200 in early 1982.

Changes in distribution included Hewlett-Packard forming marketing agreement with ComputerLand, Tandy/Radio Shack selling its Color Computer through outsiders (including RCA's distribution system), and Apple terminating a central purchasing agreement with its biggest retail account, ComputerLand. K-Mart carried the TI99/4A and Commodore Vic in 600 stores nationwide, and American Express Company sold 25,000 Sinclair ZX-81s for $99.95 each *through the mail,* in just three weeks. Sears Business Systems stores sold IBM, NEC, and Vector Graphics brands of microcomputers, and Safeway, the nation's largest supermarket chain, sold Commodore VIC 20's in twelve of its largest west-coast stores. Xerox stores reported their best-selling brand was not the Xerox 820-II, but rather the portable Osborne I. Texas Instruments opened small-computer schools to teach distributors' sales representatives and customers how to use TI equipment. Market shares in the three, major market segments continued to shift wildly as growth accelerated. The problem in all microcomputer markets continued to be access to shelf space and distinctive software in 1982.

Analysis of Strategies for Vertical Integration in the Personal Microcomputer Industry

Section one described the structure of the personal-computer industry in 1981 and section two described key events in the industry leading to its 1981 structure. This section analyzes the patterns of vertical behavior sketched above and compares the predictions of the strategy framework with outcomes observed in 1981.

In 1981 the personal-computer industry was emerging as a rapidly growing and potentially revolutionary industry, and competitors that entered the personal-computer industry were convinced that demand would continue to grow rapidly. If it did not do so, the structure of this industry was potentially volatile. Although the component manufacturers did not seem eager to exert their inherent bargaining power over microcomputer firms in 1981, distributors and specialty dealers were demanding better margins and lower prices. According to the framework proposed in chapter 2, in this industry the technological complexity of the product suggested that firms would be broadly integrated into a variety of activities and component producers would also be integrated in many stages for each activity undertaken; some internal integration would occur, especially downstream where bargaining power was weaker; and firms would tend to keep their ownership stakes low until their uncertainties were relieved but would later find increased control was necessary, due to conditions in the retail market.

Phase of Industry Development

The personal-computer industry was emerging in 1981 because demand for the product was clearly established and seemed almost recession-proof, pockets of demand were stabilizing, thereby permitting specialization to occur, many strategic postures were equally successful as ways to satisfy customer demand, technology was changing rapidly, and experience-curve economies were becoming substantial. Although there was still considerable uncertainty about how the rules of competition would eventually develop, the viability of microcomputers was assured.

When the personal-computer industry was embryonic and its structure was highly unresolved, few firms invested heavily in the infrastructure of this industry. Some firms offered microcomputer kits with sparse instructions or simple, assembled personal computers with minimal input-output devices and software, but only the semiconductor firms performed any research and development on microcomputers, and they sold most of their components elsewhere. By 1981 it had become evident that mass-marketed microcomputers required much more support from manufacturers and vendors. Software became the key to sales and firms began to experiment with programs and components that offered greater speed, memory, or novelty (such as speech). The volume of microprocessors used in personal computers had become substantial, and some internal production of components seemed advantageous. No strategic posture was clearly more successful, but increasing numbers of firms had opened retail outlets featuring their office products.

By 1981 demand for microcomputers was growing rapidly and did not appear sensitive to economic fluctuations. As the lower costs of producing electronic components and peripherals drove the cost of microcomputers down, more users entered the market, making competition more volatile, but demand seemed strong enough to absorb them in 1981 as customers increased their purchases.

Because demand was thriving, some firms felt confident that forward integration could be undertaken, and because corporate-strategy needs mandated high control over product integrity, many stages of conversion were undertaken for each activity performed in-house. Quality control had been less crucial when the consumers were engineers purchasing personal-computer kits as a hobby and could exchange defective units, work out programming bugs themselves, and needed little retailer demonstration. Little integration was needed when the industry was embryonic, but by 1981 consumers expected flawless machines and programs as well as substantial retailer support, and manufacturers integrated forward defensively.

Volatile Industry Structure

In 1981 shelf-space scarcity prompted firms to use price-cutting to gain access to consumers. Entry was relatively easy but profits were not high. Few casualties were reported in 1981, but future profit margins looked ominous.

Personal computers could be differentiated by software, speed, memory capacity, communications links, and appearance. Of these, the greatest sensitivity was to software, and as buyers grew more knowledgeable, it became a crucial selling point. Research-and-development expenditures were large because manufacturers maintained programming staffs to provide operating systems and applications software. Style changes occurred less frequently than technological changes in raw materials. Upstream industries required meticulous manufacturing precision to control quality adequately.

There were relatively few suppliers for key components of microcomputers and shortages did occur. The relative value-added of suppliers was frequently high, because their engineering content was high and manufacturers' specifications were tight. Few competitors made their own components or peripherals in 1981, but those that did had lower cost structures.

Manufacturers found the shortage of trained salespersons was a major barrier to distribution through department and discount stores. The relative value-added by distributors was high because selling personal computers required many demonstrations. Switching costs between brands that were not software-compatible was high, and software availability was frequently more important than brand names. Franchising by manufacturers did not appear to be a satisfactory way to reach consumers—nor did multiple-brand offerings. Manufacturers retrenched to company-owned retail outlets, carrying only their brands to supplement the marketing of outside distributors, and offered cooperative advertising, costly demonstration software, and other inducements to stimulate their sales efforts.

Some firms, such as Sinclair Research, used subcontractors to produce their branded microcomputers, and suppliers like Intel offered to make some or all of a customer's microprocessors. With such suppliers, manufacturing was frequently merely assembly operations using nonunionized laborers. Make-or-buy decisions for nonintegrated firms were not trivial because, although electronic components were a bottleneck, many manufacturers could not backward integrate. The output of upstream plants far exceeded the volumes needed by the emerging microcomputer industry and the capital requirements were beyond the reach of some firms. Even firms possessing the capability to manufacture components kept their engineers busy making the more-complex units while sourcing the commonplace components, rather than expand capacity without industry-wide increases in sales volume, because of the exit barriers and disequilibria such expansions could create. Finally, technology was changing too rapidly on products like disk drives or semiconductors for novices to commit assets to them.

Firms were dissimilar in their patterns of vertical integration, their strategic postures, and their parents' corporate strategies, yet they were all competing for the same scarce shelf space. They feared foreclosure from upstream and downstream firms, yet many were unable to use vertical integration as a competitive weapon. Some tried to strengthen distributor loyalties (and internal control) by erecting dealer-support centers or opening their own stores. Firms acted as though they expected historic growth rates to endure.

In summary, the structure of the microcomputer industry was potentially volatile in 1981 because the balance between upstream and downstream industries was poor, dissimilar firms were converging on the same markets, product changes were occurring rapidly, Japanese competitors and fringe firms were cutting prices to buy or maintain shelf space, and firms only partially controlled the software merchandised for their machines. Higher compatibility meant lower user-switching costs. Because future competition could become volatile, integrated firms were not expected to transfer a high proportion of their requirements in-house, and integration was advisable only if the demand that existed outside the firm could serve as a safety valve for absorbing excess output and keeping firms from incurring inflexibilities associated with older designs or technologies.

Bargaining Power

The bargaining power of suppliers over personal-computer firms was bilateral, because the volume of purchases represented by microcomputers was not important to suppliers yet, shortages of some components had delayed firms' production schedules, personal-computer firms could not force suppliers to incur research-and-development expenses on their behalf, many firms could not communicate credible threats of backward manufacture, and component manufacturers could forward integrate. To the personal-computer manufacturers' advantage, nonintegrated suppliers needed outlets for their new-component designs to attain experience-curve economies, cross-licensing alleviated some of the power of concentrated suppliers, and suppliers needed the intelligence that downstream firms could provide. Retailers had become increasingly liberated from the products of a single manufacturer by 1981, as more brands became available, more unsophisticated-market segments became customers, and increasing numbers of computer retailers bankrupted. Therefore, personal-computer firms encountered greater difficulties in dictating terms to retailers, using them to do missionary selling, or otherwise treating retailers as though they were extensions of the firm *without* risking an ownership stake in them. When manufacturers realized they could no longer control distributors as they could in the past, they created dealer-support centers or in-house wholesaling units, offered more favorable terms to dealers, and forward integrated into retailing themselves.

In summary, the phase of industry development and lack of bargaining power argued for more functions to be integrated and for the degree of internal integration to be high, but the industry's structure was potentially volatile, making high degrees of integration dangerous. This conflict between internal and external factors suggested the industry could become unprofitable for some firms and that others would be foreclosed from access to ultimate consumers.

Strategy Goals

In 1981 firms were integrating vertically to capture more value-added and to protect the integrity of their products. Firms that were capable of undertaking activities performed by adjacent industries were taper integrating to prod inside units to work harder to make a greater proportion of components in-house, or purchasing components from outsiders until the rate of technological change slowed down.

Apple Computer and many smaller competitors were assemblers seeking near-term profitability. Tandy/Radio Shack, IBM, and Commodore (among others) had their own stores, and sought long-term profitability even if losses were incurred initially to establish their new outlets. The only personal-computer firms making their own microprocessors in 1981—Texas Instruments and Commodore—were emphasizing the low-cost, home-entertainment market where price-cutting was becoming an important means of competing.

Personal computers served as market outlets for microprocessor firms, as Japanese competitors threatened to capture greater proportions of outside sales. Experience in making previous generations of semiconductors was necessary to create innovative, low-cost components in the future. Although technological leapfrogging was feasible, it was also so expensive that firms like Intel (the silicon foundry) and Texas Instruments used microcomputers as a means to vertically integrate to conserve future capabilities.

Some firms used their personal-computer businesses as outlets for related products that were already manufactured in-house. Office-equipment manufacturers sold microcomputers through pre-existing retail outlets. Computer manufacturers and others used existing peripheral equipment wherever it was cheaper to do so.

In summary, long-term benefits were anticipated because firms gained conduits to the market and intelligence useful for product improvements by forward integrating, but they also needed long-term staying power. Software appeared to be the key to long-term success.

The Need for Vertical Integration

Several, generally accepted reasons for vertical integration were not relevant in the personal-computer business in 1981. For example, firms desiring to remain on the leading edge of microcomputer technology could make their own microprocessor chips; yet the 1981 market was primarily one of unsophisticated consumers that did not require more than existing logic chips. Another motive was to protect firms' investments in technology from easy replication, but leakage of knowledge was great when transient scientists and engineers could take the knowledge of production processes needed to make high-quality products with them when changing employers. Economics and innovation were relevant motives for integration. Vertical integration reduced selling costs, handling costs, freight costs, and overhead charges. It provided firms with shorter lead times for responding to technological changes to customer needs. When the industry required greater sophistication, vertical integration would enable some firms to design their products with proprietary advantages that could not be designed as inexpensively using outside sources.

There were precedents arguing against integration, however. IBM had suffered technological lags in its large computers by relying too heavily upon internal integration, and Texas Instruments had suffered market setbacks because it did not weigh downstream units' suggestions about its personal computers as heavily as upstream units'. Moreover, the cash requirements of retailing increased firms' operating risks significantly, and could not generate all the software they needed.

Strategy Alternatives and Performance

The strategy model distinguished between ownership and the degree of internal integration firms engaged in; firms may have owned all, some, or none of the adjacent firms supplying goods and services, and transferred all, some, or none of their needs internally. Moreover, firms differed in the breadth of their integrations. In personal computers, firms could be backward integrated into all, some, or none of the components and peripherals that comprised a microcomputer system; they could also perform wholesaling and retailing tasks for some or all of their products, if these activities were justified by firms' strategic missions and competitive strengths.

Firms that used high degrees of internal integration sometimes did so to attain corporate objectives regarding market share or technological leadership. The major risks associated with doing so included asset inflexibility and loss of competitive scanning. In this industry, upstream firms usually taper integrated to remain aware of technological changes, exploit competitors' lower manufacturing costs, and diversify their customer bases. Many firms engaged in retailing activities were taper integrated to maximize their exposure to customers; even Tandy/Radio Shack began to use outsiders to reach new customers.

The number of stages of activity undertaken was determined by the product's characteristics, the nature of demand, and the mission of the personal-computer unit relative to adjacent businesses. Although personal computers was still a young industry in 1981, it had become clear that control over components, software, and retailing could provide firms with competitive advantages. Indeed, as software was becoming standardized and the personal computer was becoming a *black box,* manufacturing economies would be enjoyed by the Japanese and U.S. firms that were backward integrated to make electronic components. For firms like Texas Instruments, which were electronics firms that sold some consumer products, personal computers were conduits for selling their semiconductor memories and logic chips, and this difference in emphasis from consumer-electronic firms like Zenith or Commodore meant that such firms would use personal computers as a means to fund other high-technology businesses.

The breadth of integration—the number of activities undertaken—was determined by demand traits and competition. Firms like Texas Instruments and Zenith Data Systems made many of the components used in personal computers, because Texas Instruments expected to influence technological changes by participating in these businesses and Zenith had excess production capacity. By 1981, however, access to the market and programming were the most important advantages to possess. Thus firms like IBM and Digital Equipment joined Tandy and Zenith/HeathKit in opening stores that would showcase their computer products. As demand increased for each segment of personal computers, firms specializing in each market were enabled to undertake more in-house activities because their sales volumes justified them. During this same period, Texas Instruments abandoned consumer-electronics retailing and Tandy/Radio Shack taper integrated to reach larger market segments more economically.

The form of vertical relationships indicated the amount of asset exposure and flexibility the venture possessed. In highly uncertain or volatile environments where the performance of vertically integrated firms was sensitive to fluctuations in demand, ownership forms involving lesser amounts of asset exposure (such as quasi-integration) were used to reduce the variability of returns and increase firms' strategic flexibilities. There were few, joint ventures in this industry, however, because all components needed to enter the personal-computers business could be purchased readily, quality control had to be assured, and adjacent firms were difficult to control in this manner. Zenith Data Systems gained access by financing its distributors' inventories, Osborne Computer gained software by acting as marketing agent for programmers, Tandy/Radio Shack gained interconnection capabilities by sharing specifications with Datapoint, and Commodore gained control of a source of microprocessors by making a minority investment in MOS Technology.

The personal-computer industry was emerging in 1981 and its structure was still being developed, hence any evaluation of firms' vertical strategies must be tempered by a recognition that as demand becomes saturated, the industry structure could change to include more internal integration. Firms that formulated the more-effective, vertical-integration strategies were those that gained relatively stable access to components, raw materials, and markets while also achieving their strategic objectives, including market dominance, above-average returns of invested capital, or technological leadership.

As their name suggests, assemblers controlled neither components nor marketing channels. They used the peripherals and components developed by others and priced their systems to gain shelf space. Many incurred low overhead costs because they had no plant. This strategy would be durable for the future, provided customers did not demand more sophisticated systems than assemblers provided, assemblers absorbed slack capacity among suppliers, and retailers earned higher margins by selling their mircocomputers. Until a shortage of components halted their production schedules, their strategy was appropriate for 1981.

Commodore lacked strong dealer support in the United States and credibility among the business users it sought. To counter its weakness, Commodore had tried to reach customers using its own retail outlets, but that venture proved too costly to expand beyond the San Francisco area. Commodore had sold one of the original, and most popular, microcomputers, but by 1981 its advantages of first entry had been eroded by Apple, Tandy/Radio Shack, and IBM. Although Commodore controlled the innovative microprocessor firm, MOS Technology, it had *not* exploited this linkage adequately in the marketplace by offering features that appealed to the large customer base that Commodore sought.

Texas Instruments also lacked strong dealer support, but it offered a low-priced machine backed by national television advertising. Texas Instruments was expected to dominate future generations of the inexpensive-home-computer market because it was backward integrated and enjoyed substantial experience-curve economies in manufacturing semiconductors.

Although Tandy/Radio Shack was primarily an assembler of personal computers, its large base of consumer-electronics outlets gave Tandy a sensitivity to the market that other firms lacked. Tandy used outside suppliers to construct the components and pieces used in its TRS-80 family, and this practice gave Tandy great bargaining power over these suppliers. This was a strategy that seemed appropriate in 1981 and could be strengthened if Tandy won a healthy toehold in the office market.

Firms like IBM, Xerox, Digital, and others—that produced typewriters, copiers, and other office products such as word-processing stations and that operated retail outlets—possessed great strength in the business-user market due to their past reputations for service and reliability. By purchasing peripherals and components, they took advantage of the newest technologies available without investing the massive sums required for research and development. But firms that produced minicomputers faced a problem when using in-house resources to build microcomputers, because their market positions in minicomputers could erode each time they introduced a new microcomputer feature. Finally, these firms needed software to differentiate their microcomputer systems. Many firms made their machines CP/M compatible to use existing software, but doing so lowered switching-cost barriers and did not differentiate their systems. Although the assembler strategy was an appropriate one in 1981, these firms would be expected to use more of their in-house capabilities—as Xerox did when it achieved sufficient sales volume to justify doing so—and to exert control over the design of technological innovations in key pieces of the personal-computer system.

Apple faced a formidable challenge in IBM's entry because Apple did not possess the image needed to pursue the business-user market. It had no service personnel and had only recently created a sales force to handle national accounts. It had no computer stores and had just tried to reduce the purchasing power of its largest distributor, ComputerLand. Finally, Apple had tried to cut off supplies of its machines to mail-order distributors, but its previous success had been partially due to the selling efforts of this group. Apple was too expensive for the home market and too limited for the business market.

In summary, the leading brands in 1981 were those that were introduced early, but IBM had earned the rank of fourth place after announcing its microcomputers in August. The industry was emerging as one in which marketing and customer-support strengths would be important for success, suggesting that its structure would become predominantly forward integrated. Important criteria for long-term survival included excellent and proprietary software and documentation, reliable and resourceful service representatives, and access to the markets where systems capability would be appreciated most highly, for the following reasons. CP/M operating systems enabled firms to penetrate the personal-computer market, but not necessarily to hold their positions after initial marketing and software-development expenditures had been made, when switching costs would be low. In the area of market intelligence, field representatives could monitor the reactions of buyers to the firm's new products better than a computer-store sales representative in many cases. Finally, by 1981 the common bottleneck for all market segments was systems software, a product written by autonomous companies within a highly fragmented cottage industry. Microcomputer firms' controls over software for their machines would determine their future profitability.

References

Bernstein, Peter W., "Atari and the Video-Game Explosion." *Fortune,* July 27, 1981, pp. 40–46.

Chase, Marilyn. "Test of Time: As Competition Grows Apple Computer Inc. Faces a Critical Period." *Wall Street Journal,* November 11, 1981, pp. 1, 25.

"Computer Stores: Tantalizing Opportunity Selling Computers to Consumers." *Business Week,* September 28, 1981, pp. 76–82.

Isgur, Barbara S., "Personal Computers." Paine Webber Mitchell Hutchins Inc., September 23, 1981.

Uttal, Bro. "The Coming Struggle in Personal Computers." *Fortune,* June 29, 1981, pp. 84–92.

Webbink, Douglas W. "The Semiconductor Industry: A Survey of Structure, Conduct, and Performance." Bureau of Economics, Federal Trade Commission, January 1977.

Wiegner, Kathleen K. "Tomorrow Has Arrived." *Forbes,* February 15, 1982, pp. 111–119.

Also helpful were corporate annual reports and financial statements of the firms described in chapter 10 and conversations with seven manufacturers of personal computers, two components suppliers, and five distributors.

11

Strategies for Vertical Integration in Embryonic Energy Industries

This chapter examines vertical strategies in two embryonic energy industries—coal gasification and residential solar heating. These industries differ from the emerging industries treated in previous chapters because economic, political, and other environmental forces made demand for these industries' products so uncertain that the development of their structures has been stunted until these uncertainties can be removed. Both industries offer energy-related products, although to different types of customers. Coal-gasification plants supply fuel to industrial consumers; solar-heating systems are distributed directly to homeowners.

A Description of the Embryonic Energy Industries

The Products

Coal gasification is a process for using the energy contained in coal. Used directly, coal gasification produces fuels for heating and feedstocks for chemicals synthesis. Used indirectly, coal gasification is sometimes the first step in the coal-liquefaction process from which many useful chemicals (including gasoline substitutes) are produced. Several gasification processes existed in 1981, but the basic steps were similar in each of them. Coal was fed into a gasifier (or *reactor*) where it was reacted with steam and air, or oxygen (sometimes with all three). This produced a methane gas and other elements—primarily carbon monoxide and sulfur. The gas was desulfurized, yielding a fairly good-quality synthetic gas that, when upgraded, increased its heating content to around 1,000 British Thermal Units per cubic foot (BTU/cf.), producing a high-BTU, pipeline-quality gas. If the coal gas were not upgraded in heating content, it remained a low-BTU gas (100 BTU/cf.), but if steam and oxygen were injected, a medium-BTU gas resulted (around 300 BTU/cf.).

Background research by Paul Gelburd and Kris Ishibashi.

Solar-Heating Systems

Solar-heating systems collect the sun's energy for heating water or air in the home. The flat-plate collectors fastened on homeowners' roofs are only a portion of the solar-heating system. In addition to the collector, a solar-heating system has water tanks, controllers, heat exchangers, pumps, control valves, sensors, and specialized hardware. Although many components of the system are off-the-shelf plumbing stock, others are custom-manufactured for solar applications. The principal heat transfers in a liquid solar system are as follows: the heat exchanger brings working fluid, which is heated by the sun, into contact with circulating water used to heat potable water or air.

The most-expensive unit in a solar-water-heating system is the collector panel, a flat, rectangular box containing an absorber plate of copper or aluminum, covered with a selective coating, resting on an insulation material, covered with high-purity glass or plastic, and encased in aluminum or steel struts that make its structure rigid. The absorber plate contains a web of pipes through which water, or air, flows and is warmed by the sun's rays. The absorber plate's coating of black chrome, or paint, absorbs energy but does not reflect it back. The arteries of the absorber plate are connected to a plumbing network leading to a tank where water is heated (the *solar tank*). The physical design by which heat is transferred from one medium to another (*heat exchangers*) differs among firms and over time. In the early versions of some water-heating systems, a second absorber plate was simply wrapped around the solar tank.

The solar-heating system requires an electronic device, a *controller,* to measure the difference between the temperature at the collector and the temperature of the water in the solar tank, in order to tell the system when to turn on and collect energy from the solar panel. A circulating pump moves the working fluid through the panel to the heat exchanger and back through the system.

The major differences among competitors' solar heating systems include: warranties on the quality of manufacture and installation, relative ease of servicing (for maintenance or repairs), aesthetics (such as the packaging of components), and company name. Because consumers perceive this as a very risky purchase, the quality of installation of the solar-heating system is very important to the perceived quality of the solar system. Quality differences include the quality of the raw materials used to fabricate the collector panels and special valves needed for the solar system, as well as the engineering detail of the collector panel's design. Some collector panels contain over eighty-five different parts and minute attention to details that enable the panel to weather inhospitable climates. Solar-heating systems used in more hospitable climates, like New Mexico, do not require as much engineering detail and can therefore be produced more inexpensively.

At the end of 1981, a glut in the world availability of crude oil had dampened enthusiasm for coal-gasification projects, but some project sponsors believed the glut was temporary. First, OPEC production cutbacks could rapidly transform what had been a buyers' market for oil in 1981 back to a sellers' market in the future. Second, natural gas (which occurs in nature with crude oil) was not exported to the United States from OPEC nations in sizable quantities, and as U.S. natural gas became more costly, the economics of coal gasification looked increasingly attractive. Third, the lead time required to procure permissions, rights of way, and funding for coal gas projects would be long, and project sponsors recognized they would have to begin acting in 1981 in order to supply coal gas to customers or downstream units by the end of the decade.

The principal obstacles to commercialization for several large-scale coal-gasification projects were the risk of unknown future energy prices vis-a-vis the cost of synthetics and financial uncertainties. Briefly, the capital costs of constructing large-scale coal-gasification projects frequently exceeded amounts a single firm could afford to finance privately. The capital costs and associated risks were so high that federal loan guarantees or price supports were needed, particularly given the long gestation period of coal-gasification projects. Institutional lenders normally required assurances of repayment; yet the coal-gasification projects might never be completed or might be uneconomic when constructed, and gas-pipeline companies had little collateral to offer to satisfy these lenders.

In summary, the markets for coal gas were highly sensitive to the price of crude oil and natural gas. If the prices of these benchmark fuels rose such that coal gas became clearly cheaper, and if a plant came onstream to prove the technology was feasible for large-scale projects, more investment might occur in this industry. If a new embargo occurred in the future, or if energy prices rose abruptly and caused the public to panic, coal-gasification technologies would be desirable and even-smaller firms would try to finance coal-gas projects. At the end of 1981, however, the viability of markets for coal gas seemed questionable. Similarly, the economics of residential solar-heating systems did not look attractive without the tax incentives that were enacted during the Carter administration and repealed under Reagan. The installed price of a medium-temperature water-heating system ranged from $3,000 to $4,500, and the payback in energy savings was slow in 1981.

Markets

Low-BTU coal gas can be substituted for boiler fuels. The industries that would feel the greatest impact from substitution are the chemical, primary-metal, and petroleum industries. Low-BTU coal gas is usually consumed on-site, because it is not economical to transport low-BTU coal gas any substantial distance from the generating site.

Medium-BTU coal gas can be transported fifty miles or more economically, thereby reducing the need to build a plant at the site of coal reserves. In addition to the many applications for which low-BTU coal gas would be acceptable, medium-BTU coal gas can be used to make methanol (methyl alcohol) as a substitute for gasoline, or as a building block to making other chemicals, such as ammonia used in making fertilizer and gasoline. Medium—BTU coal gas is particularly well-suited for use as a chemical feedstock due to its high hydrogen and carbon-monoxide concentrations, and low methane content.

High-BTU coal gas is the most expensive to produce but the most suitable as a substitute for pipeline natural gas. It can be used as either feedstock or fuel, since it exhibits the same heat content, flame characteristics, and combustion behavior as natural gas, and has the potential to be transported one hundred miles or more.

Residential-solar-heating systems are used primarily to heat water, to heat air, or to cool air. Low-temperature solar-heating systems (100° Fahrenheit or less) are used primarily for heating swimming pools. Medium-temperature systems (between 90° and 180° Fahrenheit) are used in hot-water and space heating. High-temperature solar systems (temperatures exceeding 180° Fahrenheit) are used for industrial applications, such as pasteurizing beer or dyeing textiles.

Although residential and industrial sites might specify solar-heating systems in new construction, 90 percent of the sales in 1981 were to the retrofit market. The ultimate consumer of residential-solar-heating systems was the homeowner. Although annual-sales volumes grew from nearly nonexistent in the early 1970s to over $300 million in 1980, some firms complained the growth was not fast enough. Customer reticence was blamed upon unattractive economics (despite tax credits) and mistrust. Many fly-by-night operators preyed upon customers before industry standards existed.

Suppliers

The United States had large reserves of coal in 1981 that could be burned, liquified, or gasified. Coal could be shipped to the plant site and a coal-gas producer need not necessarily own coal reserves, although it could become expensive to purchase coal in the spot market. Some firms preferred short-term-contracting arrangements in order to play coal suppliers off of one another to get the lowest-possible prices, while others wanted long-term contracts specifying deliveries of a particular kind of coal, if not outright internal control of their coal reserves.

Coal-gasification processes required substantial amounts of water, particularly for high-BTU coal-gas projects, thus water rights were sought when firms contracted for supplies of coal. Water scarcity in western sites made many low- or medium-BTU coal-gasification projects uneconomic unless both water and coal were both near major population centers.

Coal gasification projects also might need abundant supplies of oxygen, depending upon the end use of the gas. Oxygen facilities could be readily constructed on-site, as they were for projects by such firms as Airco, Union Carbide (Linde), and Air Products and Chemicals. Hydrogen was produced from steam (water) and coal in processing. In summary, coal-gas firms sought control of coal reserves and water rights at their production sites. Many contracted for their oxygen (using *take-or-pay* arrangements).

Manufacturing residential-solar-heating systems was materials intensive in 1981. The largest portion of the cost of producing a solar-collector panel was that of the raw materials—copper, aluminum, and glass, among others—costing between 60 percent and 70 percent of the selling price (labor was only 10 percent of the price).

Many firms purchased preformed-copper absorber plates, although this component could have been fabricated in-house. Thin-gauge copper sheeting for absorber plates could be purchased in rolls from copper mills, or absorber plates could be purchased from solar-collector companies that had excess fabrication capacity. Backward integration from solar heating was difficult because copper milling required a plant of minimum-efficient-scale far greater than the volume of solar-collector-panel needs in 1981. Firms entering the copper-milling business would be obliged also to produce plumbing pipes, oil-drilling pipes, and other forms of fabricated product to fill plant capacity. Like copper milling, aluminum-extrusion equipment was very expensive to acquire and the minimum-efficient-plant size exceeded solar-panel needs.

Swimming pool (and other low-temperature) applications use black paint on a plastic absorber plate. Medium-temperature applications require special paints or selective coatings such as black chrome, which is applied over a plating of nickel, using an electrolysis process. There were four U.S. firms that made black-chrome coatings for solar purposes in 1981, and absorber-plate manufacturers usually shipped their preformed copper to one of these coating firms' factories for this step.

Waterwhite glass of high purity was produced by few glass companies in 1981, but backward integration was infeasible for most firms due to the high investment requirements and low volume that solar-collector panels represented. Nor were solar-heating firms likely to become producers of fiberglass or foam resins used for insulation.

Firms selling entire solar-heating systems could purchase pumps readily, and some solar-heating-equipment distributors already inventoried these pumps for other applications. Solar tanks were also readily available from firms possessing installation experience in home-ventilation and heating systems.

Plumbing hardware could be purchased readily from supply houses in 1981, as could most of the tubing and pipes required in a solar-heating system. Unusual valves (or other hardware) were supplied by the solar-collector assembler, who purchased the customized valves from a specialty producer.

Although the controller could be purchased in a customized package from outside suppliers, some solar-heating firms designed and assembled their own control panels. Unless a solar-heating firm also possessed electronics skills, the components used in a control unit were usually purchased from outside suppliers, however. Insufficient volume in solar-heating systems precluded most firms from considering backward integration for this component.

In summary, solar-heating manufacturers obtained their raw materials and components in different ways. Some assemblers had sister units which fabricated raw materials for them; others were merely assemblers. In the years prior to 1981, no residential-solar-heating firm had backward integrated to obtain a steady supply of raw materials. Rather, some raw materials suppliers entered solar-collector manufacturing as a forward integration.

Manufacturing

The capital investment needed to construct a coal gasification plant was huge in 1981, and a minimum-efficient-scale facility capable of processing 1,000 tons per day of coal cost between $200 and $300 million. A full-scale, medium-BTU coal-gas plant capable of processing 29 thousand tons per day cost $2.3 billion. The machinery was specially designed for these projects and at least five years were required to design and build a coal-gas plant. The assets were inflexible, durable, and highly specific to the production of coal gas and related chemicals.

Many firms contemplating coal-gas projects developed proprietary technologies for transforming coal into gas and licensed their processes globally. Sizable sums were invested in process improvements to bring the cost of producing coal gas closer to the cost of natural gas through economies gained from new catalysts, new technologies, and experience-curve advantages.

The price of coal gas and related products was sensitive to: (1) the capital costs associated with plant construction, (2) price escalations in raw materials, equipment, and resources needed to construct gasification plants, and (3) debt-to-equity ratios (financing costs). Raw materials, operations, and maintenance costs represented about 50 percent of the product price.

Any coal-gasification process produces both methane or hydrogen and carbon monoxide, but different gasification technologies produce differing balances of these outputs. First-generation gasifiers had been in use throughout the world since the 1940s and included (by date of first installation) Lurgi (1936), Winkler (1937), B & W (1955) Koppers-Totzek or K-T (1952), and the KBW processes. Second-generation gasifiers possessed high unit capacities as well as reduced steam and oxygen needs. No second-generation gasifiers had progressed beyond operating at pilot-plant scale in 1981. These technologies included the British Gas Corporation (BGC)/Lurgi Slagger, the Shell Coal Gasification Process, the Pressurized Winkler, and Texaco processes. Third-generation gasifiers had been demonstrated in the laboratory or in small pilot plants but none had been demonstrated in a large-scale plant by 1981. Their principal advantages over earlier generations of gasifiers included lower capital requirements, greater efficiency, and lower product prices. In situ (or underground) coal gasification was essentially a large fire that was controlled to provide useful gases.

The process steps involved in coal gasification depended upon whether the end product contained greater quantities of methane or synthesis gas. For high-BTU coal gas, the steps in production included: (1) coal preparation (sizing or screening), (2) oxygen production, (3) gasification, (4) gas purification (to remove sulfur and impurities), (5) shift reaction, (6) methanation, and (7) compression, distribution, and pipelining. The basic chemical transformations were straightforward. Coal was first converted to gas by reacting carbon with steam to create synthesis gas (carbon monoxide and hydrogen), which was either burned or converted to methane (synthetic natural gas). To make desirable liquids, either carbon was removed or hydrogen was added. In order to make high-BTU coal gas, the methane content was increased.

High strategic and economic exit barriers made coal gasification a particularly risky investment. Natural-gas-distribution companies, for example, could not walk away from their ventures for ethical as well as financial reasons. The size of the investment was large and the assets in use could not be converted easily for other businesses. Their salvage values were low and, given the remote geographical sites favored for erecting some coal-gasification projects, the costs of hauling away the assets for scrap would be high as well.

The capital investment needed to produce solar-heating systems in 1981 was low because many components could be purchased. Assemblers of collector panels needed only a basic machine shop—some special saws and punching tools, milling machines, screwdrivers and other assembly tools. Solar collectors could be assembled in a garage using welding, soldering, and brazing equipment costing less than $200,000, and a metal-forming machine (for dimpling the copper absorber plate) cost $100,000, but preformed absorber plates could be purchased instead.

The technique for making solar collectors was not very sophisticated in 1981. At the low volumes that firms experienced, the technology seemed to have a flat experience curve and few scale economies. Research-and-development expenditures emphasized product-design improvements or the substitution of more-efficient materials rather than an emphasis on improving the manufacturing process itself. Solar collectors were produced by many competitors and copying of design improvements was widespread.

There could be significant scale economies in making solar collectors if sales volumes were large; however, the necessary volumes were far in excess of 1981 sales volumes. Some firms continually redesigned their products to get costs down; they invented shortcuts in their assembly operations, or reduced the amount of expensive aluminum while maintaining the same structural integrity. By improving their manufacturing processes, by purchasing new equipment (or inventing their own) to improve productivity, and by finding new ways to produce components, some firms pushed themselves a bit further down the experience curve.

The technology used to make solar-heating systems was less sophisticated than coal gasification. Fabrication of the solar-collector panel began with the formation of absorber plates—copper creased to form troughs for the copper-tubing gridwork. The plate was sent out for black chroming, and when it returned, the gridwork was soldered in place and all joints leading to the major arteries were brazed and tested for leakage. The absorber plate, foam or fiberglass insulation, glass covering, and aluminum supports were set up on jigs to be assembled. The product's quality was determined by the number of test steps added to guarantee the collector's durability.

The shop equipment was easily reused for other production activities. The cost of the specialized jigs and customized machines was not high. Economic exit barriers were low because the salvage values of the assets used to make solar-heating systems were relatively high.

Marketing

The principal costs for the internal transfer of low- or medium-BTU coal gas were in laying pipelines to connect the gasifiers to the next stage of transformation, or to the boiler room. If coal gas were marketed as a feedstock to an outside chemicals firm, the major selling expenses involved enticing a chemical user to build an interconnected plant near the gasifiers and drafting a contract. Contracts for such transfers frequently matched the depreciable life of the facilities because they were highly specific and could not be changed easily. Multiple users could connect to large coal-gas refineries if their plants were near the gasifier sites, and joint ventures between suppliers and customers could finance coal-gas ventures (after the technology was proved).

Some coal-gas producers owned the pipelines needed to distribute the gas, but without customer contracts these firms were obliged to sell gasified coal on an incremental basis and absorb price fluctuations in the spot market for natural gas. Other firms sought long-term sales contracts for distribution arrangements if they did not own distribution channels or had never before been in the natural-gas-delivery business. Methanol-distribution channels posed similar barriers. An entire distribution system was needed before consumers felt comfortable using automobiles propelled by methanol. Automotive companies would not build engines using methanol fuel until those fuels were readily available, and coal-gas firms would not develop methanol fuels until the engines were introduced commercially.

In summary, given the enormous risks associated with coal-gas projects, firms believed their need to control their markets was great. Even in the case of coal-gasification projects that did *not* seek federal aid or regulatory assistance, coal-gas producers sought contracts binding customers and suppliers before their projects were undertaken. If the gasification projects were not suppliers to internal units of the firm, joint-venture arrangements with the consuming firms were sought.

The marketing costs associated with selling solar-heating systems included wholesaling costs, cross-country-transportation costs, instructional efforts, demonstrations, and sales aids. Solar-heating systems were sold by dealer-installers. Some dealers purchased components from distributors; others bought directly from manufacturers' warehouses. In either case, installers needed financing to install solar-heating systems, since consumers did not pay in advance. Manufacturers did not finance the installers nor the jobbers that distributed their solar-collector panels, and limited their promotional activities to advertising and providing some selling aids. They relied instead upon their dealers and distributors who varied in the amount of promotional effort they devoted to solar-heating systems. Some distributors were either home-ventilation/air conditioning (HVAC) supply houses or plumbing supply houses that offered installation services, as well as components. Others were *energy boutiques,* small stores offering an array of energy-conservation/alternative-energy products (but not necessarily installation services). Some of the most successful sales outlets for solar-heating systems were not the HVAC or plumbing houses. Rather they were experienced installers with financing abilities. In New England, Meenan Oil, an aggressive heating-oil distributor, sold and installed solar-heating systems as well as oil burners and other energy-related products, and Sears, Roebuck offered both solar-heating components and installation services. Dealers often handled more than one brand of solar collector, but distributors (the step above dealer-installers) were identified with particular manufacturers. They received special selling assistance from them and carried an inventory of their solar-heating components. Manufacturers whose plants were located in the east frequently maintained warehouses in California or

Texas because shipping heavy solar collectors (or solar tanks that weighed 300 to 400 pounds) was cheaper than operating two, underutilized plants.

The key to success in solar heating was marketing savvy and access to the customers in 1981. For some dealer-installers, this meant direct mailings or door-to-door sales calls. Others employed sales forces that spent evenings explaining the benefits of solar heating to homeowners. For distributors, market access meant having a brand name that meant reliability.

In summary, solar-heating manufacturers distributed their products in different ways. They dealt directly with homeowners, developed and trained distributors, sold directly to dealer-installers, or used all of these methods. Some firms had tried forward integration but found their sales volumes too low to sustain retail stores. Others piggybacked on their preexisting retail expertise in selling and installing HVAC or other residential products.

Competitors

Coal gasification was not a volatile industry with respect to price-cutting because of the contractual nature of coal-gas sales. Moreover, given regulated prices for sales of high-BTU coal gas in 1981, price competition was unlikely to occur in sales to public utilities until natural gas was deregulated.

Firms involved in coal-gasification projects could be grouped by market application (low-, medium-, or high-BTU coal gas for fuel or feedstocks), by whether or not they operated in a regulated-marketing environment, or by form of venture undertaken. Some firms were building sites for in-house industrial consumption while others participated in joint ventures. One group of firms produced gasification equipment or construction services and participated in coal-gas projects as a way of building the site or selling it some equipment.

Corporate Strategy Exit Barriers in Coal Gasification

Firms that had not diversified or that invested their own equity in coal gasification had higher commitments to this embryonic industry. The subset of firms that seemed to have the most urgent need for federal financing of coal-gasification projects were natural-gas-transmission and -distribution companies for whom the declining supplies of natural gas were alarming.

Summary of Competitors in Coal Gasification

In summary, the producers of gasified coal varied in their strategic postures along the following dimensions: (1) the user market served (differing BTU contents), (2) the gasifier technologies employed, (3) whether they owned coal or purchased their raw materials, (4) whether they consumed coal-gas products internally, and (5) whether they operated transmission lines for transporting the gas (or liguified products). For example, Conoco, Shell, and Texaco developed proprietary gasification technologies and possessed the capacity to consume coal gas internally or to send it by pipeline to near-by customers, but they differed in their control over coal supplies. Tenneco serviced both regulated-residential and unregulated-petrochemical users.

A Mapping of Strategic Groups in Coal Gasification

Some firms were engaged in vertically related activities—coal mining, gasification, and transmission pipelines or chemical plants—but did not transtransfer these resources internally. Rather, they purchased the supplies and services they needed for coal gasification and operated their adjacent businesses independently. Major firms could be mapped as shown in figure 11-1 to indicate where shared resources or linkages with other business units existed. In 1981 coal-gasification firms were also either gas-transmission companies serving residential markets, or industrial users with the capability to provide outsiders with coal gas. Only one firm was both a transmission and a chemical firm.

	Breadth of Nondistribution Activities		
Distribution Activities	Coal Reserves	Gasification Technology	Gasification Equipment or Construction Services
Natural-Gas Distribution Lines	(People's Energy) Pacific Gas and Electric		
Natural-Gas Transmission Lines	American Natural Resources (People's Energy) (Tennessee Gas Trans- mission, Tenneco) Pacific Gas and Electric	Tenneco	
Pipelines to Adjacent Chemical Plants	(Conoco) (General Electric) Tenneco	Conoco Koppers Shell Texaco Tenneco	(General Electric) (Bechtel)
Internal Consumption	Tenneco	Koppers Shell Texaco Tenneco	

Note: Names in parenthesis indicate that internal transfers between activities are unlikely.

Figure 11-1. A Mapping of Firms in Coal Gasification, 1981

Table 11-1
Estimated Performance of Selected Solar Firms, December 1980
(millions of dollars)

Company	1980 Solar Revenues	1980 Pretax profit (loss)
ARCO Energy Corporation	4.5	0.9 [a]
American Solar King	2.7	(0.5)[a]
Ametek, Inc.	1.5	(1.3)
Asarco	5.0	(4.5)
Atlantic Richfield	0.8	(1.2)
Grumman	10.0	(4.9)
Olin Corporation[b]	2.5	(0.3)[b]
Revere Copper & Brass	4.0	(3.)
Reynolds Metals	1.7	(0.5)
Solaron Corp.	2.5	(0.7)

Source: Industry records.
[a]Indicates estimated profit in 1981.
[b]Exited in 1981.

In 1981 the future of U.S. coal gasification was still uncertain because only one full-scale coal-gasification project was under construction, and it had required a package of federal price and loan guarantees to attain feasibility. The price or crude oil was falling and domestic efforts to find oil had uncovered several new pockets of natural gas. The surplus of natural gas reversed an ominous downward trend in marketable production of natural gas that began in the early 1970s.

Competition in Residential Solar Heating in 1981

By 1981 the rules of competition were chaotic, as a variety of vertical arrangements had been tried and often discarded. Approximately 250 companies manufactured solar-collector panels and many more firms merchandised solar-heating packages. As table 11-1 indicates, few firms were profitable in solar heating by 1981, and often their motives for entering involved sizable tax incentives that sustained them when they might otherwise have failed.

Competitors could be grouped by market application; the greatest number of firms sold low-temperature solar collectors used to heat swimming pools, and these were more likely to be privately held firms or entrepreneurial firms. Medium-temperature solar collectors were used for residential heating; thirty firms supplied approximately eighty percent of these collectors. High-temperature solar collectors were used for industrial applications. The major competitors in high-temperature applications were research-and-development intensive, publicly traded corporations.

Corporate Strategy Exit Barriers in Residential Solar Heating

Many small, undiversified proprietors were particularly unwilling to abandon the solar-heating business. Instead they were content to eke out a subsistence in the low-temperature market. Diversified corporations faced lower strategic exit barriers in solar heating than did single-business firms. Even metals-fabricating firms and HVAC companies could be less committed to competing in residential-solar-heating systems in 1981 because the product required small proportions of their upstream products.

Summary of Competitors in Residential Solar Heating

In summary, the producers of pieces of residential-solar-heating systems varied in their strategic postures along the following dimensions: the temperature applications served, whether they sold entire systems or pieces of a system, whether they produced their own solar collectors (or absorber plates), materials used in their collectors, whether private labeling was an important part of their sales volumes, and how products were distributed. Many firms used distributors to merchandise their solar collectors but a few operated their own retail outlets instead.

A Mapping of Strategic Groups in Residential Solar Heating

Some firms were fully integrated with respect to copper or aluminum in 1981, while others sold only collectors and did not merchandise the other components of the solar-heating system. They could be mapped as shown in figure 11-2 to indicate whether any shared resources or linkages with other business units existed. Many major residential-solar-heating firms used several distribution channels, including consumer-direct sales. Firms such as Reynolds, Revere Solar, Carrier, Fedders, and Lennox used existing company distributors and installers to market their solar products, while others trained distributors and supplied marketing allowances or other forms of assistance. Reynolds and Revere Solar were most broadly (metals-

Distribution Activities	Metals Fabricators	Collectors Only	Packaged Solar-Heating Systems	Solar Tanks or Pumps plus Collectors
Company-Controlled Retail Outlets	Reynolds Revere Solar			
Consumer-Direct Marketing	Reynolds	American Sunsystems Fafco Solar	Ramada Energy ACRO Solar Energy	
Dealer Direct		Ametek Harrison Radiation Energy Systems (General Motors) Gulf Thermal Colt	Novan Energy	
Exclusive Distributors		Fafco Solar	American Solar King Asarco ACRO Solar Energy ARCO Solar Grumman	Carrier Fedders Lennox
Multibrand Specialty Solar Distributors	Revere Solar	Radco		
Traditional HVAC Wholesalers		General Electric		
Private Label		Ametek	State Industries	

Figure 11–2. A Mapping of Selected Competitors in the Residential-Solar-Heating Industry, 1981

to-retailing) and fully integrated in this industry (near 95 percent of requirements). At the other extreme, there were many assemblers of solar collectors that did not fabricate any components internally.

The residential-solar-heating industry's structure was still unformed and depended heavily upon tax incentives and rising crude-oil prices if it were to be viable. Because individual sales volumes were low, no manufacturer had been able to exploit experience-curve or scale economies significantly by 1981; entry was easy and profit margins were so low that few firms had reached breakeven.

Key Events in Coal-Gasification and Residential Solar Heating

Both coal-gasification and solar-heating technologies were not new in the 1970s but their economics had been unacceptable until the oil crisis made many alternative forms of energy seem attractive. Bolstered by federal and state assistance programs, public utilities' coal-gasification programs were encouraged to begin. Many firms felt pressured to take a toehold position in the heavily subsidized solar-heating industry as well.

1971

Peoples Energy was a holding company whose activities included transmission and distribution of natural gas. It was studying a means of converting Illinois coal reserves into pipeline-quality gas with six other utilities, in a group that became the Illinois Coal-Gasification group. It was also beginning to construct a large-scale coal-gasification project in North Dakota in 1971.

American Natural Resources was a holding company with gas-transmission and -distribution companies in Michigan and Wisconsin. In 1971 American Natural Resources also initiated plans to build a coal-gasification plant in North Dakota.

1972

Tenneco was a diversified holding company originally incorporated as Tennessee Gas Transmission Company, a long-line, natural-gas-transmission company. In 1972 Tenneco was searching for feedstock coal reserves of sufficient quantity to support a high-BTU coal-gas plant for its full economic life (twenty-five years or more), but was encountering difficulties in gaining mineral and water rights in the west.

In 1972 Panhandle Eastern Pipe Line Company announced a joint venture with the Peabody Coal Company (Kennecott Copper) in Illinois to build a coal-gasification plant. It also joined two gas-transmission companies in a concerted effort to accelerate research into coal-gasification processes by building a test facility in Scotland.

In 1972 American Natural Resources announced an option, purchased from North American Coal Corporation, giving it control over one billion tons of North Dakota lignite. Under these arrangements, North American Coal would mine the coal if American Natural Resources developed a method of gasifying it.

1974

In 1974 Peoples Energy announced it would build four coal-gasification plants of 250 million cubic feet of gas per day in North Dakota in a large energy complex. Peoples Energy had negotiated rights to 2.1 billion tons of lignite in a twenty-year agreement, and applied to the North Dakota Water Commission for the necessary water rights.

In its second joint venture with Peabody Coal, Panhandle Eastern Company announced a 270 million-cubic-foot-per-day, high-BTU coal-gasification plant in Douglas, Wyoming in 1974. Panhandle Eastern later found that the capital costs of this project became too high to bear alone and Panhandle Eastern invited Ruhrgas Aktiengesellschaft, a large West German natural-gas-transmission company (which was partially owned by British Petroleum), and Pacific Gas & Electric, a San Francisco public utility, to form the WyCoalGas Inc. project.

In 1974 Texas Eastern Transmission and Pacific Lighting Corporation filed for Federal Power Commission approval of a 250 million-cubic-foot-per-day, high-BTU coal-gas plant to be located next to Utah International's coal reserves in New Mexico on a Navaho Indian reservation. The joint venture would sell 75 percent of its gas to Pacific Lighting and the remaining 25 percent to Cities Service Gas Company. Unknown to Texas Eastern and the other firms preparing coal-gasification projects, federal policies about the support of alternative-energy development had not anticipated some of the difficulties that would be encountered.

In 1974 Revere Copper & Brass sold Revere Sun-Aid solar collectors through its architectural-products subsidiary. Revere manufactured primary and fabricated aluminum, and fabricated copper and brass products. Its solar-heating products were sold in prepackaged systems or alone, through a network of national distributors, and its sales force called upon consulting engineers to persuade them to design their collectors into projects they bid upon. Revere's laminated-collector-panel design was one of the first medium-temperature solar collectors, and Revere sold other copper-collector materials to competitors in solar heating. Ninety percent of Revere's copper and aluminum needs for solar heating were furnished in-house.

Reynolds, which mined ores and produced primary and fabricated aluminum, introduced an aluminum solar collector in 1974. Reynolds distributed its prepackaged solar-heating system through existing Reynolds home-improvement stores. Previously it had sold aluminum collector panels to assemblers who packaged them under their own brands.

1975

In 1975 American Natural Resources announced a slowdown in the construction of its North Dakota coal-gasification plant, due to skyrocketing costs and regulatory delay. As it pressed onward in the regulatory process, the sunk cost of the project increased beyond $11 million and American Natural Resources began to look for additional sources of financing.

Pacific Gas & Electric (PG&E) supplied electric and natural-gas service throughout most of northern and central California. In 1975 it purchased the rights to 150 million tons of low-sulfur coal in Price, Utah, and began a coal-gasification project.

In 1975 Owens-Illinois' evacuated-tube solar collectors (high-temperature) were installed in two demonstration projects. Their design was an offshoot of Owens-Illinois' research into scientific-glassware products and found greatest acceptance for applications such as washing bottles or pasteurizing beer.

In 1975 Lennox Industries, an HVAC company, entered an agreement in which Lennox produced flat-plate solar-collector panels for Honeywell (using Honeywell technology). Lennox distributed the solar collectors through existing HVAC distributors. Honeywell used the panels in several federally funded demonstration projects.

In 1975 Ametek, a manufacturer of electromechanical devices and other industrial products, produced Sunjammer solar collectors and also sold them to Sears, Roebuck, Meenan Oil, and other private-brand customers. Ametek sold only collectors, not systems, through dealer-installers. It obtained most of its aluminum from in-house sources. It was not close to the consumer market itself.

In 1975 Exxon completed its acquisition of Daystar, a solar-collector manufacturer. After making Daystar a part of its Energy Division, Exxon performed a make-or-buy analysis of the solar-collector plates and concluded that making the plates was more economical than purchasing them. Daystar supplied a few copper absorber plates to other assemblers then because its production capacity exceeded in-house demand for solar collectors, but with time, its importance as an absorber-plate supplier grew.

Sunworks was a joint venture between a Yale professor and his associates (20 percent ownership) and Asarco's Sun Solector Corporation (80 percent). Asarco was one of the world's leading producers of nonferrous metals and owned a thirty-seven-percent interest in Revere Copper and Brass. Sunworks was not highly integrated because Revere Copper and Brass, which produced thin copper sheets for collector panels and fabricated aluminum, was an outsider with whom Sunworks did not have to deal unless it was economic to do so.

In 1975 Grumman, an aerospace company, began marketing its solar-heating systems through its own system of dealers in San Diego, Phoenix, and Houston. Its sales volume at that time was too small to support a policy of owned retail outlets, so Grumman made its best outside customers wholesale distributors to outside dealer-installers, and terminated its retail venture.

The first Grumman solar-heating systems (offered in 1974) were in a kit form. Consumers assembled the pieces according to instruction sheets, and the wooden shipping carton doubled as the structural supports that held the glass, absorber plate, and insulation in place. The heat exchanger was a bare tank wrapped with an Olin Brass copper absorber plate, and a second Olin Brass absorber plate was used in the solar collector. The cover, which used an arced acrylic glazing, gained structural strength from its curved surface. By 1975 however, Grumman solar-heating systems were assembled and packaged in-house, using as many off-the-shelf components as possible. Tanks and other components were produced and packaged according to Grumman specifications by outside suppliers. Grumman launched advertising campaigns in excess of $1 million annually to educate the public about the merits of residential-solar-heating systems, and won the Solar Engineering Industry Association prize in recognition of this educational effort that helped its competitors as much as Grumman.

ACRO Energy was one of the few major competitors in solar heating that was profitable. It sold both solar-collector plates and packaged solar water-heating systems under its brand name, Sunburst Solar Energy. ACRO was strongest in California, Arizona, and Colorado.

Fafco dominated the low-temperature solar-collector market, and eighty percent of its revenues came from California, Arizona, and Oregon. Fafco used a combination of exclusive distributors, dealers, and consumer-direct sales to market its extruded plastic collectors. Fafco usually sold turn-key solar-heating systems and had recently introduced a plastic solar collector for the medium-temperature, residential market.

Pittsburgh Plate Glass (PPG), Libby-Owens-Ford (LOF), Olin Brass, Chamberlain, Fedders, and Carrier were among the early entrants to the embryonic solar-heating industry. PPG's product was similar to the high-temperature solar collectors of Owens-Illinois, and PPG was one of the first majors to leave this industry. LOF, also a glass manufacturer, distributed its products through conventional water-pipe, plumbing, and HVAC houses, but their systems did not move out of the distributors' warehouses for years because the installers of solar-heating systems were not accustomed to calling on LOF's outlets to buy their components.

Olin Brass was an early supplier of copper absorber plates to solar-collector assemblers. Its initial design was costly, and since Olin did not improve upon it, many firms developed their own designs for collector plates to lower their costs. Chamberlain was an early entrant that manufactured storm windows and doors. It used its existing jigs to produce very small (three feet by seven feet) collectors that became the industry standard because they were among the first to be installed in a federal demonstration project. Fedders and Carrier were HVAC manufacturers with well-established distribution channels for home-ventilation and air-conditioning products. Carrier owned Day and Night, a fledgling solar-heating firm which it divested. In 1975 it purchased solar collectors from Sunworks and Revere instead. Carrier possessed one of the best distribution systems for residential-solar-heating systems but it did *not* prosper nevertheless. Fedders also purchased solar collectors from Sunworks to package with the components it produced in-house.

Companies that sold solar collectors along with their solar tanks included: Morflo Industries, of Cleveland; Rheem, of Chicago; A.O. Smith, of Chicago; and State Industries, of Ashland, Tennessee. Both Rheem and A.O. Smith purchased solar collectors from other manufacturers (Sunworks and SDI, respectively). State Industries, which produced water tanks, built its own solar collectors and sold its system through existing wholesalers that served home-construction customers and as a private-label supplier to Sears.

In summary, a number of competitors sprang into existence around 1975. Previously a few California firms operating from garages had sold systems to ecologically minded homeowners. Since there was no available experience in the best product designs or ways to distribute solar-heating systems, diverse competitors pursued dissimilar strategies.

1976

In 1976 Texaco submitted a proposal for a coal-gasification-demonstration project in response to the Energy Research and Development Administration (ERDA) request for synthetic-fuels proposals. Texaco's partners were Natural Gas Pipeline, Montana-Dakota Utilities, and Pacific Gas & Electric.

In 1976 also Conoco submitted a proposal to ERDA for a high-BTU coal-gasification plant in eastern Ohio that would be supplied by Conoco's Consolidation Coal Company and would generate gas for East Ohio Gas Company. Conoco's partners in this proposal were Consolidated Gas Supply Corporation, El Paso Company, Peoples Energy, Tenneco Inc., Tennessee Eastern Transmission Corporation, Panhandle Eastern Pipe Line Company, and Transco Company.

In 1976 a giant federal program designed to help the embryonic solar-heating industry began to take shape. ERDA and other federal agencies offered over $100 million in solar projects, but critics complained that large corporations schooled in research gamesmanship were winning most of the grants and design contracts while innovative entrepreneurs were being squeezed out. Federal-certification procedures discouraged small competitors because solar-heating systems were tested in federal laboratories before manufacturers were placed on an approved bid list for projects involving federal funding. Smaller firms could not afford the expensive testing and certification process and only firms like Sunworks, Revere, Lennox, Grumman, Daystar, Radco, and ACRO Energy were approved.

Radco Products was founded in 1976 by a retired engineer whose operations carried very-low overhead. Its solar-collector designs strongly resembled the higher-quality, medium-temperature models of other manufacturers (but sold at lower prices). It was essentially a one man show that undercut competitors' prices, and was highly profitable.

1977

As American Natural Resources gathered more information about the economics of the project, it became clear that the firm could not finance a large coal-gasification plant with its limited financial resources. Natural Gas Pipeline, a subsidiary of MidCon (Peoples Energy) had reached the same conclusion. In March 1977, American Natural Resources and Peoples Energy announced their partnership to build a coal-gasification facility near Beulah, North Dakota. The firms joined forces believing that once one coal-gasification facility was onstream, financing a second plant would be easier.

In 1977, Atlantic-Richfield acquired a minority interest in Northrup Inc. of Hutchins, Texas, the leading manufacturer of concentrating-ray solar collectors. Like the glass-tube collectors, Northrup's collector produced over twice as many BTUs per day as a flat-plate collector. Northrup also produced low-temperature flat-plate collectors, a conventional line of heating, air conditioning, and heat-pump products, and was one of several firms that comprised Atlantic Richfield's ARCO Solar Industries. It had been acquired by ARCO to develop its solar-energy-product line. Airtron, a company that installed heating and ventilation systems, became Northrup's sales channel and added other components to its solar-heating system. Frederick, a warehouser of heating and ventilation systems, expanded Airton's coverage of U.S. markets to national status, with an emphasis on the southwest.

1978

By 1978 American Natural Resources and Peoples Energy had expended $40 million in engineering studies and start-up costs and invited new partners to join the venture. These were Tenneco, Inc., Transco Gas, and Columbia Gas Systems. The new partnership was called Great Plains Gasification Associates. By November 1978, however, design and engineering work on the Great Plains project had been halted due to rapidly escalating costs and it was highly uncertain when and if the project would be approved.

In 1978, tax credits were expected to be increased and potential solar-heating customers delayed their purchases, waiting for the legislation to be enacted. Sales dropped 50 percent in the first half of 1978 and a devastating competitive shakeout followed. Grumman's advertising expenditures of $1.5 million exceeded its sales that year, and Rheem spent $1.3 million on newspaper and magazine advertising. Fafco Solar spent $1 million on direct-mail promotions as well but consumers remained hesitant because they were waiting for government rebates or other incentives to be created. Turnovers in solar heating became vigorous as, by midyear, some seventy-five small entrepreneurs dropped out of the industry, only to be replaced by many more new firms.

1979

In 1979 Federal Energy Regulatory Commission (FERC) approved the Great Plains Project's financing plan, but this approval was still subject to legal opposition. In 1980 a lawsuit was initiated by four plaintiffs challenging FERC's authority to approve the venture.

In 1979 tax credits were at last enacted and consumer purchases of solar-heating systems spurted upward. Some firms like Colt Industries experienced such high demand they had to expand their manufacturing facilities, while others, like Asarco and Exxon, consolidated their solar-heating operations. Chamberlain went bankrupt and was acquired by Solaron while firms like ALCOA entered the industry, found they had no special expertise in solar-heating systems, and exited.

1980

General Motors, the State of Michigan, the New York Public Service Commission, and the Ohio Consumers' Union argued against the cost-of-service pricing approach for the coal-gas venture in 1980. (The plaintiffs preferred a pricing scheme that permitted gas prices to rise slowly over time rather than begin at a high, but stable price that did not increase over time, and they rejected the notion that the sponsoring companies should have a guaranteed price formula that incorporated inflation and other rising costs.) A federal court decided in favor of the plaintiffs and remanded the financing case to FERC. The Great Plains partners went back to the bargaining table to create a new pricing formula and a new financing plan based on federal-loan guarantees and project-sponsor equity early in 1981.

In 1980 Texaco and Southern California Edison chose Bechtel to build their Cool Water coal-gasification plant. The partners also offered participation shares to General Electric, the Electric Power Research Institute, Pacific Gas & Electric, and an undisclosed Japanese manufacturer of large turbines.

In 1977 El Paso's partner had withdrawn from their plans to build a 72-million-cubic-foot-per-day, high-BTU coal-gasification plant in the Four Corners region of New Mexico, so in 1980 El Paso offered participation shares in its project to Pacific Gas & Electric and to Ruhrgas Aktiengesellschaft, which had been an early developer of coal-gasification technology.

In 1980 Tenneco applied to the Department of Energy for $25 million in federal funds for a Wibaux, Montana, high-BTU facility that would produce 250 million cubic feet of gas per day and for a feasibility study of a high-BTU coal-gasification plant in Mississippi. The conversion project would produce 125 million cubic feet of synthetic gas and 23,000 barrels of gasoline per day.

In July 1980, the Carter administration gave the Great Plains coal-gasification project a $250 million federal-loan guarantee to reactivate construction on the North Dakota facility. First-year construction began, predicated on the assumption that either additional loan guarantees would be granted to enable the construction of the remainder of the project or Great Plains would be successful in its defense of a ratepayer-supported-financing plan.

Conoco, the early leader in coal-gasification technology dropped out in December 1980 because it had changed the thrust of its coal-gasification efforts. Conoco's slagger demonstration project in Noble, Ohio, was dismantled in January 1981.

Propped up by federal and state incentives, the solar-heating industry began to revive. New firms like Ramada Energy Systems became national entities by offering low-cost solar collectors, while ongoing firms like Lennox Industries and Fedders introduced new solar products. Grumman lost $5 million on sales of $10 million and Olin Brass, the firm that marketed the first absorber plates, began to market Olin Solar Collectors in 1980. The collectors were manufactured for Olin Brass by an outsider, and Olin lost $300 thousand in its first year of operations and retreated.

In 1980 Meenan Oil, the nation's largest independent supplier of home heating oil, established a Solar Energy Division to merchandise Soltec heating systems to its customers in New York, New Jersey, and Pennsylvania. Its solar tanks were manufactured by Vaughn Corporation and its solar collectors came from Ametek (which also supplied Sears with a large portion of its solar-collector requirements).

In December 1980 Exxon announced it was seeking a buyer for its solar-flat-plate-collector business because the manufacturing and marketing of flat-plate systems, which were used primarily for residential-water heating, did not present an attractive business opportunity for Exxon in the foreseeable future. Also, the entire Solar Thermal Systems division had been losing money.

In 1980 Sunworks moved to a new, automated facility in Somerville, New Jersey and increased its sales volume over 1979 levels despite the decline in new-residential and commercial construction. Among the new products Sunworks introduced was a line of solar swimming-pool heaters and structural supports for large, commercial solar installations.

1981

The sponsors of the Great Plains high-BTU coal-gasification project submitted a new pricing formula to FERC in early 1981 in which they proposed to operate the coal-gas plant as an unregulated gas well. This change increased the risks to consortium partners, but it removed the regulated attributes of the project as well. In making this proposal, it was revealed that Columbia Gas Transmission had backed out as an equity partner, leaving three project sponsors.

As the operator and organizer of the Great Plains Gasification Associates, American Natural Resources lobbied Washington D.C. and the public aggressively to sell the benefits of coal gas. American Natural Resources controlled 4 billion tons of lignite deposits in North Dakota, some of which were dedicated to the Great Plains coal gasification project. In 1981, the American Natural Resources board voted to spin off the firm's remaining natural-gas utility company, making American Natural Resources a gas-transmission company only. The divestiture reduced Amercan Natural Resources' dependence on a narrow customer base, fostered arm's-length transactions in selling the coal gas, and constituted a dis-integration of American Natural Resources' distribution system.

The second partner, Peoples Energy, had also participated since 1971 in a coal-gasification partnership that proposed to build a high-BTU coal-gas plant in Perry County, Illinois under a contract with the Department of Energy. In July, 1981, that project was terminated by the government. In November 1981, the Board of Peoples Energy voted to restructure the company into regulated and nonregulated entities. Peoples Energy would continue as a parent for two gas utilities in Ilinois under this plan.

Koppers, a highly diversified chemicals company, filed three synthetic-fuel proposals that were finalists in the U.S. Synthetic Fuels Corporation's funding process. Two of these involved coal gasification. The Hampshire Energy Project proposed for Gillette, Wyoming, used an indirect process for making gasoline from coal and its partners included Northwestern Mutual Life Insurance, Koppers, Kaneb Services, Metropolitan Insurance, and Sohio.

In 1981 WyCoalGas Inc. (Panhandle Eastern, Ruhrgas, and Pacific Gas & Electric) terminated their project due to delays and uncertainties caused by the federal Synfuels Corporation. The partners had expended $16.5 million on feasibility studies for the $2.7 billion synthetic-fuels project, but they declined to provide the $88 million needed for the project to proceed without federal assistance. Although Panhandle Eastern and its partners expressed their intentions to maintain the assets they had assembled, high interest rates and unsympathetic rate-base rulings prevented them from renewing options as they expired.

In 1981, the private backers of the Cool Water generating project decided they could no longer wait for the U.S. Synthetic Fuels Corporation to act on their request for aid and committed themselves to completing the $300 million project without federal money. The sponsors—the Electric Power Research Institute (EPRI), Bechtel, General Electric, Southern California Edison, and Texaco—agreed to raise their investments to prevent further construction delays.

In 1981 Shell Oil participated in a joint venture with its parent, Royal Dutch-Shell, to build a 150-ton-per-day demonstration plant in Hamburg, Germany and announced the construction of a prototype 1,000-ton-per-day coal-gasification facility. One year later the project was shelved.

Settlement of an out-of-court dispute with the four plaintiffs who objected to an indemnification plan for the Great Plains project cleared the project for a DOE-loan guarantee, but it also forced the sponsors to assume greater risks in this project. The Great Plains project received a conditional loan guarantee for $2.2 billion from DOE that was obtained by surrendering several attributes of the financing arrangement that had made it more attractive. PG&E, whose last coal-gasification project was terminated in October 1981, expressed an interest in joining the Great Plains project.

On February 1, 1982, the government signed a $2 billion-loan-guarantee agreement for the Great Plains project. Under the terms of the new agreement, the project's sponsors put up both equity and debt (their minimum liability would be $100 million and their maximum $740 million). Federal funds would be expended only in the event that the project failed.

In early 1981 American Solar King purchased Daystar, a manufacturer and marketer of solar-water-heating systems from Exxon for $2.2 million. American Solar King's new Daystar facilities in Burlington, Massachusetts, gave it a significant market presence in New England, and Daystar had become a major supplier of copper absorber plates after Olin Brass exited. (American Solar King purchased its absorber plates from Daystar, as well.) Between the two firms, over eight collector types were produced and sold individually, or in prepackaged systems. Half of their floor space served as warehouse space for the controllers, tanks, valves, pumps, and other components that were shipped under American Solar King or Daystar brand names. Under its new management, Daystar supported a substantially lower overhead burden and a smaller management team than when it was an Exxon unit. Exxon had invested between $10 and $12 million in the development of Daystar's products, but became disillusioned about the near-term profitability of residential-solar-heating systems. Daystar had yet to turn a profit and had lost $200 thousand in 1980 on sales of $3.5 million under Exxon.

In 1981, barely a year after introducing its own solar-heating systems, Olin discontinued marketing of its collectors. Within nine months Olin announced it would also cease manufacturing the copper absorber plate that had been the core of many firms' solar collectors. Although the Olin absorber plate was efficient, it was too expensive to use in 1981. Olin Brass had been unable to compete as a marketer of solar collectors because it had never developed the network necessary to generate large sales volumes.

General Electric installed flat-plate solar-heating systems in demonstration projects in New England and marketed medium-temperature solar-heating products through traditional GE HVAC wholesalers and contractors. Despite alleged losses in excess of $5 million from its first eight years in residential solar heating, General Electric was rumored to be introducing a consumer-direct-marketing plan that included the financing of consumer purchases in 1981.

General Motors introduced a mass-produced, mass-merchandised solar collector through its Harrison Radiator Division. The General Motors solar collector was marketed by Energy Clinic and was manufactured for GM by Olympic Solar, a black-chroming firm. Distribution would be through dealer-installers, and it was rumored that purchases of the low-priced General Motors solar collector would be financed by GMAC, thereby circumventing one problem in selling solar collectors to homeowners.

1982

In 1982 federal cutbacks and policy changes severely challenged future demand for solar-heating systems. The Energy Department's solar programs were halved, the Solar Energy Research Institute was dismantled and its regional offices were closed. At the end of 1981, only 227 firms continued to manufacture solar collectors, and few of them would be capable of surviving a prolonged slump in sales.

**Analysis of Strategies for Vertical Integration in
Embryonic Energy Industries**

This section analyzes the patterns of vertical behavior sketched above and compares the predictions of the strategy framework with outcomes observed in 1981. In 1981 both industries were characterized by high uncertainty about the future viability of their products as well as uncertainty about how their structures would evolve. The coal-gasification industry did not promise to be volatile, yet profit margins threatened to be thin due to uncertainties concerning the future prices of substitute fuels. Bargaining power among coal-gas suppliers should have been high, yet economic forces reduced their abilities to exert this latent power. According to the strategy framework proposed in chapter 2, in this industry coal-gas firms could undertake several activities and stages, they would have to be more highly integrated than others in embryonic settings, and they would keep their ownership stakes in the industry low until uncertainties were reduced by using joint ventures. By contrast, the competitive environment for solar heating was volatile, largely due to widespread excess capacity and firms' differing strategic postures. The bargaining power of firms producing residential-solar-heating systems was not high with respect to raw-materials suppliers nor distribution channels. According to the strategy framework proposed in chapter 2, in this industry firms would *not* be broadly integrated into many activities or stages, they would not be highly internally integrated, and firms would keep their ownership stakes in the industry low until uncertainties about industry viability were relieved.

Phase of Industry Development

These industries were embryonic in 1981 because regulatory policies and substitute products undermined their economic viability and demand for them. The long-term need for coal-gasification facilities was substantial, but short-term demand was depressed by a glut of natural gas. Many different types of firms wanted to participate in coal gasification but the uncertainties concerning how the industry would evolve, how the large projects would be financed, and when construction could commence added to the chaos that characterized this environment in 1981. In solar heating, the viability of some firms' strategic postures was still in doubt, the competitive advantage of one form of distribution channel over another had not yet been established, and no firm enjoyed sales volumes large enough to fully automate their manufacturing process and enjoy economies of scale and experience. The industry's structure was stuck. Some clear patterns of competition were beginning to emerge, but it could assume several diverse forms.

For example, public utilities and traditional distributors of heating oil were distributing solar-heating devices to their established customer bases. Would it be long before they manufactured the technologically unsophisticated solar collector in-house? Also the fate of the packagers—firms that sold entire residential-solar-heating systems to wholesalers for resale to dealers—was murky because, in the mechanical trades of refrigeration and air conditioning the *wholesaler* had always been the packager. (A solar packager interrupted the classic distribution chain and raised prices, yet they could not purchase components more cheaply than wholesalers could.)

President Carter was shaping his energy policy during a time of doubling oil prices, a revolution in Iran, and the nuclear-reactor accident at Three Mile Island, which disrupted the possibilities for increased nuclear power. But when Reagan became president a different climate existed. Oil was temporarily in abundance, OPEC did not seem to possess the control over its members it had possessed a year earlier, and gasoline prices were declining.

In summary, although substitutes for natural gas and crude oil were generally regarded as desirable in this environment, there was great uncertainty about specific demand for coal gas and solar heating in 1981. At the end of 1981, when natural-gas supplies became available in great quantities, coal-gasification-project sponsors backed away from immediate commercialization plans. Development of this embryonic business was paralyzed by uncertainty and thus the perceived need to control many aspects of it was high. Government policies had contributed to this instability because subsidies reduced the perceived riskiness of entry for many marginal competitors in solar heating, and encouraged firms to undertake coal-gasification projects.

In 1981, the technological characteristics of coal-gasification ventures made excess capacity a significant concern, and broad ranges of integration were needed in that industry to ensure that critical throughput volumes could be maintained. Although coal-gas firms did not need integration to develop new technologies, protect product quality, or maintain operating secrecy, they desired the superior control of the project's integrity that many internal controls provided for them. By contrast, in solar heating few justifications for broad or high degrees of internal integration existed because vertical integration could not be used to control product quality effectively. Moreover, balance problems between upstream and downstream business units in solar heating were inevitable.

In summary, many of the arguments justifying broad or high vertical integration within an embryonic industry were unsupported in the experience of solar heating. There were no problems in obtaining needed supplies, there was an abundance of subcontractors ready to perform any necessary manufacturing tasks, and it would have been infeasible to reach ultimate consumers by installing the solar-heating system for the homeowner.

Volatile Industry Structure

In 1981 the outlook for profit margins on coal-gasification projects appeared gloomy due to price reductions of substitute products, not due to inherent volatility within the industry itself. Indeed, the structure of the coal-gasification industry tended to discourage the type of competitive infighting other embryonic industries might experience. Because coal-gasification plants could achieve a regional (or internal) monopolist status and because their interconnected technologies enhanced opportunities for integration economies, the industry was likely to become a stable environment where higher degrees of integration could be used successfully earlier in the industry's development. In solar heating, little price-cutting occurred, but few firms earned profits either. Entry was easy and exit should have been easy, but some firms remained despite sizable losses, making the industry become volatile rapidly. Other structural traits, taken individually, also argued against high integration in solar heating.

Coal gas was a commodity and although its processing was complex, there were relatively few trade secrets that differentiated firms' products from each other. Basic coal-gasification research was costly; firms frequently purchased this knowledge rather than developing it internally. Because the product needed little protection its traits alone did not argue for high internal integration. In solar heating, the pieces of the system were diverse, and no competitor made all of them. Therefore the most important bases for product differentiation were quality construction and quality of installation, both attributes few firms could control.

Some coal-gasification firms controlled their coal reserves or constructed gasification plants, but firms could purchase these inputs instead. Coal ownership represented the potential to capture higher value-added with less risk, thus firms frequently owned the coal they intended to gasify. In solar heating, supplies were readily available from several firms and the technology changed slowly. Thus there was little need for upstream scanning or vertical integration for the purpose of understanding competitors' cost structures. Moreover, it was not clear that firms suffered competitive disadvantages by being less integrated than their rivals at this time. Backward integration into metals fabrication would have been very expensive, and excess capacity not absorbed by solar heating would have forced potential entrants into the fabrication business inadvertantly.

Coal gas was supplied as a feedstock or fuel to chemical-process plants, industrial-fuel customers, and natural-gas-transmission companies that resold the gas to distribution companies. Since the gas was transported by pipeline, interconnection created switching-cost barriers for some customers, but since the coal-gasification firm did not need to control its intermediate customers to reach another ultimate-consumer group, the need for forward integration was less pressing than the need for strong upstream controls. In solar heating, public utilities were becoming increasingly interested in supplanting traditional HVAC outlets as distributors and installers of residential-solar-heating systems. Sales volumes in 1981 were too low to justify firms selling solar-heating systems through owned distribution channels unless the firm marketed other building or heating supplies as well. Control of this value-adding activity was important but few firms could afford to exert some form of ownership downstream.

The technology of coal gasification was capital intensive and adjacent process plants were designed to be in balance with each other. Because the assets were interconnected and could incur sizable diseconomies if no controls protected them against imbalances, a need for vertical controls was evident. By contrast, in solar heating, the technology of producing flat-plate collectors was labor-intensive and demand was insufficient to justify lower-cost, automated-assembly production processes. There was little advantage to participating in a fragmented business with low entry barriers, low technical sophistication and a relatively flat experience curve, particularly where government policies exacerbated uncertainties about demand. All of these factors argued against broad integration in 1981.

Coal gasification was unlikely to become a concentrated industry given the transportation limitations of the product, and more diverse players were expected to participate in it when the industry developed. It was not a volatile industry in 1981 because: (1) technology changed infrequently, (2) customers were few and interlinked with coal gas firms, (3) spot-market activities were less important for supplying coal-gas plants, and (4) the product was sold under long-term contracts that matched the life of the plant. The major force that instigated industry volatility was the uncertainty created by government policy changes. Thus, even in its embryonic phase, the coal-gasification industry was a stable environment in which diverse strategic groups and poor competitive signaling did not affect competition, and high customer-switching costs were guaranteed by long-term contracts and physical interconnections.

By contrast, the solar-heating industry faced a fragmented but national market in 1981 and was likely to become volatile because competitors possessed dissimilar vertical structures, expectations about the need for future integration, and corporate missions for solar-heating-business units. In brief, several different strategic groups seeking the same customers were increasing their stakes, competitive signaling was poor, fringe competitors and mavericks were using price competition, few product improvements were made (and buyers were becoming more knowledgeable), and the industry was plagued with erratic and cyclical demand. All of these created the potential for an environment in which high integration was not advisable.

Bargaining Power

Buyers and sellers in the coal-gasification industry possessed bilateral market power because coal suppliers and gasifiers needed each other. Thus, although bargaining power allowed firms to lower their ownership stakes, bilateral bargaining power seemed to force buyers' and sellers' interests to coincide, and joint ventures between partners in adjacent industries occurred in developing coal-gasification facilities. These arrangements were long-term in nature because suppliers and customers of coal-gas firms attained power over the firms due to their switching-cost barriers. Once the project was commercialized, protection of both parties was desirable. Thus the embryonic nature of demand argued against inflexible forms of vertical integration, but the industry's structure and firms' inherent bargaining positions within it were conducive to strong forms of vertical control and high degrees of asset ownership.

By contrast, the manufacturers of residential-solar-heating systems possessed little bargaining power over suppliers because their purchases represented a small portion of suppliers' sales, solar-heating firms could not credibly threaten to backward integrate, and in the case of fabricated metals, their purchases were important to the quality of solar collectors. Solar-heating firms possessed little bargaining power over distributors because there were many suppliers of solar-heating systems, suppliers could not provide demonstrations, installation and other services, distributors were relatively indifferent about selling solar-heating products in many cases, and it was clear that few manufacturers could forward-integrate. Consequently, taper integration or quasi-integration downstream would be needed by firms wishing to control quality and other aspects of product differentiation. In summary, although the embryonic nature of demand and the industry's structure argued against high internal integration, broad functional integration or high ownership stakes, few firms possessed the bargaining power necessary to control adjacent industry participants without owning them. Since they could not afford integration, these firms received very poor service at the hands of outsiders.

Strategy Goals

High and broad integration was undertaken in the coal-gasification industry to attain control, despite the high operating risks it entailed, but there were few strategic objectives that justified broad or high integration in solar heating. Firms in both industries incurred losses from high integration, but it was not necessary to do so in solar heating.

The logical firms for coal-gasification ventures were firms that owned coal or an existing pipeline, or any firm that used natural gas as a fuel, including utilities and municipalities. Yet these firms could not afford to invest in coal-gasification projects alone and used joint ventures to pool their resources. In solar heating the most promising markets were low-cost swimming-pool heating, low-cost residential heating, and high-quality residential heating, and each could be served adequately by a focus strategy rather than by high degrees of integration and a standardized product.

The decision to transfer goods between internal units is a corporate decision. In coal gasification, each firm that was a partner to a joint venture contributed special skills or assets to the project. Natural-gas-transmission companies that participated in coal-gas ventures with chemical-process firms found synergies with other continuous-process ventures they had undertaken, because joint ventures were an accepted business practice in the chemicals industry, as well. In residential solar heating, some firms carried their solar-heating businesses because they were outlets for their depressed metals-fabrication or heating-tanks businesses. Others used existing distribution outlets—distribution houses or retail stores—to market solar-heating products, but few firms exited from solar heating when it did not become profitable for them.

The Need for Vertical Integration

The benefits of vertical integration in coal gasification included opportunities for integration economies from interconnection, custom-designed plants, existing pipelines, and trading relationships. Strategic-control advantages from integration would become clearer later in the industry's development, when shutdowns and reorganizations would be easier if the venture were wholly owned. But there were also dangers associated with high degrees of integration early in this industry's development because coal-gasification plants were locked into particular operating volumes and incurred diseconomies if adjacent units became strategically sick. Technology could change substantially, leaving early entrants with obsolete plants and vertically integrated early entrants with amplified degrees of inflexibility.

In solar heating there were few economies of integration that could be enjoyed beyond the savings from handling costs, freight costs, and overhead economies common to other conversion businesses, but most solar-heating firms had yet to enjoy scale economies in manufacturing, let alone integration economies in 1981. Some firms even experienced *diseconomies* from vertical integration, when they shipped components across the country for the sake of intrafirm transfers.

Strategy Alternatives and Performance

The strategy model distinguished between ownership and the degree of internal integration that firms engaged in; firms may have owned all, some, or none of the adjacent firms supplying goods and services to them, and firms may have transferred all, some, or none of their needs internally. Moreover, firms differed in the breadth and stages of their integrations. In coal gasification, firms could be backward integrated to supply coal, oxygen, and machinery. Firms could also transmit and distribute natural gas, convert coal gas to methanol (and other chemicals), or burn coal gas as fuel. In solar heating, firms could make several components of the solar-heating system, or participate in wholesaling, retailing, and installation services. In both industries the choices depended upon firms' strategic missions and internal strengths.

The major strategic choices for coal gasification in 1981 included: (1) how to control access to coal reserves, (2) whether to build a captive-chemical-feedstock or fuel-processing linkage, and (3) whether (and when) to buy out a joint-venture partner's interest in coal gasification. Although high degrees of internal integration were tricky to manage because they required the firm to assume responsibility for upstream or downstream services or supplies that might otherwise have been purchased, the uncertainties of coal gasification made firms want to exert the control associated with these responsibilities. But the strategy matrix argued that unless firms' strategy requirements made full integration necessary, some of the responsibility for coal supplies and distribution of the coal gas and risks of vertical integration should be transferred to outside parties as in the case of the solar-heating industry.

Firms that used high degrees of internal integration sometimes did so to attain objectives of synergies or technological leadership, or to maintain control over projects of great importance to the firm. The major risks of full integration were asset inflexibility and loss of contacts among outside vendors. The degree of vertical integration—how much of each activity was performed internally—was determined by firms' relative bargaining power as well as expectations concerning future conditions, based in part on the industry's development patterns.

High market-share goals were not relevant motives for integration in the coal-gasification industry, but integration economies were. If coordinated properly, an adequate balance between each processing step and through the pipelines could be achieved. Geographic proximity to other stages in the vertical chain also seemed important in choosing the appropriate degree of internal transfer for each activity. In coal gasification, high degrees of integration were used frequently. In solar heating, the most highly integrated firms supplied either metals, heating tanks and pumps, glass, or existing distribution channels. Some synergies were enjoyed by firms in ongoing related businesses, but firms that *created* these linkages to build their residential-solar-heating businesses did not prosper because sales volumes were inadequate to support the higher overhead of owned retail outlets or other functions.

The number of stages of activity undertaken was determined by the products' characteristics, the nature of demand, and the missions of the coal-gasification or residential-solar-heating units, relative to adjacent businesses. In coal gas, some firms linked the new source of medium- or high-BTU gas with their established gas-transmission and distribution lines. Other firms were severing the corporate link between transmission and distribution during the years under study. Demand was highly uncertain for synthetic natural gas due to the price of crude oil and the increasing volumes of natural gas found as U.S. firms sought new sources of crude oil.

In residential solar heating, some metals firms hoped to create a market conduit for their copper or aluminum, but the quantity demanded for solar-collector panels in 1981 was trivial. Moreover, the nature of the solar-heating business and the way in which the product was marketed did not complement the metals firms. In summary, in these early phases of industry development it did not seem to be necessary for firms to be involved in several integrated stages. Although coal gasification offered some synergies with adjacent business, its commercial viability in 1981 was highly dubious and quasi-integration arrangements could be used to obtain the infrastructure a particular firm did not possess.

The breadth of integration—the number of different activities undertaken—was determined by demand traits and how firms competed. In coal gasification, the diverse talents of coal-gasification partners created broadly integrated joint ventures that brought together firms like, for example, Bechtel (construction services), General Electric (gas-powered electric turbines), Texaco (gasification technology), and Southern California Edison (a public utility that transported and distributed fuel and power to ultimate consumers), plus a firm that owned or controlled the needed coal reserves.

In solar heating, Reynolds Metals was one of the most highly and broadly integrated firms, supplying metals, solar controls, and retail distribution internally, but no firm was involved in all five adjacent functions that were candidates for integration. The brands of solar-heating systems mentioned most frequently as being of highest engineering quality were produced by nonintegrated firms, suggesting that early in an industry's development integration may not be necessary to ensure quality of manufacture or installation.

The form of vertical relationships employed indicated the amount of asset exposure and flexibility the venture possessed. In highly uncertain environments where the performance of vertically integrated firms was highly sensitive to fluctuating sales, lesser amounts of asset exposure were used to reduce the variability of returns and increase strategic flexibilities. The form of integration used was determined by firms' bargaining power with respect to adjacent firms and its corporate-strategy objectives.

There were many joint ventures in coal gasification because large amounts of capital were needed to erect a gasification facility, and relatively sophisticated technology was used in a highly uncertain environment. Thus quasi-integration was used where capital costs were too high for firms to venture alone. Quasi-integration arrangements were also helpful because firms wanted more control than a simple contract would provide and a joint-venture agreement could be structured to impose penalties for partners that backed out and to match asset lives with demand forecasts. But there were few joint ventures in the solar-heating industry because relatively small amounts of capital were needed to enter solar heating, relatively unsophisticated technology was used, and entry was not considered risky by many of the firms under study. Joint ventures were most likely to occur in photovoltaic or heliostat research where there was great uncertainty regarding the technology and vast amounts of capital were needed.

Evaluation of firms' vertical strategies in coal gasification must be tempered by a recognition that, if government policies stabilize, if natural-gas prices soar, and if demand rises significantly, their strategic postures could change. Similarly, solar-heating firms could change their postures if demand took off. For the purposes of this research, firms that had formulated the more-effective vertical-integration strategies were those that gained relatively stable access to raw materials and markets while also achieving their strategic objectives, including satisfaction of their market obligations, attaining above-average, long-term returns on invested capital, or retaining technological leadership.

The partners in the Great Plains project—American Natural Resources, Peoples Energy, Tennessee Gas Transmission (Tenneco), and Transco—successfully received loan assurances to guarantee an acceptable return on their capital and to obtain a source of gas to satisfy their customers. Interestingly, two partners dis-integrated from their other, regulated natural-gas operations when they found the breadth and degree of integration unworkable.

The Tennessee Gas Transmission Company was most broadly integrated, and new sources of natural gas were crucial to this firm's future ability to satisfy customer needs. Tenneco was one of the firms more likely to pursue coal-gas projects with minimal government assistance, and to do so in the most highly and broadly integrated degree and breadth.

Pacific Gas & Electric and Ruhrgas had purchased participation in several coal-gasification projects to obtain sources of synthetic natural gas and knowledge concerning the construction and operation of gasification facilities, respectively. PG&E could not venture into coal gas alone and Ruhrgas was limited by its corporate charter. Thus their involvement was appropriate in 1981.

Tennessee Eastern, Columbia Gas, and Transcontinental Transmission started coal-gasification ventures but were forced to reduce their involvement or to drop out completely. These types of companies needed the synthetic natural gas that would have been produced but lacked the financial resources to control the direction of coal gas from the surviving gasification projects.

Conoco had been the leader in coal-gasification technology, and it also owned the largest coal reserves. By 1981 Conoco backed away from coal gas and industry observers predicted Conoco's coal reserves would be sold by du Pont in the near future.

Shell announced plans to build a 1000-ton-per-day coal-gasification facility with its parent, Royal Dutch-Shell at Moerdijk in the Netherlands, but suspended construction due to rising costs in 1982. Shell had developed its own gasification technology and was well-suited to proceed when demand for coal gas looked more promising.

Texaco's major new commercial coal-gas venture, the Cool Water project, would power generators providing electricity to Californian households. Texaco's participation was as a passive investor in that venture, but it was capable of more involvement later.

Koppers, the heavy-machinery and chemicals firm, was a promoter of methanol chemicals that could be produced from synthetic gas. The coal-gasification technology proposed in its canceled Hampshire project was most likely to employ a second-generation Koppers design for coal gasification, thereby providing corporate synergies.

In summary, many coal-gasification projects were broadly integrated as well as highly integrated from upstream (and to downstream) affiliates in order to control many aspects of these very risky ventures. Firms used joint ventures to launch coal-gasification projects when they could not afford to own the investment alone. Because interconnected plants were expected to yield significant integration economies, a more highly integrated structure was expected to develop earlier in this industry than in other types of embryonic businesses.

The most profitable solar-heating firms were those that served only a regional market and incurred low overhead due to smaller plant scale and low transportation costs, such as ACRO Energy and Radco Products. Packaging firms that purchased the major components of a solar-heating system and resold them, making only a slim profit on their sales, pursued strategies that seemed to be of limited durability because wholesalers in conventional distribution channels packaged systems also, but without taking ownership as the packaging firms did.

Revere Solar had the highest brand-name awareness because Revereware was a household word that connoted quality. Revere was broadly integrated into raw materials, plumbing hardware, and retail outlets, and was also highly integrated. The solar business piggy-backed onto its established distribution channels and consulting relationships with architects and the building trade. Although Revere had increased its productive facilities, it was not believed to be profitable in 1981.

Asarco mined copper, but milled neither copper nor aluminum. Yet Asarco may be considered integrated because it owned 37 percent of Revere Copper and Brass, which milled and fabricated these metals. Sunworks operated a semiautomated factory, expanded its capacity, and was a market-share leader, but because manufacturing economies were expected at larger sales volumes than either Asarco or Revere Solar enjoyed singly, industry observers wondered why they did not consolidate their facilities in solar heating. In 1981 Sunworks was not believed to be profitable.

Critics complained that Grumman overengineered their solar-heating systems. Similarly, Grumman could be accused of having overengineered its marketing, for it won an award for its advertising. Still, Grumman lost millions because its forward integration strategy was inappropriate for its sales volumes and its sales overhead was too high.

Although American Solar King was a market-share leader, it endured high costs by shipping copper absorber plates from Burlington, Massachusetts to Waco, Texas, and entire systems (including 400-pound solar tanks) across the country for resale by distributors. American Solar King relied heavily upon the effectiveness of its wholesalers that financed inventories and distributed its products, but was not yet believed to be profitable in 1981.

In 1981 Ametek assembled solar collectors using some aluminum from sister units. At one time, Ametek had sold entire solar-heating systems as a service to its customers, but it stopped packaging systems and emphasized production of the solar collector, believing only that portion of the business offered good profitability potential for it in 1981. The other key aspect of its solar-heating strategy was its careful selection of distributors and dealers (including Sears and Meenan Oil). In 1981 Ametek's position in solar heating was believed to be improving, although it had not yet reached breakeven on this investment.

In summary, no national residential-solar-heating firm was believed to be profitable in 1981. Regional firms were marginally profitable, but only the producers of swimming-pool heaters were clearly profitable.

The industry's structure was stuck in a fragmented state. Two scenarios were possible for its future: (1) it would remain a regional ma-and-pa type of business in which large firms would never attain the critical mass of sales needed to attain scale economies; or (2) energy prices would rise while government subsidies fell, forcing mergers to occur among the smaller firms to achieve the manufacturing economies of the larger firms. Then broad and high vertical integration might be profitable.

References

Analysis of Industrial Markets for Low- and Medium-BTU Coal Gasification. DOE/RA/2625-1.

Analysis of Industrial Markets for Low- and Medium-BTU Coal Gasification. EI. 30:2625-1, July 1970. (Prepared by Booz, Allen.)

An Analysis of Petroleum Company Investments in Non-Petroleum Energy Sources—Book 1, October 1979. E3.2: Prr/3/B,1.

Detman, Roger. C.F. Braun and Company. *Preliminary Economic Comparison of Six Processes for Pipeline Gas from Coal*. Presentation to the Eighth Synthetic Pipeline Gas Symposium. Chicago, Illinois, October 18-20, 1976.

Energy Data Report, "Solar Collector Manufacturing Activity, January through June 1981." U.S. Department of Energy. September 1981.

Evolution of the Regulation of High Cost Gas Supplies. N-1435 (Rand Publication), February 1980.

Low-BTU Gas Industrial Application Analysis. November 1978. E1.28: HCP/T3012.

Oversight—Cost Estimation Techniques for Emerging Synthetic Fuels Technology. 96 Y4. Sci 2: 96/34, July 1979.

Oversight—Great Plains Gasification. 96 Y4. Sci 2: 96/60.

Oversight—Synthetic Fuels. 96 Y4. Sci 2: 96/56. September 1979.

Petroleum Industry Involvement in Alternative Sources of Energy. 95 Y4. En2:95-54. September 1977.

Prospects for the Commercialization of High-BTU Coal Gasification. R-2294-DOE. April 1978.

Also helpful were corporate annual reports and financial statements of the firms described in chapter 10 and conversations with six sponsors (or former sponsors) of coal-gasification projects, three potential coal-gas customers, one coal company, and three industry observers, ten producers (or former producers) of residential solar-heating systems, two component suppliers, three distributors and two industry observers.

12 Generalizations concerning Strategies for Vertical Integration

Some conclusions about vertical strategies in the sample industries are gathered here to generalize about the strategy matrix; the outcomes it predicted; and the effects of industry structure, demand instability, bargaining power, and corporate strategy on vertical integration. Successful uses of vertical integration in diverse settings are noted and variances between expected and observed vertical strategies are investigated in this chapter.

A Restatement of Hypotheses

It is useful to restate the key hypotheses about vertical strategies before examining each dimension of vertical integration in detail. First, because industry environments differ in their attractiveness for vertical integration, the problems encountered in coupling adjacent industries will not be homogeneous. Other things held constant, vertical strategies undertaken within volatile industry settings should involve lesser degrees of internal transfer, lower ownership stakes, and fewer integrated activities (or stages per activity) than within stable environments. Second, some embryonic industries (as well as declining industries) should not be broadly integrated due to the high uncertainties associated with the development of such industries. In these settings, successful firms will initially avoid integration, thereby avoiding errors that might create mobility barriers. Similarly, successful firms will dis-integrate their adjacent relationships early, as their industries begin to decline, to avoid exit barriers and to focus their energies on the most-lucrative remaining activities.

Third, vertical strategies suggested by industry-evolution and volatility traits will be modified by the firm's means of controlling adjacent firms' assets without owning them. This power to leverage an important market position—to control suppliers—has been demonstrated most vividly in the Japanese automobile industry's *kanban* system of minimizing inventories through close linkages with suppliers, and similar arrangements are possible with distributors. Fourth, corporate-strategy needs will also temper vertical integration. Highly and broadly integrated arrangements will occur when firms pursue low unit costs, high quality, or technological-leadership objectives. Firms using integration in this manner will sometimes endure under-utilized capacity to attain their long-range objectives. Joint ventures, or other quasi-integration arrangements, will occur when firms desire competitive or technological intelligence but can not afford to enter a new business or build a new plant alone.

Fifth, since industries differ in volatility and in demand uncertainty, and since business units vary in their relative bargaining power and the corporate-strategy directives they heed, the appropriate degree, breadth, stages, and form of their strategies will differ even within the same industry, according to the firm's needs. Finally, the strategy matrix suggested that high degrees of internal integration were difficult to manage within environments that are volatile and where demand is uncertain. Firms that do not possess the power needed to persuade suppliers or distributors to perform useful services for them are obliged to undertake these activities in-house, and when this occurs within volatile industries or when demand was unstable, firms suffer from costly excess capacity and too much vertical integration.

Findings Regarding the Research Questions

This section summarizes findings about each hypothesis. The subsequent section analyzes these data in greater detail.

The most volatile industries examined in this study included the personal-microcomputers, baby-foods, and rayon industries. Although some firms were broadly and highly integrated (for reasons suggested below), leading firms in these industries were generally less integrated than were leaders in the less-volatile coal-gasification, ethical-pharmaceuticals, or acetylene industries. Some firms in the formerly stable leather-tanning, whiskey, and receiving-tubes industries reduced their breadth and degrees of integration as their industries became more volatile. Thus the hypothesis regarding less integration in the presence of price-cutting or rounds of rapid technological (or styling) changes was supported.

Based upon findings in the whiskey, rayon, baby-foods, oil-refining, receiving-tubes, leather-tanning, acetylene, cigars, percolator-coffee-makers, and synthetic-soda-ash industries, there is support for the hypotheses about less integration within declining industries (see chapter 4 for details). Whiskey producers also dis-integrated marketing and supplying activities, and downstream breadth and degrees of integration were reduced in the oil industry. Findings from the genetic-engineering, residential-solar-heating, and mircrocomputer industries support the hypothesis that low integration will be more prevalent than higher degrees of integration in new-and un-developed-industry infrastructures. The early experiences of successful firms in the tailored-suits and pharmaceuticals industries also support this hypothesis because they were neither highly nor broadly integrated as their industries developed. Many variations of vertical strategies were tried in these industries, and firms often found that high degrees of internal transfer and broadly ranging integration did not work well for them early in their industries' evolutions.

There were exceptions to these findings, however. Interconnected technologies that were in stable environments, such as acetylene and synthetic soda ash, often began by being integrated downstream. Corn producers (whiskey) and receiving-tube manufacturers (radios) also forward integrated early in their industries' development to capture more value-added. Thus some industries may begin to develop backward or forward integration because firms integrate early in order to prove the viability of innovative or risky new products. (Recall that Celanese was forward integrated to prove acetate was a viable product, as was Corning in fiber optics.) And if there was early integration, it was more likely to be a linkage downstream if the product required complex explanations in using or selling it.

In field studies of genetic engineering, leather tanning, rayon, and ethical pharmaceuticals, some firms received marketing services, inventory financing, and manufacturing contracts from others by virtue of their bargaining power over adjacent firms. Some microcomputer manufacturers obtained much of their software from independent software houses, and suit manufacturers received styling assistance from textile producers. Although this advantageous power balance may be temporary, there was support for the bargaining-power hypothesis that argued that firms need not risk equity investments to control their suppliers or buyers, provided they sustain their market power with respect to them.

Some firms were temporarily more integrated than the strategy matrix suggested due to corporate policies on vertical transfers. Start-up businesses sometimes began vertically integrated because synergies with existing resources could be gained. Other firms became highly integrated to pursue the economies needed for cost-leadership objectives, and market-share leaders in established or successful industries, such as tailored suits, whiskey, oil refining, and microcomputers, were also vertically integrated. Firms like Texas Instruments, which was broadly integrated upstream in microprocessors (the brains of microcomputers), Hitachi, and NEC used vertical integration to exploit experience-curve economies and to pursue technological-leadership objectives. Quasi-integration, rather than full ownership, was used to leverage the productive activities of others within the genetic-engineering, coal-gasification, and acetylene industries (where *joint ventures* were used to reach the market), as well as within the ethical-pharmaceuticals, oil-refining and whiskey industries (where *contract-processing arrangements* were used to even out production schedules and maintain physical facilities). Firms' arrangements with outsiders to obtain reliable supplies were not nearly as widespread as those to reach ultimate customers and the forms of vertical arrangements they used reinforced these efforts to secure markets.

There were many satisfactory, but different, ways to leverage a firm's relationship with suppliers and distributors within any given industry. In tailored suits, for example, Hart, Schaffner & Marx and Phillips-Van Heusen merchandised suits in their men's specialty stores, but Cluett-Peabody, Genesco, and other manufacturers did not own clothing stores in 1981. Richman Brothers sold their own tailored suits while Palm Beach did not sell any suits through its own stores. In coal gasification, Ruhrgas sought participation in gasification projects *not* to distribute the resulting high-BTU gas, but rather to gain access to technological information. Shell and Tenneco prepared coal-gasification ventures on their own, while Texaco took partners (Tenneco participated in joint ventures as well). It would seem that, depending on their needs, firms in the same industry could successfully pursue different vertical strategies.

The most disastrous performance observed in an established but volatile industry was that of United Merchants and Manufacturers' Robert Hall—a retailer that was integrated from textiles to garment fabrication to retailing. It went bankrupt. Bond Industries, which also made tailored suits, suffered a similar fate, but had excellent store locations and was reorganized as a real-estate investment rather than suffer total extinction. Cluett, Peabody and Genesco, in tailored suits, also tried forward integration, again with disastrous results. Thus too much of the wrong type of integration was found to be unprofitable. In oil refining, a loss of market access pushed Commonwealth Refining (which was unintegrated) toward bankruptcy, and poor access to crude oil after decontrol created difficulties for Ashland Oil, Clark Refining, and Amerada Hess. Although they were not always physically interconnected with their own adjacent units (except in supplying their petrochemicals operations), refiners valued their traditional trading relationships as well as their ownership of adjacent products and services, and too little or the wrong kind of integration also seemed unprofitable in the refining industry.

In rayon, Avtex Fibers was backward integrated to dissolving wood pulp on a scale that resulted in substantial excess capacity when demand declined. Rayon was of central importance to Avtex, and this dependence hurt it significantly. By contrast, Swift & Company was integrated from meat packing to baby foods and leather tanning—none of which was Swift's central business—and did not suffer as significantly from excessive integration as Avtex did. Tenneco did not suffer either because chemicals was not its core business. Finally, excess capacity was a significant problem in the residential-solar-heating business, where high inventorying costs, depressed demand, and reduced government subsidies made survival difficult. Because no firms possessed adequate sales to operate a plant that enjoyed economies from automation, the industry languished—unable to attain the critical mass needed to offer solar-heating systems inexpensively (a condition that could have accelerated the growth in demand and unstuck the industry's structure) and unwilling to lower costs by further integrating in such a risky venture.

Analysis of the Findings

Industry Development

The vertical-integration study observed 16 industries and 192 firms within them. The sample was divided into consumer and industrial goods, as well as into young businesses and mature ones. The results of differences in vertical strategies in these diverse industries are discussed below.

Young businesses were linked to an established, ongoing business in this study if they were vertically integrated at all. Both embryonic businesses—coal gasification and residential solar heating—were depressed in 1981, and their infrastructures were not developing adequately to make them clearly successful industries, as microcomputers had become. The price of oil, the major substitute for these products, was declining by the end of 1981, making residential solar heating and coal gasification uneconomic forms of energy. Coal-gasification projects that had not received subsidies under the new administration, needed a mechanism to reduce the riskiness of marketing the high- and medium-BTU gas they generated, and thus market contracts and financing arrangements were created before construction began. In solar heating, some aluminum and copper firms provided their solar-collector units with flat-plate components, and some home-air-conditioning and ventilation firms used their existing distribution channels to sell heating systems, but the residential-solar-heating industry was not broadly or highly integrated overall. In coal gasification, diverse types of firms—natural-gas distributors, transmission companies, and firms that were not vertically integrated into natural gas activities—all worked together to bring a project to commercialization. Since a guaranteed market was needed before such projects were started, the industry developed as a vertically integrated one, often using joint ventures because capital costs and risks were so large.

Demand for the products of the emerging businesses—personal microcomputers and genetic engineering—was becoming strong enough for manufacturing and selling infrastructures to develop stronger patterns than within embryonic businesses. Microcomputer demand was more clearly successful and many firms were researching products using genetic engineering in 1981. The need for linkages with firms possessing access to markets for genetically altered products and the means to produce the recombined substances in commercial quantities had already become clear. Thus although the impact of genetically engineered discoveries was not expected to be widespread until the 1990s, the industry was already becoming vertically integrated through equity arrangements, joint ventures, or manufacturing contracts with firms established in related and mature industries.

In personal microcomputers, where demand was more certain, firms often made microprocessors, memory chips, or other components for microcomputers that were compatible with other established products, or they owned retailing outlets. Although some firms, such as Tandy/Radio Shack, began as retailers that eventually made their own microcomputers, by 1981 many other types of firms had also moved into retailing to sell their microcomputers and other office products. Thus as the structure of this industry evolved and demand grew more rapidly, more vertical integration occurred. Where demand uncertainty was high, by contrast, little integration occurred and access to markets seemed to be of greatest concern. The backward linkages that existed in solar heating merely represented an additional outlet for firms selling copper or aluminum products, and these were not widespread in other young industries. Similarly, in microcomputers, where some firms used their own components when it was appropriate to do so, others (like IBM) used outsiders' components initially because the industry was so volatile. When technology stabilized, higher degrees of integration could be anticipated.

The established businesses examined included ethical pharmaceuticals and tailored suits, and both had been vertically integrated. Tailored suits became less integrated as demand declined during the 1970s. The declining businesses examined were petroleum refining and whiskey, as well as the eight industries discussed in chapter 4. In both whiskey and oil, declining demand was not yet significant and could conceivably be revitalized without damage to producing assets because firms' infrastructures had not yet deteriorated. But some disintegrations had been occurring as firms eased out of activities they had previously performed and sought new distribution arrangements or other sources for low-value services or components. Firms in the whiskey industry dis-integrated from barrel making, grain elevators, and wholesaling activities as their unit volumes declined, and oil refiners shut down underutilized refineries and backed out of low value-added activities. The imminent decline of oil refining in the United States would be more like that of the U.S. leather-tanning industry than that of acetylene, however, as oil-producing nations started up their own refineries and commodity chemical plants and made the need for U.S. facilities obsolete. By 1981 several oil firms had backed away from using credit cards as marketing tools and a few firms emphasized rack selling more heavily than gasoline-station sales by 1981.

Thus, in the ten declining and six nondeclining businesses observed in this study there seems to be enough evidence to cast substantial doubt on the validity of Stigler's hypothesis regarding vertical integration.[1] Embryonic industries do not begin vertically integrated except where existing businesses offer vertical linkages, and they tend to become more vertically integrated (if at all) as the industry becomes a successful one. By endgame few vertical integrations remained in the examples this study examined. The relationship is the opposite of the one Stigler hypothesized with respect to *breadth* and *degree*.

Volatile Competition

The competitive conditions that firms encountered also affected the degree and breadth of integration they undertook. Industries that changed technologically or stylistically at frequent intervals were riskier for full integration than industries in which changes occurred slowly. Moreover, industries characterized by costly excess capacity and vicious price-cutting were less hospitable for vertical strategies than stable industries where excess capacity was not significantly costly.

If a product were differentiated by manufacturing activities, as in the case of whiskey, cigars, or ethical pharmaceuticals, firms were more likely to be backward integrated to control the ingredients and processes that made their products special. Similarly, the presence of trade secrets for some pharmaceuticals or microprocessor logics increased the likelihood of upstream control. By contrast, if a product were differentiated by marketing activities as in the case of some ethical pharmaceuticals, tailored suits, petroleum refining, microcomputers or residential-solar-heating systems, firms were more likely to employ specialty sales forces, open their own stores, or become otherwise involved in marketing their own products. Competitive scanning was improved, especially in the pharmaceuticals and microcomputers industries, by having downstream intelligence as well as basic research facilities in-house, but few *fully* integrated strategies were observed downstream. The exceptions included Upjohn, which sold primarily through its own distribution facilities, and Tandy/Radio Shack, which sold only through its computer stores in 1981. Most forward integrations were tapered rather than full transfers of materials or services downstream, and this partial involvement was sufficient to gather the needed intelligence.

Backward integration was expected where the value-added of suppliers was substantial, as in the cases where high-value components were supplied by manufacturers of bulk pharmaceuticals, microprocessors, and solar-collector panels, but the entry barriers upstream were too high for unintegrated firms in the ethical-pharmaceutical, microcomputer, or residential-solar-heating industries to backward integrate (except by acquisition) in 1981. By contrast, in oil exploration, where entry barriers were low, many previously unintegrated refineries became so when the price of U.S. crude oil was decontrolled and exploration became a high value-added activity. Whiskey producers backward integrated to make barrels when government price controls created a shortage of barrel suppliers, and many whiskey distillers were also grain merchants initially. No tailored-suit manufacturers were backward integrated to textiles, however, because the minimum-efficient scale of a mill was too large for their needs. In the ethical-pharmaceuticals industry, integration moved both downstream from medicinal chemicals and pharmaceutical preparations and upstream from pharmaceutical wholesaling over time to capture value-added. Patented drugs offered the largest proportion of value-added and thus most pharmaceutical firms made their own bulk preparations if not their own fine chemicals by 1981. Most frequently, the scale of upstream operations exceeded those of the business under study, and vertically integrated firms often supplied raw materials or components to outsiders as well as to sister units when economies dictated doing so.

Forward integration was more likely where the value-added of consuming industries was attractive and could be captured easily, as in radios and television, several organic and inorganic chemicals, flat glass, shoes, gasoline, men's-specialty retailing, computer software, and computer stores. (Forward integration could occur into pharmaceuticals and specialty chemicals by firms using genetic-engineering techniques if they could overcome entry barriers.) Wholesalers had added value by distributing pharmaceuticals, heating oil, gasoline, whiskey, cigars, baby foods, electric percolator coffee makers and electronic receiving tubes, and at least one competitor had once been a wholesaler of these products in many of these industries at one time. Detailed demonstrations and explanations were most important in adding value to ethical pharmaceuticals, microcomputers, and residential-solar-heating systems, but firms employed their own selling personnel primarily in the pharmaceuticals business. (Tandy/Radio Shack's computer stores and a few solar stores owned by manufacturers were the exceptions in other industries.) Hart, Schaffner & Marx sold its own tailored suits through its retail outlets successfully, but Phillips-Van Heusen's retailing linkage was less successful. (PVH specialized in tailored suits of a lower quality grade and price level and its retail outlets were mismatched in the quality of PVH merchandise they handled.) Replacement parts were a lucrative market for receiving tubes, and manufacturers wholesaled their own components and assisted their authorized dealers to capture this value.

(Broadly integrated firms like Texas Instruments also used various forms of dealer assistance to capture a large portion of the after-market sales for those microcomputer components they manufactured.)

Integration went from the target businesses to downstream—except in ethical pharmaceuticals and coal gasification—and forward integration was more likely to occur where the distribution activity or next production stage provided brand-name recognition or special attributes that added substantial value to the final products. Retailing outlets dedicated primarily to declining products were rare, and thus it was not surprising to observe some petroleum refiners changing their gasoline and heating-oil-marketing policies to emphasize bulk sales in 1981. (Their integrated positions gave refiners cost structures that rivaled the off-brand marketers' costs and enabled them to use small distributors as the most-effective way to minimize asset inflexibility while maximizing sales in endgame.)

Make-or-buy decisions were possible in most of the industries because private branding, plant leasing, and contract manufacturing were available to firms in all but the coal gasification industry, and these arrangements were used to balance firms' capacity utilizations while satisfying seasonal peaks in demand. Sometimes manufacturers made products for each other while their plants were down for maintenance. Osborne Computer purchased its subassembled components and built them into microcomputers, and Sinclair Research (which had no factory) hired Timex to manufacture its microcomputers. Thus, a firm's decision to purchase subassembled components or finished products from others was not limited to the early and late evolutionary phases of an industry, and contract manufacturing was used in established industries as well as within unstable ones. The use of integration to keep skilled personnel was most significant in the genetic-engineering, oil-exploration, and pharmaceutical industries, and not surprisingly these firms tried to be highly integrated *and* fully utilized where these critical personnel were employed.

The skills needed to control outside subcontractors varied according to a product's technological complexities. Purchasers of genetic-engineering services and microcomputer software needed to understand the products they desired, and these products' traits changed rapidly. To control them, firms needed in-house, parallel projects staffed with skilled personnel that could evaluate their subcontractors' activities. By contrast, production of residential-solar-heating systems was not a high-technology process, and scale economies were most important to lower costs and automate procedures. Pooling requirements to let one firm manufacture for the others was the logical way to attain these economies, but the large number of solar-collector manufacturing sites in operation in 1981 suggested the industry had not yet become rationalized.

The pattern of integrated plants seemed to be one of decreasing scale for downstream facilities, except in oil production. Other integrated industries had larger upstream plant capacities than the target business did and downstream facilities were often geographically dispersed in fragmented industries. Thus when a firm contemplated exit from vertically integrated businesses, it began by divesting or terminating low-margin, downstream operations to ease its way out.

There were few significant exit barriers created by vertical integration, even where interconnected plants were used, because large write-offs were a normal part of those industries' risks. Dis-integration frequently progressed from the marketing outlets upstream, with downstream units (the smaller-sized facilities) divested first, and vertical integration created no special exit barriers that would not have been faced also by unintegrated competitors in the target businesses.

Firms used vertical integration differently because they belonged to dissimilar strategic groups, their parents had differing policies on integration, and they possessed dissimilar expectations about demand and rates of technological change. Due to these differences some firms expanded their degree, or breadth, of integration while others took actions to strengthen their suppliers or distributors. The worst type of industry to be in was one in which uncertainty was creating chaos. In oil refining, the eighteen largest firms were all vertically integrated, but they differed greatly in their crude-self-sufficiency ratios and in how they distributed their refined products. Some firms used primarily owned service stations, while others used leased stations operated by independent parties. Unbranded gasoline stations also purchased refined products, and some refiners emphasized unbranded sales (in addition to petrochemicals production) instead of branded sales because they expected price competition would again become rampant in the industry's endgame.

In whiskey, the eight largest firms had similar vertical strategies by 1981. Only Seagram, Brown-Forman, and Glenmore Distilleries retained their barrel-making units, and only the distribution companies of whiskey firms in major markets like New York City remained. All other liquor distribution was done by outsiders and the industry's competition had not yet become volatile. In pharmaceuticals, the twelve largest firms had very similar vertical-integration strategies, differing primarily in their use of drug wholesalers, and competition was not on the basis of price-cutting. In genetic engineering, most research firms were unintegrated (except Bio-Logicals, Novo Industri, Bethesda Research Laboratories), and major customers like Abbott Labs, Rohm & Haas, Allied Chemical, Johnson & Johnson, Monsanto, Schering-Plough, National Distillers & Chemicals, Campbell Soup, Koppers, and American Cyanamid used equity investments in and research contracts with genetic-engineering firms to control this technology. Shell, Eli Lilly, International Minerals & Chemicals, and Hoffman-

LaRoche, among others, had research contracts only, and competition was expected to develop on a nonprice basis, as in the ethical-pharmaceuticals industry, despite firms' diversities.

Firms used vertical integration quite differently in tailored suits and personal microcomputers, where firms were forward-, backward- or non-integrated, and these industries became very price competitive in 1982. In tailored suits, there were many small competitors who contracted for all aspects of manufacturing and marketed their suits in-house, while others like Rapid-American were primarily private-label manufacturers with no downstream facilities. Tailored suits were very price competitive in the lower-quality-grade markets, but less so where quality was important.

The most volatile industries had the greatest variety of vertical strategies. Stable environments, where superior products were protected by patents or other nonprice means of competing, had very similar vertical-integration strategies among leading competitors. Some firms were broadly integrated in volatile environments, but very few were highly integrated. Those that sold internally risked costly excess capacity, exit barriers, and other costs to obtain the control, intelligence, and other corporate objectives they desired.

Bargaining Power

Bargaining power was used to persuade suppliers to give firms price reductions during hard times, as General Motors did with some of its suppliers in spring 1982 (or as one of its squeezed suppliers negotiated to do with Illinois Power after granting GM's price rollback). Bargaining power could also persuade distributors or customers to provide extra services. If firms did not possess bargaining power, they absorbed price increases or provided extra services to customers without compensating concessions. If the firms in this sample did possess bargaining power, they could obtain these special services without integrating, but if the task were important enough they might perform it in-house even if the margins gained in doing so were low. For example, taper-integrated petroleum refiners could set prices for purchases of domestic crude oil and for rack pricing of refined products, but they were vertically integrated because otherwise they had no way to ensure they would have the supplies and outlets they needed when they were desired. Similarly, whiskey distillers were once backward integrated to barrel making because there was no other economic way to obtain the barrels they needed. Thus integration was undertaken from necessity and was abandoned when providing these goods or services became too costly to be justified in endgame. (Whiskey producers subsidized surviving barrel makers that were in decline to avoid having to produce barrels themselves.)

In tailored suits, manufacturers did not make their own textiles because they obtained a wider variety of colors and patterns by patronizing several firms, yet suit producers placing large orders could have exclusive runs of patterns and colors created for them under this arrangement. Suit producers whose brands were valued by customers were the only ones who could maintain high prices, and brands without that market power were degraded in quality or abandoned as competition grew intense. Pharmaceutical houses had market power only through their patented ethical drugs, and they safeguarded the perceived value of these patents by using their own medical-detail-sales forces. Upstream, pharmaceutical houses used outsiders primarily for difficult or dangerous manufacturing steps requiring costly capabilities that would be underutilized if firms performed them in-house, or to even out excess demand for tableting and labeling facilities. Bargaining power was not a major factor in these ventures because pharmaceutical firms did most bulk synthesis themselves.

Genetic-engineering firms used outsiders to market their products (and often to mass-produce them), and in making such arrangements they often "gave away their birthrights" because their bargaining power was so low in 1981. Diversified firms had their own active in-house-research programs in genetic engineering and could use traditional distribution channels when they commercialized their new products. This gave them substantial power over the research firms in creating quasi-integrated ventures. Microcomputer firms were similarly dependent on retailers to demonstrate and explain their products, and gross ignorance prevailed in many department stores where microcomputers were sold. To avoid this weakness, some manufacturers opened their own retail outlets staffed with knowledgeable personnel to assist first-time buyers, while others let "how-to-do-it" books instruct their users because their electronic boxes used other manufacturers' supported software. Similarly, some microcomputer firms created their own software as well as operating systems while others relied heavily upon outsiders to create compatible software for their machines.

In coal gasification, early projects usually had customer commitments to purchase gas and leases to mine coal before they commenced, and firms that needed new sources of natural gas were among those who pioneered coal-gas projects. But medium- or high-BTU gas from later coal-gas projects might be sold on the open market under contracts like those used in the oil industry and then forward integration would not be necessary because much uncertainty in marketing would be removed. In residential solar heating, few firms forward integrated to retailing because the market was too fragmented and too costly to cover if a firm were not already in retailing. Moreover, no chain of solar-specialty stores the magnitude of a ComputerLand sprang up to distribute solar products, and the undercapitalized marketing efforts of the solar-heating firms that tried retailing were ineffective. Grumman had tried operating its own retail outlets and discovered that the control over sales representatives gained by doing so in an embryonic environment did not justify the costs. Forward integration did not appear to be a good solution in this industry in 1981.

One advantage to owning downstream operations was suggested by the example of acetylene firms that found that physically interconnected facilities were easier to shut down if both stages of production (for example, acetylene feedstock and monomer plants) were owned by one firm. Outside customers made exits more difficult to achieve because both firms had to agree on the timing of shutdowns.

In summary, the use of market power to reduce asset investments in low value-added industries was only partially illustrated in the industries observed because corporate-strategy considerations encouraged more integration than may have been necessary in order to accomplish certain manufacturing tasks in a timely fashion. The most successful firms in residential solar heating, personal microcomputers, and genetic engineering were *not* highly or broadly integrated, though, and firms in the rayon, baby-foods, electric-percolator-coffee-makers, and leather-tanning businesses also found it was not necessary to be integrated in order to be successful.

Corporate-Wide Strategies

Corporate-wide policies to own adjacent business units and encourage them to transfer materials or services are major strategic decisions, but sister units often preferred to deal with outsiders because they feared that affiliated suppliers or distributors would take unfair advantage of them in the name of intracorporate links. This reticence to trade with sister units was due primarily to a short-term perspective and overlooked the long-run intelligence-gathering advantages of vertical linkages. Few managers interviewed in this study indicated that vertical integration was explicitly a part of parent-company-strategy objectives, and few firms maintained vertical relationships when excess capacity in one stage became costly, even if their industry was thriving in general and the imbalance seemed temporary. It would seem that integration was often foregone because sister units could not adequately negotiate with each other or their managers did not share in the long-term strategic visions of the top management that coupled them. For lack of an effective strategic coordinating system, integration economies were being foregone. For example, some exploration and production companies suggested their sister, oil-refinery and distribution businesses should be divested to improve their parent corporations' performance, and other firms ignored the need to forge global strategies when criticizing integration policies. Short-term perspectives like these overlooked the need for secure customers, a steady diet of technological breakthroughs, and balanced risks among vertically linked business units.

Forward integration helped microcomputer makers Tandy/Radio Shack, IBM, and Digital Equipment to reassure customers, inform them, and understand their needs when their product was not well-understood. When customer education became less critical, other types of outlets became useful in selling branded microcomputers without damaging their perceived quality. Then even Tandy/Radio Shack changed its degree of forward integration. In genetic engineering where few research firms had the manufacturing or marketing capabilities needed to commercialize their discoveries, few firms could survive except as contract-research entities, while the vertically integrated pharmaceutical, food processing, and chemical firms which did possess these capabilities could prosper by contrast. In ethical pharmaceuticals, leading firms depended upon new products that were developed, tested, and commercialized in company facilities. Without these linkages between upstream and downstream businesses, pharmaceutical firms could not maintain the scarce personnel that comprised their crucial competitive edge, and their products became commoditylike faster.

In summary, several corporate goals were served well by vertical integration. Often it was the means of attaining lowest operating costs or of capturing high value-added. Long-run market-share and innovation goals were served well by vertical integration over a longer time horizon and shared experience-curve economies gave firms blocking positions in several markets. Thus it is useful to recognize that some firms perpetuated vertical linkages to gather intelligence but that poor cooperation among linked business units nullified the benefits they should have enjoyed. In brief, in addition to the contract failures Williamson[2] described between the firm and outsiders, there were also internal market failures, in which business units that were consciously linked for strategic reasons did not cooperate. In these cases, firms would often be better served by going outside to obtain their needs until these disputes could be resolved through a better system of intracorporate transfers and controls because the costs of vertically integrating badly would be high.

Firms' Performances and Vertical Integration

This section charactertizes firms' vertical strategies and performances in the sixteen industries observed. The dimensions of strategy reviewed are the degree, breadth, stages, and form of internal transfers, and the performance dimensions include profitability and competitive responsiveness.

The degree of integration considers how much of a particular need was satisfied by internal transfers, and highly integrated firms transferred almost 100 percent of a particular material or service in-house. Since many upstream plants had larger breakeven points than the volumes downstream plants required, it was often possible for upstream business units to satisfy downstream sister units as well as outsiders. Petroleum-refining firms were moving toward higher internal transfers in 1981 in order to lower operating costs and stabilize operations, and they seemed to perform better when they were less sensitive to the risks of availability of overseas crude-oil supplies. Pharmaceutical companies that were highly integrated upstream performed well, and downstream access to an effective medical-detail-sales force was a necessity.

At the other extreme, Osborne Computer was very successful in 1981 with a strategy of buying subassemblies because software and systems were the heart of Osborne's microcomputers, and the physical origins of its machine components were of lesser importance than the delivery of a low-priced, portable microcomputer. Similarly, some successful pharmaceutical firms purchased bulk product for tableting and labeling, but did not perform any other manufacturing steps in-house, and some residential solar-heating firms successfully assembled solar collectors and packaged them with other purchased components rather than build their own plants. In summary, high integration worked best when premium prices could be sustained and integration economies were available. Low integration worked well when firms were not seeking positions of technological leadership or could not manage complexity well.

The number of stages undertaken depended upon the types of businesses that vertical integration linked. Firms' objectives to capture value-added frequently meant that they performed tasks in-house to keep their critical people and resources occupied and farmed out low value-added activities whenever feasible to free plant space for tasks that utilized their scarce human resources. This was the case in the production of microprocessors, for example, where microcomputer firms purchased commonplace electronic components but manufactured their logic chips in-house, or in toxicology studies which many pharmaceutical firms preferred to perform in-house to occupy crucial research personnel. But for other functions, such as oil-well drilling, firms found it more economical to purchase services rather than invest in facilities to perform them in-house, and these tasks were usually not central to firms' corporate missions. Some firms on the fringes of an industry could perform fewer steps in the production process by purchasing crude oil, aged whiskies, bulk pharmaceuticals, piece-work garment-construction services, or assembled microcomputers from others. Their nonintegrated postures often permitted the other, broadly integrated firms to dispose of excess capacity when their upstream and downstream capacities were not balanced.

In summary, firms performed many stages for activities when they could enjoy synergies with other business units, when a task was important to their business mission, or when it represented high value-added. Firms performed numerous steps in making a component (such as semiconductors) or in obtaining raw materials (such as ores) when these were of strategic importance to the corporation.

The breadth of integration—the number of activities undertaken—depended on demand traits and how firms competed. Firms engaged in fewer activities when demand was highly uncertain or was either embryonic or declining. Where products were complex or firms needed to be aware of the implications of each technological improvement, firms were more likely to be broadly integrated. Firms concerned with controlling the quality of components, manufacturing and how their product was represented to customers were more likely to be broadly integrated. But being too broadly integrated at the wrong time was risky and unprofitable. Thus, although demand for ethical pharmaceuticals justified firms being engaged in the production of fine chemicals, pharmaceutical bulks, dosage-form pharmaceuticals, and in wholesaling, for example, demand for whiskey in 1981 no longer justified firms being involved in grain brokerage, timber lands, barrel-stave production, barrel making, bottle making, and wholesaling.

The form of a venture referred to its ownership pattern—contract, joint venture or wholly owned—and the form that firms used was determined by their corporate-strategy needs as well as their bargaining power. For example, offshore oil exploration was always done as a joint venture on federally leased lands because firms preferred to place small bets on several drilling prospects rather than bet heavily on a single drilling site. Joint ventures were used to hurdle entry barriers where capital costs were high, absolute-cost advantages must be surmounted, or combined efforts created a differentiated product that could not be made alone. Joint ventures were a means of preempting suppliers or customers from entering in a manner unfavorable to the firm, and they blunted the retaliation of ongoing firms if a venture was forged with an established competitor. Joint ventures enabled firms to share development risks and gain access to technological knowledge and manufacturing experience. They were an effective means to leverage synergies with firms' established distribution channels or other skills. Finally, joint ventures were an effective means to marry dissimilar cultures, as in genetic engineering, where research scientists preferred to work in small organizations and look at many recombinant-DNA problems rather than be part of a large corporation.

Import licenses were used in whiskey to extend product lines, and manufacturing licenses were used in tailored suits to brand products that a designer did not manufacture in-house. Marketing contracts were used in ethical pharmaceuticals to distribute products manufactured by foreign firms, or to obtain distribution services for highly specialized products. Drug firms also used contract manufacturing arrangements to produce off-

patent drugs, and manufactured private-label generic drugs for retail outlets. Marketing contracts were also used in genetic engineering and residential solar heating by firms that did not possess the resources to distribute
their own products but these firms did not gain as much by using outsiders
to perform this service as did those firms (like pharmaceutical companies or
whiskey distillers) that controlled brand names and patents. In summary,
firms performed tasks in-house that were important to them and that they
could not otherwise control to their satisfaction. They purchased services
that were less important or that were performed economically and satisfac-
torily by outsiders. Joint ventures, exclusive-distribution arrangements, and
other quasi-integrations were ways of extending firms' controls over others'
assets without risking full equity ownership and for fledgling firms were a
means of penetrating difficult markets with lower expenditures.

*A Comparison of the Strategic Matrix's Predictions
with Observed Performances*

The strategy matrix predicted that certain alternatives would be more
appropriate to achieve vertical control than others, and these differed in
degree, breadth, stages, and form of integration employed. As chapter 2
had predicted, some firms did use high degrees of integration to control
their upstream and downstream activities. The use of other vertical strategies is less clear, however, and will be discussed at length in this section.
For example, the framework predicted that firms would be most broadly
integrated in mature and stable environments and perform those functions
of greatest importance to their corporate strategies. (For example, whiskey
distillers once grew, traded, and processed grain into mash for distilling,
and then recovered it to sell as a livestock feed.) The framework also predicted that the degree of internal transfers would be higher in stable environments where firms possessed low bargaining power, and that the proportion of equity ownership a firm invested in a function depended on bargaining power as well as the strategic importance of the activity. The smallest
amount of internal transfers and equity ownership were expected in declining industries and in those where demand was not yet healthy enough to risk
much investment in the business. Vertically integrated structures could
create exit barriers, therefore firms were expected to ease out of vertical
arrangements as sales volumes began to deteriorate.

Competition Was Stable—Firm Possessed Power

The most stable industry observed was the ethical-pharmaceuticals business
where the greatest bargaining power was held by firms who sold the most-

frequently-prescribed drugs. Roche, Smith Kline, and Lilly relied exclusively on wholesalers to distribute their products in 1981, and Merck, Sharpe & Dohme (MSD) was not highly dependent upon its own distribution facilities, although it used dual methods of distribution. Of these firms, only MSD had a strong fine-chemicals position. The extent of the others' integrations were historically not as broad and they did not feel a need to backward integrate to many stages by 1981, but MSD, Lilly, and Roche had extensive toxicology and other research facilities in-house, consistent with their leadership positions. Lilly and Roche operated parallel genetic-engineering laboratories and had joint ventures with Genentech to develop new ethical pharmaceuticals.

In whiskey, strong brand names gave firms like Seagram, Hiram Walker, Brown-Forman and James Beam Distilling bargaining power over distributors, and consequently they obtained the services of the strongest wholesale houses in each geographic region. In tailored suits, where the strongest firms had brand names that commanded prices commensurate with the quality of their manufacture or the celebrity of their designers, firms like Hart, Schaffner & Marx distributed both through their own stores and through others', while the products of firms like Oxford, Ralph Lauren, and other designer labels were sold through exclusive, but non-owned, outlets. Moreover, designer clothes were often manufactured by subcontractors for the designers' licensees. In genetic engineering, there were hundreds of research firms but only a few had the personnel, track records, or research reputations needed to create advantageous vertical arrangements with larger venture partners. These firms included Novo Industri and BioLogicals (which were backward integrated), and Biogen, Cetus, Genentech, Genex, IPRI, and BRL (which had good track records). Agrigenetics was the only leading genetic-engineering firm that did not use research contracts to fuel its growth, largely because it had its own distribution channels (seed-supply outlets). In residential solar heating, lower-priced systems were the most profitable because consumers were price sensitive. Fafco Solar dominated the swimming-pool-heating market with its inexpensive plastic collector, and ACRO Solar Energy offered a low-priced heating system that it assembled from several vendors' components. Neither firm was vertically integrated upstream or downstream, and both firms sold directly to consumers from their factories or through exclusive distributors. Solar heating was not a high-volume business for most firms.

Competition Was Stable—Firm Did Not Possess Power

The less powerful firms in the ethical-pharmaceuticals industry included Alza, Astra, and Organon, all firms that had not successfully launched patented products on their own and were using joint ventures and market-ing arrangements to obtain the distribution they needed. The tableting and capsuling firms, which were often dependent on the manufacturers of bulk pharmaceuticals to provide raw materials and on wholesalers to sell their generic-drug products, had thin profit margins because they did not have the wherewithal to capture the high value-added of research activities in pharmaceuticals.

In whiskey, there were few successful firms that did not also possess brand-name strength. The weaker firms were not broadly or highly inte-grated, and thus they mitigated the damage that vertical relationships could have created for them. In the volatile tailored-suits industry the most-inte-grated firm, United Merchants & Manufacturers, suffered the most-painful failure. Other weak competitors in the low-priced segment, like Bond Industries and the firms acquired by Rapid-American, survived, but their business missions were often radically changed. In genetic engineering, there were many small firms that had little bargaining power to prevent their loss of autonomy and equity control when they obtained capital from larger firms. The contracts they agreed to often assigned near-term patent, licensing, and marketing rights to their ventures partners, giving them only enough cash to cover their expenses. In coal gasification, no firm possessed the strengths needed to leverage other firms' resources in 1981. Shell and Tenneco were comtemplating ventures in which they carried the full risks of financing and securing markets for their gas, while firms like American Natural Resources and Peoples Energy worked with others to develop their Great Plains project. Meanwhile greater volumes of natural gas were dis-covered as domestic-oil exploration increased, pushing further away the day when synfuels became economic. In residential solar heating, few of the best-known firms possessed the bargaining power needed to create exclusive distribution channels or had attained profitability in 1981. State Industries, which sold solar collectors to Sears, was the most profitable among this group because it had an effective distribution system, albeit one the firm could not control.

Competition Was Volatile—Firm Possessed Power

The most volatile industries were the declining ones where there were clearly too many plants and insufficient demand. Firms' performances within them were discussed in chapter 4. Changing lifestyles, technologies, or demand uncertainty made most of these declining industries volatile, but price-cutting erupted most viciously in the baby-foods, rayon, leather-tanning, and other declining environments.

In petroleum refining, access to crude oil became the most significant competitive advantage in 1981 and Getty, Sohio, and other self-sufficient firms were in the best competitive positions after decontrol. Balanced integration gave refiners cost economies and therefore they strived to rationalize their physical assets and bring refining capacity back into balance with supplies. In personal microcomputers, access to the best software gave firms bargaining power, and Apple and Tandy/Radio Shack were the strongest competitors until IBM entered. Apple had been neither backward- nor forward-integrated, and Tandy/Radio Shack had not made its own microcomputer components initially. For IBM, its new retail outlets shared space with other IBM office products and these synergies made the investment justifiable. In summary, the most powerful firms in volatile environments were not broadly nor highly integrated. They relied upon outsiders to perform tasks for them unless the adjacent business possessed strategic importance for them at the corporate level.

Competition Was Volatile—Firm Did Not Possess Power

Volatile environments were the most difficult in which to succeed because vertical integration was unwise, yet the low bargaining power of these firms forced them to perform many tasks themselves or else accept lower service levels, slower rates of technological innovation, and spottier distribution by using outsiders. SOCAL, Tenneco, and ARCO are examples of firms whose domestic crude supplies were a high proportion of their refinery needs and yet they were not market leaders. ARCO's retreat from credit cards and Tenneco's retreat from marketing territories represent circumspect attempts to manage a volatile environment by altering competitive postures to create positions of strength. SOCAL, by contrast, increased its exposure in marketing, an activity the strategy matrix would not recommend. In personal microcomputers, weaker firms like Commodore and Zenith Data Systems lacked the brand identification, software, or marketing channels needed for enduring success, yet both firms were broadly and highly integrated when compared with the rest of the industry, and both firms supplied components to other microcomputer firms as well as in-house to mitigate the damage their vertical postures could create.

In summary, it was possible to have too much internal integration and to undertake too many functions in-house in volatile settings. Firms that were overly integrated faced problems in finding buyers for their businesses or customers for their outputs when they tried to dis-integrate because they lacked contact with outside markets. Successful firms minimized their vertical ownership and sought to make more of their cost structure variable, as opposed to fixed, while maintaining a window on their markets or suppliers through other arrangements.

Table 12-1 presents a statistical model of the vertical strategies firms

Table 12-1
Regressions on Degree, Breadth, Stages, and Form of Vertical Integration

	Dependent Variables				
Independent Variables	Degree of Backward Integration	Degree of Forward Integration	Breadth of Integrated Activities	Stages per Integrated Activity	Form of Integrated Relationship
Uncertainty	.25	-.30	-.69**	.12	-.66**
Concentration	.22*	-.24*	—	—	—
Value-Added Upstream	.35***	—	—	.48***	.5***
Value-Added Downstream	—	-.16	—	.85***	.61***
Competitors' Backward Integration	.25***	—	—	—	—
Market Share	-.30**	-.12	.17	-.28**	—
Height of Exit Barriers	.29***	-.02	.22***	—	.28***
Relative Price	.05	-.77***	—	—	-.24
Relative Quality	.42*	.41	.18	—	.21
Synergies with Upstream Businesses	.20**	—	—	—	-.09
Synergies with Downstream Businesses	—	.02	—	—	.12*
Minimum-Efficient Scale	-.08	—	—	-.31**	—
Alternate-Supply Availability	.02	—	—	—	—
Alternate-Selling Availability	—	.49**	—	—	—
Percentage of Three Largest Suppliers' Sales	-.38***	—	—	—	—

Table 12-1 continued

| | Dependent Variables | | | | |
Independent Variables	Degree of Backward Integration	Degree of Forward Integration	Breadth of Integrated Activities	Stages per Integrated Activity	Form of Integrated Relationship
Percentage of Three Largest Distributors' Sales	—	-.06	—	.52***	—
Rate of Technological Innovation	-.08	-.14	—	—	—
Product Differentiability	-.28**	-.17	—	—	—
Broad Product Line	—	.02	—	—	—
Height of Customer-Switching Costs	—	.39***	—	—	—
Complexity of Selling Product	—	.17	.21***	.43***	—
Competitors' Forward Integration	—	.23***	—	—	—
Proprietary Knowledge	—	—	-.20***	—	—
Interconnected Technology	—	—	—	.21***	—
Mean (Standard Deviation)	.35 (.34)	.37 (.38)	.64 (.28)	.86 (.45)	.87 (.26)
Intercept	-.35	.31	.30	.49	.34
Coefficient of Multiple Determination—R^2	.4099	.3438	.2515	.3459	.27
F-Statistic	8.78***	5.73***	10.36***	5.14***	8.32***
Degrees of Freedom	177	175	185	183	183

*** Significant at the .01 level using a student's t-test of the null hypothesis that the coefficient equals zero.
** Significant at the .05 level using a student's t-test of the null hypothesis that the coefficient equals zero.
* Significant at the .10 level using a student's t-test of the null hypothesis that the coefficient equals zero.

embraced in light of the presence of certain environmental and corporate traits. The model indicates that demand uncertainty was a statistically significant predictor of the breadth and form of integration, and product traits explained much of the difference in the stages of firms' integrations. Value-added, bargaining power, and product differentiability were statistically significant predictors of the degree of forward or backward integration.

In table 12-1 the *degree* of backward (or forward) integration was measured as the percentage of upstream material sold in-house or output sold downstream. The *breadth* of integration was estimated as the number of activities a particular firm engaged in, divided by the number of activities it was possible to perform, and the stages of integration were estimated by an index in which the average equaled 100 percent. The *form* of integration was measured as the percentage of ownership with wholly owned ventures coded as 99 percent.

From these limited statistical findings it would appear that when adequate supplies or distribution channels were available from outsiders, firms were more likely to be taper integrated, if at all, unless economies from interconnection were available. This finding suggests that firms should carefully consider inflexible investments in volatile industries where vertical-integration-exit barriers could become difficult to surmount, and seek a means of scanning these industries without surrendering their abilities to reposition instead. Higher degrees and broader stages of integration may best be undertaken in stable environments where demand uncertainty is low.

From these results and the findings concerning the strategy matrix, some general conclusions about vertical integration and the use of this strategy as a competitive weapon can be offered that may be of interest to the business practitioner, the student of business administration, and public policy makers. Conclusions are contained in the chapter that follows.

Notes

1. George J. Stigler, "The Division of Labor is Limited by the Extent of the Market," *Journal of Political Economy,* vol. LIX, no. 3 (June 1951), pp. 185–193. The Stigler hypothesis was confirmed by Tucker and Wilder, "Trends in Vertical Integration in the U.S. Manufacturing Sector," *Journal of Industrial Economics,* vol. 26 (September 1977), pp. 81–94. Their data was aggregated at the SIC group level and did not allow for differences in vertical strategies within an industry.

2. Oliver Williamson, *Markets and Hierarchies* (New York: The Free Press, 1975).

13

Policy Implications of the Vertical-Strategies Study

The findings of this study offer substantial evidence that vertical-integration strategies differ across industries, and that firms use differing degrees, breadths, stages, and forms of integration to control the supplies and services they need. Discussion of the industry examples suggests that firms within the same industry could use different vertical linkages successfully and that they change these linkages at dissimilar times. Vertical integration is a corporate decision about whether to encourage or allow intrafirm transfers of goods and services that takes many shapes and is used differently by many firms.

Insights and Questions Raised by Research Results

The findings from this study have offered some insights into the relationships of industry volatility, demand instability, company strategies, and the bargaining power of business units to suppliers or downstream units. They have suggested where high degrees of internal transfers work best. These findings are valuable to managers in making informed strategy decisions about vertical integration. Since the characteristics of industry demand and structure do differ, and since there have been different patterns of ownership, intrafirm transfers, and functions integrated across industries, it would seem that the analysis above could offer important suggestions about the use of vertical integration as a competitive weapon. In particular, the principal implications of the factual findings from the sixteen industries observed suggest the need for attention in the areas of analysis discussed in the following paragraphs.

Managers may wish to create technological jump-off points for reexamining their vertical strategies to determine whether they could enjoy lower costs or superior competitive intelligence by creating vertical linkages. Alternatively, broadly and highly integrated firms may wish to investigate whether some activities could be performed more advantageously by outsiders, or whether a portion of the firms' needs for a particular item should be provided in-house to gain better insights into customer and supplier industry conditions.

339

An enlightened understanding of the narrow and low degrees of integration many firms favored could create opportunities for adjacent business units—insiders and outsiders—to offer more value to these firms by performing the activities they wished to avoid. By producing especially for their needs and by retaining highly skilled personnel, satellite firms could develop their specialty processes into defensible, competitive products that could become lucrative market niches for them. Reinforced by their successes, these specialized suppliers or distributors could approach integrated firms and help them to dis-integrate by taking over either some of their activities or partial production of some supplies, components, or services for them.

Many firms entered embryonic businesses to have an additional outlet for disposing of excess materials or products. Although one milling firm once entered the breakfast-cereal industry successfully in that way, within the residential-solar-heating industry this practice was highly unprofitable because demand for residential solar products did not grow as had been expected. Consequently, it seems that firms should investigate the viability of the businesses with which they will forge linkages before introducing vertical integration imprudently.

This study was exploratory because the existing theories of vertical integration seemed inadequate for strategic-planning purposes and previous studies of the phenomenon omitted important variables, thereby showing only a portion of the dynamic forces afoot in vertical strategies. Given the nature of the data gathered in this study of vertical integration and of the different ways in which firms coped with their needs to secure reliable supplies and distribution, the study's findings must be subject to certain qualifications and limitations. For example, this study has focused on the patterns of activity in vertical strategies, not upon the processes leading to the choice of a strategy. The forecasts of strategic conditions that emanate from this study must be modified in some cases (such as whiskey or petroleum refining) to accommodate some variations in strategy alternative explained best by industry eccentricities and regulations that eliminated any integration economies. Wherever possible in the industry studies, proper recognition of firms' corporate policies toward, for example, intrafirm transfers or other considerations such as their histories (which may have created dissimilarities in firms' perceptions of the same events), has been accorded to the firms in analyzing their vertically related behaviors.

Since the studies are based on interviews and library research there are limitations, of course, to what can be learned about the long-run success of particular vertical arrangements. Moreover, the behaviors of some of the 192 competitors studied were reconstructed from the reports of competitors and published information. These limitations in the study's conclusions and others are treated as they were encountered in the sections which follow.

Summary of Findings

The need for vertical control changes as an industry evolves and as a firm's position within it changes. Technological innovation can change primary demand for industries' products; it can also change cost structures in manufacturing and firms' bargaining strengths. Firms that have enjoyed competitive advantages in the past may lose them if they do not continually upgrade their products, processes, and vertical arrangements. Each new investment decision is also an appropriate time to review current strategies regarding vertical integration. If firms could identify how their industries will develop—whether specialized distribution channels will become important, whether imported technologies will be required, or which customer groups will be important—they could make investments early to position themselves to serve the most-promising markets appropriate for their mix of competitive skills.

The study's findings suggest that effective use of vertical integration can make markets more competitive by accelerating the rate of information exchange. Joint ventures and other forms of shared experience can be used to gather technical expertise, to compete in an area in which firms may be weak alone, or to obtain other proficiencies, thereby lowering firms' entry barriers in businesses such as wholesaling or retailing that were previously unfamiliar to them. But the strategic window for the successful use of joint ventures closes rapidly and substantial organizational sophistication is needed to manage such ventures, particularly where firms' asset sizes are symmetrical, their skills are evenly matched, and the joint-venture project is an interfacing of upstream and downstream firms in an arena that neither has entered before. U.S. firms avoided the use of joint ventures long after their Japanese and European counterparts mastered the secrets of managing such complexity. This knowledge is also applicable to managing vertical integration in cases where shared productive capabilities cannot be bounded by markets and the control system must coordinate the supply side of a firm's strategic response as well as the more frequently monitored market side of its strategy.

Many unanswered questions about the use of joint ventures remain. Although firms could spread their influence across more business ventures if they shared the costs and risks of doing so, this study's findings suggest that within dynamic environments, firms must guard against erecting exit barriers because their vertical arrangements may require rapid modification to respond to new challenges. (Thus joint ventures must dissolve in a timely fashion if they could later create exit barriers.) Finally, effective use of vertical integration requires fine tuning of the degree of internal transfers between various functions performed in-house as well as a review of the ownership form used to control these exchanges.

Thus, there is more to the analysis of vertical-integration strategies than an economic calculation involving input-output tables, multiplicative indices, or other aggregative devices might suggest. The conclusions drawn from this study relied heavily upon an analysis of demand and competitive conditions as well as historic relationships between suppliers and customers. It suggests that smaller firms need not copy the integrated strategies of larger firms but they should be aware of them in order to recognize when firms that used vertical integration imprudently created unprofitable competitive arenas so that they may avoid them. The implications of these findings are explained below.

Implications for Business Strategists

Integration can be a means of lowering both capital and operating costs where there are integration economies such as joining technological, complementary production processes, coordinating separate plants' operations (kanban), creating standardized parts useful in geographically remote sites, and reducing requirements for slack inventories. It can also be a means of supplementing weaknesses, developing bargaining power (if tapered, not fully integrated), adding value to an otherwise indistinguishable product, and controlling materials flows. If used effectively, vertical integration provides insights into where future resource allocations should be made and how to reduce capital inflexibility, *if* firms' degrees, breadths, stages, and forms of vertical integration are revised to exploit changing environmental conditions.

The way in which firms integrate matters unless they face: (1) competitive conditions where errors do not matter, (2) demand that is perfectly balanced upstream and downstream, (3) exclusive access to a scarce and costly resource, (4) ineffective competitors, (5) no significant diseconomies, and (6) no threats of work stoppages or materials shortages. Most firms face hostile environments in which they could easily overintegrate as the steel producers have done, instead.

In this study, the first firm to integrate vertically often enjoyed the cost advantages of access to lower-priced raw materials, superior distribution channels, and experience-curve economies, but there was also great uncertainty in being the first firm to integrate upstream or downstream due to the larger fixed costs that doing so created. Pioneers like Commodore International in microcomputers, or Conoco in coal gasification, were surpassed by firms that waited until some of the uncertainties regarding vertical relationships had been resolved and then entered, using the most-advantageous vertical-integration strategy.

The key to effective use of vertical integration is moderation, even at those times when the strategy matrix recommends the highest degrees of internal transfer. By keeping the high value-added functions in-house and purchasing the low value-added materials or services from outsiders, firms maximize their returns on vertically integrated activities. By taper-integrating, firms learn about their suppliers' or distributors' cost structures. By having intelligence antennae in the markets of firms' customers, they can ascertain whether certain customers merit extra attention on the basis of their future promise. Moreover, since most plants' minimum-efficient-scale sizes are larger upstream than downstream (except oil production and refining), many firms taper integrate downstream to sell excess outputs.

The study found that backward integration was used like an insurance payment to ensure a stable supply of materials and components. Forward integration far downstream was used initially to create credibility for new products like residential-solar-heating systems, microcomputers, rayon, and acetate. The flow of integration was usually downstream initially, then upstream after the benefits of forward linkages had been explored. Firms moved in and out of functions and materials that had low entry and exit barriers, and they adjusted their degree of integration by using outside parties, both as a spur to inside business units and to reduce operating costs.

When firms began to dis-integrate, one of the administrative devices that changed first was a policy that discouraged internal transfers. There were some firms, like Textron, that owned adjacent business units but did not encourage them to trade or to become dependent on internal services, but most firms encouraged integration. The primary advantage of vertical arrangements where trade did not occur was a knowledge of costs and of the competitive milieu faced by adjacent business units. Firms that did not at least collect and process the information available in such situations overlooked a significant opportunity for competitor analysis.

When the vertical relationship was severed by divesting one formerly linked business unit, the accounting system was often changed to ensure two accounting entities were created where there may have been only one. (The shared facilities that gave firms integration economies when the vertical relationship was desirable could become an exit barrier if an early provision to prevent this was not made.) That meant introducing duplicate assets or services in several cases to make their divestitures easier to conceptualize and carry out.

When dis-integrations are decided upon, the firms' will often wish to retain scarce and skilled personnel, of course, but the units being divested must not be gutted of management talent lest they become difficult to sell. The logical buyer of divested units could be existing suppliers or customers that would welcome the opportunity to attain a broader integration, but competitors and the existing management team of divested units are also potential customers for divestiture. All of these (as well as many outside buyers) will expect the divesting firm to purchase services or products from the spun-off units for some time after dis-integration to help the orphaned units survive. If there are good reasons to avoid continued dealings after divestiture, selling firms should recognize them before the issue is raised in negotiations. After business units have been dis-integrated, their former parents can continue to exert power over them because they know the business units' costs and how to improve upon them. This knowledge of how to lower costs can be used to encourage suppliers or distributors to undertake recommended manufacturing or operating changes to lower their costs and pass on their savings to these firms.

In summary, major technological changes transformed industries such as steel, petrochemicals, meat packing, flour milling, cigarette manufacturing, cement and concrete, aluminum, rubber, copper, wood and paper products, and inorganic chemicals not merely by replacing labor with capital. Rather, these innovations changed the nature of operations by integrating tasks. Future changes from chemical synthesis to fermentation technologies, or to a greater use of microprocessors to guide complementary tasks, could again revolutionize manufacturing operations, making a review of firms' vertical strategies mandatory. The review milestones that firms create for monitoring their vertical strategies will be spaced according to how volatile their industries are.

Implications for Academic Research

The findings from this study of vertical integration supplement previous studies of integration as well as works that illuminated the nature of competition within an industry. This study develops what is known about competition within strategic groups—competitors that address their markets using similar generic strategies, strengths, and tactics—and it isolated strategic groups in eight industries to trace their dynamic vertical strategies through two decades. It also builds upon research on the endgame in declining industries, where few competitors that had been vertically integrated remained so, by ascertaining why and how firms in such environments dis-integrated. It found that the characteristics of firms' strategic postures—particularly which degree, breadth, stages, and form of vertical strategy firms embraced—could be analyzed not only in terms of other firms in the adjacent industries but also in terms of firms' corporate strategies. As such, it represents an important linkage between business-unit- and corporate-level-strategy research.

This study of vertical strategies offered several dimensions of the decision not considered heretofore, and observed how firms adjusted those dimensions over time. It illustrated a variety of the arrangements that firms used to control their rates of technological innovation and their market coverage. It showed (with company examples) the rarity of a broad and fully integrated vertical strategy, where firms perform many tasks and where most of the transfers of these goods or services were made in-house. Even where the stages of firms' integrations included several levels of in-house activities, they still used outsiders for infrequent supplementary processing or to obtain additional raw materials. Indeed, the presence of these outsiders represented an important service to the large, integrated firms.

In presenting the data compiled from field and library research, this study used a format that facilitated comparisons of firms' behaviors longitudinally and cross-sectionally. The format ensured uniformity of presentation for the key variables and facilitated the replicability of results. Use of such research designs creates an opportunity for large sample studies (which have been difficult to obtain in corporate-strategy studies) without losing the fine-grained attention to detail and nuances that individual case studies provided.

Areas for Further Research

This exploratory study of vertical strategies has mapped out some factors that affected vertical strategies over time. Further research of a diagnostic nature could investigate other predictive aspects of this dynamic problem. For example, this study investigated only one truly new industry—genetic engineering—where the manufacturers were themselves primarily new entrants and where few parts of the infrastructure needed to support a sizable biotechnology industry were extant in 1981. In such industries a further study of questions regarding vertical integration and both industry development and organizational development should be undertaken.

The research methodology employed in this study used a hybrid design comprised of library data, public-source information (press releases, local-newspaper announcements, trade-association publications, and so on), and field interviews with the actual participants in the sample industries explored. The nest step in testing the framework would be a statistical study that gathered the financial and qualitative data required to test more fully the entire system of regression equations that has been described in chapter 2.

Implications for Public Policymakers

These findings on the use of vertical integration question some long-held assumptions about this economic strategy that have formed the base of antitrust and other economic-regulation policies. In light of these findings, questions about market power and competition are raised which these policies address only in part. For example, vertical integration has been considered a barrier to entry and exit from markets, but the findings of this study suggest that neither barrier need be particularly high in vertical arrangements, because both joint ventures or significant technological breakthroughs can provide a means of entering established industries in ways that reduce capital requirements for entry and that leapfrog the experiences of ongoing firms, respectively. Exit barriers can be reduced early and consciously through reductions in the degree, breadth, stages, or form of integration. An orderly and incremental withdrawal of investments from units that have been suppliers, retailers, or have provided other services could enable firms to hurdle exit barriers easily while maintaining access to the services these units once provided.

Vertical integration was believed to give firms market power and increase industry concentration, but this study's findings suggest it would be difficult to extend the competitive strengths from one stage to what has usually been a more fragmented stage downstage. Given the lower minimum-efficient scales of downstream units, it would be difficult for them to exploit their market power *upstream*. Thus market power is intransitive and temporary.

Bargaining power, like market power, is temporary. Firms have it when they can obtain the products or services desired at satisfactory prices without integrating. Firms lose it when they become highly integrated because they can no longer use their formerly effective threats to perform the tasks they seek to buy in-house, instead. Moreover, technological change can upset the balance of bargaining power or totally disrupt previous trade relationships. In the case of franchise arrangements, however, firms sometimes spurred franchisees on to do better by threatening to revoke their franchises, but only if they were already richly endowed with other distribution outlets or the promise of finding better franchisees. (Poor use of forward integration has been blamed—among other factors—for the poor performances of Chrysler and American Motors.) Thus a distinction needs to be made between *forms* of vertical integration and bargaining power. Firms in declining industries, like petroleum refining for example, may prefer to reduce their dependence on outsiders and to own their distribution outlets in order to respond more effectively to declining demand, especially if doing so means eliminating these outlets. One pattern this behavior has assumed is for refiners to back out of branded sales and use short-term contracts to sell their gasoline to service stations thereafter. Firms in developing industries, by contrast, may need their capital to expand primary capacity and spur their future growth. They may use their market successes to bargain for the services of outsiders, instead of performing certain tasks themselves.

Vertical integration can increase competition by giving firms listening posts in several industries. The accelerated exchange of information and improved coordination of resources that effective vertical integration can provide fosters more rapid technological changes and a faster response to consumer preferences.

Finally, although the satellite-industry structure that has proven effective in the industries examined herein suggests that firms need not be integrated to enjoy a profitable existence, there is one circumstance under which vertical integration seems to offer important competitive advantages—that is, global competition. Frequently one efficient-sized plant is sufficient to serve global demand for products at a particular time and the logistics of distribution become of paramount importance to competition, as in the microcomputer and ethical-pharmaceuticals industries. Forward integration through joint ventures, wholly owned marketing companies, or other arrangements that permit firms to control the distribution of their products becomes important when introducing technological innovations in products and processes throughout the globe. Thus public policymakers should consider the economic realities of increasingly competitive environments and global industries before attacking a business strategy that offers so many advantages to consumer welfare and technological innovation.

Bibliography

Ackerman, R.W. "Influence of Integration and Diversity on the Investment Process." *Administrative Science Quarterly* 15:341-351, 1970.

Adams, W., and Dirlam, J. "Steel Imports and the Vertical Oligopoly Power." *American Economic Review,* vol. 54, September 1964, pp. 640-655.

Adelman, M.A. "Concept and Statistical Measurement of Vertical Integration." in National Bureau of Economic Research (conference report), *Business Concentration and Price Policy.* Princeton: Princeton University Press, 1955.

Adelman, M.A. "Integration and Anti-trust Policy." *Harvard Law Review,* vol. 63, November 1949, pp. 27-77.

Adler, Lee. "How to Tell If You Need the Services of an Outside Research House." *Sales & Marketing Management,* vol. 120, no. 5, pp. 74-76, April 1978.

Allen, Bruce T. "Vertical Integration and Market Foreclosure: The Case of Cement and Concrete." *Journal of Law and Economics,* vol. 14, April 1971, pp. 251-274.

Alluvine, F.C. "Thoughts on Breaking Up the Petroleum Industry." *Business Horizons,* vol. 19, no. 4, August 1976, pp. 41-51.

Altschuler, Stuart. "Sylvania, Vertical Restraints, and Dual Distribution." *Antitrust Bulletin,* vol. 25, no. 1, pp. 1-102, 1980.

Ammer, Dean S. "Top Management View of the Purchasing Function." *Journal of Purchasing,* vol. 10, no. 3, pp. 5-15, 1974.

Anderson, Earl V. "Divestiture is a Four-Letter Word, to Some." *Chemical & Engineering News,* vol. 54, no. 23, pp. 8-9, 1976.

Ansoff, H. Igor. "Strategies for Diversification." *Harvard Business Review,* September-October, 1957, pp. 113-124.

"Antitrust Treatment of Intraband Territorial Restraints Within a Dual Distribution System." *Texas Law Review,* vol. 56, no. 8, 1978, pp. 1486-1511.

Arbose, J. "Shoe Firm Fits into One-Site Operation." *International Management,* vol. 33, no. 11, 1978, pp. 50-53.

Armour, Henry Ogden, and Teece, David J. "Vertical Integration and Technological Innovation." *Review of Economics and Statistics,* vol. 62, 1980, pp. 470-474.

Arrow, K.J. "Vertical Integration and Communication," *The Bell Journal of Economics,* vol. 6, no. 1, 1975, pp. 173-183.

Bain, Joe S. *Industrial Organization,* 2nd Edition. New York: John Wiley, 1968.

Bain, Joe S. *Barriers to New Competition,* Cambridge, Mass.: Harvard University Press, 1956.

Baker, H. Kent; Miller, Thomas O.; Ramsperger, Brian J. "An Inside Look at Corporate Mergers and Acquisitions." *MSU Business Topics,* vol. 29, no. 1, pp. 49–57, 1981.

Baker, Kenneth R., and Taylor, Robert E. "A Linear Programming Framework for Cost Allocation and External Acquisition When Reciprocal Services Exist." *Accounting Review,* vol. 54, no. 4, 1979, pp. 784–790.

Balderston, Frederick E. "Scale, Vertical Integration and Costs in Residential Construction Firms." (Unpublished doctoral dissertation, Princeton University, 1953).

Bentley, Jerome Thomas. *The Effects of Standard Oil's Vertical Integration into Transportation on the Structure and Performance of the American Petroleum Industry, 1872–1884.* New York: Arno Press, 1979.

Bentley, Trevor. "Added Value and Contribution." *Management Accounting* (UK), vol. 59, no. 3, 1981, pp. 17–21.

Berg, S.V., and Fiedman, P. "Joint Ventures in American Industry." *Mergers & Acquisitions,* 13:28–41, 1978.

Bernhardt, I. "Vertical Integration and Demand Variability." *Journal of Industrial Economics,* vol. 25, no. 3, 1977, pp. 213–229.

Blaich, Oswald Paul. "Vertical Integration in Theory." (Unpublished doctoral dissertation, University of Minnesota, 1962).

Blair, Roger, and Kaserman, David L. "Uncertainty and the Incentive for Vertical Integration." *Southern Economic Journal,* vol. 26, July 1978, pp. 266–272.

Blair, Roger, and Kaserman, David. "Vertical Integration, Tying and Antitrust Policy." *American Economic Review,* vol. 68, June 1978, pp. 397–402.

Blair, R.D., and Kaserman, D.L. "Vertical Control with Variable Proportions: Ownership Integration and Contractual Equivalent." *Southern Economic Journal,* vol. 46, no. 4, April 1980, pp. 1118–1128.

Blauvelt, Howard W. "Petroleum Divestiture—an Untenable Solution to a Non-Existent Problem." *Vital Speeches of the Day,* vol. 42, no. 12, pp. 380–383, April 1, 1976.

Blois, K.J. "The Pricing of Supplies by Large Customers." *Journal of Business Finance and Accounting,* vol. 5, no. 3, Autumn 1978, pp. 367–379.

Blois, K.J. "Quasi-Integration as a Mechanism for Controlling External Dependencies." *Management Decision* (UK), vol. 18, no. 1, pp. 55–63, 1980.

Blois, K.J. "Supply Contracts in the Galbraithian Planning System." *The Journal of Industrial Economics,* vol. 24, no. 1, September 1975, pp. 29–39.

Blois, K.J. "Vertical Quasi-Integration." *Journal of Industrial Economics,* vol. 20, July 1972, pp. 253–272.

Bock, B. "Concentration as an Economic Scapegoat." *The Conference Board Record,* vol. 12, no. 6, pp. 6–12.

Bock, B. "The Lizzie Borden Solution." *Across the Board,* vol. 14, no. 3, March 1977, pp. 46–53.

Bolch, Ben W., and Damon, William. "The Depletion Allowance and Vertical Integration in the Petroleum Industry." *Southern Economic Journal,* vol. 26, July 1978, pp. 241–249.

Bolch, Ben W., and Damon, William. "The Windfall Profit Tax and Vertical Integration in the Petroleum Industry." *Southern Economic Journal,* vol. 47, no. 3, pp. 788–791, January 1981.

Bomers, Gerard B.J., and Peterson, Richard B. "Multinational Corporations and Industrial Relations—The Case of West Germany and the Netherlands." *British Journal of Industrial Relations,* vol. 15, no. 1, pp. 45–62A, March 1977.

Bork, Robert. "Vertical Integration and the Sherman Act: The Legal History of an Economic Misconception." *University of Chicago Law Review,* vol. 22, Autumn 1954, pp. 157–201.

Bourke-White, M. "Copper in the Mills." *Fortune,* vol. 101, no. 3, February 11, 1980, pp. 76–79.

Bowersox, Donald J.; LaLonde, Bernard J.; and Smykay, Edward W. (Eds.). *Readings in Physical Distribution Management,* New York: Macmillan Company, 1969.

"Braced for the Worst." *Financial World,* vol. 149, no. 7, April 1, 1980, pp. 24–25.

Brand, John Peter Henry. "Vertical Integration Theories Applicable to the Growth of Ownership Integration in the Egg Industry." (Unpublished dissertation, Purdue University, 1963).

Brekelmans, W., and Jonsson, B. "The Diffusion of Work Design Changes in Volvo." *Columbia Journal of World Business,* vol. 11, no. 2, Summer 1976, pp. 96–99.

Brookshire, Michael L., and Carroll, Sidney. "Patents and Vertical Integration as a Source of Monopoly Power—The Photographic Industry." *Antitrust Law & Economics Review,* vol. 7, no. 1, pp. 49–60, 1974.

Brown, J.R. "Toward Improved Measures of Distribution Channel Conflict." *American Marketing Association Proceedings,* no. 41, 1977, pp. 385–389.

Brown, P.I. "Diversifying Successfully." *Business Horizons,* vol. 19, no. 4, August 1976, pp. 84–87.

Cady, J.F. "Structural Trends in Retailing: The Decline of Small Business." *Journal of Contemporary Business,* vol. 5, no. 2, Spring 1976, pp. 67–90.

Cairns, James Pearson. "Acquisitions, Concentration and Vertical Integration in Food Retailing." (Unpublished dissertation, Johns Hopkins University, 1960).

"Can Semiconductors Survive Big Business?" *Business Week,* vol. 2614 (Industrial Edition), pp. 66-81, December 3, 1979.

Cannon, James. "Why Electric Utilities Are Buying into Coal." *Business & Society Review,* vol. 36, pp. 53-59, Winter 1980-81.

Carlton, Dennis. "Vertical Integration in Competitive Markets Under Uncertainty." *Journal of Industrial Economics,* vol. 27, March 1979, pp. 189-209.

Chandler, Alfred D., Jr. *The Visible Hand: The Managerial Revolution in American Business.* Cambridge, Mass.: Harvard University Press, 1977.

"The Chip Revolution: A Candid Conversation." *Datamation,* vol. 25, no. 7, pp. 98-107, June 1979.

Clarke, William Alan. "Vertical Integration in the Aluminum Industry." (Unpublished doctoral dissertation, Rutgers University, 1974).

Clevenger, Thomas C., and Campbell, Gerald R. "Vertical Organization: A Neglected Element in Market Structure-Performance Models." *Industrial Organization Review,* vol. 5, no. 1, 1977, pp. 60-66.

Coase, Ronald H. "The Nature of the Firm." *Economica,* November 1937, pp. 386-405.

Cole, Robert H. "Vertical Integration in the Carolina Textile Industry, with Particular Reference to the Marketing Aspects." (Unpublished doctoral dissertation, University of North Carolina at Chapel Hill, 1953).

Colenutt, D.W., and O'Donnell, P.O. "The Consistency of Monopolies and Mergers Commission Merger Reports." *Antitrust Bulletin,* vol. 23, no. 1, Spring 1978, p. 51082.

Comanor, William. "Vertical Mergers, Market Power, and Antitrust Laws." *American Economic Review,* vol. 57, May 1967, pp. 259-262.

"Competition in the Telephone Equipment Industry—Beyond Telerent," *The Yale Law Journal,* vol. 86, no. 3, pp. 538-560, January 1977.

Crandall, Robert. "Vertical Integration and the Market for Repair Parts in the United States Automobile Industry." *Journal of Industrial Economics,* vol. 16, July 1968, pp. 212-234.

Crandall, Robert Warren. "Vertical Integration in the United States Automobile Industry." (Unpublished doctoral dissertation, Northwestern University, 1968).

"Cutting Loose from the Wholesaler." *Dun's Review,* vol. 75, pp. 48-49, June 1960.

"Data Processing—Philips' Latest U.S. Toehold." *Business Week* (Industrial Edition), pp. 92D, 92I, 92L, September 10, 1979.

Day, Charles R., Jr. "Hydraulic Hose Firms Shift Marketing Gears." *Industry Week,* vol. 206, no. 3, pp. 84, 87, August 4, 1980.

Dayan, David. "Vertical Integration and Monopoly Regulation. (Unpublished dissertation, Princeton University, 1973).

Deutsch, Claudia H. "Tough Purchasing Pays Off." *Purchasing,* vol. 72, no. 6, pp. 37–40, March 21, 1972.

Dirks, Harlan John. "Technological and Market Forced Influencing Vertical Integration in the Swine Industry." (Unpublished doctoral dissertation, University of Minnesota, 1963).

Donohue, J. "Vertical Integration Can Ease Supply Woes." *Purchasing,* 78:34–35 + , March 4, 1975.

Doyle, Michael Thomas. "A Flexible Management System for Vertical Integration of Feeder Cattle Production and Feedlot Operation." (Unpublished doctoral dissertation, University of Nebraska, Lincoln, 1977).

Draper, Gerald. "What Future for the Airlines." *Marketing,* September 1973, pp. 27–29.

Duncan, Ian D. "Make-or-Buy Decisions." *RIA Cost and Management,* vol. 49, no. 5, pp. 44–49, September/October 1975.

Dyloe, Turner Leo. "A Study of Vertical Integration in the Minnesota Turkey Industry." (Unpublished doctoral dissertation, University of Minnesota, 1965).

Eckard, E.W., Jr. "A Note on the Empirical Measurement of Vertical Integration." *Journal of Industrial Economics* (U.K.), vol. 28, no. 1, September 1979, pp. 105–107.

"The Economics of Vertical Integration." *Petroleum Economist,* vol. 213, August 1976, pp. 290–291.

Edwards, D.C. "American and German Policy toward Conduct by Powerful Enterprises: A Comparison." *Antitrust Bulletin,* vol. 23, no. 1, Spring 1978, pp. 83–146.

Ellis, Howard S. "Fact and Fancy About the Oil Industry." *Columbia Journal of World Business,* vol. 12, no. 2, pp. 50–63, Summer 1977.

Etgar, M. "Differential Strategies in Interchannel Competition," *Journal of Business Administration,* vol. 8, no. 2, Spring 1977, pp. 39–52.

Etgar, M. "The Effects of Foward Vertical Integration on Service Performance of a Distributive Industry." *Journal of Industrial Economics,* vol. 26, March 1978, no. 3, pp. 249–255.

Etgar, M. "Effects of Administrative Control on Efficiency of Vertical Marketing Systems." *Journal of Marketing Research,* vol. 13, no. 1, February 1976, pp. 12–24.

Etgar, M. "A Test of the Stigler Theorem." *Industrial Organization Review,* vol. 5, nos. 2 & 3, 1977, pp. 135–137.

"Fairchild Camera: An Ideal Target for Gould." *Business Week,* no. 2586, May 21, 1979, pp. 28–29.

Federal Trade Commission, *Economic Report on the Influence of Market Structure on the Profit Performance of Food Manufacturing Companies.* Washington, D.C.: 1969.

Flaim, Theresa. "The Structure of the U.S. Petroleum Industry: Joint Activities and Affiliations." *Antitrust Bulletin,* vol. 24, no. 3, pp. 555–572, Fall 1979.

Flaim, Theresa. "The Structure of the U.S. Petroleum Industry: Concentration, Vertical Integration and Joint Activities." (Unpublished doctoral dissertation, Cornell University, 1977).

"The Flaky Arguments Over Breaking Up Big Oil." *Business Week,* no. 2445, August 16, 1976, pp. 93–98.

Ford, David. "A Methodology for the Study of Inter-Company Relations in Industrial Market Channels." *Journal of the Market Research Society,* vol. 22, no. 1, pp. 44–59, January 1980.

Formby, John P., and Amato, Louis. "State Policy Regulating and Controlling Milk Markets: The Case of North Carolina." *Studies in Economic Analysis,* vol. 3, no. 1, pp. 3–26, Spring 1979.

Foster, G. "How Inversek Climbed Back." *Management Today,* May 1978, pp. 50–57 +.

Fusfeld, Daniel R. "Joint Subsidiaries in the Iron and Steel Industry." *American Economic Review,* vol. 48, May 1958, pp. 578–587.

Gambino, Anthony J. "The Make-or-Buy Decision." *Management Accounting,* vol. 62, no. 6, pp. 55–56, December 1980.

"GE Shifts to Direct Selling for Line of Universal Appliances." *Advertising Age,* vol. 36, p. 66, May 31, 1965.

"General Host: Vertical Integration to Save a Subsidiary It Couldn't Sell," *Business Week,* vol. 2671 (Industrial Edition), pp. 103–104, January 18, 1981.

Globerman, Steven. "Markets, Hierarchies, and Innovation," *Journal of Economic Issues,* vol. 14, no. 4, pp. 977–998, December 1980.

Globerman, S., and Diodati, J. "Market Structure, Internal Organization, and R&D Performance in the Telecommunications Industry." *Quarterly Review of Economics & Business,* vol. 20, no. 4, Winter 1980, pp. 70–85.

Gould, J.P. "Inventories and Stochastic Demand: Equilibrium Models of the Firm and Industry." *Journal of Business* (University of Chicago), vol. 51, no. 1, January 1978, pp. 1–42.

Gould, J.R. "Price Discrimination and Vertical Control: A Note." *Journal of Political Economy,* vol. 85, October 1977, pp. 1063–1071.

Granfield, M., and Nicols, A. "Economic and Marketing Aspects of the

Direct Selling Industry." *Journal of Retailing,* vol. 51, no. 1, Spring 1975, pp. 33-50 + .

Greenhut, M.L., and Ohta, H. "Related Market Conditions and Interindustrial Mergers." *American Economic Review,* vol. 66, June 1976, pp. 267-277.

Greenhut, M.L., and Ohta, H. "Vertical Integration of Successive Oligopolists." *American Economic Review,* vol. 69, March 1979, pp. 137-141.

Greening, Timothy Scott. "Oilwells, Pipelines, Refineries and Gas Stations: A Study of Vertical Integration." (Unpublished doctoral dissertation, Harvard, 1976).

Gross, Harry. *Make or Buy: Detailed Guidelines to Assist in Analyzing, Formulating, and Concluding Make or Buy Decisions.* Englewood Cliffs, N.J.: Prentice-Hall, 1966.

"Growing Room Lies to the South." *Executive,* vol. 20, no. 2, February 1978, pp. 20-21.

"Growing Taller in the Electrical Repair Business." *Iron Age,* 219:27-30, May 16, 1977.

"GTE Feels the Sting of an Antitrust Ruling." *Business Week,* no. 2526, March 20, 1978, pp. 37-38.

Haas, Robert, and Wotruba, Thomas. "Marketing Strategy in a Make-or-Buy Situation." *Industrial Marketing Management,* vol. 5, no. 2/3, pp. 65-76, June 1976.

Hanan, M. "How Manpower Management Helps Sales—Using Services to Bail Out Commodity Products." *Sales Management,* vol. 115, no. 3, pp. 87-88, August 4, 1975.

Hansen, Robert Shields. "Vertical Integration and Control." (Unpublished doctoral dissertation, University of Florida, 1978).

Harding, B., and Round, J.I. "Input-Output Analysis and Management Accounting: An Application Concerned with Scrap Recycling." *Omega,* vol. 6, no. 6, 1978, pp. 507-513.

Harrigan, Kathryn Rudie. "A Framework for Looking at Vertical Integration Strategies." *Journal of Business Strategy,* Winter 1982 (forthcoming).

Holmes, Stanley Robert. "Predatory Vertical Integration and Petroleum Firms in Economic Space." (Unpublished doctoral dissertation, Texas A & M University, 1978).

Howe, R.J., and Norwood, A.W. "Merging OD with Planning as a Response to Change," *Management Review,* vol. 64, no. 6, June 1976, pp. 16-23.

Huber, Robert F. "Service Centers—Customers Talk It Out." *Production,* vol. 79, no. 6, pp. 74-78, June 1977.

Hurdle, James A. " 'Bottlers Bill' Still Getting Congressional Scrutiny,

Will It Up Prices, Competition?" *Marketing News,* vol. 9, no. 3, p. 3, August 1, 1975.

Hurnanen, Roy R.; Hawkins, M.; and Manning, T. "Vertical Integration and Concentration in the Alberta Broiler Industry." Distributed by the Department of Extension, University of Alberta, 1978.

"Implications of Nationalization." *The Petroleum Economist,* vol. 42, no. 4, pp. 122–123, April, 1975.

Irland, L.C. "Do Giants Control Timber-Based Industries in North America?" *Forest Industry,* 103:22–23, August 1976.

"Issues on Trial in the Westinghouse Lawsuits." *Business Week,* N2502, pp. 125–131, September 26, 1977.

Jantsch, Erich. "Enterprise and Environment." *Industrial Marketing Management,* vol. 2, no. 2, pp. 113–128, February 1973.

Jauch, Lawrence R., and Wilson, Harold K. "A Strategic Perspective for Make or Buy Decisions." *Long Range Planning,* vol. 12, no. 6, pp. 56–61, December 1979.

Johnson, H.T. "The Role of Accounting History in the Study of Modern Business Enterprise." *Accounting Review,* vol. 50, no. 3, July 1975, pp. 444–450.

Jones, Russell Owen. "Vertical Integration, Cartel Coordination and the Petroleum Industry." (Unpublished doctoral dissertation, University of California, Santa Barbara, 1977).

Jud, G.D. "The Multinational Expansion of U.S. Business: Some Evidence on Alternative Hypotheses." *Mississippi Valley Journal of Business and Economics,* vol. 10, no. 2, Winter, 1974–75, pp. 37–51.

Kahn, Alfred E. U.S. Congress, Senate, Subcommittee on Antitrust and Monopoly Hearings. "Governmental Intervention in the Market Mechanism: The Petroleum Industry." Part 1, 91st Congress, 1st Session, March 1969, pp. 132–142.

Karg, Robert Lawrence. "A Theory of Crude Oil Prices: A Study of Vertical Integration and Percentage Depletion Allowance." (Unpublished doctoral dissertation, University of Pittsburgh, 1962).

Kaserman, David. "Theories of Vertical Integration: Implications for Antitrust Policy." *Antitrust Bulletin,* vol. 23, Fall 1978, pp. 483–510.

Kelly, J.S., and Peters, J.I. "Vertical Conflict: A Comparative Analysis of Franchisees and Distributors." *American Marketing Association Proceedings,* no. 41, 1977, pp. 380–384.

Khandwalla, Pradip N. "Mass Output Orientation of Operations Technology and Organizational Structure." *Administrative Science Quarterly,* vol. 19, no. 1, pp. 74–79, March 1974.

Kindleberger, C.P. "Quantity and Price, Especially in Financial Markets." *The Quarterly Review of Economics & Business,* vol. 15, no. 2, pp. 7–19, Summer 1975.

Kintner, E.W.; Henneberger, L.F., and Fleishacker, M.L. "Reform of the Robinson-Patman Act: A Second Look." *Antitrust Bulletin,* vol. 21, no. 2, Summer 1976, pp. 203-236.

Kobrin, Paul Richard. "Vertical Integration and Efficiency in the Petroleum Industry." (Unpublished doctoral dissertation, New York University, 1976).

Koenen-Austin, V. "Changing Structure of the Municipal Public Power Industry in the United States." *Local Finance,* vol. 5, no. 4, pp. 24-29, August 1976.

Krebs, A.V. "A Galloping Oligopoly in Food." *Business and Society Review,* no. 28, Winter 1978-1979, pp. 60-65.

Kummer, Donald R. "Valuation Consequences of Forced Divestiture Announcements." *Journal of Economics and Business* (Temple University), vol. 30, no. 2, pp. 130-136, Winter 1978.

Laffer, Arthur B. "Vertical Integration by Corporations, 1929-1965," *Review of Economics and Statistics,* vol. 51, February 1969, pp. 91-93.

Larson, D.A. "An Empirical Test of the Relationship between Market Concentration and Vertical Integration," *Industrial Organization Review,* vol. 6, no. 1, 1978, pp. 71-74.

Leff, Nathaniel H. "Industrial Organization and Entrepreneurship in the Developing Countries: The Economic Groups." *Economic Development and Cultural Change,* vol. 26, no. 4, pp. 661-675.

Leister, D.V., and Stram, B.N. "Vertical Integration, Intermodality, and the Public Interest Through 'Deregulation' of the Domestic Air Cargo Industry," *American Marketing Association, Educators' Proceedings,* Series 43, 1978, pp. 244-248.

Levey, Gary D. "The Second Aim," *Management Accounting,* vol. 55, no. 12, pp. 47-49, June 1974.

Levitt, T. "Dinosaurs Among the Bears and Bulls." *Harvard Business Review,* vol. 53, no. 1, January-February 1975, pp. 41-53.

Litman, Barry Russell. "Vertical Integration and Performance of the Television Networks." (Unpublished doctoral dissertation, Michigan State University, 1976).

Lombard North Group. The Common Ownership of Land, Agricultural Processing and Marketing Facilities in Alberta, Edmonton, Alta.: Alberta Land Use Forum, 1974.

Louis, Martin B. "Vertical Distributional Restraints Under 'Schwinn' and 'Sylvania'—an Argument for the Continuing Use of a Partial Per Se Approach." *Michigan Law Review,* vol. 75, no. 2, pp. 275-310, December 1976.

Louis, Martin B. "Vertical Distribution Restraints After 'Sylvania': a Postscript and Comment." *Michigan Law Review,* vol. 76, no. 2, pp. 265-280, December 1977.

Lundquist, E. "Bell: Vertical Integration Should Not be Disrupted." *Electronic News,* 26:78+, September 15, 1980.

Lusch, R.F. "Franchise Satisfaction: Causes and Consequences," *International Journal of Physical Distribution,* vol. 7, no. 3, 1977, pp. 128-139.

McCollum, James Bobby. "Information, Vertical Integration, and Antitrust Policy." (Unpublished doctoral dissertation, Tulane University, 1968).

McGee, John S., and Bassett, Lowell R. "Vertical Integration Revisited." *Journal of Law and Economics,* vol. 19, April 1976, pp. 17-38.

McGucklin, Robert, and Chen, Heng. "Interaction between Buyer and Seller Concentration and Industry Price-Cost Margins." *Industrial Organization Review,* vol. 4, no. 3, 1976, pp. 123-132.

McGugan, Vincent J., and Caves, Richard E. "Integration and Competition in the Equipment Leasing Industry." *Journal of Business,* vol. 47, July 1974, pp. 382-396.

McLean, John G., and Haigh, Robert William. *The Growth of Integrated Oil Companies.* Boston: Division of Research, Graduate School of Business Administration, Harvard University, 1954.

McLellan, Vin. "SBS Partnership May be Doomed." *Datamation,* vol. 25, no. 1, pp. 90, 101, 104, January 1979.

MacMillan, K. and Farmer, D. "Redefining the Boundaries of the Firm." *Journal of Industrial Economics,* vol. 27, pp. 227-287, March 1979.

Maddigan, Ruth Jean. "The Impact of Vertical Integration on Business Performance." (Unpublished doctoral dissertation, Indiana University, 1979).

Maddigan, Ruth Jean. "The Measurement of Vertical Integration." *Review of Economics and Statistics,* August 1981, pp. 328-335.

Madison, Jim. "The Make or Buy Decision." *Management Accounting,* vol. 57, no. 3, pp. 32-34, February 73.

Mallele, Parthasaradhi, and Nahta, Babu. "Theory of Vertical Control with Variable Proportions." *Journal of Political Economy,* vol. 88, no. 5, pp. 1009-1025, October 1980.

Mancke, Richard B. "Iron Ore and Steel: A Case Study of the Economic Causes of Vertical Integration." *Journal of Industrial Economics,* vol. 20, July 1972, pp. 220-229.

Margolis, James. "Vertical Integration: No Sure Ladder to Profit." *Chemical Week,* vol. 84, pp. 84-89, April 18, 1959.

Marx, Thomas G. "An Analysis of the Economic Issues Raised in Continental TV versus GTE Sylvania." *Akron Business and Economic Review,* vol. 10, no. 1, pp. 7-11, Spring 1979.

Marx, T.G. "Vertical Integration in the Diesel-Electric Locomotive Building Industry: A Study in Market Failures." *Nebraska Journal of Economics and Business,* vol. 15, no. 4, Autumn 1976, pp. 37-51.

Mead, D.E. "The Effect of Vertical Integration on Risk in the Petroleum Industry." *Quarterly Review of Economics and Business,* vol. 18, no. 1, Spring 1978, pp. 83-90.

Meehan, James W., comment on Allen, Bruce T. "Vertical Integration." *Journal of Law and Economics,* vol. 15, October 1972, pp. 461-471.

"Melville Steps into the Billion-Dollar Class." *Business Week,* no. 2478, April 11, 1977, pp. 58-62.

Menge, John Alexander. "Internal Transfer Pricing and Vertical Integration in the Automotive Assembly Industry," (Unpublished Dissertation, MIT, 1959.)

Metzger, Michael B. "Schwinn's Swan Song." *Business Horizons,* vol. 21, no. 2, pp. 52-56, April 1978.

Mighell, R.L. and Hoofnagle, W.S. "Contract Production and Vertical Integration in Farming," 1960 and 1970, U.S. Department of Agriculture, Economic Research Service (1972).

Miller, Richard A. "Exclusive Dealing in the Petroleum Industry: The Refiner-Lessee Dealer Relationship." *Yale Economic Essays,* vol. 3, Spring 1963, pp. 223-247.

Minihan, Michael J. "Persistent Inflation—Its Effects on Small Business." *Journal of Small Business Management,* vol. 14, no. 3, pp. 34-35, July 1976.

Mitchell, E.J. "Busting Up Big Oil: Too High a Price." *MBA; Master in Business Administration,* vol. 11, no. 1, January 1977, pp. 41-44.

Mitchell, Edward J., ed. *Vertical Integration in the Oil Industry.* Washington: American Enterprise Institute for Public Policy Research, 1976.

Mommsen, Jack Terman. "Vertical Integration in the Nuclear Fuel Cycle." (Unpublished doctoral dissertation, University of Santa Clara, 1977.)

Moyer, M.S. "Toward More Responsive Marketing Channels." *Journal of Retailing,* vol. 51, no. 1, Spring 1975, pp. 7-19 + .

"A New Role for Marketing." *Industry Week,* vol. V, 184, no. 11, pp. 32-38, March 17, 1975.

Nikolai, Loren A., and Bazley, John D. "An Analysis of the Organizational Interaction of Accounting Departments." *Academy of Management Journal,* vol. 20, no. 4, pp. 608-621, December 1977.

"Obligational Markets and the Mechanics of Inflation." *Bell Journal of Economics,* vol. 9, no. 2, pp. 549-571, Autumn, 1978.

Pakrul, Herb A. "A Decision Maker's Perspective on How the Accounting System Can Meet User Needs." *RIA Cost and Management,* vol. 51, no. 5, pp. 12-19, September/October 1977.

Parker, Russell Clayton. Vertical Integration by Grocery Retailers: A Market Structure. (Unpublished dissertation, University of Wisconsin, Madison, 1962).

Parsons, Donald O., and Ray, Edward J. "The United States Steel Consolidation: The Creation of Market Control." *Journal of Law and Economics,* vol. 18, April 1975, pp. 181–219.

Patterson, James M., and Allvine, Fred C. "Shortages and Gasoline Marketing." *Business Horizons,* vol. 17, no. 2, pp. 5–17, April 1974.

Peck, Merton J. *Competition in the Aluminum Industry, 1945–1958.* Cambridge, Mass.: Harvard University Press, 1961.

Perry, Martin K. "Forward Integration by Alcoa: 1888–1930." *Journal of Industrial Economics,* vol. 29, September 1980, pp. 37–53.

Perry, Martin K. "Vertical Integration: The Monopsony Case," *American Economic Review,* vol. 68, September 1978, pp. 561–570.

Perry, Martin Kent. "The Theory of Vertical Integration by Imperfectly Competitive Firms." (Unpublished dissertation, Stanford University, 1976.)

Peterson, R.D. "Galbraith's Obviated Market: Some Empirical Evidence." *Journal of Economic Issues,* vol. 14, no. 2, June 1980, pp. 291–308.

Pfeffer, J., and Phillip, N. "Patterns of Joint Venture Activity: Implications for Antitrust Policy," *Antitrust Bulletin,* vol. 21, no. 2, Summer 1976, pp. 314–339.

Philips, Louis, and Francois, Jacques. "Pricing, Distribution and the Supply of Storage." *European Economic Review* (Netherlands), vol. 15, no. 2, pp. 225–243, February 1981.

Pickering, J.F. "The Abandonment of Major Mergers in the U.K., 1965–75." *Journal of Industrial Economics,* vol. 27, no. 2, pp. 123–131, December 1978.

Piette, Michael John. "The U.S. Petroleum Pipeline Industry: A Study of Vertical Integration," (Unpublished doctoral dissertation, Florida State University, 1977.)

Porter, Michael E. *Competitive Strategy: Techniques for Analyzing Industries and Competitors.* New York: Free Press, 1980.

Porter, Michael E. "Consumer Behavior, Retailer Power, and Market Performance in Consumer Goods Industries." *Review of Economics and Statistics,* 56 (November 1974), pp. 419–436.

Porter, Michael E. *Interbrand Choice, Strategy, and Bilateral Market Power.* Cambridge: Harvard University Press, 1976.

Porter, Michael E. "The Structure within Industries and Companies' Performance." *Review of Economics and Statistics,* vol. 60, May 1979, pp. 214–227.

Posner, Richard A. "The Next Step in the Antitrust Treatment of

Restricted Distribution: *per se* Legality." *University of Chicago Law Review,* vol. 48, no. 1, pp. 6–26, Winter 1981.

Pulikonda, Nagabhushanam. "The Impact of Vertical Integration on Firms Subject to Regulatory Constraints," (Unpublished doctoral dissertation, University of Illinois at Urbana-Champaign, 1979.)

Raunick, Donald A., and Fisher, Armen G. "A Probabilistic Make-or-Buy Model." *Journal of Purchasing,* vol. 18, no. 1, pp. 63–80, February 1972.

Reed, S.F. "Corporate Growth by Strategic Planning: Developing a Plan." *Mergers & Acquisitions,* 12:4–27, Fall 1977.

Reese, Bud. "Pratt and Whitney to Sell Through Distributors." *Industrial Marketing,* vol. 45, pp. 45–47, August 1960.

Reese, R.M., and Pruden, H.O. "A Chance-Constrained Distribution Model—An Application to the Forest Products Industry." *International Journal of Physical Distribution and Materials Management,* vol. 8, no. 2, 1977, pp. 119–128.

Reid, Marvin. "Midwest—Jobbers Now Find That Controls Hurt a Lot More Than They Help." *National Petroleum News,* vol. V68, no. 6, p. 22, June 1976.

Reinharth, Leon; Shapiro, H. Jack; and Kallman, Ernest A. "Planning for Change in the Organizational Structure." *Planning Review,* vol. 8, no. 2, pp. 27–31, March 1980.

Renner, Elmer J. "Plant Capacity—Physical or Financial." *Management Review,* vol. 65, no. 2, pp. 4–14, February 1976.

"Rented Furniture: A New Design for Living." *Business Week,* no. 2474, March 14, 1977, pp. 107–109.

Richards, Eric L., and Krider, Charles E. "The States' Assault on Oil: Special Interests v. Consumer Welfare." *American Business Law Journal,* vol. 18, no. 4, pp. 477–510, Winter 1981.

Robinson, E.A.G. *The Structure of Competitive Industry,* rev. ed. Chicago: University of Chicago Press, 1958, pp. 20–29.

Roe, P.A. "Modeling a Make or Buy Decision at ICI." *Long-Range Planning,* vol. 5, no. 4, pp. 21–26, December 1972.

Rothwell, Geoffrey. "Market Coordination by the Uranium Oxide Industry." *Antitrust Bulletin,* vol. 25, no. 1, pp. 233–268, Spring 1980.

Rumelt, Richard P. *Strategy, Structure, and Economic Performance.* Boston: Division of Research, Graduate School of Business Administration, Harvard University, 1974.

Salter, Malcom S., and Weinhold, Wolf A. *Diversification through Acquisition: Strategies for Creating Economic Value.* New York: The Free Press, 1979.

Salverson, M.E. "Business Strategy: Pinning the Blame for Strategy Failures on the CEO." *Planning Review,* vol. 4, no. 5, September 1976, pp. 1, 4–7, 24.

Saxton, W.A. "Vertical Integration—AT + T Style—An Influence on Datacomm. Usage." *Communications News* 15:42–43, March 1978.

Schaffner, David John. An Economic Analysis of Vertical Integration and New Technology in the California Iceberg Lettuce Industry. (Unpublished dissertation, Golden Gate University, D.B.A. 1980.)

Scherer, Frederic M. "The Determinants of Industrial Plant Sizes in Six Nations." *Review of Economics and Statistics,* May 1973, pp. 135–195.

Scherer, Frederic M. *Industrial Market Structure and Economic Performance.* New York: Rand McNally (2nd ed.), 1980.

Scherer, Frederic M.; Beckenstein, Alan; Kaufer, Erich; and Murphy, Dennis R. *The Economics of Multi-Plant Operation: An International Comparison Study.* Cambridge: Harvard University Press, 1975.

"Schick's New Direct Selling Irks Wholesalers." *Advertising Age,* vol. 30, January 19, 1959, p. 97.

Schineller, R.J. "Financial Planning for Vertical Integration." *Financial Executive,* vol. 47, no. 8, August 1979, pp. 44–50.

Scott, Bruce. "The Industrial State: Old Myths and New Realities." *Harvard Business Review,* March-April, 1973, pp. 133–148.

Scott, Bruce. "Stages of Corporate Development, Part I." Boston Intercollegiate Case Clearinghouse, 1965.

Shepherd, William G. *The Economics of Industrial Organization.* Englewood Cliffs, N.J.: Prentice-Hall, Inc., 1979.

Shepherd, William G. "The Elements of Market Structure." *Review of Economics and Statistics,* February 1972, pp. 25–37.

Shepherd, William G. "What Does the Survivor Technique Show About Economies of Scale?" *Southern Economic Journal,* July 1967, pp. 113–122.

Sichel, Warner. "Vertical Integration as a Dynamic Industry Concept." *Antitrust Bulletin,* vol. 18, Fall 1973, pp. 463–482.

Spengler, Joseph J. "Integration and Antitrust Policy." *Journal of Political Economy,* vol. 68, August 1950, pp. 347–352.

Schmalensee, Richard. "A Note on the Theory of Vertical Integration." *Journal of Political Economy,* vol. 81, March-April 1973, pp. 442–449.

"A Statistical Estimation of an Operating Cost Function for Municipal Refuse Collection," *Public Finance Quarterly,* vol. 4, no. 1, January 1976, pp. 56–76.

Stetinius, Wallace. "Be Adaptable and Specialize, or Kiss the Future Goodbye." *Printing Impressions,* vol. 20, no. 4, pp. 16, 19, 95, September 1977.

Stewart, I.C. "Merger Regulation in the United States." *Management International Review,* vol. 18, pp. 43-48, March 1978.

Stigler, George J. "The Division of Labor is Limited by the Extent of the Market." *Journal of Political Economy,* vol. LIX, no. 3, June 1951, pp. 185-193.

Stigler, George J. "The Economies of Scale." *Journal of Law and Economics,* October 1958, pp. 54-71.

Stigler, George J. *The Organization of Industry.* Irwin, Homewood, Illinois, 1968.

Strong, Jerome C. "Product Diversification by Medium-Large Manufacturing Companies, 1928-1954." (Unpublished doctoral dissertation, Columbia University, 1961.)

Sturdivant, Frederick David. An Historical Analysis of the American Hospital Supply Corporation with Special Attention Given to the Backward Vertical Integration of a Channel of Distribution, 1922-1956. (Unpublished dissertation, Northwestern University, 1964.)

"Supplier Suggestions Aid Virginia Buying Team." *Purchasing,* vol. 72, no. 8, pp. 51-52, April 18, 1972.

"Tandy Corp: Back on a Fast-Growth Track." *Business Week,* no. 2530, April 17, 1978, pp. 117-118.

Teece, David J. "Vertical Integration and Vertical Divestiture in the U.S. Oil Industry." Stanford, California: Institute for Energy Studies, Stanford University, 1976.

Temin, Peter. "Technology, Regulation, and Market Structure in the Modern Pharmaceutical Industry." *Bell Journal of Economics,* vol. 10, no. 2, pp. 429-446, Autumn, 1979.

Teresko, John. "Make or Buy? New Issues Force the Decision." *Industry Week,* vol. V198, no. 5, pp. 34-37, September 4, 1978.

Thieme, Carl W.; Wilson, Thomas E.; and Long, Dane M. "Strategic Planning for Hospitals under Regulation." *Health Care Management Review,* vol. 6, no. 2, pp. 35-43, Spring, 1981.

Thomas, Christopher R. "A Theory of the Vertically Integrated Input Monopolist with a Depletion Allowance." *Southern Economic Journal,* vol. 47, no. 3, pp. 799-804, January 1981.

Tsaklanganos, A.A. "Peers, Persuasion, and Horizontal Management." *Management Accounting,* vol. 60, no. 2, August 1978, pp. 33-37.

Tucker, Irvin B., and Wilder, Ronald P. "Trends in Vertical Integration in the U.S. Manufacturing Sector." *Journal of Industrial Economics,* vol. 26, September 1977, pp. 81-94.

U.S. Bureau of the Census. *Census of Manufactures, 1973-1977.* Washington, D.C., U.S. Government Printing Office, 1977.

U.S. Congress, Senate, Committee on Government Operations, Permanent

Subcommittee on Investigations. "Preliminary Federal Trade Commission Staff Report on Its Investigations of the Petroleum Industry." 93rd Congress, 1st session, July 1973, pp. 25–27, 60–62.

U.S., Congress, Senate, Committee on Interior and Insular Affairs Hearings. Oil Price Decontrol, Federal Trade Commission Staff Report. "The Effects of Decontrol on Competition in the Petroleum Industry," 94th Congress, 1st Session, September 5, 1975, pp. 359–394.

United States Federal Trade Commission, Bureau of Economics. "Economic Report on Mergers and Vertical Integration in the Cement Industry." Staff Report to the Federal Trade Commission, Washington: U.S. Government Printing Office, 1966.

Upton, Molly. "Lines Blended, Trends Continued in 1976." *Computerworld,* vol. 11, no. 1, p. 35, January 3, 1977.

"Using Accounting Information to Make Better Decisions." *Business,* vol. 15, no. 2, pp. 24–27, March/April 1981.

Varadarajan, P., and Dillon, William R. "Competitive Position Effects and Market Share: An Exploratory Investigation." *Journal of Business Research,* vol. 9, no. 1, pp. 49–64, March 1981.

Vernon, John M. *Market Structure and Industrial Performance: A Review of Statistical Findings.* Boston: Allyn & Bacon, 1972.

Vernon, John M., and Graham, Daniel A. "Profitability of Monopolization by Vertical Integration." *Journal of Political Economy,* vol. 79, July/August 1971, pp. 924–925.

"Vertical Agreements to Terminate Competing Distributors: Oreck Corp. v. Whirlpool Corp." *Harvard Law Review,* vol. 92, no. 5, pp. 1160–1169, March 1979.

Vesey, J.T. "Vertical Integration: Its Effect on Business Performance." *Managerial Planning,* vol. 26, no. 6, May/June 1978, pp. 11–15.

Warren-Boulton, F.R. "Vertical Control by Labor Unions." *American Economic Review,* vol. 67, pp. 309–322, June 1977.

Warren-Boulton, F.R. "Vertical Control with Variable Proportions." *Journal of Political Economy,* vol. 82, July/August 1974, pp. 783–802.

Wasson, Chester R. *Dynamic Competitive Strategy and Product Life Cycles.* St. Charles, Illinois: Challenge Books, 1974.

Weisberg, David E. "Continental TV v. GTE Sylvania: Implications for Horizontal as Well as Vertical Restraints on Distributors." *Business Lawyer,* vol. 33, no. 3, pp. 1757–1769, April 1978.

Weiss, E.B. "The Manufacturer Gets Closer to the Consumer." *Advertising Age,* vol. 35, p. 74, June 29, 1964.

Weiss, E.B. "Will Direct Retail Accounts Now Top Out?" *Advertising Age,* vol. 34, pp. 64+, August 12, 1963.

"What's Mobil Up To in the Southwest and Southeast?" *National Petroleum News,* vol. 68, no. 5, pp. 30–31, May 1976.

White, L. *The Automobile Industry Since 1945.* Cambridge, Mass.: Harvard University Press, 1971.

"Who Won?—The Recent FCC Decision Was Tougher on Western Electric than AT&T Has Acknowledged." *Forbes,* vol. 119, no. 9, p. 46, May 1, 1977.

"Why Chemical Companies Are Nervous." *Forbes,* vol. 120, no. 12, December 15, 1977, p. 68.

"Why They're Integrating into Integrated Circuits." *Business Week,* September 28, 1974, pp. 55–56+.

Wiek, James Lohren. An Analysis of the Relation of Vertical Integration and Selected Attitudes and Behavioral Relationships in Competing Channel Systems. (Unpublished dissertation, Michigan State University, 1969.)

Williamson, Oliver E. *Markets and Hierarchies.* New York: Free Press, 1975.

Williamson, Oliver E. "The Vertical Integration of Production: Market Failure Considerations." *American Economic Review,* vol. 61, May 1971, pp. 112–123.

Wiseman, Toni. "Rigid Disk Drive Revenues Seen Peaking in 1979." *Computerworld* vol. 11, no. 37, p. 93, September 12, 1977.

Wolfe, E. "Reform or Repeal of the Robinson-Patman Act—Another View: A Response in Park to Messrs. Kinter, Henneberger and Fleishaker." *Antitrust Bulletin,* vol. 21, no. 2, Summer 1976, pp. 237–270.

Zelek, Eugene F., Jr.; Louis W. Stern; and Thomas W. Dunfee. "A Rule of Reason Decision Model after Sylvania." *California Law Review,* vol. 58, no. 1, pp. 13–47, January 1980.

Zelenitz, A. "The Attempted Promotion of Competition in Related Goods Markets: the Ford-Autolite Divestiture Case." *Antitrust Bulletin,* vol. 25, no. 1, Spring, 1980, pp. 103–124.

Index

About the Author

Kathryn Rudie Harrigan is an assistant professor at the Columbia University School of Business and is an editor on the boards of the *Academy of Management Journal* and the *Journal of Business Strategy*. She received the D.B.A. from Harvard University and the M.B.A. from the University of Texas at Austin. Professor Harrigan received the General Electric Award for Outstanding Research in Strategic Management in 1979 and received an IBM research fellowship for her study of declining industries. Her research interests include industry and competitor analysis, strategic management, global management, and business-government relations.

Professor Harrigan is the author of *Strategies for Declining Businesses* (Lexington Books 1980) and numerous journal articles. She is a member of the Strategic Management Society and has acted as a consultant to both public and private organizations.